THE PAGEANT OF

GREECE

THEATRE AT EPIDAURUS, built by the
architect Polycleitus c. 350 B.C.

THEATRE AT ATHENS, from the East

The
Pageant of
GREECE

Edited by

R. W. LIVINGSTONE

President of Corpus Christi College
Oxford

OXFORD
AT THE CLARENDON PRESS

Oxford University Press, Amen House, London E.C. 4

GLASGOW NEW YORK TORONTO MELBOURNE WELLINGTON
BOMBAY CALCUTTA MADRAS KARACHI CAPE TOWN IBADAN

Geoffrey Cumberlege, Publisher to the University

FIRST PUBLISHED 1923
REPRINTED 1924, 1928, 1935
1942, 1945, 1947, 1953
PRINTED IN GREAT BRITAIN

PREFACE

I HAVE given in my first chapter some judgements on Greek thought and literature by famous men of letters. If there is any truth in them, no one interested in the achievements of the human mind should be content to pass through life without forming some idea of what the Greeks achieved, and no education can be complete which ignores Hellenism.

This book is intended for those who know no Greek, but wish to form some idea of its great writers and of what they wrote. It is meant for the ordinary educated reader, as well as for pupils at the universities and in the upper forms of schools, who will never learn the language but need not be left in total ignorance of the literature and thought of Greece ; and it may be used to give the weaker student, while he struggles with individual authors, a view of the literature as a whole and an idea of the doors which knowledge of the language will open to him. It is not a book *about* the Greeks : such books can be at best pale reflections of the central fire at which they are lit. It consists of selections from the greatest Greek writers, with such a sketch of their lives and works as may give an idea of what they were and did.

But it is not a mere anthology of selections. I have tried, as far as possible, to piece the passages together in a continuous whole, and, further, to trace the growth of Greek literature, and indicate the historical background in which it is set. Any one who reads these pages will not merely read famous or typical extracts from the great Greek writers, but will also follow in outline the most important part of that vast intellectual development which started with Homer and outlasted the Roman empire. I do not think that I have included any writer who is definitely second-class, unless Xenophon is so considered, or ignored any one before 300 B.C. who is definitely first-class

2574

and whose works survive otherwise than in fragments. Yet a reader will form a false idea of the richness of Greek literature who forgets that the authors here quoted are probably less than 10 per cent. of the surviving writers of Greece and less than 1 per cent. of the original total. Want of space has prevented me from doing justice to later authors, who may be dealt with in a second volume.

Some critics will object to the study of literature either in selections or in a translation. I sympathize. Every scholar knows what is lost by those who approach Greek by any other door than its own. They lose the language, 'the first of languages' (Gibbon), 'which contains the excellences of all languages' (Coleridge), 'a type of the understanding of which it was the creation and the image—in variety, in simplicity, in flexibility, and in copiousness excelling every other language of the western world' (Shelley).[1] They also inevitably lose much of the literature. Most is lost in lyric poetry ; next comes drama. In Homer we lose the metre and much of the beauty of the language. In prose our losses vary with the literary quality of the work translated. Thus Aristotle has no graces to forfeit, but Plato is robbed of the magic of his style. It is infinitely better to be able to read the originals, and no lover of literature within whose grasp this power lies will be content with less.

But for very many the choice is between Greek literature in an English dress and nothing ; and only a pedant would deny that it is far better to read Greek in a translation than not to read it at all.[2] Though much is taken, much remains, and

[1] What language could rival the subtlety of Xenophon's description of a trustworthy messenger as one who reported τά τε ὄντα ὡς ὄντα καὶ τὰ μὴ ὄντα ὡς οὐκ ὄντα ? No English can give the effect of the varied negative, yet the words could not be simpler. Or what language could extract as much from a particle as the same writer's description of men disguised as women—αἱ δὴ γυναῖκες ?

[2] The use of translations was strongly recommended by the Prime Minister's Committee on Classics for those unable to study the original languages.

any one who doubts this can read the following pages and say
if he does not get profit and enjoyment from the translations
they contain. And there is a sense in which the study of the
Greek language may be helped by the study of translations
from it. We may reasonably hope that the small percentage
of students who at present learn Greek in this country may
be increased. But it will increase only as the general public
comes to realize what treasures Greek contains, and it may be
hoped that there is some truth in Goethe's saying: ' Translators
are like match-makers; they sing the praises of some half-
veiled beauty and arouse an irresistible longing for the original.'
A similar plea may be urged for selections. At best they lead
to deeper reading. At worst, in an age when no man can hope
to cover the wide territories of knowledge, they are the only
means by which a student can gain some acquaintance with
districts that are not in his province but of which no educated
man remains willingly ignorant.

I have given some helps to pronunciation, marking long
syllables where any doubt can arise as to their quantity and
where mispronunciation matters, but not otherwise. I have
not marked short vowels nor final syllables. The latter should
always be sounded and are long (e. g. Socratēs, Andromachē).
On these principles I have not marked such words as e. g.
Pēnĕlŏpē or Ēurīpĭdēs. The quantity once shown, I have not
in general repeated the mark.

A reader who knows no classical mythology should buy
a dictionary of it : there is one in the Everyman Series.

I could not have carried out this work without the generous
help of translators and publishers. I gratefully acknowledge
my debt to the following for leave to use copyright translations :

Homer, *Iliad*, Lang, Leaf, and Myers (Macmillan), *Odyssey*,
Dr. Mackail (John Murray) : Aeschylus, *Agamemnon*, and
Euripides, *Electra*, Prof. Murray (Allen & Unwin) ; Aristo-
phanes, *Frogs*, Prof. Murray (Allen & Unwin), other plays,
Dr. Rogers (Bell & Sons) : Herodotus, Dr. Godley (Loeb Series,

Heinemann) : Aristotle, *Rhetoric*, Dr. Welldon (Macmillan) :
Theophrastus, Sir A. Hort (Loeb Series, Heinemann). I have also
to thank the following for leave to quote versions from the Greek
Anthology : Sir Rennell Rodd, *Love, Worship, and Death*, 2nd ed.
(E. Arnold), Dr. J. A. Pott, *Greek Love Songs and Epigrams*
(Kegan Paul, Trench, Trübner), Dr. R. Garnett, *A Chaplet from
the Greek Anthology* (Fisher Unwin), Dr. G. B. Grundy, *Ancient
Gems in Modern Setting* (Blackwell), H. Macnaghten, *Verses
Ancient and Modern* (Allen & Unwin). One or two other debts
are acknowledged in the notes. I am much indebted to Mr.
J. D. Beazley for kindly selecting the portraits here reproduced.

LIST OF ILLUSTRATIONS

TABLE OF CONTENTS

SHORT BIBLIOGRAPHY

THE books here mentioned can all be recommended. Students are strongly advised to purchase *The Claim of Antiquity* (Oxford Univ. Press, 1s.), a list of the best translations and books on the classics for the general reader, with their publishers and prices, and with comments. My own list is largely taken from it. In making it I have preferred to recommend inexpensive translations where they are also good.

The chief series of classical translations are:

Loeb Classical Library (Heinemann). Prints the original and the translation opposite.

Oxford Library of Translations (Oxford Univ. Press).

Everyman Library (J. M. Dent).

Bohn Library (G. Bell & Sons).

World's Classics (Oxford Univ. Press).

HOMER. *Iliad* (prose) by Lang, Leaf, and Myers (Macmillan). W. Leaf, *A Companion to the Iliad for English Readers* (Macmillan), is useful.

Odyssey (prose) by Butcher and Lang (Macmillan).

Odyssey (verse) by J. W. Mackail (Murray, 3 vols.), and by Caulfeild (G. Bell & Sons).

AESCHYLUS, by E. D. A. Morshead (Macmillan, 2 vols).

The Agamemnon, Choephoroi, Eumenides, Prometheus Bound, Suppliant Women, by Gilbert Murray (Allen & Unwin).

Four Plays of Aeschylus, by G. M. Cookson (Blackwell).

SOPHOCLES, by L. Campbell (World's Classics), fair.

Oedipus, King of Thebes, by Gilbert Murray (Allen & Unwin), and by J. T. Sheppard (Cambridge Univ. Press), excellent.

EURIPIDES, *Alcestis, Bacchae, Electra, Hippolytus, Iphigeneia in Tauris, Medea, Rhesus, Trojan Women*, by Gilbert Murray (Allen & Unwin), *Iphigenia in Aulis*, by F. M. Stawell (G. Bell & Sons).

Complete translation (Everyman, 2 vols.).

ARISTOPHANES, by B. B. Rogers (G. Bell & Sons).

The Frogs, by Gilbert Murray (Allen & Unwin).

HERODOTUS, by A. D. Godley (Loeb, 4 vols.).

by G. Rawlinson (Everyman, 2 vols.).

THUCYDIDES, by R. Crawley (Everyman).

by B. Jowett (Oxford Univ. Press, 2 vols.).

XENOPHON, *Socratic Discourses* (Everyman), contains the *Memorabilia*, &c., as well as the *Apology* and other Platonic dialogues.

Various works by H. G. Dakyns (Macmillan).

PLATO. *Dialogues*. Translated by Benjamin Jowett (Oxford Univ. Press, 5 vols.).

Euthyphro, Apology, Crito, and Phaedo, published as *The Four Socratic*

Dialogues of Plato (Oxford Univ. Press), and as *The Trial and Death of Socrates* (Macmillan).

Phaedrus, Lysis, and Protagoras (id.).

The Republic (id.). Best read with *Lectures on the Republic of Plato*, by R. L. Nettleship (Macmillan).

The Laws, tr. A. E. Taylor (G. Bell & Sons).

A. E. Taylor, *Plato* (Constable), a good short introduction.

ARISTOTLE *Nicomachean Ethics*, by H. Rackham (Loeb), good, J. E. C. Welldon (Macmillan), and F. H. Peters (Kegan Paul); *Chapters from Aristotle's Ethics*, by J. H. Muirhead (Murray), selections and good discussions.

Politics, by B. Jowett (Oxford Univ. Press).

Rhetoric, by J. E. C. Welldon (Macmillan).

Poetics, by I. Bywater (Oxford Univ. Press).

Other works (Oxford Univ. Press).

A. E. Taylor, *Aristotle* (People's Books, T. C. Jack), a good short introduction.

The Aristotle translations in Everyman are not recommended.

THEOPHRASTUS, by Sir A. Hort (Loeb).

DEMOSTHENES. *Public Orations*, by A. W. Pickard-Cambridge (Oxford Univ. Press, 2 vols.).

A good selection in Everyman.

THEOCRITUS, by C. S. Calverley (G. Bell & Sons).

GREEK ANTHOLOGY. For translations see acknowledgement in preface. There are good selections by G. R. Tomson (Walter Scott), G. B. Grundy (Blackwell), and (prose) J. W. Mackail (Longman).

PLUTARCH (Everyman, 3 vols.). For those who enjoy Elizabethan English and are not particular about accuracy North's translation (Temple Classics, 9 vols.) is recommended.

LITERATURE. *Ancient Greek Literature*, by Gilbert Murray (Heinemann), highly recommended.

Histoire de la littérature grecque, by A. and M. Croiset (Fontemoing, 5 vols.). The standard history, and itself a work of literature.

Ancient Greek Literature, by C. M. Bowra (Home University Library), good.

HISTORY. J. H. Breasted, *Ancient Times* (Ginn & Co.). Excellent sketch of the history of the ancient world.

A Short History of Greece, by M. A. Hamilton (Oxford Univ. Press), elementary but well illustrated.

Everyday Life in Greece, by C. E. Robinson (Oxford Univ. Press).

Bury, *History of Greece* (Macmillan). The standard history.

SCIENCE. Essays in *Legacy of Greece* (Oxford Univ. Press). *Greek Biology and Greek Medicine*, by C. Singer (Oxford Univ. Press), reprinted from above. *Science and Mathematics in Classical Antiquity*, by J. L. Heiberg (Oxford Univ. Press).

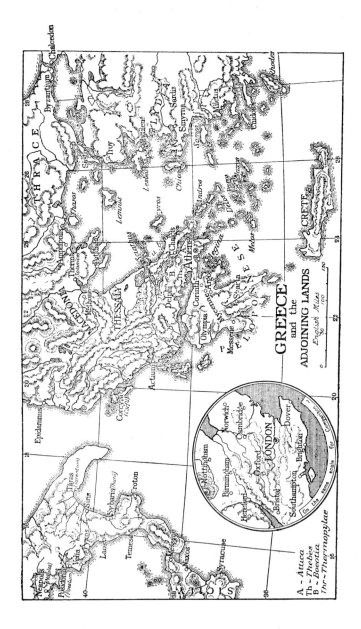

GREECE
and the
ADJOINING LANDS

English Miles

A - Attica
Th - Thebes
B - Boeotica
Thr - Thermopylae

I

INTRODUCTION

Je sais maintenant combien je dois . . . aux Grecs à qui je dois tout, à qui je voudrais devoir davantage, car ce que nous savons de raisonnable sur l'univers et l'homme nous vient d'eux.—ANATOLE FRANCE.

IF we trace the life of Europe to its origin, we shall come to three sources. Rome gives us a great legal system, the vision of a highly organized and partly successful world-empire, splendid examples of great men of action, and some noble works in poetry and prose. Our spiritual and intellectual life we owe chiefly to Judaea and Greece. Besides the specific gift of Christianity, Judaea shows us a strong sense and hold of the unseen world, the stubborn persistence which in the Bible is called Faith, and that most difficult and rare of all virtues, which S. Paul defined in the thirteenth chapter of his first letter to the Church at Corinth. Greece is the author of the intellectual life of Europe and of one of its two greatest literatures ; but though in the following pages I shall deal almost entirely with these, it must not be forgotten that she represents an outlook on the world and a way of life.[1]

A man walking down Shaftesbury Avenue from Piccadilly to Charing Cross Road passes the *Lyric Theatre*. If it is the evening, a *dramatic* performance is probably taking place inside. It may be a *tragedy*, or some form of *comedy*. If it is a *musical comedy* and he enters, he will see elaborate *scenery* and a play which may open with a *prologue* and which is partly composed of *dialogue* between the various *characters*, partly of songs in various *metres* sung by a *chorus* to the accompaniment of an *orchestra*. As the words in italics indicate, our imaginary passer-by will have seen, though he may not have suspected it, a symbol of the indelible mark which the Greeks have set on the aesthetic and intellectual life of Europe, and of the living presence of Greece in the twentieth century. An ancient Athenian might be startled at the sight of a musical comedy and its chorus, but

[1] I have tried to deal with this in *The Greek Genius and Its Meaning to Us*, where the subjects treated in this chapter are more fully discussed. The chapter itself is largely abbreviated from my essay in *The Legacy of Greece*.

B

he would be looking at his own child, a descendant, however distant, degenerate, and hard to recognize, of that chorus which with dance and song moved round the altar of Dionysus in the theatre of his home.

The same imprint, clear or faint, is on all our literary forms, except perhaps one. Epic, lyric, elegiac, dramatic, didactic, poetry, history, biography, rhetoric and oratory, the epigram, the essay, the sermon, the novel, letter writing and literary criticism are all Greek by origin, and in nearly every case their name betrays their source. Rome raises a doubtful claim to satire, but the substance of satire is present in the Old Comedy, and the form seems to have existed in writings now lost. There are even one or two *genres*, such as the imaginary speech, which Greece invented and which are not, fortunately, found in modern literature. When the curtain rose on Homer, European literature did not exist : long before it falls on the late Byzantines, the lines were laid on which it has moved up to our own day. This is the entire work of a single people, politically weak, numerically small, materially poor—according to the economy of nature which in things of the mind and the spirit gives a germinating power to few. The Greeks are justly admired for individual poems, plays, and pieces of writing ; but it was something even greater to have explored the possibilities of literature so far that posterity, while it has developed Greek *genres*, has not hitherto been able to add to them.

It is the same with the rest of our intellectual life. Modern civilization largely rests on the will to give a rational account of things: this will originates in Greece. All branches of modern philosophy, from metaphysics to psychology, and many of the sciences, spring from seeds that first germinated in Hellas. ' The students of nature (at the Renaissance) picked up the clue to her secrets exactly as it fell from the hands of the Greeks a thousand years before. The foundations of mathematics were so well laid by them, that our children learn their geometry from a book written for the schools of Alexandria more than 2,000 years ago. Modern astronomy is the natural continuation and development of the works of Hipparchus and Ptolemy ; modern physics of that of Democritus and Archimedes ; it was long before modern biological science outgrew the knowledge bequeathed to us by Aristotle, by Theophrastus, and by Galen.' [1] This is one part of the Greek Legacy.

[1] Huxley, *Science and Culture*, p. 16.

Another part are the works themselves. Literature can only be judged by reading it, and certainly it cannot be characterized in a few pages. But a man ignorant of Greek and anxious to estimate its value might form some idea by inquiring the opinion of qualified judges. He would find them unanimous : I suppose it is true that no man of eminence qualified to speak has ever spoken of Greek literature in any tone but one. The first testimony is that of the Romans. It is borne by their literature, starting in translations from Greek, adopting one after another of their *genres*, permeated through and through (and most of all in the greatest writers) by imitations, reminiscences, influences of Greek, confessing and glorying in the debt. ' In learning,' says Cicero, ' and in every branch of literature, the Greeks are our masters.' [1] A Roman boy should begin his studies with Greek, Quintilian thought, ' because Latin learning is derived from Greek '.[2] The same note is repeated in the literature of the Renaissance, and re-echoed by the most various voices of our own century.

' Beside the great Attic poets, like Aeschylus and Sophocles, I am absolutely nothing.' [3]

' He spoke with great animation of the advantage of classical study, Greek especially. "Where," he said, "would one look for a greater orator than Demosthenes ; or finer dramatic poetry, next to Shakspeare, than that of Aeschylus or Sophocles, not to speak of Euripides."' Herodotus he thought ' the most interesting and instructive book, next to the Bible, which had ever been written '.[4]

' The period which intervened between the birth of Pericles and the death of Aristotle is undoubtedly, whether considered in itself or with reference to the effects which it has produced upon the subsequent destinies of civilized man, the most memorable in the history of the world. . . . The wrecks and fragments of these subtle and profound minds, like the ruins of a fine statue, obscurely suggest to us the grandeur and perfection of the whole. Their very language . . . in variety, in simplicity, in flexibility, and in copiousness, excels every other language of the western world.' Then, after some words on their sculpture, he adds : ' their poetry seems to maintain a very high, though not so disproportionate a rank, in the comparison ' (with other literatures).[5]

---

[1] Tusc. iii. 1. 2.   [2] Inst. Or. i. 1. 12.
[3] Goethe, *Gespräche*, iii. 443.   [4] Wordsworth, *Tabletalk.*
[5] Shelley, *On the Manners of the Ancients.*

' The Greeks are the most remarkable people who have yet existed. . . . They were the beginners of nearly everything, Christianity excepted, of which the modern world makes its boast. . . . They were the first people who had a historical litera- ture ; as perfect of its kind (though not the highest kind), as their oratory, their sculpture, and their architecture. They were the founders of mathematics, of physics, of the inductive study of politics, of the philosophy of human nature and life. In each they made the indispensable first steps, which are the foundation of all the rest.' [1]

' From quotations I had seen I had a high notion of Aristotle's merits, but I had not the most remote notion what a wonderful man he was. Linnaeus and Cuvier have been my two gods . . . but they were mere schoolboys to old Aristotle.' [2]

' I have gone back to Greek literature with a passion quite astonishing to myself. . . . I felt as if I had never known before what intellectual enjoyment was. Oh that wonderful people ! There is not one art, not one science, about which we may not use the same expression which Lucretius has employed about the victory over superstition " *Primum Graius homo* ". I think myself very fortunate in having been able to return to these great masters while still in the full vigour of life and when my taste and judgement are mature. Most people read all the Greek that they ever read before they are five-and-twenty. . . . A young man, whatever his genius may be, is no judge of such a writer as Thucydides. I had no high opinion of him ten years ago. I have now been reading him with a mind accustomed to historical researches and to political affairs ; and I am astonished at my own former blindness, and at his greatness. I could not bear Euripides at college. I now read my recantation. He has faults undoubtedly. But what a poet ! ' [3]

These men—and there is no difficulty in adding to their number —are not only qualified but unprejudiced witnesses. They have no *parti pris*. They cannot be accused, as schoolmasters and dons are sometimes accused, of holding shares in a great Trading Bank of Greece and Rome Unlimited, and having a personal motive for their enthusiasm. Nor can it be said that they admired Greece because they knew nothing better. All—Goethe no less than the others—had English literature in their hands, knew it well and appreciated its greatness. Yet this, given in their

[1] Mill, *Dissertations*, ii. 283 f.   [2] Darwin to Ogle in 1882.
[3] Macaulay, *Life and Letters*, i. 431.

own words, is the impression which Greek made on them. *Securus iudicat orbis terrarum*; and the verdict here is plain. The Greeks created our intellectual life; they laid down the lines which European literature has followed; they wrote a body of prose and poetry which has won the homage of the world and which is of unique interest to any one who cares for literature.

A climber used to Welsh hills must accustom himself to a change of atmosphere if he is successfully to judge distances in Switzerland. A modern who reads Greek literature must adjust himself to similar differences, in style as well as in mood and mental views. Certain characteristics of Greek writing are a delight to those familiar with it, a stumbling-block to those who are not. If a reader new to the classics opened Thucydides, his first impression would probably be one of jejuneness, of baldness. If, fresh from Shelley or Tennyson, he came across the epigram of Simonides on the Spartan dead at Thermopylae, ' Stranger, tell the Spartans that we lie here, obeying their words,' he might see little in it but a prosaic want of colour. This exceeding simplicity or economy is a stumbling-block to those who are accustomed to the expansive modern manner. Yet such a reader would have been making the acquaintance of some of the finest things in Greek literature, which is always at its greatest when most simple, and he would have been face to face with a characteristic quality of it.

We may call this quality Economy and illustrate it by comparing an epitaph on a Greek boy with Ben Jonson's lines on a child actor. The former runs : ' His father Philip laid here to rest his twelve-year-old son, Nicoteles, his high hope.' Ben Jonson writes :

> Weep with me, all you that read
>   This little story ;
> And know, for whom a tear you shed,
>   Death's self is sorry.
>
> 'Twas a child that so did thrive
>   In grace and feature,
> As heaven and nature seemed to strive
>   Which owned the creature.
>
> Years he numbered scarce thirteen
>   When Fates turned cruel ;
> Yet three filled zodiacs had he been
>   The stage's jewel :

And did act (what now we moan)
  Old men so duly,
As sooth the Parcae thought him one,
  He played so truly.

So, by error, to his fate
  They all consented ;
But, viewing him since, alas, too late !
  They have repented.

These lines—and they are not the whole of the poem—are enough to illustrate the difference between the Greek method and the English, the latter rich and profuse, following the flow of an opulent fancy, the former reticent and restrained, leaving the reader's imagination room and need to play its part. There are materials for half a dozen epigrams in Ben Jonson's poem. Had he been Simonides or Plato, he would have stopped after the fourth line and, in the opinion of some critics, by saving his paper he would have improved his poem.

In their theory and in their practice the Greek writers were true to this principle of Economy. Their proverbs proclaim it : ' the half is greater than the whole ' : ' sow with the hand and not with the whole sack'. The great passages of their literature illustrate it. It is to be found no less in Thucydides' account of the siege of Syracuse (p. 225 f.) and in the close of the *Republic* (p. 318) than in the death of Hector (p. 40).

Closely allied to Economy is another mark of Greek writing. Like the Biblical writers, the Greeks tend to narrate events or facts without comment, leaving them to make their own impression, where a modern will develop and dwell on them. Thus Plato tells the death of his master with severe economy of detail, and adds only one brief comment on this great tragedy of his life : ' Such, Echecrates, was the death of our friend, the best man, I think, that I have ever known, the wisest too and the most just ' (p. 282). Thus the writer of the epitaph on Nicoteles says nothing directly of the sorrow or loss, but gives the boy's name and age and states that he was his father's high hope. Thus Sappho describes the fall of evening : ' Star of evening, that brings all things which bright Dawn scattered, you bring the sheep, you bring the goat, you bring the child back to its mother.'

This seems bald to us. We prefer Byron's amplification, bringing out the moral and telling us what to feel :

O Hesperus, thou bringest all good things—
Home to the weary, to the hungry cheer,
To the young bird the parent's brooding wings,
The welcome stall to the o'erlaboured steer ;
Whate'er of peace about our hearthstone clings,
Whate'er our household gods protect of dear,
Are gathered round us by thy look of rest ;
Thou bring'st the child too to its mother's breast.

Yet in the end we may come to prefer the Greek way. Something of course may be said for both methods. Amplitude of treatment and fullness of detail enrich the imagination ; economy stimulates it. The latter may become jejune, and is safe only in the hands of great writers : the former may provide too rich a feast and leave the full-fed mind inert. Everything is done for it and nothing left for it to do. Economy, on the other hand, throws the reader on his own resources, and sets the mind wandering in the fields of infinity.

It has a further advantage. It leads a reader to see and feel what is described instead of wallowing in vague emotion. Sound counts more than sense for many readers of literature. The meaning of a poem or piece of prose may be null or false, yet, if their ears are filled with sounding phrases, thunderous rhetoric, musical lines, they are satisfied. This weakness is likely to exclude them from understanding the greatest things in literature, and it certainly secures the popularity of many bad poems, plays, and novels. They may admire

I loved thee,—hark, one tenderer note than all—
Atthis, of old time, once—one long low fall,
Sighing—one long low lovely loveless call,
Dying—one pause in song so flamelike fast—
Atthis, long since in old time overpast—
One soft first pause and last.
One,—then the old rage of rapture's fiercest rain
Storms all the music-maddened night again.

But they will see little in Sappho's words that inspired Swinburne : ' I loved thee once, Atthis, long ago.' They will appreciate the greatness of Macbeth's speech

To-morrow, and to-morrow, and to-morrow,
Creeps in this petty pace from day to day ;

but not Macduff's reply to the comforter who tells him to face
the death of his wife and children like a man :

> I shall do so ;
> But I must also feel it as a man :
> I cannot but remember such things were,
> That were most precious to me.

In Homer they may be taken by the rich language and the roll
of the hexameter ; but they will think nothing of Priam's words
to the man who killed his son : ' I have had the heart to do what
no other mortal man has ever done—to stretch out my hand to
the face of my son's slayer' (p. 43). From translations of Greek
poetry, they will get little, for in a translation the original music
is almost always lost, and they will go away disappointed. Or
else they will learn that sense is greater than sound, and that (so
far as the two can be separated) what a writer sees and feels is of
more importance than the words in which he clothes it.

We will now glance at certain other qualities of Greek literature.
Some of these are difficult to appreciate in an English version.
The high level of technique, the literary art, which is an obvious
quality of Greek literature, is a volatile essence that escapes in
translation. But we may note that all the writers quoted in this
book, except Aristotle, Plutarch, and, in part, Thucydides, are
not only great writers, but masters of the art of writing.

Nor again can justice be done in a translation to that Beauty,
in which critics of past generations found the glory of Greece.
Those critics exaggerated; and we now know that the greatness
of Herodotus, Thucydides, or Aristotle (who have none of it)
is independent of beauty, and that there are other qualities in
Greek literature greater or as great. Yet even a translation reveals
its presence in Homer or the poets, and the extracts from Plato
will show it associated with the closest dialectical reasoning—
a rare bird in the drab aviary of philosophy. For the rest we
may remember that it was a Greek vase which inspired in Keats
the paradox

> Beauty is truth, truth beauty—that is all
> Ye know on earth and all ye need to know.

Two qualities, however, of Greek literature are as conspicuous
in a translation as in the originals. First is simplicity. It is not
only that Greek writings are briefer than ours, that the *Oedipus*

Tyrannus has fewer lines than the first two acts of *Hamlet*, and that Thucydides could be printed in a 24-page issue of *The Times*; but they show a firmer hold on the fundamental issues of life. As civilization moves further from its origin, it receives a thousand tributaries that continually augment its volume, and colour and confuse its streams. The interests of an early age are the principal interests of man, and the literature of such an age presents them unalloyed and uncomplicated by lesser issues. The poets make their poetry from emotions as old as the world, and have none of the refinements and elaborations which education and a long inheritance of culture superadd to the essential stuff of human nature. Like the Bible, Homer deals with feelings shared by mankind twenty centuries before Christ and twenty centuries after him, common equally to Shakespeare or Napoleon and to the stupidest and least educated of men. But Thucydides, Plato, Aristotle, with all their depth of feeling and analysis, are in their kind equally simple. They take us straight to those fundamental problems of morals and politics, which rise out of human nature, and continue so long as the world is peopled by men. The brevity of their writings is secured by the omission of lesser interests ; the great issues are left, standing out like forest trees which no undergrowth of brushwood masks. This explains the paradoxical fact that, with all their superficial disadvantages, the *Republic* and the *Politics* are still perhaps the best *introductions* to the study of morals and politics.

It would be foolish to demand that modern writers should have the simplicity of Homer or of the age of Pericles, or to pretend that they cannot be great without it. Every age must and will have its own literature, reflecting the minds and circumstances of those who write it. Nor is the advantage entirely on the side of the Greeks. A drama of Shakespeare or a novel of Tolstoi, with their long roll of *dramatis personae*, are more like life than a Greek tragedy with its absence of byplot and its few, central, characters. A modern historian would have recorded and discussed aspects of the history of fifth-century Greece which Thucydides ignores. Modern literature may claim that, with less intensity, it has greater amplitude and a more faithful presentation of the complexity of life. On the other hand the Greeks are free from that dominance of the abnormal which is one danger of modern literature ; they do not explore sexual and other aberrations or encourage their readers to explore them. They are also free from that dominance of the unessential, which, in life as in literature, is a more innocent but more subtle and perhaps equally ruinous vice. Read some of the great writers of modern England such as Browning, Meredith, Hardy, Henry James, Conrad : then turn to Homer or Herodotus or some Greek play. The reader will surely discover the meaning of Goethe's words : ' In the presence of antiquity the mind feels itself placed in the most ideal state of nature ; and even to this day the Homeric hymns have the power of freeing us, at any rate for moments, from the terrible burden which the tradition of many hundreds of years has rolled upon us.' *Porro unum necessarium.* In life human beings return from a distracting variety of interests to a few simple things. In literature, which is life's shadow, they need to do the same.

Of a third quality of Greek Literature we have already seen something, its Truthfulness : and this can be perfectly appreciated in a translation. The Greeks told no fewer lies than other races, but they had the desire and the power to see the world as it is. So they came to give Europe the conceptions of philosophy and science. These we inherit from them alone ; Palestine and our German ancestors neither created them, nor show any signs of the temper which creates them, and Rome received her share from Greece.

We shall understand Greek ' truthfulness ' best, if, dropping philosophical terms, and forgetting modern meanings, we remember a saying of Anaxagoras, who, when asked for what purpose he was born, replied : ' To contemplate the works of nature.' The disinterested passion for contemplating things, which gathered inquiring groups round Socrates to discuss what justice and friendship mean, or whether goodness is knowledge and can be learnt, has its counterpart in literature. The Greeks were fascinated by the spectacle of man and the world, and their fascination is seen not only in their formal philosophy. Of their poets it may be said that they were born to see the world and human life—not to moralize or to indulge in sentiment or rhetoric or mysticism about it, but to see it. Keats's description of the poetic temperament fits them closely : ' It has no self, it is everything and nothing. . . . It enjoys light and shade. . . . A poet is the most unpoetical of anything in existence, he is continually in, for, and filling some other body.' In such a mood men will write literature that may justly be called truthful. Avoiding the didactic, they will not distort truth to suit personal bias ; avoiding rhetoric, they will not sacrifice it to fine phrases ; avoiding sentiment and fancy, they will not gratify their own or their hearer's feelings at the expense of truth ; avoiding mysticism, they will not move away from facts into a world of emotions. Their care will be to see things, and their delight will be in the mere vision. They will echo the words of Keats, ' If a sparrow comes before my windows, I take part in its existence and pick about the gravel ' : they will not treat it as Shelley treats the skylark, or even as Keats and Wordsworth treat the nightingale. Herein is one of the secrets of Greek poetry, for the Greek poets, more than any others, bring us in a manner entirely simple and natural into immediate contact with what they describe, and thus escape the thousand distortions for which epigram, rhetoric, sentiment, fancy, mysticism, and romanticism are responsible. This secret may be called ' directness '. It is the habit of looking straight and steadily at things, and describing them as they are, the very contrary of the habit of didactic comment and of rhetorical or emotional inflation. The ' direct ' writer, in the fullest extent that is possible, keeps himself and his feelings in the background. He does not allow the mists which rise from a man's personality to come between him and his subject.

A few instances of directness will give a better idea of it than many definitions. Compare the two epitaphs on p. 5 and note how much more real a sorrow the Greek enshrines. The fancies, of which Jonson made his verse, are pretty ; but they are false and incompatible with deep feeling. The Greek neither plays with fancies nor indulges in the half justifiable extravagances of grief. It never loses from sight the dead child, and with perfect truth to fact sees that and the father's sorrow.

The following extract deals with a very different subject, but illustrates directness equally well. The scene is the Athenian colony of Amphipolis on the Struma ; the dramatis personae are the Spartan general Brasidas who wishes to capture it, and the Athenian Thucydides who was then at Thasos, distant half a day's sail from Amphipolis. ' As soon as Thucydides heard the news about Brasidas, he sailed quickly to Amphipolis . . . in order to garrison it if possible before it could capitulate, or at any rate to occupy Eion (its seaport). Meanwhile Brasidas, fearing the arrival of the Athenian fleet at Thasos and hearing that Thucydides . . . was one of the leading men of the country, did his utmost to get possession of the city before he arrived. . . . He therefore offered moderate terms. . . . These terms were

accepted, and the city was surrendered to him. On the evening
of the same day Thucydides and his ships sailed into Eion, but
not until Brasidas had taken possession of Amphipolis: another
night, and he would have seized Eion.' [1] The gist of the story
contained in this extract is plain. The Spartan general Brasidas
seized the important town of Amphipolis, and the Athenian
general came too late to save it. But who would guess that
the Athenian general Thucydides was the historian Thucydides
who wrote these words, and that the episode which he here
describes with such detachment and neutrality earned him perpetual exile under pain of death from the country which he
passionately loved ? Thucydides has told the bare facts, objec-
tively, as if they related to some one else, without a comment,
without a word of protest, excuse, explanation or regret on the
crowning disaster of his life. He writes of himself in the third
person. This is not the way in which modern generals describe
their mishaps, but it is the Greek way. Thucydides has forgotten
himself and his feelings ; he sees only the disastrous day when
he sailed up the Struma with his ships and found the gates of
Amphipolis closed against him. He ignores himself so far that he
does not call it disastrous, though disastrous it was for himself
and his country. With the same detachment he speaks of the
enslavement of Melos (p. 223 f.) and the tragedy of Syracuse
(p. 240), though he thinks, and makes us feel, that the one was
the crowning crime, the other the crowning disaster of his country.
He narrates the plain facts and leaves the reader to draw his
inferences. If we did not know that he was an Athenian, we
could hardly tell from his history whether he took the side of
Athens or Sparta in the war ; so entirely are he and his feelings
kept in the background. Yet he was an ardent patriot, and he
is describing the war in which his country lost supremacy and
empire. No historian of the war of 1914–18, whether on the
Allied or the German side, is likely to write of it in this way.

The art of Homer has the same quality of detachment. He
is a Greek, writing of a ten years' war between Greeks and
Asiatics, yet most of his readers sympathize with Hector rather
than with Achilles. He himself preferred neither, but saw and
felt equally for both ; with the hero who fought the losing battle
for Troy, and with him who lost his friend, and, intoxicated
with sorrow, could see and feel nothing but a passion of revenge.
It would seem hardly possible to write the close of the 22nd Book of

[1] Thuc. iv. 104, 105, 106 (tr. Jowett, mainly).

the *Iliad* (p. 33 f.), where the heroes meet, without taking sides; we, no doubt, should take Hector's side. But Homer stands apart from the quarrel, and sees both men and the feelings of both, writing with the pen of the Recording Angel, not of the Judge. What he or Thucydides thought in each case can only be guessed at. They have presented the facts without comment, and the facts tell their own tale, explain themselves, carry with them the feelings they should evoke, and shine by their own light, like the phosphorescence of the sea.

I have laid special stress on Greek ' truthfulness'. It is the parent, not only of Greek science and philosophy, which are the children of a desire to see things in themselves as they are, and not as the seer wishes them to be, but also, in part, of Greek Literature, where truth is never sacrificed to beauty or sentiment or emotion, and where neither the light nor the shade on the canvas of life is ignored, but both are depicted with an even-handed justice. It is the lesson which Europe began at the Renaissance to relearn from Greece, and which she has been perfecting ever since.

There are of course other teachers of this lesson. But the Greeks were the first to bring ' truthfulness' into the world, and they are peculiarly free from its dangers. For, like all qualities, it has its defects. It may be exclusive, blind, dour : and modern veracity, because it has to fight its way against falsities and obscurantism, has often worn the shape of an un-lovely protestantism. Not science only, but those writers who have reflected the scientific spirit in literature, have often been narrow and hard. Truth has not come naturally to them, but has been achieved by a struggle, of which they bear the marks. Thus the truthfulness of French realists and of their English followers has often been ' struggling and tasked', and their world barren of the colour of real life. The Greeks escaped these dangers. They did not have to establish the claims of truth against a hostile world and they are unscarred by conflict. Their truthfulness is not a protest, but a gift of nature. Homer does not force himself to do justice to Hector ; Thucydides and Hero-dotus are not consciously struggling to be impartial to the national enemy. They are following the natural bent of their minds. And it is this spontaneous and effortless veracity that they teach us.

But it is dangerous to talk of qualities and to dissect a writer or a people. The living being vanishes, and isolated limbs remain on the dissecting table. We shall see the Greeks as they were, if we think of them, not as incarnations of simplicity or beauty or truthfulness, but as human beings, entering on the common inheritance of life with the clear eye, the open mind, the eager enjoyment, the generous receptivity of children, and yet with the faculties of full-grown men. Such are the beings who will meet us in the following pages.[1]

[1] The gods are a stumbling-block to some modern readers of Greek Literature, though only in the early stages of their study. Any one who feels this difficulty may remember three things. First, we witness in Greek Literature the rapid advance of a people from a crude polytheism to a monotheism as lofty, in its way, as our own. Thus we meet many stages of the theological belief. In Homer the gods are beings with human passions and superhuman power: Thucydides, Plato, and Aristotle regard God much as we might. Second, the theme of Homer, of Tragedy, of Greek Literature as a whole, is not theology, but the fortunes of the human spirit moving among the changes and chances of life. Theological machinery is far more integral a part of *Paradise Lost* than it is of any Greek poem. It is on the human beings that the Greeks' eyes were fixed, and that our eyes should be fixed in reading them. Third, in Greek Tragedy, where the legends drew after them the old theology, though the poet might not believe in it, a reader who wishes can often substitute for the deity in any play some such conception as the Power behind the Universe, the Moral Law, the Laws of Nature, without any loss to the total effect.

II

HOMER

Si on me demandoit le chois de tous les hommes qui sont venus à ma connoissance, il me semble en trouver trois excellens au-dessus de tous les autres. L'un, Homère.—MONTAIGNE.[1]

Homer,
Whose poem Phoebus challenged for his own.
MILTON.

By great Homer set,
Not to impugn his undisputed throne,
The many-hearted by the mighty-hearted one.
R. BRIDGES : *Ode on the Tercentenary Commemoration
of Shakespeare.*

*We are high in the air ; beneath us a blue sea studded with
islands. On its eastern shore fertile valleys ascend from the sea-
coast to the high table-land of Asia Minor. In the west, across some
120 miles of water, is the Balkan Peninsula, ' an Alpine land set
in the sea'—in the north high mountains ; then ancient Greece
commences in the plain of Thessaly ; then more mountains ; then,
across a strip of sea, the Peloponnese.*

*We can prophesy something about the inhabitants of these lands.
The mountains of the north will breed a hardy, wild race, remote
from the influences of civilization. But in the south and east the
people of the sea-girt and indented coasts will be sailors, with all
that this implies of intercourse with other nations, and stimulus
from the sight of strange habits and men. Yet when they return from
the sea, each to his own green valley, they will find themselves cut
off from their neighbours by mountain walls, and, in the seclusion
of small communities, will develop their own nature and grow to be
individualists at heart. They will never be a rich people ; there is
too much rock and too little cornland or pasture. But in compensation, if scenery counts for anything, they will learn what beauty is
from the bright and clear air, the vivid sea, and the sharp outlines of
their hills.*

*Let us now see the inhabitants of Greece. It is the year 2000 B.C.
In the island of Crete we see a city and a rich palace with frescoed
walls, the home of the rulers of a maritime empire. Elsewhere, in
this ' Minoan Age', mists hide the life of these lands. Five hundred years pass, and we are at the opening of the ' Mycenaean Age'.*

---

[1] *Essays,* ii. 36. The essay contains an admirable tribute to Homer.

The civilization of Crete has developed and spread. On the hill-tops of Mycenae and Tiryns, in the swamps of Boeotia, and, built above the ruins of older cities, on a low hill called Troy at the mouth of the Dardanelles, we see elaborate fortresses of huge, unmortared stones. They are inhabited by a dark-haired race, skilful in goldsmith's work, wearing bronze armour.

Now turn the eyes northwards to Macedonia, and note those tribes on the move before the pressure of other tribes. We can see them moving with their herds down the Vardar valley; later following the sea-coast under the snows of Olympus, among which their imagination will place heaven, and through the defile of Tempe into Thessaly, where some find a home. More follow and yet more, breaking successively over valley after valley, and filling them as the sea fills rockpools, till, hundreds of years after the time when we first saw the wanderers, Greece is theirs from Olympus to Cape Malea.

These invaders are governed by kings supported by a council of chiefs; their decisions must be brought before the tribesmen and ratified by them. We recognize the elements of our own constitution, though their relative importance has changed.

The tribal names are perhaps preserved in the Greek lands which they conquer—Hellenes, Thessalians, Boeotians, Achaeans, Phocians, Dorians. They mix with the inhabitants of the land in various proportions; in Attica the natives predominate, in Sparta the invading Dorians keep their race pure. Mycenae is destroyed; Mycenaean culture is submerged; and the native languages give way to the Aryan tongue of the invaders, which we call Greek.

Greece once conquered—the conquest takes centuries—the migrating tribes push across the sea, to the western coast of Asia Minor, where three groups of settlements, Aeolian, Ionian, Dorian, preserve the name of tribes. In one of these migrations Troy is destroyed, and its siege, blended with memories of earlier battles, forms the subject of the first epic of Europe, sung in the metre that its conquerors had brought with them from the north.[1]

Greek literature begins with Homer and presents us at once with a great poem and an unsolved problem. When and where was 'Homer' written? Is it a composite work of many poets or, in the main, from one hand? Probably the *Iliad* dates from the ninth century and was written on the coast of Asia Minor, but no one has yet proved whether it was composed by one or by many poets. The more general view is that it is composed of

---

[1] The historical sketches are printed in italics.

different strata from different dates, and perhaps was given its final form by one great poet. But interesting as the problem is, we shall ignore it, and pass to the poems.

Step three thousand years back and walk into the palace of King Alcinoüs of Phaeãcia.

THERE was a gleam as it were of sun or moon through the high-roofed hall of great-hearted Alcinous. Brazen were the walls which ran this way and that from the threshold to the inmost chamber, and round them was a frieze of blue, and golden were the doors that closed in the good house. Silver were the door-posts that were set on the brazen threshold, and silver the lintel thereupon, and the hook of the door was of gold. And on either side stood golden hounds and silver, which Hephaestus wrought by his cunning, to guard the palace of great-hearted Alcinous, being free from death and age all their days. And within were seats arrayed against the wall this way and that, from the threshold even to the inmost chamber, and thereon were spread light coverings finely woven, the handiwork of women. There the Phaeacian chieftains were wont to sit eating and drinking, for they had continual store. Yea, and there were youths fashioned in gold, standing on firm-set bases, with flaming torches in their hands, giving light through the night to the feasters in the palace. And he had fifty handmaids in the house, and some grind the yellow grain on the millstone, and others weave webs and turn the yarn as they sit, restless as the leaves of the tall poplar tree: and the soft olive oil drops off that linen, so closely is it woven. And without the courtyard hard by the door is a great garden, of four ploughgates, and a hedge runs round on either side. And there grow tall trees blossoming, pear-trees and pomegranates, and apple-trees with bright fruit, and sweet figs, and olives in their bloom. The fruit of these trees never perisheth neither faileth, winter nor summer, enduring through all the year. Evermore the West Wind blowing brings some fruits to birth and ripens others. Pear upon pear waxes old, and apple on apple, yea and cluster ripens upon cluster of the grape, and fig upon fig.

There too hath he a fruitful vineyard planted, whereof the one part is being daily dried by the heat, a sunny plot on level ground, while other grapes men are gathering, and yet others they are treading in the wine-press. In the foremost row are unripe grapes that cast the blossom, and others there be that are growing black to vintaging. There too, skirting the furthest line, are all manner of garden beds, planted trimly, that are perpetually fresh, and therein are two fountains of water, whereof one scatters his streams all about the garden, and the other runs over against it beneath the threshold of the courtyard, and issues by the lofty house, and thence did the townsfolk draw water. These were the splendid gifts of the gods in the palace of Alcinous.[1]

Such was a Homeric palace and garden ; so sat its princes, and in such a scene did the minstrel ' Homer ' recite his poems, to pass the long evening hours when men sat over their wine. The first and greatest of these poems is the *Iliad*, the story of a few days in the ten years' war, that the allied princes of Greece under Agamemnon fought against Troy to recover Helen, wife of Meneläüs of Sparta, whom the Trojan Paris had carried off. At its outset Achilles, the chief Greek champion, has retired from the fighting, indignant at the injustice of Agamemnon, who took from him a slave girl, his portion of the spoil. In consequence the Greeks suffer defeat, till Patroclus, the dearest friend of Achilles, is killed, and Achilles re-enters the fighting and kills Hector, the leader of the Trojans. The poem is in twenty-four books and written in hexameters (of which Kingsley's *Andromeda* and Bridges's *Ibant Obscuri* afford different examples in English, but the hexameter does not suit our language). Unlike the early writing of other peoples, it is a perfect work of art : the Greeks themselves never surpassed its diction and metre. The story is simple, centring on war, and elementary in its plot. What did Homer make out of it to deserve the title of greatest of epic poets ?

To answer these questions we must enter the Homeric world, and see it first at its favourite occupation. The scene is set at dawn in a plain two miles broad at the mouth of the Dardanelles :

[1] Odyssey, vii. 84 ff., tr. Butcher and Lang. Elsewhere I have quoted the Iliad in the famous prose version of Lang, Leaf, and Myers (Macmillan & Co.), the Odyssey in Dr. Mackail's brilliant verse rendering (John Murray).

on the beach the Greek ships are drawn up, and the camp in front of them is protected by a stockade and trench ; some four miles away, on a low hill, stands the city of Troy. Homer begins his fighting by a vision of the goddess who presides over all war.

BUT Zeus sent forth fierce Discord unto the fleet ships of the Achaians, and in her hands she held the signal of war. And she stood upon the huge black ship of Odysseus, that was in the midst, to make her voice heard on either side, both to the huts of Aias, son of Telamon, and to the huts of Achilles, for these twain, trusting in their valour and the might of their hands, had drawn up their trim ships at the two ends of the line. There stood the goddess and cried shrilly in a great voice and terrible, and mighty strength she set in the heart of each of the Achaians, to war and fight unceasingly. And straightway to them war grew sweeter than to depart in the hollow ships to their dear native land.[1]

In the following scene the Trojans attack the Greek ships. Troy is also called Ilios. The Greeks are also called Argives, Achaians, and Danaans.

AND Hector was raging, like Ares, the brandisher of the spear, or as when ruinous fires rage on the hills, in the folds of a deep woodland ; and foam grew about his mouth, and his eyes shone beneath his dreadful brows, and around the temples of Hector as he fought his helm shook terribly. For Zeus out of heaven was his ally, and gave him honour and renown, he being but one man against so many. For short of life was he to be, yea, and already Pallas Athēne was urging against him the day of destiny, at the hand of Achilles. And fain he was to break the ranks of men, trying them wheresoever he saw the thickest press, and the goodliest harness. Yet not even so might he break them for all his eagerness. Nay, they stood firm, and embattled like a steep rock and a great, hard by the hoary sea, a rock that abides the swift paths of the shrill winds, and the swelling waves

[1] Iliad, xi. 3 ff.

that roar against it. Even so the Danaans steadfastly abode the Trojans, and fled not away. But Hector shining with fire on all sides leaped on the throng, and fell upon them, as when beneath the storm-clouds a fleet wave reared of the winds falls on a swift ship, and she is all hidden with foam, and the dread blast of the wind roars against the sail, and the sailors fear, and tremble in their hearts, for by but a little way are they borne forth from death, even so the spirit was torn in the breasts of the Achaians. But he came on like a ravening lion making against the kine, that are feeding innumerable in the low-lying land of a great marsh, and among them is a herdsman that as yet knoweth not well how to fight with a wild beast concerning the slaughter of the kine of crooked horn, and ever he paces abreast with the rear or the van of the cattle, but the lion leaps into the midst, and devours a cow, and they all tremble for fear, even so the Achaians all were made terribly adread by Hector and father Zeus.

Now were they come between the ships, and the prows protected them, the prows of the ships drawn up in the first line, but the Trojans rushed in after them. And the Argives were compelled even of necessity to give back from the foremost ships, yet there they abode in close rank beside the huts, and did not scatter throughout the camp. For shame and fear restrained them and ceaselessly they kept shouting each to other. Now Gerēnian Nestor above all, the Warden of the Achaians, implored each man by the memory of them that begat him, and spake beseechingly : ' O friends, play the man, and set shame of other men's contempt in your hearts. Let each also be mindful of children and wives, and of his possessions, and of them that begat him, whether any have parents yet alive or they be already dead. For their sake do I here beseech you, for the sake of them that are not with us, to stand stoutly, nor turn to flight.'

Nor yet did it please the spirit of high-hearted Aias, to stand in the place whereto the other sons of the Achaians had withdrawn, but he kept faring with long strides, up and down the decks of the ships, and he wielded in his hands a great pike for

sea-battles, jointed with rings, two and twenty cubits in length.
And always with terrible cries he summoned the Danaans to
defend the ships and the huts. Nor did Hector abide in the throng
of well-armed Trojans, but even as a tawny eagle rushes on a flock
of winged fowl, that are feeding by a riverside, a flock of geese, or
cranes, or long-necked swans, even so Hector made straight for a
black-beaked ship, rushing right on it, and mightily Zeus urged
him on from behind with his strong hand, and roused on the host
along with him.

So again keen battle was set by the ships. Thou wouldst deem
that unwearied and unworn they met each other in war, so eagerly
they fought. And in their striving they were minded thus ; the
Achaians verily deemed that never would they flee from the danger,
but perish there, but the heart of each Trojan hoped in his breast,
that they should fire the ships, and slay the heroes of the Achaians.
With these imaginations they stood to each other, and Hector
seized the stern of a seafaring ship, a fair ship, swift on the brine,
that had borne Protesilāos to Troia, but brought him not back
again to his own country. Now round his ship the Achaians
and Trojans warred on each other hand to hand, nor far apart
did they endure the flights of arrows, nor of darts, but standing
hard each by other, with one heart, with sharp axes and hatchets
they fought, and with great swords, and double-pointed spears.
And many fair brands, dark-scabbarded and hilted, fell to the
ground, some from the hands, some from off the shoulders of
warring men, and the black earth ran with blood. But Hector,
after that once he had seized the ship's stern, left not his hold,
keeping the ensign in his hands, and he called to the Trojans :
' Bring fire, and all with one voice do ye raise the war-cry ; now
hath Zeus given us the dearest day of all—to take the ships that
came hither against the will of the gods, and brought many woes
upon us, by the cowardice of the elders, who withheld me when
I was eager to fight at the sterns of the ships, and kept back the
host. But if even then far-seeing Zeus did harm our wits, now he
himself doth urge and command us onwards.'

So spake he, and they set yet the fiercer on the Argives. And Aias no longer abode their onset, for he was driven back by the darts, but he withdrew a little—thinking that now he should die —on to the oarsmen's bench of seven feet long, and he left the decks of the trim ship. There then he stood on the watch, and with his spear he ever drave the Trojans from the ships, whosoever brought unwearied fire, and ever he shouted terribly, calling to the Danaans : ' O friends, Danaan heroes, men of Ares' company, play the man, my friends, and be mindful of impetuous valour. Do we deem that there be allies at our backs, or some wall stronger than this to ward off death from men ? Verily there is not hard by any city arrayed with towers, whereby we might defend ourselves, having a host that could turn the balance of battle. Nay, but we are set down in the plain of the mailèd men of Troy, with our backs against the sea, and far off from our own land. Therefore is safety in battle, and not in slackening from the fight.'

So spake he, and rushed on ravening for battle, with his keen spear. And whosoever of the Trojans was coming against the ship with blazing fire, to pleasure Hector at his urging, him would Aias wound, awaiting him with his long spear, and twelve men in front of the ships at close quarters did he wound.[1]

Homeric society is essentially aristocratic ; which does not mean that its common people are without shining virtues, but that the princes, though their kingdoms are small, stand out above the masses, like mountain peaks rising from an undistinguished plain. The English counterpart is the life of the Highlands, portrayed for example in *Waverley*. But Homer portrays a darker and harder world than Scott. We may read the *Iliad* for its poetry or for its pictures of adventurous, heroic, many-coloured life ; but, beneath all its gaiety and zest, sound very different notes: epic in form, in spirit it is a great tragedy. These chiefs spend their time in fighting and adventure, under conditions where the weak go to the wall, and we hear

> Sounds of insult, shame and wrong,
> And trumpets blown for wars.

[1] Il. xv. 605 ff.

Life is difficult and often disastrous, and death is the door to a dim world where men are bloodless and impotent ghosts. Over all are the gods, immortal and stronger than men, but capricious with human passions, and vaguely dominated by something called Fate. Hence, in a sense, these men are pessimists, and their view of life is expressed in the famous reply of one of them to the adversary who asked his name: ' Great-hearted son of Tȳdeus, why inquirest thou of my generation ? Even as are the generations of leaves, such are those likewise of men ; the leaves that be, the wind scattered on the earth, and the forest buddeth and putteth forth more again, when the season of spring is at hand : so of the generations of men, one putteth forth and another ceaseth.' [1]

How are human beings to live worthily in a world where life is hard, death certain, and there is no promise beyond ? Homer's answer to this question is the character which he was the first to create ; in creating it he gave the world a word and a conception which is still central in the ideals of the ordinary man of to-day. Three thousand years have enlarged the field of heroism, but hardly improved his portrait of a hero. To understand it, we may take a few passages which reveal the spirit of these heroes. Glaucus, who gave that gloomy verdict on life quoted above yet ends his speech : ' Hippolochus begat me, and of him do I declare myself sprung ; he sent me to Troy, and bade me urgently to be ever the best and to excel all other men, nor put to shame the lineage of my fathers that were of the noblest blood in Ephyre and in wide Lycia.' [2] Achilles, speaking to the horse that carries him into battle, says : ' Xanthus, why prophesiest thou my death ? Well know I of myself that it is appointed me to perish here, far from my father dear and mother ; howbeit anywise I will not refrain till I give the Trojans surfeit of war.' He spoke, and with a cry among the foremost drove on his whole-hooved steeds.[3] Hector, urged by his brother to bow to unfavourable omens and retreat, replies : ' One omen is best— to fight for our country '.[4] Odysseus thus rebukes Agamemnon, when disaster threatens, and he proposes to abandon the camp : ' Son of Ātreus, what a word has escaped your lips' barrier. Unhappy man, would that you commanded some other, paltry, army, and were not king over us, to whom, methinks, from youth to age Zeus has given to wind the web of grievous war, till we perish,

---

[1] Il. vi. 145 ff.   [2] Il. vi. 206 ff.   [3] Il. xix. 420 ff.
[4] Il. xii. 243.

all of us.'[1] Clearest of all is the speech of Sarpēdon to Glaucus, both Lykian chiefs, who were fighting on the Trojan side.

GLAUKOS, wherefore have we twain the chiefest honour—seats of honour, and messes, and full cups in Lykia, and all men look on us as gods ? And wherefore hold we a great demesne by the banks of Xanthos, a fair demesne of orchard-land, and wheat-bearing tilth ? Therefore now it behoveth us to take our stand in the first rank of the Lykians, and encounter fiery battle, that certain of the well-corsleted Lykians may say, ' Verily our kings that rule Lykia be no inglorious men, they that eat fat sheep, and drink the choice wine honey-sweet : nay, but they are also of excellent might, for they war in the foremost ranks of the Lykians. Ah, friend, if once escaped from this battle we were for ever to be ageless and immortal, neither would I fight myself in the foremost ranks, nor would I send thee into the war that giveth men renown, but now—for assuredly ten thousand fates of death do every way beset us, and these no mortal may escape nor avoid—now let us go forward, whether we shall give glory to other men, or others to us.'[2]

None of these speakers has any of the civilian's illusions about war. They make no fine speeches about glory and romance. They know that ' ten thousand fates of death hover over their heads' and that they have to wind the endless web of battle till each of them is dead. None the less they will not cease till they have given their enemies surfeit of war. That is heroism, in the plains of Troy or in the trenches of France.

We will now watch from the walls of Troy some of the heroes who are fighting below, and we shall see the woman about whom they are fighting, for she is on the wall. Her name has become a symbol for beauty and has passed as a tradition even into the songs of Irish fiddlers who know nothing else of Greek or Greece. Homer has never told us what she looked like, but in spite of that he gives us an impression of her beauty such as no painting could give. He does it in the simplest way (and it shows how well he understood the art of description), by telling the impression

---

[1] Il. xiv. 83 ff   [2] Il. xii. 310 ff.

that she made on the Trojans ; there could be no greater witness to her than the admiration wrung from the men to whose land she had brought ruin. The elders of Troy are on the wall, watching the armies below ; Helen enters. Priam is King of Troy.

THESE old men had now ceased from battle for old age, yet were they right good orators, like grasshoppers that in a forest sit upon a tree and utter their delicate voice ; even so sat the elders of the Trojans upon the tower. Now when they saw Helen coming to the tower they softly spake winged words one to the other : ' Small blame is it that Trojans and well-greaved Achaians should for such a woman long time suffer hardships ; marvellously like she is to the immortal goddesses to look upon. Yet even so, though she be so goodly, let her go upon their ships, and not stay to vex us and our children after us.'

So said they, and Priam lifted up his voice and called to Helen : ' Come hither, dear child, and sit before me, that thou mayest see thy former husband and thy kinsfolk and thy friends. I hold thee not to blame ; nay, I hold the gods to blame who brought on me the dolorous war of the Achaians—so mayst thou now tell me who is this huge hero, this Achaian warrior so goodly and great. Of a truth there are others even taller by a head ; yet did mine eyes never behold a man so beautiful nor so royal ; for he is like unto one that is a king.'

And Helen, fair among women, spake and answered him : ' Reverend art thou to me and dread, dear father of my lord ; would that sore death had been my pleasure when I followed thy son hither, and left my home and my kinsfolk and my daughter in her girlhood and the lovely company of mine age-fellows. But that was not so, wherefore I pine with weeping. Now will I tell thee that whereof thou askest me and inquirest. This is Ātreides, wide-ruling Agamemnon, one that is both a goodly king and mighty spearman. And he was husband's brother to me, ah shameless me ; if ever such an one there was.'

And next the old man saw Odysseus, and asked : ' Come now, tell me of this man too, dear child, who is he, shorter by a head than Agamemnon son of Atreus, but broader of shoulder and of chest to behold ? His armour lieth upon the bounteous earth, and himself like a bell-wether rangeth the ranks of warriors. Yea, I liken him to a thick-fleeced ram ordering a great flock of white ewes.'

Then Helen sprung of Zeus made answer to him : ' Now this is Lāertes' son, crafty Odysseus, that was reared in the realm of Ithaka, rugged though it be, and is skilled in all the ways of wile and cunning device.'

Then sage Antēnor made answer to her : ' Lady, verily the thing thou sayest is true indeed, for erst came goodly Odysseus hither also on an embassage for thee, in the company of Menelāos dear to Āres ; and I gave them entertainment and welcomed them in my halls, and learnt the aspect of both and their wise devices. Now when they mingled with the Trojans in the assembly, while all stood up Menelaos overpassed them all by the measure of his broad shoulders ; but when both sat down, Odysseus was the more stately. And when they began to weave the web of words and counsel in the face of all, then Menelaos harangued fluently, in few words, but very clearly, seeing he was not long of speech, neither random, though in years he was the younger. But whenever Odysseus full of wiles rose up, he stood and looked down, with eyes fixed upon the ground, and waved not his staff whether backwards or forwards, but held it stiff, like to a man of no under-standing ; one would deem him to be churlish, and naught but a fool. But when he uttered his great voice from his chest, and words like unto the snowflakes of winter, then could no mortal man contend with Odysseus ; then marvelled we not thus to behold Odysseus' aspect.'

And thirdly the old man saw Aias, and asked : ' Who then is this other Achaian warrior, goodly and great, pre-eminent among the Argives by the measure of his head and broad shoulders ? '

And long-robed Helen, fair among women, answered : ' This is huge Aias, bulwark of the Achaians. And on the other side amid the Cretans standeth Īdomeneus like a god, and about him are gathered the captains of the Cretans. Oft did Menelaos dear to Āres entertain him in our house whene'er he came from Crete. And now behold I all the other glancing-eyed Achaians, whom well I could discern and tell their names; but two captains of the host can I not see, even Kastor tamer of horses and Polydeukes the skilful boxer, mine own brethren, whom the same mother bare. Either they came not in the company from lovely Lakedaimon; or they came hither indeed in their seafaring ships, but now will not enter into the battle of the warriors, for fear of the many scornings and revilings that are mine.'

So said she; but them the life-giving earth held fast there in Lakedaimon, in their dear native land.[1]

We will look closer at two Homeric heroes, taking first Hector, who is the more attractive, partly because he fights bravely a hopeless battle. Here he is not on the battle-field, but in his home with his wife, Andromache.

ANON Hector came to his well-stablished house. But he found not white-armed Andromache in the halls; she with her boy and fair-robed handmaiden had taken her stand upon the tower, weeping and wailing. And when Hector found not his noble wife within, he came and stood upon the threshold, and spake amid the serving women: 'Come tell me true now, my serving women. Whither went white-armed Andromache forth from the hall? Hath she gone out to my sisters or unto my brothers' fair-robed wives, or to Athēne's temple, where all the fair-tressed Trojan women propitiate the awful goddess?'

Then a busy housedame spake in answer to him: 'Hector, seeing thou straitly chargest us to tell thee true, she went to the great tower of Ilios, because she heard the Trojans were hard pressed, and great victory was for the Achaians. So hath she come in haste to the wall, like unto one frenzied; and the nurse with her beareth the child.'

So spake the housedame, and Hector hastened from his house

[1] Il. iii. 149 ff.

back by the same way down the well-builded streets. When he had passed through the great city and was come to the Skaian gates, whereby he was minded to issue upon the plain, then came his dear-won wife, running to meet him, even Andromache daughter of great-hearted Eëtion, Eëtion that dwelt beneath wooded Plakos, and was king of the men of Kilikia; for his daughter was wife to bronze-harnessed Hector. So she met him now, and with her went the handmaid bearing in her bosom the tender boy, the little child, Hector's loved son, like unto a beautiful star. Him Hector called Skamandrios, but all the folk Astyanax; for only Hector guarded Ilios.[1] So now he smiled and gazed at his boy silently, and Andromache stood by his side weeping, and clasped her hand in his, and spake and called upon his name. ' Dear my lord, this thy hardihood will undo thee, neither hast thou any pity for thine infant boy, nor for me forlorn that soon shall be thy widow; for soon will the Achaians all set upon thee and slay thee. But it were better for me to go down to the grave if I lose thee; for never more will any comfort be mine, when once thou, even thou, hast met thy fate, but only sorrow. Moreover I have no father nor lady mother: my father was slain of goodly Achilles, for he wasted the populous city of the Kilikians, even high-gated Thēbe, and slew Eëtion; yet he despoiled him not, for his soul had shame of that, but he burnt him in his inlaid armour and raised a barrow over him; and all about were elm-trees planted by the mountain nymphs, daughters of aegis-bearing Zeus. And the seven brothers that were mine within our halls, all these on the selfsame day went within the house of Hādes;[2] for fleet-footed Achilles slew them all amid their kine of trailing gait and white-fleeced sheep. And my mother, that was queen beneath wooded Plakos, her brought he hither with the other spoils, but afterward took a ransom untold to set her free; but in her father's halls was she smitten by the archer Artemis.[3] Nay, Hector, thou art to me father and lady mother, yea and

---

[1] Astyanax = ' City King '.   Scamander was one of the rivers of Troy.
[2] i. e. were killed.   [3] i.e. died.

brother, even as thou art my goodly husband. Come now, have pity and abide here upon the tower, lest thou make thy child an orphan and thy wife a widow. And stay thy folk beside the fig-tree, where best the city may be scaled and the wall is assailable. Thrice came thither the most valiant that are with the two Aiantes and famed Īdomeneus and the sons of Ātreus and Tȳdeus' valiant son,[1] and essayed to enter ; whether one skilled in sooth-saying revealed it to them, or whether their own spirit urgeth and biddeth them on.'

Then great Hector of the glancing helm answered her : ' Surely I take thought of all these things, my wife ; but I have very sore shame of the Trojans and Trojan dames with trailing robes, if like a coward I shrink away from battle. Moreover mine own soul forbiddeth me, seeing I have learnt ever to be valiant and fight in the forefront of the Trojans, winning my father's great glory and mine own. Yea of a surety I know this in heart and soul ; the day shall come for holy Ilios to be laid low, and Priam and the folk of Priam of the good ashen spear. Yet doth the anguish of the Trojans hereafter not so much trouble me, neither my mother, Hekabe's, neither king Priam's, neither my brethren's, the many and brave that shall fall in the dust before their foemen, as doth thine anguish in the day when some mail-clad Achaian shall lead thee weeping and rob thee of the light of freedom. So shalt thou abide in Argos and ply the loom at another woman's bidding, and bear water from fount Messēïs or Hypereia, being grievously entreated, and sore constraint shall be laid upon thee. And then shall one say that beholdeth thee weep : " This is the wife of Hector, that was foremost in battle of the horse-taming Trojans when men fought about Ilios." Thus shall one say hereafter, and fresh grief will be thine for lack of such an husband as thou hadst to ward off the day of thraldom. But me in death may the heaped-up earth be covering, ere I hear thy crying and thy carrying into captivity.'

So spake glorious Hector, and stretched out his arm to his boy.

[1] Greek chiefs.

But the child shrunk crying to the bosom of his fair-girdled nurse, dismayed at his dear father's aspect, and in dread at the bronze and horse-hair crest that he beheld nodding fiercely from the helmet's top. Then his dear father laughed aloud, and his lady mother ; forthwith glorious Hector took the helmet from his head, and laid it, all gleaming, upon the earth ; then kissed he his dear son and dandled him in his arms, and spake in prayer to Zeus and all the gods, ' O Zeus and all ye gods, vouchsafe ye that this my son may likewise prove even as I, pre-eminent amid the Trojans, and as valiant in might, and be a great king of Ilios. Then may men say of him, " Far greater is he than his father " as he returneth home from battle ; and may he bring with him blood-stained spoils from the foeman he hath slain, and may his mother's heart be glad.'

So spake he, and laid his son in his dear wife's arms ; and she took him to her fragrant bosom, smiling tearfully. And her husband had pity to see her, and caressed her with his hand, and spake and called upon her name : ' Dear one, I pray thee be not of oversorrowful heart ; no man against my fate shall hurl me to Hades ; only destiny, I ween, no man hath escaped, be he coward or be he valiant, when once he hath been born. But go thou to thine house and see to thine own tasks, the loom and distaff, and bid thine handmaidens ply their work ; but for war shall men provide, and I in chief of all men that dwell in Ilios.'

So spake glorious Hector ; and took up his horse-hair crested helmet ; and his dear wife departed to her home, oft looking back, and letting fall big tears. Anon she came to the well-stablished house of man-slaying Hector, and found therein her many hand-maidens, and stirred lamentation in them all. So bewailed they Hector, while yet he lived, within his house : for they deemed that he would no more come back to them from battle, nor escape the fury of the hands of the Achaians.[1]

We see in this passage the dark and the bright sides of the Homeric world. There is the raid, like a border foray, in which

[1] Il. vi. 370 ff.

Andromache's home was destroyed, and there is the shadow of her future. There is also a glimpse of home life and of the relations of husband and wife, in which three thousand years have made little change. As a character study the portraiture of the pair is perfectly true ; the woman in her distress thinks only of her husband and asks him for an impossibility ; the man knows that he is going to death, but also that he must go. Notice his motives. He sees her point of view ; but *aidos* (a sense of honour), his own instinct, and his family traditions bid him go. Of the three figures here, the husband and child will be dead, the woman a slave, before the year is out.

Of the rival heroes, Hector is the more sympathetic character, but Achilles is the greater creation. He has much in common with Shakespeare's Hotspur—youth, prowess, a passion for honour, a personal wrong to resent. But Achilles is a far more tragic figure. Handsome, young, the son of a goddess, the greatest of the Greek warriors, he is doomed to a life not only short but full of sorrow, embittered, through his own fault, by the death of the friend whom he passionately loves. He belongs to a far more primitive age than Hotspur, and is a far more primitive being. He has the intense passions of a child or a savage. Like a child, his soul has room for one emotion only at a time, and that emotion is proportionately intense. He is consumed, now with acute resentment of injustice, now with grief for his dead friend, now with a passion of revenge. It is a type which no one could draw to-day, so remote are we from it, but we can recognize its truth and power. I quote his reply to the Greek envoys who brought gifts and offers of reconciliation from Agamemnon. In antiquity it was admired as a speech, and it is admirably direct, forcible, dignified. The irreconcilable spirit may shock us, but three thousand years have passed since then, and it is fair to remember that the Greek host was not a national army in our sense, but a collection of independent chiefs. It is the voice of such a chief (we can see a modern equivalent in the opening scene of the *Legend of Montrose*) : the mood is resentment of wrong and contempt of the wrongdoer.

HEAVEN-sprung son of Lāertes, Odysseus of many wiles, in openness must I now declare unto you my saying, even as I am minded and as the fulfilment thereof shall be, that ye may not sit before me and coax this way and that.

For hateful to me even as the gates of hell is he that hideth one
thing in his heart and uttereth another : but I will speak what
meseemeth best.   Not me, I ween, shall Agamemnon son of
Atreus persuade, nor the other Danaans, seeing we were to have
no thanks for battling with the foemen ever without respite.   He
that abideth at home hath equal share with him that fighteth his
best, and in like honour are held both the coward and the brave ;
death cometh alike to the untoiling and to him that hath toiled
long.   Neither have I any profit for that I endured tribulation of
soul, ever staking my life in fight.   Even as a hen bringeth her
unfledged chickens each morsel as she winneth it, and with herself
it goeth hard, even so I was wont to watch out many a sleepless
night and pass through many bloody days of battle, warring with
folk for their women's sake.   Twelve cities of men have I laid
waste from shipboard, and from land eleven, I do you to wit,
throughout deep-soiled Troy-land ; out of all these took I many
goodly treasures and would bring and give them all to Agamemnon
son of Atreus, and he staying behind amid the fleet ships would
take them and portion out some few but keep the most.   Now
some he gave to be meeds of honour to the princes and the kings,
and theirs are left untouched ; only from me of all the Achaians
took he my darling lady and keepeth her.' [1]

He rejects the offer of Agamemnon's daughter in marriage, and
continues :

'MANY Achaian maidens are there throughout Hellas and
Phthīa, [2] daughters of princes that ward their cities ;
whomsoever of these I wish will I make my dear lady.
Very often was my high soul moved to take me there a wedded
wife, a help meet for me, and have joy of the possessions that my
father Pēleus possesseth.   For not of like worth with life hold
I even all the wealth that men say was possessed of the well-
peopled city of Ilios in days of peace gone by, before the sons

---

[1] Il. ix. 307 ff.   [2] The home of Achilles.

of the Achaians came; neither all the treasure that the stone threshold of the archer Phoebus Apollo encompasseth in rocky Pytho. For kine and goodly flocks are to be had for the harrying, and tripods and chestnut horses for the purchasing; but to bring back man's life neither harrying nor earning availeth when once it hath passed the barrier of his lips. For thus my goddess mother telleth me, Thetis the silver-footed, that twain fates are bearing me to the issue of death. If I abide here and besiege the Trojan's city, then my returning home is taken from me, but my fame shall be imperishable; but if I go home to my dear native land, my fame is taken from me, but my life shall endure long while, neither shall the issue of death soon reach me.'[1]

Achilles has his will, gratifies his resentment, and pays a tragic penalty for its gratification : while he keeps away from the battle, his friend Patroclus is killed by Hector, and in a passion of grief and revenge he returns to war and in the following scene meets Hector. All our sympathies go to Hector. But we shall not understand Achilles, unless we feel too with this primitive hero, who has lost his dearest friend, and now finds himself face to face with his slayer.

THUS saying toward the city Achilles was gone in pride of heart, rushing like some victorious horse in a chariot that runneth lightly at full speed over the plain; so swiftly plied Achilles his feet and knees. Him the old man Priam first beheld as he sped across the plain, blazing as the star that cometh forth at harvest time, and plain seen his rays shine forth amid the host of stars in the darkness of night, the star whose name men call Orīon's Dog. Brightest of all is he, yet for an evil sign is he set, and bringeth much fever upon hapless men. Even so on Achilles' breast the bronze gleamed as he ran. And the old man cried aloud and beat upon his head with his hands, raising them on high, and with a cry called aloud beseeching his dear son; for he before the gates was standing, all hot for battle with Achilles. And the old man spake piteously unto him, stretching

[1] Il. ix. 395 ff.

forth his hands : ' Hector, beloved son, I pray thee await not this man alone with none beside thee, lest thou quickly meet thy doom, slain by the son of Pēleus, since he is mightier far, a merciless man. Would the gods loved him even as do I ! then quickly would dogs and vultures devour him on the field—thereby would cruel pain go from my heart—the man who hath bereft me of many valiant sons, slaying them and selling them captive into far-off isles. Have compassion on me, the helpless one, who still can feel, ill-fated ; whom Zeus will bring to naught by a grievous doom in the path of old age, having seen full many ills, his sons perishing and his daughters carried away captive, and his chambers laid waste and infant children hurled to the ground in terrible war, and his sons' wives dragged away by the ruinous hands of the Achaians. Myself then last of all at the street door will ravening dogs tear, when some one by stroke or throw of the sharp bronze hath bereft my limbs of life—even the dogs I reared in my halls about my table and to guard my door, which then having drunk my blood, maddened at heart shall lie in the gateway.'

Thus Priam with wailing spake to his dear son, beseeching him sore, yet persuaded not Hector's soul, but he stood awaiting Achilles as he drew nigh in giant might. As a serpent of the mountains upon his den awaiteth a man, having fed on evil poisons, and fell wrath hath entered into him, and terribly he glareth as he coileth himself about his den, so Hector with courage unquenchable gave not back, leaning his shining shield against a jutting tower. Then sore troubled he spake to his great heart : ' Ay me, if I go within the gates and walls, Polydamas will be first to bring reproach against me, since he bade me lead the Trojans to the city during this ruinous night, when noble Achilles arose. But I regarded him not, yet surely it had been better far. And now that I have undone the host by my wantonness, I am ashamed before the men of Troy and women of trailing robes, lest at any time some worse man than I shall say : " Hector by trusting his own might undid the host." So will they speak ; then to me would it be better far to face Achilles and either slay him and go home, or myself die gloriously before the city.'

Thus pondered Hector as he stood, but nigh on him came Achilles, peer of the war-god, warrior of the waving helm, brandishing from his right shoulder his terrible spear ; and all around the bronze on him flashed like the gleaming of blazing fire or the Sun as he ariseth. And trembling seized Hector as he was aware of him, nor endured he to abide in his place, but left the gates behind him and fled in fear. And the son of Peleus darted after him, trusting in his swift feet. As a falcon upon the mountains, swiftest of winged things, swoopeth fleetly after a trembling dove ; and she before him fleeth, while he with shrill screams hard at hand still darteth at her, for his heart urgeth him to seize her : so Achilles in hot haste flew straight for him, and Hector fled beneath the Trojan's wall, and plied swift knees. They past the watch-place and wind-waved wild fig-tree sped ever, away from under the wall, along the wagon-track, and came to the fair flowing springs, where two fountains rise that feed deep-eddying Skamandros. The one floweth with warm water, and smoke goeth up therefrom around as it were from a blazing fire, while the other even in summer floweth forth like cold hail or snow or ice that water formeth. And there beside the springs are broad washing-troughs hard by, fair troughs of stone, where wives and fair maidens of the men of Troy were wont to wash bright raiment, in the old time of peace, before the sons of the Achaians came. Thereby they ran, he flying, he pursuing. Valiant was the flier, but far mightier he who fleetly pursued him. For not for beast of sacrifice or for an ox-hide were they striving, such as are prizes for men's speed of foot, but for the life of horse-taming Hector was their race. And as when victorious whole-hooved horses run rapidly round the turning-points, and some great prize lieth in sight, be it a tripod or a woman, in honour of a man that is dead,[1] so thrice around Priam's city circled those twain with flying feet, and all the gods were gazing on them.

[1] At funeral games.

The gods watching from heaven allow Athene to descend to help Achilles.

BUT after Hector sped fleet Achilles chasing him vehemently. And as when on the mountains a hound hunteth the fawn of a deer, having started it from its covert, through glens and glades, and if it crouch to baffle him under a bush, yet scenting it out the hound runneth constantly until he find it ; so Hector baffled not Peleus' fleet-footed son. Oft as he set himself to dart under the well-built walls over against the Dardanian gates, if haply from above they might succour him with darts, so oft would Achilles gain on him and turn him toward the plain, while himself he sped ever on the city-side. And as in a dream one faileth in chase of a flying man—the one faileth in his flight and the other in his chase—so failed Achilles to overtake him in the race, and Hector to escape. But when the fourth time they had reached the springs, then the Father[1] hung his golden balances, and set therein two lots of dreary death, one of Achilles, one of horse-taming Hector, and held by the midst and poised. Then Hector's fated day sank down, and fell to the house of Death, and Phoebus Apollo left him. But to Peleus' son came the bright-eyed goddess Athene, and standing near spake to him winged words : ' Now verily, glorious Achilles dear to Zeus, I have hope that we twain shall carry off great glory to the ships for the Achaians, having slain Hector, for all his thirst for fight. No longer is it possible for him to escape us. But do thou now stand and take breath, and I will go and persuade this man to confront thee in fight.'

Thus spake Athene, and he obeyed, and was glad at heart, and stood leaning on his bronze-pointed ashen spear. And she left him and came to noble Hector, like unto Deïphobos his brother in shape and in strong voice, and standing near spake to him winged words : ' Dear brother, verily fleet Achilles doth thee violence, chasing thee round Priam's town with swift feet : but come let us make a stand and await him on our defence.'

[1] Zeus.

Thus saying Athene in her subtlety led him on. And when they were come nigh in onset on one another, to Achilles first spake great Hector of the glancing helm : ' No longer, son of Peleus, will I fly thee, as before I thrice ran round the great town of Priam, and endured not to await thy onset. Now my heart biddeth me to stand up against thee ; I will either slay or be slain. But come hither and let us pledge us by our gods, for they shall be witnesses and beholders of covenants : I will entreat thee in no outrageous sort, if Zeus grant me to outstay thee, and if I take thy life, but when I have despoiled thee of thy glorious armour, O Achilles, I will give back thy dead body to the Achaians, and do thou the same.'

But unto him with grim gaze spake Achilles fleet of foot : ' Hector, talk not to me, thou madman, of covenants. As between men and lions there is no pledge of faith, nor wolves and sheep can be of one mind, but imagine evil continually against each other, so is it impossible for thee and me to be friends, neither shall be any pledge between us until one or other shall have fallen and glutted with blood Ares, the stubborn god of war. Bethink thee of all thy soldiership : now behoveth it thee to quit thee as a good spearman and valiant man of war. No longer is there way of escape for thee, but Pallas Athene will straightway subdue thee to my spear ; and now in one hour shalt thou pay back for all my sorrows for my friends whom thou hast slain in the fury of thy spear.'

He said, and poised his far-shadowing spear and hurled. And noble Hector watched the coming thereof and avoided it ; for with his eye on it he crouched, and the bronze spear flew over him, and fixed itself in the earth ; but Pallas Athene caught it up and gave it back to Achilles, unknown to Hector shepherd of hosts. Then Hector spake unto the noble son of Peleus : ' Thou hast missed, so no wise yet, godlike Achilles, hast thou known from Zeus the hour of my doom, though thou thoughtest it. Cunning of tongue art thou and a deceiver in speech, that fearing thee I might forget my valour and strength. Not as I flee shalt thou plant thy spear in my reins, but drive it straight through my breast as I set on thee, if God hath given thee to do it. Now in thy turn avoid my spear of bronze. O that thou mightst take it all into thy flesh ! Then would the war be lighter to the Trojans, if but thou wert dead, for thou art their greatest bane.'

He said, and poised his long-shadowed spear and hurled it, and smote the midst of the shield of Peleus' son, and missed him not : but far from the shield the spear leapt back. And Hector was wroth that his swift weapon had left his hand in vain, and he stood downcast, for he had no second ashen spear. And he called with a loud shout to Deïphobos of the white shield, and asked of him a long spear, but he was no wise nigh. Then Hector knew the truth in his heart, and spake and said : ' Ay me, now verily the gods have summoned me to death. I deemed the warrior Deïphobos was by my side, but he is within the wall, and it was Athene who played me false. Now therefore is evil death come very nigh me, not far off, nor is there way of escape. This then was from of old the pleasure of Zeus and of the far-darting son of Zeus,[1] who yet before were fain to succour me : but now my fate hath found me. At least let me not die without a struggle or ingloriously, but in some great deed of arms whereof men yet to be born shall hear.'

Thus saying he drew his sharp sword that by his flank hung great and strong, and gathered himself and swooped like a soaring eagle that darteth to the plain through the dark clouds to seize a tender lamb or crouching hare. So Hector swooped, brandishing his sharp sword. And Achilles made at him, for his heart was filled with wild fierceness, and before his breast he made a covering with his fair graven shield, and tossed his bright four-plated helm ; and round it waved fair golden plumes. As a star goeth among stars in the darkness of night, Hesperos, fairest of all stars set in heaven, so flashed there forth a light from the keen spear Achilles poised in his right hand, devising mischief against noble Hector, eyeing his fair flesh to

---

[1] Apollo.

find the fittest place. Now for the rest of him his flesh was covered by the fair bronze armour he stripped from strong Patroklos when he slew him, but there was an opening where the collar bones coming from the shoulders clasp the neck, even at the gullet, where destruction of life cometh quickliest ; there, as he came on, noble Achilles drave at him with his spear, and right through the tender neck went the point. Yet the bronze-weighted ashen spear clave not the windpipe, so that he might yet speak words of answer to his foe. And he fell down in the dust, and noble Achilles spake exultingly : ' Hector, thou thoughtest, whilst thou wert spoiling Patroklos, that thou wouldst be safe, and did reck nothing of me who was afar, thou fool. But away among the hollow ships his comrade, a mightier far, even I, was left behind, who now have unstrung thy knees. Thee shall dogs and birds tear foully, but his funeral shall the Achaians make.'

Then with faint breath spake unto him Hector of the glancing helm : ' I pray thee by thy life and knees and parents leave me not for dogs of the Achaians to devour by the ships, but take good store of bronze and gold, gifts that my father and lady mother shall give to thee, and give them home my body back again, that the Trojans and Trojans' wives give me my due of fire after my death.'

But unto him with grim gaze spake Achilles fleet of foot : ' Entreat me not, dog, by knees or parents. Would that my heart's desire could so bid me myself to carve and eat raw thy flesh, for the evil thou hast wrought me, as surely is there none that shall keep the dogs from thee, not even should they bring ten- or twenty-fold ransom and here weigh it out, and promise even more, not even were Priam Dardanos' son to bid pay thy weight in gold, not even so shall thy lady mother lay thee on a bed to mourn her son, but dogs and birds shall devour thee utterly.'

Then dying spake unto him Hector of the glancing helm : ' Verily I know thee and behold thee as thou art, nor was I destined to persuade thee ; truly thy heart is iron in thy breast. Take heed now lest I draw upon thee wrath of gods, in the day when Paris and Phoebus Apollo slay thee, for all thy valour, at the Skaian gate.'

He ended, and the shadow of death came down upon him, and his soul flew forth of his limbs and was gone to the house of Hades, wailing her fate, leaving her vigour and youth. Then to the dead man spake noble Achilles : ' Die : for my death, I will accept it whensoever Zeus and the other immortal gods are minded to accomplish it.'

Then Achilles devised foul entreatment of noble Hector. The tendons of both feet behind he slit from heel to ankle-joint, and thrust therethrough thongs of ox-hide, and bound him to his chariot, leaving his head to trail. And when he had mounted the chariot and lifted therein the famous armour, he lashed his horses to speed, and they nothing loth flew on. And dust rose around him that was dragged, and his dark hair flowed loose on either side, and in the dust lay all his once fair head, for now had Zeus given him over to his foes to entreat foully in his own native land.

How the news came to Andromache.

BUT Hector's wife knew not as yet, for no true messenger had come to tell her how her husband abode without the gates, but in an inner chamber of the lofty house she was weaving a double purple web, and broidering therein manifold flowers. Then she called to her goodly-haired handmaids through the house to set a great tripod on the fire, that Hector might have warm washing when he came home out of the battle—fond heart, and was unaware how, far from all washings, bright-eyed Athēne had slain him by the hand of Achilles. But she heard shrieks and groans from the battlements, and her limbs reeled, and the shuttle fell from her hands to earth. Then again among her goodly-haired maids she spake : ' Come two of ye this way with me that I may see what deeds are done. It was the voice of my husband's noble mother that I heard, and in my own breast my heart leapeth to my mouth and my knees are numbed beneath me : surely some evil thing is at hand against the children of Priam. Would that such word might never reach my ear ! yet terribly I dread lest noble Achilles have cut off bold Hector from the city by himself and chased him to the plain and ere this ended his perilous pride that possessed him, for never would he tarry among the throng of men but ran out before them far, yielding place to no man in his hardihood.'

Thus saying she sped through the chamber like one mad, with beating heart, and with her went her handmaidens. But when she came to the battlements and the throng of men, she stood still upon the wall and gazed, and beheld him dragged before the city :—swift horses dragged him recklessly toward the hollow ships of the Achaians. Then dark night came on her eyes and shrouded her, and she fell backward and gasped forth her spirit.[1]

Two things will strike every reader of these passages. He will observe the art with which Homer tells the story, preparing us by hints and forebodings, making it doubtful first whether Hector will fight at all, then whether the gods will save him, and so keeping us in suspense. Note how the story of the pursuit is broken by two scenes on Olympus ; this affords Homer an opportunity of describing it in such a way that the description is drawn out, giving a sense of the long chase, without becoming monotonous. Observe how he brings the scene before our eyes. For this purpose he has no minute description of the place or people ; the long preambles of Scott, the precise realism of Flaubert were not his way. But the speeches and story are broken by phrases that make us see the heroes as they run or fight, and in the crises Homer throws in a few words that bring before us the scene or person—once in the race, when we see the steaming spring and the water-troughs, once just before Hector's death, when we see the helmet of the man who kills him. The poet has nothing to learn in the art of telling a story.

The other thing that will strike the reader is the savagery of Achilles, and he may wonder why a Greek poet should enlist our

[1] Extracts from Il. xxii. 21–467, with omissions.

sympathies on the side of a Trojan. The answer is that here, at the very outset of their history, we have met one of the most remarkable qualities of Greek literature, to which I have already referred. More than any people, the Greeks seem to have had a power of being spectators of life, looking at it with open eyes, recording exactly what they saw, whether it suited their tastes, views, and wishes or not. They are as faithful and impartial as a mirror, which has no preferences or sympathies, or at any rate conceals them. The writer disappears from his writings. Morally this is a dangerous gift, but it enables a man to see life as it is, without prejudice, fear, or superstition, and we can prophesy that its owners will achieve the greatest things in the world of art and thought where truth is at least half the battle. Here Homer is simply telling us what happened; he shows us this primitive savage chief, on fire with grief at the death of his friend, and occupied only with the vision of revenge; he makes us feel how powerful and formidable he is—Hector's forces pale before him like a flame in the sunlight. Homer is deeply conscious of the tragedy. But he takes no side and passes no judgement; he says simply, ' Thus it was.'

The *Iliad* closes, as Greek works of art always close, with a lessening of the strain; we pass out of the fighting to private sorrow, and something like reconciliation. Priam drives across the Trojan plain and into the camp of his enemies to beg the body of Hector from Achilles. Homer's description conveys without effort the terror of that drive across No-man's-land by night, and the suspense when they meet a stranger by the river. He proves to be Hermes, and guides Priam to the tent of Achilles. There are few passages in literature more audacious and tragic in conception than the scene that follows—the meeting of Priam with the man who killed his son—and any one who wishes to test its greatness can do so by trying to write it himself, and then comparing his draft with Homer. Homer opens quietly with a description of the scene; and what follows does not achieve its effect by heroics or elaborate or passionate writing. Sorrow meets sorrow, and in the soul of Achilles pity and a delicate considerateness is born. No passage could illustrate better the high courtesy of the heroic age; and there is something more than courtesy. Yet throughout Homer gives us a sense of fires burning beneath the ashes; we are on the edge of an outbreak of ungovernable passions; and at the close Priam steals away while Achilles is sleeping.

BUT Priam leapt from the car to the earth, and left Ĩdaios in his place ; he stayed to mind the horses and mules ; but the old man made straight for the house where Achilles was wont to sit. And therein he found the man himself, and his comrades sate apart : two only, the hero Automedon and Alkimos, were busy in attendance ; and he was lately ceased from eating and drinking : and still the table stood beside him. But they were unaware of great Priam as he came in, and so stood he anigh and clasped in his hands the knees of Achilles, and kissed his hands, terrible, man-slaying, that slew many of Priam's sons. And as when a grievous curse cometh upon a man who in his own country hath slain another and escapeth to a land of strangers, to the house of some rich man, and wonder possesseth them that look on him—so Achilles wondered when he saw god-like Priam, and the rest wondered likewise, and looked upon one another. Then Priam spake and entreated him, saying : ' Bethink thee, O Achilles like to gods, of thy father that is of like years with me, on the grievous pathway of old age. Him haply are the dwellers round about entreating evilly, nor is there any to ward from him ruin and bane. Nevertheless while he heareth of thee as yet alive he rejoiceth in his heart, and hopeth withal day after day that he shall see his dear son returning from Troy-land. But I, I am utterly unblest, since I begat sons the best men in wide Troy-land, but declare unto thee that none of them is left. Fifty I had, when the sons of the Achaians came. Now of the more part had impetuous Ares unstrung the knees, and he who was yet left and guarded city and men, him slewest thou but now as he fought for his country, even Hector. For his sake come I unto the ships of the Achaians that I may win him back from thee, and I bring with me untold ransom. Yea, fear thou the gods, Achilles, and have compassion on me, even me, bethinking thee of thy father. Lo, I am yet more piteous than he, and have braved what none other man on earth hath braved before, to stretch forth my hand towards the face of the slayer of my sons.'

Thus spake he, and stirred within Achilles desire to make

lament for his father. And he touched the old man's hand and gently moved him back. And as they both bethought them of their dead, so Priam for man-slaying Hector wept sore as he was fallen before Achilles' feet, and Achilles wept for his own father, and now again for Patroklos, and their moan went up throughout the house. But when noble Achilles had satisfied him with lament and the desire thereof departed from his heart and limbs, straightway he sprang from his seat and raised the old man by his hand, pitying his hoary head and hoary beard, and spake unto him winged words and said : ' Ah hapless ! many ill things verily thou hast endured in thy heart. How durst thou come alone to the ships of the Achaians and to meet the eyes of the man who hath slain full many of thy brave sons ? of iron verily is thy heart. But come then, set thee on a seat, and we will let our sorrows lie quiet in our hearts, for all our pain, for no avail cometh of chill lament. This is the lot the gods have spun for miserable men, that they should live in pain ; yet themselves are sorrowless. For two urns stand upon the floor of Zeus filled, one with evil gifts, and one with blessings. To whomsoever Zeus dealeth a mingled lot, that man chanceth now upon ill and now again on good, but to whom he giveth but the bad kind him he bringeth to scorn, and evil famine chaseth him over the goodly earth, and he is a wanderer honoured neither of gods nor men. Even thus to Peleus [1] gave the gods splendid gifts from his birth, for he excelled all men in good fortune and wealth, and was king of the Myrmidons, and mortal though he was the gods gave him a goddess to be his bride. Yet even on him God brought evil, seeing that there arose to him no offspring of princely sons in his halls, save that he begat one son to an untimely death. Neither may I tend him as he groweth old, since very far from my country I am dwelling in Troy-land, to vex thee and thy children. And of thee, old sire, we have heard how of old time thou wert happy, even how of all these folk, men say, thou wert the richest in wealth and in sons, but after that the Powers of Heaven brought this bane on thee, ever are battles and

[1] Father of Achilles.

man-slayings around thy city. Keep courage, and lament not unabatingly in thy heart. For nothing wilt thou avail by grieving for thy son, neither shalt thou bring him back to life.'

Then made answer unto him the old man, godlike Priam: Bid me not to a seat, O fosterling of Zeus, so long as Hector lieth uncared for at the huts, but straightway give him back that I may behold him with mine eyes; and accept thou the great ransom that we bring. So mayst thou have pleasure thereof, and come unto thy native land, since thou hast spared me from the first.'

Then fleet-footed Achilles looked sternly upon him and said: ' No longer chafe me, old sire; of myself am I minded to give Hector back to thee, for there came to me a messenger from Zeus, even my mother who bare me, daughter of the Ancient One of the Sea. And I know, O Priam, that some god it is that hath guided thee to the swift ships of the Achaians. For no mortal man, even though in prime of youth, would dare come among the host, for neither could he escape the watch, nor easily thrust back the bolt of our doors. Therefore now stir my heart no more amid my troubles, lest I leave not even thee in peace, old sire, within my hut, albeit thou art my suppliant, and lest I transgress the commandment of Zeus.'

Thus spake he, and the old man feared, and obeyed his word.

Achilles goes out to tell the attendants to wash and dress Hector's body.

THUS spake noble Achilles, and went back into the hut, and sate him down on the cunningly wrought couch whence he had arisen by the opposite wall, and spake a word to Priam: ' Thy son, old sire, is given back as thou wouldst and lieth on a bier, and with the break of day thou shalt see him thyself as thou carriest him. But now bethink we us of supper. For even fair-haired Niobe bethought her of meat, she whose twelve children perished in her halls, six daughters and six lusty sons. The sons Apollo, in his anger against Niobe, slew with arrows from his silver bow, and the daughters archer Artemis, for that Niobe matched

herself against fair-cheeked Lēto,[1] saying that the goddess bare but
twain but herself many children : so they though they were but
twain destroyed the others all.   Nine days they lay in their blood,
nor was there any to bury them, for Zeus turned the folk to
stones.   Yet on the tenth day the gods of heaven buried them, and
she then bethought her of meat, when she was wearied out with
weeping tears.   And somewhere now among the cliffs, on the
lonely mountains, even on Sīpylos, where they say are the
couching-places of nymphs that dance around Achelōös, there
she, albeit a stone, broodeth still over her troubles from the gods.
But come let us too, noble father, take thought of meat, and
afterward thou shalt mourn over thy dear son as thou carriest
him to Ilios ; and many tears shall be his due.'

But when they had put off the desire of meat and drink, then
Priam son of Dardanos marvelled at Achilles to see how great he
was and how goodly, for he was like a god to look upon.   And
Achilles marvelled at Priam son of Dardanos, beholding his noble
aspect and hearkening to his words.   But when they had gazed
their fill upon one another, then first spake the old man, godlike
Priam, to Achilles : ' Now presently give me whereon to lie,
fosterling of Zeus, that of sweet sleep also we may now take our
fill at rest : for never yet have mine eyes closed beneath their
lids since at thy hands my son lost his life, but I continually
mourn and brood over countless griefs, grovelling in the court-
yard-close amid the mire.   Now at last have I tasted bread and
poured bright wine down my throat, but till now I had tasted
naught.'

He said, and Achilles bade his comrades and handmaids to
set a bedstead beneath the portico, and to cast thereon fair
shining rugs and spread coverlets above and thereon to lay
thick mantles to be a clothing over all.   And the maids went
forth from the inner hall with torches in their hands, and
quickly spread two beds in haste.   Then said fleet-footed
Achilles unto Priam : ' Lie thou without, dear sire, lest there

---

[1] Mother of Apollo and Artemis.

come hither one of the counsellers of the Achaians, such as ever take counsel with me by my side, as custom is. If any of such should behold thee through the swift black night, forthwith he might haply tell it to Agamemnon shepherd of the host, and thus would there be delay in giving back the dead. But come say this to me and tell it true, how many days' space thou art fain to make funeral for noble Hector, so that for so long I may myself abide and may keep back the host.'

And the old man, godlike Priam, answered him saying : ' If thou art verily willing that I accomplish noble Hector's funeral, by doing as thou sayest, O Achilles, thou wilt do me grace. For thou knowest how we are pent within the city, and wood from the mountain is far to fetch, and the Trojans are much in fear. Nine days will we make moan for him in our halls, and on the tenth we will hold funeral and the folk shall feast, and on the eleventh we will make a barrow over him, and on the twelfth we will do battle if need be.'

Then again spake the fleet noble Achilles unto him saying : ' All this, O ancient Priam, shall be as thou biddest ; for I will hold back the battle even so long a time as thou tellest me.'

Thus speaking he clasped the old man's right hand at the wrist, lest he should be anywise afraid at heart.[1]

On the grounds of small differences of style, theology, geographical knowledge, and general atmosphere, the *Odyssey* is generally dated one or two generations later than the *Iliad* and ascribed to a different author. A sequel to the *Iliad*, it tells the adventures of the Greek chief Odysseus, as he returned after the sack of Troy to his island home in Ithaca, and how he dealt with the lawless chiefs who had seized his house and were wooing his wife. Its subject is not war, its interests are ' travel and home-coming ', and it shows another side of life in the heroic age.

Its hero, too, is very different from Achilles, though not less living. Achilles is young, passionate, fated to unhappiness and an early death—a figure of tragedy. Odysseus is none of these things. He is a middle-aged man, making his way back from war

---

[1] Extracts from Il. xxiv. 469–672.

to his home. He is not superhuman in wisdom, courage, acts, or glory. Two constant epithets express him—'the much-enduring', 'the man of many devices'. Worldly prudence, resource, and a stubborn persistence, which in spite of discouragement and even despair keeps a tenacious life, bring him home through endless difficulty and misadventure. Incidentally he is the first great traveller. He is ' much-enduring ', and travel in the Homeric age needed and developed courage as much as war. He is a ' man of many devices ', and there is no such school for resourcefulness as travel. But his wisdom goes deeper than mere fertility of expedient, for travel to him means 'seeing the cities of men and knowing their thoughts'. Hence he is the most open-minded and genial of men, for he has learnt to understand and live with kings and swineherds, princesses and maid servants, giants and enchantresses and gods, rogues and fools (of the latter he has plenty in his crew), indeed with every kind of being, except the disloyal and the bully. Hence he is the best of talkers, for to anecdote and reminiscence he adds knowledge of men and the widest sympathy. Hardship has not left him harsh or cynical or tired, but merely wiser and with

> Wonder not dead and thirst not dried,
> Still gazing on the never full,
> Eternal, mundane spectacle.

Yet he has a passion for home that draws him across the seas to rugged Ithaca, and makes him desert a goddess for Penelope. *Vetulam suam praetulit immortalitati* ; and nobody has said better things about home. But Greek legend and Tennyson were right when they made him take again to the road in old age, for the love of roaming is one of the few passions inextinguishable by time.

Let us see the kind of adventures that might have befallen us, had we sailed the seas in the Homeric age ; we shall see something of Odysseus by the way. We might have come to an island like this, where Odysseus sat on the rocks and looked over the barren sea, weeping ' because a fair-tressed goddess stayed him there, and there is no more delightful sight than the smoke going up from one's native land '. Yet it was a beautiful place.

HOLDING it now, the Shining One[1] with might
Took wing, and mounting the Pierian height,
Out of the sky on ocean darted down,
And swift across the billows urged his flight.
As a sea-eagle that his finny prey
Chases, his thickset plumage wet with spray,
Through the dread gulfs of sea unharvested,
Over the thronging waves he sped his way.
And now that island far amid the foam
Reaching, from out the violet sea he clomb
Over the mainland, to the cavern great
Wherein the fair-tressed nymph had made her home.
Within he found her in the cavern-cell;
Where from a brazier by her, burning well,
A fire of cloven cedar-wood and pine
Far through the island sent a goodly smell.
And in it she with voice melodious sang,
While through the warp her golden shuttle rang
As to and fro before the loom she went.
But round the cave a verdurous forest sprang
Of poplars, and sweet-scented cypresses,
And alders; and long-pinioned birds in these
Nested, owls, falcons, chattering cormorants,
And all that ply their business in the seas.
But round the hollow cavern trailing went
A garden-vine with heavy clusters bent;
And rising all arow, four springs abroad
This way and that their shining water sent.
And on both sides fair-flowering meads were set,
Soft-clad with parsley and with violet.
Even an immortal, if he came, that sight
Marvelling might view and joy thereof might get.
There stood the fleetfoot Shining One, that sight
Marvelling to view; and when to his delight

[1] Hermēs, sent by Zeus to tell the goddess Calypso to release Odysseus.

All he had viewed, into the cavern wide
He entered ; but Calypso, Goddess bright,
Failed not to know him, seeing him face to face ;
For never do the Gods' immortal race
Fail one to know another when they meet,
How far soe'er apart their dwelling-place.
But therewithin Odysseus high of heart
He found not then ; who, sitting far apart
On the sea-beach, as oftentimes before,
Fretted with tears and sighs and bitter smart,
Out seaward to the barren ocean-rim
Kept gazing, and his eyes with tears were dim.[1]

Or we might have come to an island hardly less beautiful.

'NOW on that coast an island makes a bar
   Across a bay's mouth, neither very far
   From the Cyclopes' land nor close to it :
And all about it tangled woods there are.
And there innumerable goats are bred ;
For no man's footprint scares them, nor the tread
Of hunters with their hounds, who in the woods
Range, faring hard, on many a mountain-head.
For no poor land it is, but fit to bear
All fruits in season, set with meadows fair,
Well-watered, soft, beside the grey sea-banks ;
And vines would flourish never-failing there.
And level tilth it has, whence harvests deep
Men at the season evermore might reap,
So rich the soil is under ; and thereby
A haven, ships at anchorage to keep
Unmoored, not needing anchors to let go
Or mooring-cables from the stern to throw,
But to lie beached until the sailors' mind
Moves them to voyage, and the breezes blow.

[1] Od. v. 49 ff.

But at the haven's head with water bright
A spring beneath a cavern leaps to light
Amid a grove of poplars. Thither we
Came sailing on, and through the darkling night
Some God directed us ; for not a ray
Glimmered, but round the ships a thick mist lay,
And the moon showed no light out of the sky,
But muffling clouds had hidden her away.
So that no outlook of the island told,
Nor the long waves upon the beach that rolled
Could we discern, until upon the strand
Our beached galleys grated and took hold.
And when they grounded, all the sails therefrom
We lowered, and on the edge of the sea-foam
Ourselves we disembarked and fell asleep,
And waited for the shining Dawn to come.'[1]

Odysseus and his men row across to a neighbouring island.

'BUT as across the narrow strait we drew,
A cave upon the headland came in view,
High-vaulted, nigh the sea, with laurel trees
Shaded, and flocks about it not a few
Of sheep and goats lay sleeping, and around
Were reared great boulders sunk into the ground
To make a courtyard wall, filled up between
With tall-stemmed pines and oak trees lofty-crowned.
And there a giant man was wont to sleep,
Far and alone who shepherded his sheep,
Nor went among his fellows, choosing there
A lonely life in lawlessness to keep.
Mighty of frame he was, a monster dread,
Not like a man of them who live on bread,
But like some wooded crag that high aloft
Among the mountains rears its lonely head.

[1] This and the following extracts are from Od. ix. 116 ff., with omissions.

E 2

So to the giant's cave apace came we,
Nor found him in it : for his fat sheep he
Was pasturing afield ; and we the cave
Entered, and looked about it curiously.
With cheeses mats were full as they could hold,
And lambs and kids were crowded up in fold
All sorted separately, the first-born,
The halflings, and the young but few days old.
And the wrought vessels that he milked in lay,
Both pails and pans, all brimming up with whey.
Then was the counsel of my fellows first
To lift some cheeses thence and go our way ;
And next, that opening the pens with speed
To the swift ship for plunder we should lead
The lambs and kids, and over the salt sea
Sail forth ; but to their words I gave not heed ;
As had been better far for them and me :
Being desirous his own self to see
And haply get gifts from him : but no joy
For my companions was that sight to be.
Then kindled we a fire below the rock
And sacrificed, and cheeses from his stock
We took and ate, and sat abiding him
Till he came on us shepherding his flock.
A monstrous faggot of dry wood he bore
For supper-firing, and on the cave-floor
Down with a clatter cast it ; and in dread
We huddled inward farther from the door.
But into the wide cave the fatted sheep
He drove, that he was wont for milk to keep,
But left their males, the he-goats and the rams,
Outside within the courtyard sunken deep.
Then a huge slab he lifted up and set
Against the doorway, such as labourers met
With two-and-twenty goodly four-wheeled wains,

All harnessed, from the threshold could not get.
On the cave's mouth that towering slab he slid,
And, sitting down his bleating flocks amid,
His ewes and his she-goats milked all in turn,
And set to each her suckling lamb or kid.
Half the white milk he curdled, and laid by
The curd in wicker frails to drain it dry,
And half he set in vessels to take up
And drink from when his supper-time drew nigh.
But when his task was finished and made good,
He lit a fire, and spied us where we stood,
And questioned us : Who are you, strangers ? whence
Sail you across the pathways of the flood ?
Over the seas on traffic do you sail,
Or cruising idly on a random trail
Like pirates, who at hazard of their lives
Wander, to outland people carrying bale ?
So said he, and our hearts within us brake ;
For his deep voice and his gigantic make
Wrought terror in us.'

Odysseus answers the questions of the Cyclops :

'SO said I, and he answered not again
With ruthless heart, but leapt upon my men,
And at a single clutch a pair of them
Caught, and like puppies dashed them on his den,
So that their brains were spattered on the floor,
Wetting the earth ; then limb from limb he tore,
And like a mountain lion supped on them
Devouring, and left nothing, less or more,
Entrails and flesh and marrowy bones ; while we
Hold up to God our hands most wretchedly,
Weeping to see such deeds of wickedness,
Helpless to succour their extremity.
But when the Cyclops with the flesh of men

Had filled his ravening maw, and swallowed then
Great draughts of his raw milk, amid his flocks
He stretched him out to sleep within his den.
Then, taking courage, my sharp sword I planned
To draw, and creeping nigh his breast to stand
And, feeling where the liver lies enwrapped,
Strike ; but a second thought held back my hand.
For there we likewise had been doomed to die,
Since our hands could not from the doorway high
Push the vast rock-slab he had laid on it :
So we abode bright Dawn with many a sigh.'

The Cyclops next evening repeats his meal : after it Odysseus
gives him wine.

' SO said I, and he took the cup from me
And drank it off ; and right well pleased was he
With the sweet drink, and for a second draught
Asked me again : Now give me presently
Yet more of this, nor grudge it : and repeat
Your name, that I may give you guesting meet
To make you glad : for the Cyclopes' land
Likewise among the acres of the wheat
Bears wine rich-clustered, when the rain of Zeus
Gives increase to us : but a branch cut loose
From the immortal deathless tree is this.
So said he ; and I poured the fiery juice
Again ; and thrice the cup to him gave I,
And thrice in witlessness he drained it dry.
Then in soft-flattering words I spake to him :
Cyclops, you ask the name men call me by :
That will I utter forth ; and likewise you
Give me a guest-gift as you sware to do.
Noman my name is ; Noman am I called
By them who bare me and by all my crew.
So said I ; and he answered me straightway

With ruthless heart : Then Noman shall my prey
Be after all his fellows, and they first :
This gift I give you as my guest to-day.
These words he spake, and rolling backward leant,
Lying along, his thick neck sideways bent :
For sleep that conquers all laid hold on him :
While from his gullet jets of wine there went,
And gobbets of man's flesh mixed therewithal
That in his drunken vomit he let fall.
Then in the embers piled I thrust a stake
To heat it, cheering on my fellows all,
That none might falter, but with courage good
Stand by : but when the stake of olive-wood
All through glowed fiercely, and began, though green,
To kindle, then amid the rest I stood,
And pulled it from the fire and bore it nigh,
While in our hearts a God breathed courage high.
Then the sharp-pointed stake of olive-wood
They took and thrust it deep into his eye.
And I leant hard above it, with a will
Twirling it round, as with a boring-drill
A man drills through the timbers of a ship
While two below him keep it running still,
Handling the strap both ways to make it go
Backward and forward swiftly : even so
The fiery-pointed stake we twirled, and round
Its heated end the blood began to flow.
And all his lids and brows were scorched and marred
In the fierce vapour, as the eyeball charred
And the nerves shrank and crackled in the fire ;
And even as when a blacksmith, to make hard
Broad axe or adze, in the cold water-flood
Dips it with hissing scream (for that makes good
The strength of iron), tempering it : so
His eye hissed round the stake of olive-wood.

Then from his lips a great and awful shout
Brake, that the rock-walls echoed round about,
And we in terror fled away, while he
The stake bespattered all with blood pulled out
With both his hands and cast it far away,
And called out loudly, wallowing where he lay,
For help to the Cyclopes who in caves
Dwelt on the wind-swept headlands round the bay
Hearing him call, they came from far and nigh
And questioned him what ailed him, standing by
About the cave, and asked : What ails you so,
O Polyphēmus, that aloud you cry,
To break our sleep, through the immortal night ?
Is any mortal man in your despite
Driving away your flocks ? is any man
Slaying yourself, by treachery or by might ?
And mighty Polyphemus from the den
Answered : O friends, Noman it is of men
Slays me, by treachery nor by any might.
Then answered they in winged words again :
Now then if no man does you violence
And all alone you are, upon your sense
Some malady is come from Zeus on high,
Against the which there is no sure defence.
Then to your father, Lord Poseidon, pray
To heal you. So they said, and went their way.
But in my heart I laughed, because my name
And pure device had led him quite astray.
But racked with agony and groaning sore
The Cyclops, groping blindly to the door,
Took off the stone from it and sat him down
With outspread hands the cavern mouth before ;
That aught among the sheep that issued he
Might pounce on : such a fool he reckoned me !
But I was planning how I best might deal

My fellows and myself from death to free.
And all my wisdom and my wiles I dressed,
Since the task was my very life to wrest
From swift and utter ruin : whereupon
This counsel to my mind appeared the best.
Males were there, waxen fat among the sheep,
Both great and goodly, clad with fleeces deep
Dusk as a violet : these in twisted withes
Pulled from the bed whereon was wont to sleep
That monster, full of lawlessness and pride,
The Cyclops, three by three I caught and tied
Together, and the midmost bore a man,
While the two others went on either side,
And held my fellows hid, that safely so
Beneath each three of them a man might go :
But I one ram, the foremost of the flock,
Caught round his back, and climbing up below,
Close to his shaggy body clung with mine,
Twisting both hands amid his fleece divine,
And held on grimly with enduring heart :
So sighing we abode for Dawn to shine.
But when rose-fingered Dawn of Morning shone,
The males of all the flocks went forth anon
To pasture, but the females round the pens
Stayed bleating, for they long unmilked had gone,
And their swoln udders pained them. But their king,
Racked with fierce pangs, ran over fingering
The backs of all the sheep as up they stood
Before him : yet he noted not this thing,
Fool, that beneath their woolly breasts they bore
Men bound. Then last among them to the door
The leader ram went pacing, laden down
With his thick fleece and me and all my lore.
And mighty Polyphemus felt him go,
And said : O ram beloved, why so slow

Last through the cave's mouth come you ? not your wont
It was behind the sheep to linger so.
But striding far before them in the mead
Upon the tender flowering grass you feed,
And first you reach the riverside, and first
The flock at evening to the fold you lead.
Yet now you loiter last of all the line.
Surely for your protector's eye you pine,
That with his cursed crew an evil man
Has blinded, having drugged my sense with wine :
Noman, who has not yet methinks outrun
His doom ; but if your sense and mine were one,
And you could speak intelligible words,
To tell me where he lurks my wrath to shun,
Once I had caught and dashed him to the ground,
His brains were spattered all the cave around,
And my heart lightened of the woes wherein
Noman, that man of naught, my life has bound.
So saying, out of doors the ram sent he :
And when from cave and courtyard gone were we
A little way, from underneath his fleece
I slipped out first, and then the rest cut free.
Down to the ships we quickly drove thereat
The sheep, long-striding, thickly clad with fat,
Heading them off all round ; and when we came
To our good fellows a glad sight was that.'

Then again we might have sailed to the great river that flows
round the world, the deep stream of Ōceänus, and beyond it to
the place of the dead where Odysseus saw the heroes and heroines
of the past, and dead friends in whose company he fought at
Troy.

' THEREBY a tribe of men their city keep,
        Cimmerians, round whom mist and cloud are deep,
        Nor ever does the shining sun on them
Dart down his rays when up the skyey steep

Star-strewn he climbs, nor when he turns once more
To earth descending from the heavenly floor ;
But baleful night upon those wretched men
Lies brooding : there we ran the ship ashore.'[1]

Then they sacrificed sheep, for the dead are pale phantoms and cannot speak until they have tasted blood.

'BUT when the lordly nations of the dead
With vows and prayers I had propitiated,
Taking the sheep, their throats above the pit
I cut, and into it their dark blood shed.
Then swarmed from out the darkness where they lay
Ghosts of the dead that had fulfilled their day :
Striplings and brides and aged men outworn ;
And tender maids whose grief was young as they ;
And many smitten with the bronze-topped spear,
Famed warriors, who still wore their blood-stained gear,
With awful clamour all about the pit
Circling in swarms, that I waxed wan for fear.
Then straitly bade I them who stood around
The sheep that lay sword-slaughtered on the ground
To flay, and burn them, calling on the Gods,
Strong Hades and Persephone renowned.
But I, the sharp sword drawing from my thigh,
Sat still, and let not to the blood thereby
The strengthless people of the dead approach,
Ere of Tīresias I might win reply.'[2]

In the following he tells how he met his mother among the dead.

'STRAIGHTWAY she knew me then, and grieving sore
A winged word she spake : O child I bore,
How came you hither to the misty West
Alive ? for living men this dusky shore
Hardly may see, which mighty floods enclose

---

[1] Od. xi. 14 ff.   [2] Ib. 34 ff

And awful rivers, and before it flows
The Ocean-stream, that none afoot may cross,
Except in a well-builded ship he goes.
So spake she, but I answering said: Alas,
My mother, strong constraint has made me pass
Down into darkness, to the ghost to seek
That was the Theban seer Tiresias.
Not yet have I come nigh Achaean land,
Nor set my foot upon my native strand,
But ever have been wandering wearily
Since with bright Agamemnon hand in hand
To Ilium, nurse of steeds, I took my way,
Against the Trojans battle to array;
Now tell me this thing plainly: by what fate
Did Death the Leveller bring you to decay?
Did a long sickness waste from you the bliss
Of life, or arrow-showering Artemis
With shafts that hurt not strike you down and slay?
And of my father likewise tell me this;
And of the son I left behind me then:
Do they yet keep my honour among men?
Or has it fallen into stranger's hands
Who say that I return not home again?
So said I: and the Queen returned reply,
My mother: Sure within your palace high
Abides she[1] steadfast-hearted, and the days
And nights wears through with many a tear and sigh.
Nor does a stranger hold your honour fair;
But still Tēlemachus untroubled there
Keeps the domain that is his heritage,
And in the banquets has an equal share
That for the lawgiver are duly spread;
For all men bid him. But in lonelihead
Your father keeps his farm, nor to the town

---

[1] i.e. Penelope. Telemachus is Odysseus' son.

Goes in at all, nor covered is his bed
With rugs and broidered blankets ; by the fire
Where they that in the household serve for hire
Among the ashes lie, in wintertide
He sleeps, his body clad in mean attire ;
But when the summer comes and fruits abound
In autumn, then his lowly bed is found
Where all about his terraced vineyard-plot
The fallen leaves lie thick upon the ground.
There lies he mourning, and his heart is sore,
Day after day, that you return no more,
While grievous eld comes over him : for thus
I likewise perished and my life outwore.
For neither me where in my halls I lay
Did the keen-sighted Arrow-Showerer slay
With shafts that pain not, nor was I assailed
By any sickness, such as takes away
The life out of the limbs with wasting sad ;
But died of longing that for you I had,
And for your wisdom and kind-heartedness,
Noble Odysseus, that my life made glad.
So said she : but I inly for a space
Mused and was full of longing to embrace
The soul of my dead mother. Thrice I sprang
Toward her, fain to clasp her face to face ;
And thrice from out my hands to clasp her spread
Like to a shadow or a dream she fled.
And grief waxed ever keener at my heart.'[1]

The fairy islands have vanished, the Sirens sit no longer on their white islands off the Sorrento coast, the steamers from Marseilles to Greece pass unharmed between Scylla and Charybdis ; but you may yet meet a storm like this. There is no finer piece of description in Homer than what follows, so simple, so full of the irresistible power of wind and sea.

[1] Od. xi. 153 ff.

EVEN as he spoke, a monstrous wave abaft
   Came towering up, and crashed into the raft :
   And the raft reeled, and off it far he fell,
And from his hand shot out the rudder-shaft.
And in one whirling gust the hurricane
Snapped the mast midway ; far into the main
Fell yard and rigging : and beneath the surge
He sank, nor for a while his head again
Out of the overwhelming wave could lift :
For now the raiment, bright Calypso's gift,
Weighed heavy on him : but at last he rose,
And with abundant-streaming head made shift
Out of his mouth to spit the salt sea-spray.
Yet withal marking where the wrecked raft lay,
He plunged amid the waves and caught at it,
And crouched amidships, keeping death at bay :
While the raft helpless on the tideway spun,
As down the plain when Autumn is begun,
Before the North wind tufts of thistledown
Entangled close together twirling run,
So him across the sea in furious race
Hither and thither the winds bore apace ;
And now South wind to North its plaything tossed,
And now East wind to West gave up the chase.[1]

If you are as fortunate as Odysseus and can swim for two days
and nights, you may see a coast like this—M. Bérard believes it
to be Corfu, but an English reader can think of Cornwall—

TWO days and nights upon the long smooth swell
   He drifted on, nor could his heart foretell
   Aught but destruction ; but when fair-tressed Morn
Brought the third day to birth, the tempest fell,
And windless grew the calm ; and now anigh
He saw the land, with keen and forward eye

[1] Od. v. 291 ff.

Gazing, as lifted on the swell he rose :
And with such joy as children may descry
Hope for a father's life who long has lain
Wasted by sickness, bearing grievous pain
Beneath some grim God's hand, and gladly they
See him by kinder Heaven restored again :
So joyfully Odysseus saw appear
Forest and shore, and strongly swam to near
The mainland : but when now no farther off
Than a man's voice will carry, he could hear
Upon the reefs the thunder of the sea,
Where the great wave on dry land horribly
Belched roaring, and in spindrift all the coast
Was wrapped, nor any landing-place saw he,
Nor harbourage where ships might find relief,
But all was jutting fang of rock and reef.
Thereat Odysseus trembled, heart and limb,
And to his mighty soul he spoke in grief :
'Woe's me ! when now beyond my hope to-day
Zeus grants me sight of land, and all this way
Throughout the sea-gulf I at last have pierced,
I see no issue from the ocean grey.
For sharp rocks rise far out, and all around
Welters the breaker with a roaring sound,
And the cliff runs up sheer, and under it
The sea is deep, nor may I take the ground
Or foothold find among the waves, lest one
Might catch and hurl me on a ridge of stone
As forth I clomb : poor work were that : and yet
If I swim farther up to light upon
Some shoaling beach or haven of the main,
I fear lest yet once more the hurricane
May sweep me out on the fish-pasturing sea,
And all my heavy woe begin again :
Or lest heaven loose on me some monster dread,

Such as in Amphitrīte's halls are bred
Full many : for I know how sore the great
Shaker of Earth [1] with me is angered.'
While he debated thus his heart within,
A great wave lifted him and bore him in
Upon a jagged rock, that there and then
Had shattered all his bones and stripped his skin,
But that the Goddess with the eyes of grey,
Athena, put it in his heart to lay
Both hands tight-clutched upon the rock, and there
Cling gasping till the great wave passed away.
Over his head it went, but backward whirled
Bore down on him and struck him full and hurled
Far out to sea : as when a cuttlefish
Out of its hole is dragged with suckers curled
And clinging round the pebbles of its bed,
So from his mighty hands the skin was shred
Against the rocks ; and in the whelming wave
Quite hidden, then Odysseus had been dead
Before his day, in grievous wise and grim,
But that grey-eyed Athena put in him
Counsel, uprising from beneath the flood
That burst upon the land, far out to swim,
Still keeping on the land a sidelong eye,
Some shoaling beach or haven to descry :
Until he, swimming onward, to the mouth
Of a fair-flowing river drew anigh.[2]

In the end you may land and, like Odysseus, pass the night
sheltered in a thicket covered by fallen leaves, ' like a firebrand
hidden under the embers of a fire ' ; but you will not meet the
Homeric princess, the frank, the brave, the modest, the wise
Nausicaä, daughter of Alcinoüs, King of Phaeācia, in whose

---

[1] i.e. Poseidon, the sea-god, father of the Cyclops whom Odysseus had
blinded.   Amphitrite is a sea-goddess.   [2] Od. **v.** 388 ff.

kingdom Odysseus had landed. It was a dream that sent her
to wash the household linen in the rock pools.

THE grey-eyed goddess, inly counselling
    Odysseus mighty-hearted home to bring,
    Then to the richly-carven chamber went
Where slept a maid, the daughter of the king,
Like any deathless Goddess fair and bright,
Nausicaa : and two handmaids lay by night,
Dowered by the Graces' hands with comeliness,
On either side the doorway left and right.
Shut were the shining chamber doors : but she,
Like to a breath of wind, invisibly
Passed through them, and above the maiden's head
Stood by her pillow, in the shape to see
Of Dymas' daughter, a great lord of fame
Among that sea-folk : of their age the same
Were the two girls, and loving playfellows.
Taking her shape grey-eyed Athena came :
And uttering speech, ' Nausicaa,' said she, ' why
Thus idly does your mother's daughter lie,
The garments wrought with bright embroideries
Unheeded ? yet your wedding-day draws nigh ;
When clad in goodly raiment you must go,
And on your marriage train the like bestow.
For so a favourable speech goes forth
Among the people, and your father so
And royal mother glad at heart you make.
Go we a-washing soon as dawn shall break,
And I myself will bear you company,
That the work shared less time and toil may take.
Not long shall yet your maidenhood be worn.
Even now, amid the land where you were born,
Phaeacia's princes woo you. Up, and bid
My lord your father yoke at break of morn
A mule-team and a cart whereon to lay

Girdles and gowns and broidered blankets gay.
You too had better ride than go afoot ;
The washing-pools from town are far away.'
So saying, Athena to Olympus passed,
The grey-eyed Goddess : where, they say, set fast
For ever is the Gods' unchanging seat,
Wet with no rain and shaken by no blast,
And by no snowflake touched ; but very bright
It stretches cloudless, and a splendour white
Broods over all its borders, and therein
The blessed Gods live ever in delight.[1]

Nausicaa obtains her father's leave.

THEN into the wain
Mounting, she took the whip and broidered rein,
And lashed the mules ; and they with clattering feet
Bore girl and raiment up the road amain,
Her women hasting by her side to go ;
Until they reached the lovely river's flow,
Where never-failing water brims the pools,
Bright and abundant gushing from below,
Soilure to cleanse however deep in grain :
And there, the mules unyoking from the wain
Beside the eddying river, turned them loose
To graze the honeyed herbage of the plain.
Then from tne cart the clothes their hands among
They fetched and into the dark water flung,
And trod them in the trenches busily
Contending : but when all were washed and wrung,
By the seashore they spread them on a reach
Where the waves cleanest washed the pebbled beach.
And now, when they had bathed and oiled themselves,
In the hot sun they left the clothes to bleach,
While by the river bank they sat and fed.

[1] This and the following extracts are from Od. vi. 15 ff., with omissions.

But when their hearts with food were comforted
Their kerchiefs they undid to play at ball :
And in the game white-armed Nausicaa led.
Artemis the Arrow-showerer even so
Rejoices on the mountain side to go
All down the long slope of Taÿgetus
Or Erymanthus, while before her bow
Wild boar and fleetfoot deer flee fast away,
And round her move the wildwood nymphs at play,
Daughters of Zeus the Lord of Thunder-clouds ;
And Lēto joys at heart : for fair are they,
Yet fairest of them all the child she bred ;
And over all the rest her brows and head
Rise, easily known among them : even so
Among her women shone the maid unwed.
But when for faring homeward she was fain
To fold the fair clothes up, and yoke the wain,
The grey-eyed Goddess counsel took once more
That now Odysseus might awake again,
And see the fair maid who his way should tell
On to the town where the Phaeacians dwell.
Thereat the princess to a handmaiden
Threw the ball wide, and missed her, and it fell
In a deep eddy.   From them all outbroke
A long shrill cry : and bright Odysseus woke :
And sitting up he pondered inwardly :
' O me ! what land is this of mortal folk ?
Are these fierce savages and men of blood,
Or hospitable and of godly mood ?
And are these voices as of womenkind,
That echo round me now, the maiden brood
Of nymphs who haunt the crags that top the hill
And grassy meads and fountains of the rill ?
Or am I nigh to folk of human speech ?
Come, for myself now make essay I will.'

Odysseus approaches them.

> Dreadful to them the sea-stained man drew nigh :
> And up and down they ran dispersedly
> Along the jutting beaches : only then
> The daughter of Alcinoüs did not fly :
> Such courage put Athena in her breast :
> Unfaltering she stood up and undistressed,
> And faced him.
>   Then subtle-soft said he :
> ' I kneel to you, Protectress : God are you
> Or mortal ? if a God indeed you be
> Of those who in wide heaven abide in bliss,
> Unto none else than very Artemis,
> Daughter of Zeus Most High, I liken one
> So tall and fair and beautiful as this :
> But if a mortal, such as dwell on earth,
> Thrice fortunate are they who gave you birth,
> Father and mother, and thrice fortunate
> Your brethren : surely evermore great mirth
> And joyance fills them, while with hearts elate
> They see a thing so lovely-delicate
> Upon the dancing floor.   But far beyond
> All others is that man most fortunate,
> Who loading you with many a precious thing
> May woo you and to share his home may bring :
> For never mortal man or woman yet
> Mine eyes have gazed on with such marvelling.
> Once on a time indeed a young palm tree
> In Dēlos by Apollo's sanctuary
> Upspringing thus I saw—for thither too
> I voyaged, and much people followed me,
> When on that journey evil-starred I went
> That brought me woe—and in astonishment
> Long gazed I on it ; for in all the world

No shaft so stately up from earth is sent.
So wondering now I stand at gaze once more,
Lady, and fear to clasp your knees, and sore
Is mine affliction : for but yesternight
Out of the purple deep I won to shore.
Nor may I reckon yet my labour done,
Till the Gods finish that they have begun.
Pity me then, Protectress ! for to you
Out of woes manifold I first have won,
And beside you naught else I understand,
Nor know what folk possess this town and land.
Then guide me to the city, and bestow
From such clothes-wrappings as lie here at hand,
A rag for covering. So what you require
May the Gods grant you to your heart's desire ;
Husband and house, and in your household ways
Fair concord : since no height of bliss is higher
Than this, when in one house according well
A husband and a wife together dwell :
Great grief to foes, and joy to well-wishers ;
But their full bliss themselves alone can tell.'
And to his word made answer straightway then
White-armed Nausicaa : ' Stranger, to my ken
Nor knave nor fool you seem : but Zeus himself
Ruling from heaven allots their weal to men,
After his pleasure, be they good or ill :
And your own burden you must carry still.
Yet coming to our land and city now
Raiment you shall not lack nor what you will,
Such as a suppliant in his need might claim
From far-off people to whose hands he came.
And I myself will guide you to the town,
And tell you what the people have for name.'
Then to her fair-tressed maidens cried she thus :
' Stand still, my women ! why so timorous

At a man's face ? you do not surely think
This man is here with ill intent to us ?
That living mortal is not, nor shall be,
Who to Phaeācia bearing enmity
May come : for very dear to heaven we are,
And dwell apart amid the surging sea,
At the world's end, where never foot has trod
Of other mortals. But to our abode
We must make welcome this poor wanderer.
Strangers and beggars all are dear to God.
How small soe'er, the grace to them we show
Is precious. With this stranger be it so.
Give him to eat and drink, and make him bathe
In shelter, down the windswept bank below.'

The *Odyssey* may not move on such heroic heights as the *Iliad*, but it is pleasant for the modern reader, who has not the natural interest which Homer's contemporaries took in detailed descriptions of men being killed in battle, to see the reverse and peaceful side of Homeric life. And the *Odyssey* takes us not only to the homely palaces of these simple kings, but to the country-side where we meet the common people, who in the *Iliad* serve merely as spear-fodder for the chiefs. This is a Homeric farm, kept by a servant of Odysseus, Eumaeus. On his return to Ithaca, Odysseus makes for the farm, but tells nobody who he is.

BUT from the harbour to the rough ascent
Setting his face, among the rocks he went
Up through the woodland, where Athena told
That he should find the swineherd excellent ;
Who for his substance cared the most of all
The folk whom bright Odysseus had in thrall.
Him in the forecourt of the house he found
Sitting within the high-built courtyard wall,
Both great and goodly, giving ample bound
Of prospect, with a clearing all around ;
That he for his long absent master's swine

Had built with boulders gathered from the ground,
Far from his mistress and Lāertēs old,
And coped it with dry thorn to make a fold,
With stout posts driven outside it every way
Into the ground as close as they could hold,
Made of split oaken core ; and in the yard
Twelve styes he framed each nigh to each, and barred
Fifty brood-swine in each : but less in tale
Were the boar-pigs that slept in the outer ward.
And by them four hounds alway made their bed,
Half savage, by the master swineherd bred.
But he was cutting shoes to fit his feet
From a tanned ox-hide by his side outspread.[1]

Homer is an aristocrat, in that he wrote for, and mainly about,
the great men of his day, a democrat in that his poor men have
as many virtues and as much manly independence as their lords.
This is how the farm people dined and talked.

SO saying, with the axe-edge logs he[2] cleft,
While a fat hog of five years old they brought
Where on the hearth the swineherd stood ; and he
The Gods forgot not in his piety,
But cutting bristles from the white-tusked head
Into the fire he cast them reverently
With prayer addressed to all the Gods that they
Should compass wise Odysseus' homeward way ;
And lifting up an oaken billet left
From cutting, smote it down, that dead it lay.
Then the rest fell to work and cut its throat
And singed it and in pieces quickly smote ;
But from each joint the swineherd cut raw bits
And wrapped them up in fat as in a coat.
Then this he threw, to make burnt-offering fit,
With flour of barley sprinkled over it,

---

[1] Od. xiv. 1 ff.   [2] Eumaeus.

Into the fire ; and all the residue
They cut up small and stuck it on the spit,
And broiled it well ; and off the spits they drew
The meat and all of it on trenchers threw.
And up the swineherd rose to carve the meat,
For equal dealings in his mind he knew.
In seven parts he dealt it share by share ;
And one of these he set apart with prayer
For Hermēs, son of Maia, and the nymphs,
And portioned out the rest to each man there.
But for Odysseus from the white-tusked swine
He cut long slices all adown the chine
In special honour ; and his master's heart
Waxed high within him at the favouring sign.
And subtle-souled Odysseus hailed him so :
' Eumaeus, may our father Zeus bestow
His love on you as I do, since to me
Honour you render though my state be low.'
And answering spake you, herder of the swine,
Eumaeus : ' Eat, O luckless guest of mine,
And let your heart be gladdened with this fare.
God, as the heart within him shall incline,
This thing or that will give or will withhold ;
For by his power is all the world controlled.'
So spake he, while first-offering to the Gods
He made that are for ever from of old.
And flame-bright wine the sacrifice to crown
He poured, and to the Stormer of the town,
Odysseus, dealt it, as he sat beside
His share, and bread upon the board set down.
So to the ready food before them spread
They reached their hands ; and after they had fed
Hunger and thirst to quench, Mesaulius cleared
The food away ; and filled with flesh and bread
They turned to rest. Now night upon them set

Stormy, with clouds across the moon that met,
And all night long poured down the rain, and blew
The strong west wind that ever brings the wet.
And to the swineherd then Odysseus spoke,
Trying if haply he would strip his cloak
To lend him, since he cared for him so well,
Or move thereto some other of his folk :
‘ Eumaeus, you and all your fellows now
Hearken to me while something I avow,
Urged on by witless wine, that drives a man
To what his wisdom oft would disallow ;
To sing and to laugh loosely and to dance,
And many a word to utter that perchance
Were better left unsaid : but since my word
Is launched, I will allow it utterance.
Would I were young and my old force unspent,
As once when under Troy an ambushment
We fashioned, and Odysseus in command
With Menelāus son of Ātreus went.
And with these captains twain the third was I
At their own instance. Now when we drew nigh
The sheer wall of the city, round the town
Into a thicket we crept close to lie ;
Among the swamps and reedbeds crouching low
Under our arms : and night came on to blow
Foul, with an icy wind out of the North,
And all the air was thick with frozen snow.
And on our armour icicles congealed.
Then all the others in the open field
Slept comfortably, clad in shirt and cloak,
And to his shoulders each drew close his shield.
But I, who deemed not that the cold would hurt
So sore, had gone forth with them in my shirt
Leaving my cloak behind among my men,
With my bare shield and shining girdle girt.

Now when the third part of the night was gone
And the stars drew to westward, I thereon
Odysseus with my elbow, as he lay
Beside me, touched, and he lent ear anon.
And thus I whispered : O Laertes' son,
High-born Odysseus, subtle-hearted one,
No more among the living shall I be,
But by the wintry tempest am undone.
A cloak I have not, for by heaven made blind
Stripped to the shirt I started, and I find
This cold beyond endurance. So said I ;
And straightway then a counsel in his mind
He found : such ever was he wont to be
In council as in battle. Then spake he
And in a low voice answering me said :
Keep silence now ; let no man saving me
Among the Achaeans hear you. Thus he said,
And on his elbow lifting up his head
He spake aloud : Listen, O friends ; a dream
Has come to me from heaven upon my bed :
Far from the ships we lie ; now who will run
With word to Agamemnon Atreus' son,
The shepherd of the people, bidding him
Send reinforcement, lest we be fordone ?
He spake, and swiftly to the ships a man,
Thoas, Andraemon's son, arose and ran,
Casting his crimson cloak away from him ;
And so till golden-throned Dawn began
I lay beneath his covering, well content.
Would I were young now and my strength unspent !
For in this cottage then assuredly
One of the swineherds would his cloak have lent ;
And such kind service and regard were mine
As good men get : but now they let me pine
Because I wear mean rags.' Then answering him

Spake you, Eumaeus, herder of the swine :
'No fault is in the story you have told,
O aged man, and not ill-timed I hold
The word you say, nor idle : therefore now
Raiment you shall not lack against the cold,
Nor aught of what distressful men should claim
From one to whom in suppliant wise they came,
As for this night : but with the dawn of day
In your own rags you needs must play the game ;
Since here we have not many cloaks to spare
Or change of shirts, but one for each man's share.
But when Odysseus' son comes home again,
Himself shall give you cloak and shirt to wear,
And wheresoever you would fain be gone
Shall send you forth.' So said he, and anon
Got up and laid for him beside the fire
A bed with sheep and goat-skins piled thereon.
So there Odysseus laid him down anew ;
And over him a cloak the swineherd threw
Large and close-woven, that he kept by him
For change of raiment when the storm-wind blew.
So there Odysseus took his rest, while near
By him the young man slept ; but little cheer
The swineherd had far off his swine to lie,
And going forth he clad him in his gear ;
(But in his heart Odysseus then was glad
That for his absent lord such care he had)
And first about his shoulders the sharp sword
He slung, and in a cloak his body clad,
That kept the wind from off him, nowise thin,
And over all a great and goodly skin
Stripped from a shaggy goat ; and in his hand
He took a good sharp-pointed javelin,
Both dogs and men aloof from him that kept,
And going forth he laid him down where slept

The white-tusked swine beneath a hollow rock
Sheltered, while overhead the north wind swept.[1]

One more scene, this time in a palace yard, but the interest
centres round a dog-kennel. It is the home-coming of Odysseus ;
the insolent suitors are in possession of his house, and he comes
in secret and unrecognized.

EACH to the other while these words they said,
A dog that lay near by lift up his head
And pricked his ears : Odysseus' hound was he,
Argus, whom that man much-enduring bred ;
But got no profit of his rearing ere
To holy Troy he overseas must fare ;
Therefore the young men took him with them once
To hunt the pricket or wild goat or hare :
But then, his master being far astray,
Before the gate thrust out of doors he lay
Upon a dunghill where the dung of mules
And oxen was heaped up to take away
To the great field that was Odysseus' plot,
That there the thralls might spread it out to rot.
There the dog Argus full of vermin lay ;
Yet then to know his master failed he not ;
And wagged his tail and both his ears laid low,
But nearer to his lord he could not go.
And he turned sidelong to wipe off a tear
Privily, that Eumaeus did not know :
And thus inquired : ' Eumaeus, to mine eyes
This hound that here upon the dunghill lies
Is goodly-shaped and marvellous to see :
But I would be assured of my surmise,
If as in beauty he excelled in speed,
Or was but such a plaything as men breed
For show, and princes keep for luxury

[1] Od. xiv. 418 ff.

Beside them at the table where they feed.'
And answering spake you, herder of the swine,
Eumaeus: 'This indeed as you divine
Was the man's hound who far away has died.
Had but his limbs and deeds not known decline
From what he was of old when Troyward-bound
Odysseus left him, you would be astound
To see his strength and speed : no beast of chase
Escaped him in the tangled woodland ground ;
And he excelled in scenting of the slot ;
But now has fallen on him an evil lot :
His master from the land is far away,
Dead, and the careless women tend him not.
As servants, when their lords no more bear sway,
Will not endure their service due to pay ;
For of man's virtue when he is enslaved
Zeus the Far-Sounder takes the half away.'
So saying, to the fair-built house anon
Among the haughty suitors he passed on.
But black death fell on Argus, having seen
Odysseus after twenty years were gone.[1]

The following extract describes how the suitors become fey
before their slaying, and how the prophet Theoclymenus foresees
their end. It may be compared with the scene in hell in Wandering Willie's tale in *Redgauntlet*.

SO spake Telemachus, and Pallas Athēne sent laughter
unquenchable on the suitors and made them distraught.
And they laughed at each other with unnatural faces, and
the meat they ate was dabbled with blood, and their eyes were
filled with tears and their hearts' thought was of lamentation.
Then godlike Theoclymenus spake among them : Wretched men,
what ails you ? Your heads and faces and your knees are
wrapped in night, and a cry of wailing is kindled, and your

---

[1] Od. xvii. 290 ff.

cheeks are wet with tears, and the walls and the bases of the pillars are splashed with blood. The porch is full of ghosts and the courtyard is full of them—ghosts hurrying to the gloom of the nether darkness; and the sun has perished out of heaven, and an evil mist is spread abroad. So he spoke; and they all laughed at him merrily.[1]

These quotations should have shown why the world calls Homer great, why, for instance, the present Poet Laureate places him by the side of Shakespeare. It is impossible to put the reasons on paper, and critics who have attempted the task really do little beyond quoting from the poems, and saying, ' Isn't that good ? ' We may indeed say with Matthew Arnold that Homer is noble, plain and direct, and by dwelling on these words and making them real to ourselves we shall learn much about Homer, but it will not be his inmost secret. So I will only beg the reader to ask himself : Are these scenes real ? has Homer made us see them—the storm, Calypso's island, the old men watching Helen on the wall, Achilles and Hector face to face ? Does he show us the tragic and the heroic, the ' true pathos and sublime of human life ' ?

The difficulty of expounding Homer comes from one of his greatest qualities, his simplicity ; it has been said that he is distinguished by ' grandeur of effect associated with simplicity of means '. Look at the great passages, the scenes between Hector and his wife, Hector and Achilles, Achilles and Priam, and see whether that is not true. Nothing could be simpler in idea or language. That is why Homer's greatness defies analysis ; we cannot analyse an element. Virgil and Milton may yield up some of their secret to the chemist of literature : not so *Genesis* or the *Iliad*. Homer taught the Greeks, as the Bible teaches us, that literature is not fine writing and that the greatest things are the simplest.

[1] Od. xx. 345.

III

LYRIC POETRY: PINDAR

> May I . . . thy smiles
> Seek as they once were sought, in Grecian isles,
> By bards who died content on pleasant sward,
> Leaving great verse unto a little clan !
>
> KEATS : *Ode to Maia.*

Let us again hover above the Greek lands. We see the clustering of their population into those poleis, *or city centres, which are of the essence of Greek civilization, and to which our own owes one of its most important words. These cities are the centres of districts mostly smaller than an ordinary English county (Attica has 700 sq. miles, Lancashire 1,700; fourth-century Athens had about 30,000 male citizens); and in studying the wars and rivalries of Greek history the smallness of the scale must not be forgotten. From the seventh century onwards these cities swarm, and the swarms go out and form colonies that retain an attachment to the parent hive. Tiny fleets move across the Greek seas, to seize one after another of the great commercial sites of the Mediterranean. In the Crimea, at Trebizond, Constantinople, Cyrene, Syracuse, Naples, Marseilles, and at countless other places small Greek cities appear. The Black Sea, Sicily, and South Italy are fringed with these colonies, hereafter to be the conduits from which Greek civilization will flow into the outer world. Meanwhile in the cities of the homeland, kings are supplanted by aristocracies, and, except at Sparta, disappear. There follow struggles between the nobles and people. In most cities strong individuals use these to establish autocracies which the Greeks called tyrannies (the word has originally no bad meaning). These are overthrown, and in many cases democracies, the first in the world, are established. The years of struggle are hard and difficult.*

Though ultimately conscious of common Hellenic blood, these Greek states are vividly individual, divided against their neighbours. Primarily a man is a Spartan, an Athenian, a Theban, and so on. Secondarily he belongs to one of the great rival groups, Ionians, Dorians, Aeolians. Thirdly, and that chiefly at the great festivals, at the national religious centre, the Oracle at Delphi, and in times of foreign invasion, he is a Greek.

*Five states specially engage our attention. Four are Dorian :
Thēbes, the centre of Boeotia (the use of the word Boeotian in English
preserves its reputation) ; Corinth, a great commercial centre ;
Argos, though Dorian, a jealous enemy of its greater Dorian neighbour Sparta ; Sparta, a byword for conservatism and for such
a militarism as the world has never seen. The Spartans were the
best soldiers in Greece ; their town, unwalled in those ages of war,
reveals the spirit of its inhabitants ; their name has become a
synonym for hardy simplicity, and thinkers in other Greek states,
like Plato, weary of self-indulgent democracy, at times envied the
austere discipline of Sparta, as Carlyle admired Prussia. But
these virtues were paid for by the extinction in Sparta of art,
literature, and thought. In this period she becomes the dominant
state in the Peloponnese. Finally there is the Ionian Athens. In
these years we see her developing from kingship through oligarchy
and tyranny to a democracy, in which freedom of opportunity is
secured to all, and the people has the deciding voice in the law courts
and the ecclesia, or political assembly of the nation. Of these five
states, Thebes is to produce one great poet ; the militarist Sparta,
the commercial Corinth are and remain insignificant in everything
but war and trade : Athens as yet shows no signs of what she is
to be. The centres of poetry and, from the seventh century, of
thought are on the coast of Asia Minor, and in a less degree in the
Italian and Sicilian colonies. Greece herself is struggling with
a poor soil and political upheavals, and literature flowers first in
the richer communities across the sea. To this literature we must
now turn.*

Homer is the greatest and the only survivor of a crowd of epic
poets, who wrote on different episodes of the Trojan War and
on other subjects of mythology. Passing over these, and over
Hesiod, the father of didactic poetry, whose *Works and Days*
treated in hexameters of the farmer's life, we come, two centuries
after Homer, to the age of lyric poetry. It is characteristic of
the Greeks that the different poetic *genres* develop in turn, and
are separated from their predecessors by a clearer dividing-line
than can be drawn in modern literatures. In Greece the lyric
supersedes the epic and holds the stage completely for some
150 years, till it in turn fades before the age of drama. These
divisions reflect the development of the national mind. Epic is
the offspring of its childhood, delighting in stories for their own
sake ; lyric, of which the essence is the expression of personal

feelings, represents its adolescence, the age of emotion, conscious of itself and at moments touched by reflection ; drama is its manhood, facing the problems of the world and life with all the forces of a full-grown mind.

Any one glancing at the fragmentary remains of Greek lyric poetry would be struck by two qualities, characteristic of the Greek genius, rich creativeness and an instinct for system. Starting in the seventh century without external models or inspiration, the Greeks produced this amazingly rich and various harvest, one crop following another for two hundred years without intermission or check. With this amazing fertility goes an instinctive systematization. That gift of method, which later taught the Greeks to map out the field of human knowledge under the various sciences and the different sections of philosophy, is seen at work here. Apart from the ode, the song, and the sonnet, it is difficult to assign modern lyrics to clearly defined classes. An index to the works of an English poet will show lyrics of some three types. An index to Greek lyric poetry will show infinitely more species. Of Pindar alone we possess fragments in ten distinct varieties. And each variety of Greek lyric has its special characteristics and use ; some have special metres, some special instruments—the harp with four strings, the harp with twenty, the flute, &c.—some are performed with dance, some with marching ; some are sung by one performer, others by choirs.

An ancient critic divided Greek lyric, or, as it is called, ' melic ', poetry into twenty-one different varieties. Of these the *threnos* or dirge, the hymn, the elegy,[1] and the epithalamium have survived in our literary vocabulary, which bears other marks of this period in words like dithyrambic, ode, lyric, choric. The simpler metres are the property of all languages : the more complicated and characteristic ones do not lend themselves to English use, though elegiacs, Sapphics, and Alcaics make occasional appearances. We need not trouble about either the different types of lyric or their history, except to note that in the one hundred and fifty years between Archilochus, the creator of the elegy, and Pindar, the greatest master of the choral ode, the Greeks created and developed type after type of lyric with a wonderful combination of system and freedom.

---

[1] Strictly speaking, the Greeks did not include it in ' melic ' poetry. Its mark was the elegiac metre: and it was not confined to laments, as with us.

In that century and a half a small seed grows into a tree with many branches, each loaded with fruit.

If we possessed a tithe of this poetry, we should know the inner life and emotions of men and women on the shores of the Mediterranean from the seventh century to the Persian Wars. Most of the singers were Ionians from the coast of Asia—Lesbos is a famous centre—where life blossomed earlier than in Greece. But there are representatives from Greek towns in Italy ; the Athenian statesman Solon put his thoughts on life into elegies ; and even Sparta, not yet hardened into mere militarism, has its poets. In the tiny fragments that survive we have the complaints of an aristocratic *émigré* against the democracy, the war songs of a Spartan general, the lampoons of a Samian politician against the female sex, glimpses into the thoughts of several women, confidences of exiles and adventurers, the private quarrels, loves, regrets, and moralizings of a generation that felt passionately and wrote frankly.

Of these lyric poets, Pindar and Sappho never disappoint. Apart from these, few of the fragments are great as poetry, though nearly all have a peculiar freshness and vigour, and show an instinct for form : most of them were preserved by grammarians and scholars, who had other things in view than literature. If we possessed the poems entire, we should find their range narrower than that of the modern lyric. The moderns express ' the emotions of a soul, more complex, more rich morally and spiritually than that of the seventh-century Greek '.[1] It is with the songs of Shakespeare or Burns or Scott that we must compare these lyrics—I am thinking here of the song writers, not of poets like Pindar—and the best of them are worthy of the comparison. They have not the compass or variety of Shelley or Keats, any more than a bird has the compass of a piano ; but many have in the original the clearness, purity, and beauty of a bird's song.

Lyric poetry is notoriously untranslatable ; and the simpler it is, the more difficult to translate. A literal rendering is almost certain to miss its delicate grace, and the translator is forced to amplify and develop : then the simplicity is lost. I shall therefore only quote a few specimens.

ALCMAN (seventh century). Born at Sardis in Lydia but spent his life at Sparta. One of the founders of Greek choral poetry.

---

[1] Croiset, *Hist. de la Litt. grecque*, ii. 265.

NIGHT IN THE VALLEY

SLEEP broods o'er the mountain crest,
　And the folds of the hill,
Hollow and headland rest,
　　Silent and still.
All things are slumbering,
　　Not a leaf is stirred,
Of insect or creeping thing
　　No rustle is heard.
The beasts of the mountain sleep,
　　And the murmuring bees,
And the monsters that haunt the deep
　　Of the purple seas ;
The swift winged tribes of the air
　　Have ceased from their flight. . . .[1]

THE AGED POET

VOICES of honey-sweet, haunting music,
　Maidens, your poet is tired and gray ;
O for the wings of the bird that hovers
　Where the crest of the salt wave flowers in spray,
Sea-blue bird of the April weather,
　Careless at heart, where the halcyons play.[2]

MIMNERMUS of Colophon in Ionia (late seventh century).
Fragment of an elegy.

THE LABOUR OF THE SUN

SURELY the Sun has labour all his days,
　And never any respite, steeds nor god,
Since Eōs first, whose hands are rosy rays,
　　Ocean forsook and Heaven's high pathway trod ;

[1] Fr. 60, tr. J. A. Pott, *Greek Love Songs and Epigrams*. It shows the haphazard way in which these fragments have survived, that this one has been preserved by a Greek lexicographer, who quoted it to illustrate the meaning of the word translated ' monsters '.
[2] Fr. 26. Alcman was famous for *partheneia*, songs written for choruses of girls.

At night across the sea that wondrous bed
  Shell-hollow, beaten by Hephaestus' hand,
Of wingèd gold and gorgeous, bears his head
  Half-waking on the wave, from eve's red strand
To the Ethiop shore, where steeds and chariot are
Keen-mettled, waiting for the morning star.[1]

We know little of Sappho except that she lived in Lesbos in
the early sixth century and was married, that she was exiled,
returned, and had a school of young poetesses. It is difficult for
her admirers to speak of her with moderation. ' A wonderful
creature,' says one ancient writer ; ' you will look through
history in vain to find a woman even distantly comparable to
her.' ' Her speech is mixed with fire,' says another. She shares
with a few poets the power of writing magical poetry while using
the simplest language. We possess some short fragments by her,
and a few fragmentary poems. I quote one of the latter in
a prose rendering.[2] It gives us a glimpse of the poetess, sitting
with a companion in Mitylēne, her home, and talking of an old
friend, Arignōta,[3] now married and living in Sardis some ninety
miles away. The poem shows the hour and scene.

FROM Sardis her thoughts often turn hither. When we lived
together, she held you ever as a goddess and loved your singing above all. Now she shines among the women of Lydia,
as the rosy-fingered moon, when the sun sets, shines brighter
than all the stars. The light falls on the salt sea and on the fields
deep in flowers. The dew descends in beauty, and the roses are
in bloom and the clovers and flowering grasses. Arignota wanders
up and down and thinks of gentle Atthis, and her thoughts are
heavy with longing and her heart with distress. She calls aloud
for us to come to her, but Night with the thousand eyes does not
carry the words across the sea, and we cannot hear.[4]

[1] Fr. 12, tr. G. Murray. The poem alludes to the story that during the
night the sun was carried in a golden bowl across the sea to his place of
rising in the East. Eos is the Dawn.
[2] Most of the fragments, with English versions and imitations of them
can be read in Wharton's *Sappho*.
[3] If this is a proper name.   [4] Berlin fragment.

A NIGHT SCENE

THE stars about the lovely moon
Fade back and vanish very soon
When round and full her silver face
Swims into sight, and lights all space.[1]

ON THE HILLS

LIKE the wild hyacinth flower, which on the hills is found,
Which the passing feet of the shepherds for ever tear and
wound,
Until the purple blossom is trodden into the ground.[2]

THE UNRETURNING

SWEET Rose of May, sweet Rose of May,
Whither, ah whither fled away ?
What 's gone no time can e'er restore—
I come no more, I come no more.[3]

THE GIFTS OF EVENING

THOU, Hesper, bringest homeward all
That radiant dawn sped far and wide,
The sheep to fold, the goat to stall,
The children to their mother's side.[4]

TWO DRINKING SONGS [5]

DRINK from my cup, Dear ! live my life—be still
Young with my youth ! have one heart, word and will,
One love for both ; let one wreath shade our eyes ;
Be mad when I am—wise when I am wise.

[1] Fr. 3, tr. Sir E. Arnold.
[2] Fr. 94, tr. D. G. Rossetti. From an epithalamium.
[3] Fr. 109, tr. J. H. Merivale. Also from an epithalamium. A girl
apostrophizes the unwedded life, which she is exchanging for marriage.
Quoted by an ancient scholar to illustrate the effectiveness of repetition.
[4] Fr. 95, tr. Sir Rennell Rodd, *Love, Worship, and Death.*
[5] Skolia, fr. 21, tr. Sir E. Arnold : and Anacreontea, 21, tr. J. H. Merivale.
The first is early and perhaps by a Dorian poetess, Praxilla. The second
is from the collection of *Anacreontea.* Anacreon was a song-writer of the
sixth century from Teos in Ionia, who became for later ages the typical
poet of wine and love. It became a fashion to compose poems in his
style : a collection of these has survived in a Byzantine anthology of the
eleventh century A. D.

THE black earth drinks the falling rain,
   Trees drink the moistened earth again ;
Ocean drinks the streams that run
Only to yield them to the sun ;
And the sun himself as soon
Is swallowed by the thirsty moon.
All Nature drinks : if I would sip,
Why dash the goblet from my lip ?

To us the word lyric suggests a book of poetry. But these lyrics were not written to be read. They take us back to halls like those of Alcinous (p. 17), with the listening feasters and solitary singer : to marriages, to dinners, to celebrations of athletic victories, to processions, to the innumerable festivals which brightened Greek life.[1]

Who are these coming to the sacrifice ?
   To what green altar, O mysterious priest,
Lead'st thou that heifer lowing at the skies,
   And all her silken flanks with garlands drest ?
What little town by river or sea-shore,
   Or mountain-built with peaceful citadel,
      Is emptied of this folk, this pious morn ?

Keats's picture might well have included a choir, chanting a hymn, written by Alcman or Stēsichorus in honour of the god.

We have to read these poems in a book, but we should see behind its pages the scenes in which they were born. Here, as always at its greatest, Greek literature is closely connected with national life ; and unless we remember that these poems are not mere flowers of the study, but rooted in everyday life, we shall not understand the vitality of the Greek choral lyric. Most of the poems hitherto quoted were written for a single singer. But the strong corporate life of Greek communities gave a field to hymns, odes, and other poems, composed for choirs to sing on the occasions mentioned above. Dryden's Odes for St. Cecilia's Day are exact parallels. The type has never flourished with us, though Wales, with its local eisteddfodau, is a soil where it might well grow. But in Greece the choral ode became an important

[1] Cp. the scene described on p. 381 f. The date is later.

branch of lyric poetry, and developed very elaborate metrical patterns.

The only Greek lyrist of whom we possess any considerable remains happens to have been the greatest writer of the choral lyric. He is perhaps the most difficult Greek author for a modern to appreciate. In the original he is hard enough; but the reader who studies him in English will miss the magic of his language and find himself in an impenetrable wood, following pathways that seem to have no plan with their sudden turns and abrupt endings. Pindar (521–441) is the great representative in Greek literature of Thebes, the chief town of Boeotia. Born of an aristocratic and priestly family, he began at once to write poetry and became a classic in his lifetime. He is not, like Sappho or Alcaeus, a song-writer. His *métier* was to write these elaborate choral odes; four books of them have survived, all belonging to one type—the epinīkian ode, in honour of athletic victories. The four books correspond to the four great athletic festivals of Greece—at Olympia, Delphi (Pythian games), Nemea, and the Isthmus of Corinth. He wrote these poems to order and for pay, and we find him in Sicily, in Macedonia and Africa, at the court of Greek or Hellenized monarchs, superintending their performance. They were sung when the successful athlete returned home or at a dinner in his honour, ' while the lovely beams of the fair-faced moon lit up the evening, and all the place rang with feasting and delight '.[1]

Pindar is interesting for his influence. The elaborate odes of Dryden and Gray were inspired by him, and he is responsible for many less successful imitations in a *genre* which has always been an exotic in European literature. He is interesting as an ideal poet laureate, who could write great poetry to order; his secret being that he kept his independence, wrote what he felt, and had his heart in his work. The poet of aristocracy, he is the last representative of an ideal which Greece was to know no more, and which has found few such ardent interpreters. On one side he saw the undistinguished many; on the other the ardent few, born to great achievement, spiritual kin of those Argonauts who felt ' the sweet and overpowering desire, not to nurse a life sheltered from danger, but, even at the price of death, in their peers' company to make valour, fairest of charms, their own '.[2] If he wrote of the *élite* for the *élite*, at least his ideal for them is noble.

[1] Ol. x. 73 f.   [2] Pyth. iv. 184 f.

He is one of the great lyric poets of the world, unlike any other, and, in his kind, unrivalled. His style, with its allusiveness, rapid transitions, and abrupt flashes of imagination, resembles lightning. No other simile can express its sudden, dazzling quality. I quote his last Isthmian Ode, written in honour of a young Aeginetan, Cleander, who had won the prize at the Isthmus in the mixed boxing and wrestling contest, called the *pancratium*. It is an example of Pindar's average work, not one of his masterpieces. (It ends, for instance, rather weakly.) Cleander was only a well-to-do young Greek, and Pindar kept his best for kings and important persons. But it is the more interesting as showing what poetry Pindar put into his ordinary work, what immortal verse a commonplace prizewinner in the fifth century could command. The scheme is this. The Persian War is recently ended. Thebes had played an inglorious part in it, and Pindar alludes to his personal distress at this. He will, however, celebrate Cleander's victory—the more so because in legend the nymph Aegīna who gave her name to Cleander's home was a sister of Theba after whom Thebes was called. This recalls to his mind famous descendants of Aegina—Aeacus, and Pēleus who married Thetis and was the father of Achilles. With these explanations and the foot-notes and marginal comments the plan of the ode should be clear.[1]

FOR CLEANDER OF AEGINA, WINNER OF THE BOYS' PANCRATION (478 ? B. C.)

CLEANDER in his April prime to free   Pindar's
    From toil's effect with ransom of renown,   subject.
    And pay the pains that won his Isthmian crown
As erst his Nemean,[2] let one of ye,
Young men, awake for him the chant of victory,
Soon as your revel-choir are come
To the pranked portal of his home.
Thither even I, albeit with heart bowed down,

---

[1] I have to thank Miss W. M. L. Hutchinson for very kindly allowing me to use her brilliant translation. I should not have thought, till I saw it, that any English rendering could do justice to Pindar's 'grand style' or so well recapture his unique mixture of austerity and human feeling.

[2] He had won already at the Nemean games.

At friendship's bidding not refuse
To call the golden Muse—
Nay, when redeemed are all from giant woe,
Why should one head without its garland go ?

Nor court thou Care, my soul, but since we gain
Surcease of harms that passed all wit to heal,
Publish we now unto the commonweal
Matter for mirth, though in the wake of pain ;
For lo, the labour Hellas else had dared in vain,
Some god achieved, who turned from us
The incumbent stone of Tantalus.[1]
That peril fled, my spirit finds repeal
From tyrannous fears ; enough for man
The present hour to scan ;
For Life, the cheat, blows such a shifting gale
That none may keep the course he thinks to sail.

Yet for the sorest blows of mortal fates
They lack not salve, who lose not Liberty ;
Hope is a man's right work, whoe'er he be—
But if withal the Muse he meditates,
And had for kindly nurse the town of Seven Gates—
Theban and bard, let him essay
Before AEGINA's feet to lay
In homage due, a rose of poesy ;
For twinborn in that sisterhood
Sired by the Asōpus [2] flood
Were she and THEBA, youngest of their race,
And both with Zeus the king found equal grace.

Unto one sister gave the god in fee
A city of chariots,[3] hard by Dirce's well ;
And one he wafted to the island-fell,[4]

After touching on contemporary events,

Pindar speaks of the legendary origin of Aegina, Cleander's home.

[1] i.e. the Persian invasion. Tantalus was a legendary sinner, punished by having a stone, always threatening to fall, hung over him.
[2] Asopus and Dirce were Theban streams.
[3] i.e. Thebes.   [4] i.e. Aegina.

Oenōne's namesake erst, but thine to be,
Aegina, since a bed it made for Zeus and thee.
There from thy travail sprang to birth
The Thunderer's [1] dearest son on earth—
Just Aeacus,[2] whose sentence could compel   And of its
At need the very gods on high   first great
To lay their discords by ;   son.
From him began a great heroic line,
Peerless in war, wise-hearted, half divine.

Whereof kept mind the synod of the Blest [3]   Of how the
When Zeus and bright Poseidon fell to strife,   son of Aeacus
Each fain of loveliest Thetis for a wife,   married
Desire so thralled him ; but to speed their quest Thetis.
The Immortals willed not, when from Her who counsels best—
Even Themis—their full session heard
How it was that Sea-Nymph's weird
To bear a son, of princely lot in life,
Who must his sire in might excel—
So ran the oracle—
And thus would bolt or trident overbear,
If King of Sea or Sky her bridegroom were.

This rede then spoke grave Themis to the twain—
' Forgo your quarrel, both ; let the Sea-Fay
Taste human love, and bear as women may
To look upon a son in battle slain—
Her beautiful, low lying, not to stir again
The hands like Ares' hands, the feet
Radiant as lightnings and as fleet.

[1] Zeus.
[2] Aeacus, for his justice, became after death one of the three judges in the Underworld.
[3] The legend alluded to in this and the following stanzas is that Zeus and Poseidon wished to marry the Nereid, or sea-nymph, Thetis. Their dispute was referred to Themis (Justice), whose answer made them decide that she should marry a son of Aeacus, Peleus, to whom she bore Achilles. This passage shows with what poetry Pindar can transform a legend that in itself is primitive and crude.

My further counsel if ye list obey,
Bless with the boon of wedding her
Your devout worshipper,
Aeacid Pēleus, whom all tongues declare
The saintliest soul that draws Iolcos' air.

And straightway to the cave of timeless stone
Where Chīron [1] houses, swift commands address,
Ere twice upon our palms the Nereid press
Dissension's ballot-leaves ; [2] your pleasure known,
That Centaur sage will see her bride-bed duly strown.
So, when yon rounding moon doth ride
Full-orbed through the eventide,
She shall put off her lovely shamefastness,
And in the hero's first embrace
Her virgin zone unlace.'
The goddess ended ; those Olympians bent
Their deathless brows in token of consent.

Nor failed her word of fruit ; both kings, men say,
Took place among the children of the Sky
Who Thetis' bridal feast did beautify,
What time the Muses sang her marriage lay,
Unfolding things to come, as lips immortal may.
ACHILLES' fame they prophesied,
Peer ere his prime of warriors tried—
Achilles' fame we too conspire to magnify ;
For this was he whose valour crude
Spilled Tēlephus' best blood,
And drenched with that dark dew the Mysian vines
Ere yet Troy town beheld the Grecian lines.

Of their son Achilles, and his great deeds.

His attack on Telephus, the Mysian king,

'Twas he enfranchised Helen ; only he
The longed-for homeward path did pioneer
For the Atridae ; his dividing spear

and on Troy.

---

[1] The Centaur, by whom Peleus was brought up.
[2] Olive leaves were used at Athens for balloting.

Unstrung Troy's very sinews utterly—
Bold Hector, Memnon proud, and all their chivalry ;
Yea, naught availed those chiefs of pride
To stay the work Achilles plied,
Heaping the field with havoc far and near ;
He to Persephone's dim bourne
Piloted each in turn,[1]
Famousing so Aegina, and their name,
Those island princes, of whose blood he came.

Him even in death forsook not minstrelsy ;
For at his pyre and place of burial
The Heliconian Maidens [2] gathered all,
Outpouring their full-throated threnody.
So to this precept gods themselves gave warranty—
The valiant man, though cold his clay,
As ever-living theme to lay
In keeping of the choir celestial.
Still is that saw in high account,
For lo, the Muses mount
Their car, and hither speed to memorize
The tomb where Nicocles [3] the boxer lies.
Honour to him, whom Dorian parsley [4] crowned
In the Isthmian vale ; for in his day and land,
He also with inevitable hand,
Achilles-like, his foemen did confound.
Yet this our athlete shames not kinsman so renowned.
And therefore now let one of ye,
Youths that his own age-fellows be,
Enwreathe Cleander's hair with myrtle bland,
Betokening many a garland won
In the pancration.

The thought of Achilles brings Pindar back to Aegina, and turns his mind to the immortality of heroic deeds,

and to a great athlete of Cleander's family,

and so to Cleander himself.

[1] i.e. killed them. Persephone was queen of the Underworld.
[2] The Muses.
[3] Cousin of Cleander, victor in boxing at the Isthmian games.
[4] The parsley crown was given to the victor.

Good men shall say—' This was a mettled boy ;
No stay-at-home, that skulked from brave employ.' [1]

Without some guidance the reader's first feeling about this poem would probably be mere bewilderment. He would see indeed that the poem is in honour of Cleander. But what have Theba and Aeacus and Achilles to do with him, and why, above all, does the poet flit from subject to subject like a butterfly in a garden ? Look closer. As a piece of complicated metre, the poem clearly shows great technical skill : it is more elaborate and highly wrought than the great English Odes of Milton, Dryden, Gray, or Keats. A reader who follows the quick turns of Pindar's thought will find method in his madness, and may discern that, if he has the quick movements of a butterfly, he draws honey from the flowers. But the uniqueness of the poem is not in any of these things. Where it lies, we can learn if we turn to the *Sportsman,* and then compose an ode on any of the successful athletes or horse-owners whose names are to be found there. For there is nothing remarkable about Cleander : achievements as great as his can be found most days in the sporting columns of the newspapers, and Queen's Club, though less picturesque, is as important as the Isthmus. But the light in which Pindar saw Cleander's victory, and the poem which he wrote about it, are remarkable. Read the words again. Cleander and the pancration vanish as Pindar writes, and the fires of his imagination shape themselves into less ephemeral visions. We see Cleander's island home in Aegina and heroic figures from its past—Aeacus and his sons and grandsons, great fighters and wise and good men, ' whose virtues the gods remembered '—then a glimpse of Achilles, unforgotten in death, because of his deeds, and to whose funeral the Muses came ; then gliding into real life, we hear of another athlete of Cleander's family and at the close are told why Cleander may be named with these famous names. The poem was sung at the athlete's home-coming or at a dinner in his honour ; when it was finished, he had remembered the history and heroes of his home, had praised the great and wise of the past whose traditions he inherited, had recalled their fame, virtues, and shining example, had felt the link which binds together all human beings who rise above the crowd by strength of mind or character or body, and through his small achievement had known himself a part of that splendid company.

[1] Isthmian, vii, tr. W. M. L. Hutchinson.

This is a better gift than is given to the winners of a Cup Tie or the Diamond Sculls or the Grand National—a paragraph in the stop-press of the evening ' specials ', and the praises of the sporting editor. In every corner of life's tapestry—even in athletics—the Greek saw the threads of poetry and read the pattern of splendid virtues. He fell into neither of the extremes between which we waver—those of deifying athletes and denouncing athleticism. He knew that it was an excellent thing to be physically strong and skilful, and he paid his tribute to these gifts without supposing them supreme or ignoring others. They were *aretai*, ' virtues ', of the body and he admired them, and in admiring was led on, as Pindar is led here, to think of other and greater virtues.

Pindar's life, if not his thought, takes us into the age of the Attic drama : so with his elder contemporary and rival, Simonides (556–468), who was born in the Ionian island of Ceos and died in Sicily. Lessing called him the Greek Voltaire, a phrase suggested by his travels, his friendships with contemporary princes and statesmen, his vein of worldliness, and his love of money ; [1] but he was also a great poet. He wrote in many styles of lyric, though perhaps his greatest works were his epigrams, remarkable even in Greek for their union of power and simplicity (p. 385 f.). The following fragment of a lyric deals with Danäe and her infant son, Perseus, who were turned adrift in a chest by her father.

' WHEN in the carven chest,
   The winds that blew and waves in wild unrest
Smote her with fear, she, not with cheeks unwet,
Her arms of love round Perseus set,
   And said : O child, what grief is mine !
But thou dost slumber and thy baby breast
Is sunk in rest,
Here in the cheerless brass-bound bark,
Tossed amid starless night and pitchy dark.
   Nor dost thou heed the scudding brine
Of waves that wash above thy curls so deep,
Nor the shrill winds that sweep,—

[1] Asked whether it was better to be a philosopher or rich, he replied : Rich ; for I see the philosophers hanging about the doors of the wealthy.'

Lapped in thy purple robe's embrace,
Fair little face !
But if this dread were dreadful too to thee,
Then wouldst thou lend thy listening ear to me :
Therefore I cry,—Sleep babe, and sea be still,
And slumber our unmeasured ill !
 Oh, may some change of fate, sire Zeus, from thee
Descend, our woes to end !
But if this prayer, too overbold, offend
Thy justice, yet be merciful to me.[1]

[1] Fr. 37. Tr. J. A. Symonds, *Studies of the Greek Poets*, which has other translations from Greek Lyric Poetry. I have to thank Messrs. Black for leave to quote this specimen.

IV [1]

TRAGEDY: AESCHYLUS, SOPHOCLES, EURIPIDES

Aeschylus' bronze-throat eagle-bark at blood
Has somehow spoilt my taste for twitterings.
R. BROWNING.

Be his
My special thanks, whose even-balanced soul
Business could not make dull nor passion wild;
Who saw life steadily and saw it whole;
The mellow glory of the Attic stage,
Singer of sweet Colonus and its child.
MATTHEW ARNOLD.

Euripides is the most precious thing left us—the most like Shakespeare.
CHARLES JAMES FOX.

A few years after Sappho was singing at Lesbos, a storm-cloud gathers on the uplands of Persia: it descends on the Mesopotamian plain and takes shape over the ruins of the kingdoms of Lydia (546) and of Babylon (538) as the Persian Empire. Its shadow moves westward engulfing the Asiatic Greeks. In 500 they revolt, are overthrown by Darius, King of Persia, and lose their independence. Eight years later Persian envoys are demanding

---

[1] In the following chapters I have grouped the authors according to their literary *genres* and not their chronological order. The reader will be able to make the necessary adjustments with the following table of dates. He will notice that Euripides, Socrates, Thucydides, and Aristophanes are contemporaries. He should also remember that Greek thought is transformed during the fifth century, largely by the sophists (p. 252 f.); and that Aeschylus and Herodotus, though deeply influenced by the new movement, belong in part to the older Greece, whereas Thucydides and Euripides are as modern in thought as ourselves.

Aeschylus 525–456.   Aristophanes 446–385.
Sophocles 496–406.   Xenophon 434–354.
Herodotus 484–425.   Plato 427–347.
Euripides 480–406.   Aristotle 385–322.
Thucydides 471–?   Demosthenes 384–322.
Socrates 469–399.   Menander 343–292.

The great sophists are active from the middle to the end of the fifth century.

*earth and water in token of submission from the states of Greece.
Athens and Sparta refuse. In 490 a Persian army of some 50,000
men lands in the bay of Marathon in Attica, while 10,000 Athenians
and 1,000 Plataeans watch them from the hills. The Greek army
charges, and we see the defeated Persians sail back home. Eight
years pass and an immense Persian army of nearly half a million
assembles at Sardis under Xerxes, the son of Darius. In 480 we see
it moving northward accompanied by a huge fleet, crossing the Dardanelles on a bridge of boats, creeping round the coast of Thrace and
Thessaly and receiving the submission of many Greek states. At
the Pass of Thermopylae a few thousand Greeks block its way. For
six days the army is checked, then floods onwards. The scene shifts
to the island of Salamis in the narrow seas between Attica and the
Peloponnese. Xerxes from a hill watches the clash of the Persian
and Greek navies ; the unwieldy Persian fleet is outmanœuvred
and destroyed, and Xerxes abandons his attempt. Next year the
army he leaves behind is defeated at Plataea, and Europe is left to
freedom.*

*479–431. Inspired by this brilliant triumph, Athens takes the
political and intellectual leadership in Greece. From leader of
a league of states against Persia she becomes its mistress, and the
league becomes her empire. In 459, Athenians (and Athens has
not more than 30,000 citizens) fell fighting in Cyprus, Egypt,
Phoenicia, Aegina, and at Halieis and Megara. At home under
Pericles her trade develops, her government progresses still further
to complete democracy, her city is crowned with splendid buildings,
immortal plays are acted in her theatres, and she becomes the
intellectual centre of Greece.*

*431–404. But her subjects begin to resent their lost independence,
Greece outside is jealous of her power, and in 431 the Peloponnesian
war breaks out. It is a struggle of Ionians against Dorians, of
democracy against oligarchy, of Athens and her empire against Sparta,
Corinth, Thebes, and most of the Peloponnese. For eleven years
the tides of invasion break over Attica and fall back before the walls
of Athens, till after a struggle with varying fortunes the tired rivals
make peace in 421. Meanwhile Pericles, the intellectual aristocrat
who led the democracy, is dead, and his power is disputed between
a number of lesser men—chief among them the respectable and
mediocre Nicias, the brilliant and unscrupulous Alcibiades and
a succession of violent democrats.*

*In 415 the greatest fleet that ever left Athens sails to extend her
empire to Sicily : by 413 she has lost it, and the reinforcements*

that followed it, under the walls of Syracuse. Her enemies see their chance and the Peloponnesian war is resumed. Struggling with oligarchic sedition at home, deserted by subjects who resent the growing tyranny of her empire, she yet maintains the struggle till 404, when her last fleet is destroyed, the corn-ships that bring her food from the Black Sea are cut off, and she surrenders at discretion. Her walls are destroyed and her empire is lost. This century is the supreme age of Greek creative activity ; political and literary greatness go together—as they have ever gone—the creators in art, literature, and thought are mainly Athenians, and, where they are not, are drawn to Athens.

404–338. For fifty years we witness meaningless parochial struggles, first Sparta, then Thebes leading Greece, and Athens recovering a shadow of her lost power. The most significant incident, though none thought it so at the time, is the march of 10,000 Greek mercenaries to the heart of the Persian Empire and their retreat, unharmed, to the Black Sea. From 360 clouds begin to gather in the half-savage northern kingdom of Macedonia. Its king, Philip, diplomatic, far-sighted, unscrupulous, devises the famous phalanx formation, armed with lances 21 feet long, a human cheval de frise. He conquers the surrounding tribes, then begins to enclose Greece in the tentacles of his intrigues. Athens is roused by the genius of Demosthenes from its fourth-century occupation of balancing budgets, reducing military costs, and spending money on social ends, and becomes again the leader in the struggle for Greek independence. We hear furious debates in the assembly between the parties of peace and war, headed respectively by Aeschines and Demosthenes. Twenty years of struggle end in 338 on the battle-field of Chaeronea, where the allied Athenian and Theban forces are routed, and Greece loses her freedom. In this period Plato's political writings reflect the discontents of the time, though his vital inspiration is drawn from the fifth century ; Xenophon's Anabasis *throws the shadow of the future before ; through the speeches of Demosthenes we see the drama of a peaceful democracy threatened by foreign aggression and unwilling to face the fact.*

In dealing with Greek Tragedy, I shall follow a new plan ; no play can be judged from quotations, it must be read as a whole ; and assuming that one or more plays from each of the great tragedians will be studied independently, I shall try to give some estimate of Greek Drama and its writers, and to prepare the reader for what he will find there. The following pages must not be taken for an account of the subject. They are simply intended to point out some of the peculiarities of Greek Drama, and to indicate the particular genius of its three chief writers. The reader can then turn to the plays themselves. If in reading them he sees at each moment the figures on the stage, enters into their thoughts and feelings, forms a conception of their characters, and divines the idea which was in the mind of their creators and which lies behind each play, he will have read to some purpose.

The subjects of Greek Tragedy are taken from Greek legend and legendary history ; fiction and even contemporary history were avoided, though the *Persians* of Aeschylus deals with his own times. The plays were acted in the great theatre of Dionysus at Athens. Thirty-three of them have survived, a tiny fraction of the whole, from the hands of three Athenians, Aeschylus, Sophocles, and Euripides. But the wealth and quality of the dramatic output of the time may be judged from the fact that every March twelve new plays were exhibited, and that the extant plays in many cases were defeated by others now lost.[1] New plays continued to be written even into the Christian era, but it is not likely that anything of real value was produced after the fourth century, and the great dramas are earlier still.

Let the reader imagine himself sitting on a cushion, which he has brought with him to soften his stone bench, in the great open-air theatre pictured in the text. It is the end of March, but spring comes early and warm in the South. The theatre is packed, and holds perhaps 20,000 spectators, who have been there since dawn and will sit till nightfall, for three poets are competing (selected out of a larger number) and each poet is presenting four plays. In the front row sit priests and important political personages, on marble seats, of which the photograph shows some remains. Just beyond them is a circular ' orchestra ' or ' dancing place ', in the centre of which stands the altar of Dionysus, god of wine and of the vegetation, just now burgeoning in the spring weather ; behind that is a long, low, narrow stage, backed by buildings which serve as green room, and on whose wooden wall is roughly painted a palace, or temple, or whatever may be the setting of the play.

The play begins, and seems as foreign and strange as its setting. There are three actors only, never more. They wear

---

[1] The *Medea* got the third prize, the *Oedipus the King* the second prize, though they are among the greatest of surviving Greek plays,

a cothurnus or buskin (a curious wooden sole, some six inches high), and padding on their chest, to make them look tall and impressive ; on their heads are linen masks, with wide mouths, a great cone-shaped projection above and exaggerated features. These actors move on the stage and are supplemented by fifteen other persons called a chorus, who execute dances and elaborate evolutions in the orchestra, singing at intervals in the play choral songs, and through their leader sometimes engaging in dialogue with the actors. There is no curtain ; breaks in the action are filled with choric songs. The speeches are longer than in an English play, and the dialogue is apt to take the form of what the Greeks called stichomythia—conversations in alternate lines. There is always a Messenger's speech, extending often to fifty or sixty lines or more, and generally used to narrate the catastrophe, which is never enacted on the stage. The scenery is of the simplest, and if it is necessary to show characters inside the house, who are sleeping or dead, they are rolled out on a trolley (eccyclema). It seems a curious mixture of a play and an opera, and, in form at least, primitive and crude. The first play is followed by two other tragedies, and then, curiously, by a ' satyric ' drama, a comic play with satyrs, or wild men of the woods, for chorus. Originally the four plays deal with different stages of the same story : later, their subjects may have no connexion.

The first question an intelligent spectator would ask is, Where does it all come from, the mask and cothurnus, the singing and dancing, the long speeches, the limited number of actors, the curious tail of buffoonery attached to a body of tragedy? The question goes deep, for we have here the distant ancestors of our modern play. We are standing beside the cradle of European drama, of *Hamlet* and *Faust*, and of those complex and elaborate phenomena which may be seen any day in modern theatres.

Drama springs from a primitive and universal instinct—the instinct to imitate. At religious feasts men ' imitated ' or acted the sacred legends ; at the local hero's shrine they acted his feats. Among the most important religious celebrations were those of Dionysus, the god of vegetation and more especially of the vine, particularly important to an agricultural people in a wine-growing country like Greece. The Greek Drama was a religious service in honour of Dionysus ; his altar stood in the centre of the theatre, and it is probably in his worship that tragedy, no less than comedy, originates. The first stage is a song called a dithyramb, sung by countrymen, later by regular choirs of fifty performers. Out of these beginnings, with nothing to guide or help them, the Greeks made tragedy. There is no more striking sign of their genius than that in a few generations they had evolved in its essentials the most complex form of literature that the human genius has created, and were writing plays that Shelley ranks with *King Lear*. What steps lead from these fifty singers dressed in goatskins to the *Agamemnon* ?

At first, in the intervals of the dithyrambic song, the leader of the chorus tells some story about Dionysus in recitative. There is our drama in germ. The chorus of Greek Tragedy is the developed song ; the rest of the play is the developed recitative. At first the chorus is almost everything ; the recitative grows, two people take part in it instead of one, finally a third is added, and we have the three actors. The chorus diminishes in proportion. Its members fall to twelve, then are fixed at fifteen. It still forms half of the earliest extant play of Aeschylus ; in the time of Euripides it is cut down to a fraction, and its songs sometimes become musical interludes without reference to the subject of the play. That is the origin of Greek, and of European, Drama ; there we see why the former has a chorus, few actors, and long speeches : the masks are survivals of the old religious service, in which the human being must not be himself, but change his face and take the mask of a hero or a god. The 'satyric' drama is a relic of the buffoonery and revelry of the vintage festival, and recalls the god of wine in whose worship drama begins. Of course, in a sense, the Greeks were not writing drama ; the poet did not say to himself : ' I am going to portray human life ; let me make the portrait convincing and realistic.' He was simply telling a story in honour of the god at a religious service. But through the Greek artistic genius the literature encroached on the religion, the story became in essentials the drama we know, and the poet evolved the principles of Unity of Action, Development to a Climax, Tragic Character, &c., which the modern playwright finds ready to his hand and sanctified by the approval of ages, but which the Greek had to discover for himself, and to which he felt his way with the sure instinct of genius. It is part of the interest of Greek Drama that we can watch its development and rapid progress from the *Suppliant Women* of Aeschylus to the finest work of Sophocles or Euripides. From start to finish we see development, experiment, change.

There are two great differences which we have not yet mentioned between Greek and modern acting : one in the use of the
voice, the other in gesture and movement. The history of Greek
Drama shows that the voice was considered the actor's chief
instrument. We are told that ' acting lies in the voice, in the
method of using it to express each emotion ', that ' actors should
be judged by their voices, as statesmen by their wisdom ', that
tragic actors used to spend years in training their voices, and
used to test them before each performance by running over all
their notes.[1] Here we have one reason why modern representations of Greek plays are often disappointing. The difficult art of
declamation, on which the Greeks relied, is almost unknown on
the English stage ; it is the weakest weapon of our actors. The
long speeches of Greek Drama which need perfect declamation,
and without it are as tedious as with it they are superb, are
often delivered with indistinctness or monotony or ranting. In
consequence they are ruined. To this is often added a further
weakness. Transferring the methods of the English stage to
a very different type of art, modern actors are rapid and violent
in their gestures. It is quite clear that the quick movement of
the modern stage was impossible in the Greek theatre. The
buskin in itself made it impossible ; tie a six-inch clog under
your boot, and see how fast you can move. Further, the dress,
with its emphasis on stateliness and dignity, the long speeches,
the distance from the audience, which would have made rapid
movements difficult to follow, all point to slowness of movement,
a statuesque and almost sculptural style of acting. Those who
saw the Aeschylean Trilogy represented in this style at Cambridge
in 1921 by an amateur company of young men, who naturally
lacked the experience and long training necessary for perfect
acting, will agree not only that the effect was most impressive,
but that the play was quite as ' realistic ' as if in moments of
emotion the violent gestures had been used which we are accustomed to regard as signs of strong feeling.
     Let us now review the chief peculiarities of Greek Drama and
prepare ourselves for its chief differences from our own. If we
are to call up before our eyes the scene in the Great Theatre, we
must think of slow movement and statuesque tableaux, of lines
perfectly delivered, with clearness, emphasis, and fullness of meaning. We must remember that the technique of drama is not
completely evolved, that a touch of the narrative form of its

[1] Haigh, *Attic Theatre*, p. 272 f.

original clings about it, that there is less acting in an ancient than in a modern play and more tendency to describe things than to show them on the stage. We must be prepared, especially in Euripides, for long speeches in which opponents state their respective points of view. These are interesting as studies of character and motive, but they are not dramatic in our sense, and drama had yet to outgrow them. We must expect the plays to be much shorter than Shakespeare's. The *Electra* of Euripides is a story not unlike that of *Hamlet*. In both the hero (Hamlet, Orestēs) is the son of a king (Hamlet the Elder, Agamemnon), who has been murdered and succeeded on the throne by a younger kinsman (Claudius, Aegisthus). The dead king's wife (Gertrude, Clytaemnestra) has married the murderer. The hero is driven by supernatural commands (the Ghost, Apollo) to exact vengeance. The play in both cases shows how this murder is accomplished.[1] But the *Electra* has 1,359 lines, while the first two acts of *Hamlet* alone have over 1,600. The reason for this difference is that the construction of the Greek play is simpler; it has no comic relief, no under-plot. It is, as it were, a *Hamlet* without Polonius, Laertes, Ophelia, the grave-diggers and other characters. Both plays move to a final catastrophe, but the *Electra*, like a rapid stream, follows a straight course, while *Hamlet* flows with checks and wide meanders. Undoubtedly we should prefer the English form, which has more of the variety and richness of life, but the Greek has some compensation in its greater intensity. In a Greek play the reader has the main characters perpetually under his eyes; their figures and changing fortunes never leave him. There are no sub-plots or relief scenes to relax the tension. He never escapes from the presence of the tragedy that first overshadows and finally confronts him. English Drama is richer and more true to life, but this sustained intensity it lacks.

Another peculiarity of Greek Drama lies in the choric songs. These in good translations strike us as fine pieces of lyrical poetry, but we shall miss their real significance if we see nothing else in them. They are more than mere music. Sometimes they are used to sound the *leit-motif* of the play. If, for instance, the story is the working of an inherited taint which brings ruin on the members of a family, that *motif* will be sounded in the chorus. The death of Agamemnon, in the play of that name, is the direct result of the criminal sacrifice of his daughter Īphigenīa, and the indirect result of evil deeds in the history of his house whose

[1] G. Murray, *Hamlet and Orestes*.

poison taints the third and fourth generation. Hence the first
chorus is full of ominous hints of punishment and vengeance,
and closes with a description of Iphigenia's death. We are shown
the invisible background of human life, and hear the echoes of the
unseen spiritual forces that direct and create the tragic events on
the stage. At other times the chorus gives us the atmosphere in
which the play is moving at the moment. It sums up in music
and song the meaning of what we have just seen or are about to
see. In the previous scene certain events have been enacted or
described in conversation and formal speech. The chorus pass
from this rational, everyday world of prose into a realm of pure
emotion, where the dominant feeling of the play at the moment
finds a sublimated, purified feeling in poetry. The first and
second songs of the *Oedipus the King* are fine examples of this
use of the chorus. A third use of the chorus is for contrast and
relief. Where Shakespeare breaks the tension by comic relief,
the Greek poet broke it by pure poetry. A scene of horror is
succeeded by some exquisite song. Thus the third song of the
Hippolytus, which follows an agonizing scene, is a prayer by the
chorus for the wings of a bird on which they might escape to
some magic land of beauty. Of this Professor Murray writes :
' This lovely song seems to me a good instance of the artistic
value of the Greek chorus. The last scene has been tragic to the
point of painfulness : the one thing that can heal the pain without spoiling the interest is an outburst of pure poetry.'

Greek Drama in its evolution moved towards the elimination
of the chorus, and in Euripides its songs seem often to be mere
musical lyrics unconnected with the play. Something was lost
thereby. The Greek tragedian had an instrument which the
dramatist of our own day has lost, and could produce effects which
are absent from the modern stage. He had a peculiar and powerful means of expression in this union of song with plain verse, of
music with speech—song and music taking up, re-expressing, and
reinforcing in their own medium the thoughts and feelings of the
play. It is interesting to compare Mr. Thomas Hardy's revival
of the chorus in the *Dynasts*, where it is employed for purposes
and effects akin to those of Greek Drama.

Passing from the form of these plays to their contents, we find
ourselves in a land that seems more foreign than it is. Perhaps
the strangest feature is the mixture of crude polytheism with high
moral conceptions. We meet Apollo and Ares, Artemis and
Aphrodite, and other deities tarnished with human frailties and

vices. Then suddenly we are surprised by a piece of theology as lofty as anything in Shakespeare and more subtle and speculative. The explanation is simple. Between 480 and 400 Athenian thought was transformed. Criticism and science have profoundly changed our own view of the world in the last eighty years ; but these changes are nothing to the transformation of Athenian ideas within the lifetime of Sophocles. At the beginning of the period we see a people of keen sensibility and sharp wit, but with many primitive and savage notions. The stimulus of their victory over Persia and of intellectual influences from Asiatic Greece acted like a tropical sun on Athens, and produced luxuriant vegetation of thought. Thus we have a nation with many primitive and superstitious ideas which are rapidly purged by the play of criticism ; and even when the work of criticism is almost done, and superstition is melting away in the sunlight, isolated fragments are left, like drifts and patches of snow in a thaw. We need not, then, pay much attention to the polytheism of Greek Tragedy. Its many deities are in progress of becoming aspects of a single God, and God is ceasing to be, as he is to the savage, mere power that can do anything, and that does do anything, carrying off mortal women and arbitrarily killing those who annoy him. He is becoming the god who is justice, who does right himself and sees that it is done. Aeschylus and Euripides are monotheists, and the older religious ideas survive in them, because these are inextricably inwoven in the stories which they treat, just as traces of a primitive conception of God might survive in the works of a modern dramatist who took his subjects from the Pentateuch. We shall speak of other peculiarities of idea in these plays when we come to the individual dramatists.

We can, as I said, disregard the primitive element : partly because it is passing away, partly because the substance of which these tragedies are woven is our common human nature, and the faces in their tapestry are like our own. A man whose character and ability have raised him to the highest place in the state suddenly discovers that he has unknowingly committed terrible crimes : we see his good and bad qualities, his downfall, how he supports life after it, and how through patience and endurance he is redeemed. Another, the incarnation of indomitable personality, rebels against the injustice that oppresses him, and faces the extreme of suffering rather than compromise where he knows that he is right. We see a woman tormented by a passion which she cannot conquer and may not satisfy ; we hear the tempter telling her to bow to the inevitable ; we hear her reply, and we are shown the tragic end. Another woman has left her home and quarrelled with her family to marry a Greek stranger. He abandons her and marries a princess of his own country. We hear his motives, and her reproaches, and his reply, and see the spirit that enters her, and what she does. Another woman has to choose between breaking the law of duty and the law of the land ; we see her choice, and in what spirit (by no means stoical) she faces death.[1] There is nothing exotic or antiquated about these characters and situations. They are made of the permanent stuff of human nature. Matthew Arnold has thus defined the quality that gives literature a lasting value. ' The poet ', he says, ' has in the first place to select an excellent action ; and what actions are the most excellent ? Those, certainly, which most powerfully appeal to the great primary human affections ; to those elementary feelings which subsist permanently in the race, and which are independent of time. Those feelings are permanent and the same ; that which interests them is permanent and the same also. The modernness or antiquity of an action, therefore, has nothing to do with its fitness for poetical representation ; this depends upon its inherent qualities. To the elementary part of our nature, to our passions, that which is great and passionate is eternally interesting ; and interesting solely in proportion to its greatness and to its passion.' This test Greek Tragedy satisfies.

Our specimens of Greek Tragedy come from three authors : seven plays by Aeschylus, seven by Sophocles, and nineteen [2] by Euripides have survived. These were the greatest dramatists of the Attic stage, and, after Shakespeare, of the world. Further, not only are they in themselves interesting and dissimilar personalities, but they represent different phases in a rapidly changing world, and, like shafts sunk into a geological formation, they reveal the intellectual structure and development of an age of thought. The following plays may be particularly recommended. The *Oresteia*, or the Trilogy as it is sometimes called, consisting of the *Agamemnon*, the *Libation-Bearers* (*Choëphoroi*), and the *Furies* (*Eumenides*), is the only example of a Trilogy that has survived and is the greatest achievement of the genius of Aeschylus. It is a story of sin visited on the third

---

[1] Oedipus, Promētheus, Phaedra, Mēdēa, Antigonē.
[2] Including the *Rhēsus*.

and fourth generation, of a wife that murdered the triumphant leader of the Greek armies, of the duty of vengeance that fell on her son, of his fate when he had killed his mother, and of how he found release. The *Prometheus Bound*, which inspired Shelley, is the picture of the resistance of Prometheus to the unjust strength of Zeus. It would be difficult to find anything in literature which equally portrays ' the abysmal depths of personality ', the untameable power of the will. The *Persians* is inspired by the great victories of 480 B.C. over the Persians. (One might compare it to a drama on the Armada or on 1918, or to Tchaikowski's ' 1812 '.) For Aeschylus Salamis is less a national triumph than the god-ordained victory of Right over Insolent Power.

Oedipus the King, by Sophocles, is a story of a man who unknowingly committed terrible sin, and whose sin found him out in the days of his greatness as King of Thebes. Apart from its tragic quality, the plot of this play is of unsurpassed perfection. Its sequel, the *Oedipus at Colōnus*, tells of the last days of Oedipus. The *Antigonē* is a tale of a girl who has to choose between breaking the laws of God and those of the State. The *Electra* deals with the same subject as the *Libation-Bearers*—the murder of Clytaemnestra by her son. The *Philoctētes* is a study of three men—Philoctetes, a generous nature in whom illness has bred a warped and morbid spirit, Odysseus, seen as a sinister and unscrupulous man of affairs, and the generous-hearted son of Achilles—the play shows how this boy is overpersuaded by Odysseus into treachery, and how he comes to himself again.

I have chosen the plays of Euripides which have been translated by Professor Murray, because the reader has his excellent introduction and notes to help him in understanding them : they need not therefore be specially characterized here. Every student should read the *Medea* and the *Bacchae*. Next, perhaps, should be placed the *Trojan Women*, the *Electra*, and the *Alcestis*, the first as a portrait of war seen from the angle of the conquered, the second for comparison with the plays on the same subject by Aeschylus and Sophocles, the third as a portrait of an egoist and a heroic woman. The *Iphigenīa among the Taurians* is a happier play than Euripides usually wrote. The *Ion* and the *Hercules Mad* (neither translated by Professor Murray) are powerful and original plays. The latter is a story in its essentials resembling the *Oedipus*, a picture of a great man overwhelmed by undeserved misfortune, yet saving his soul. The *Cyclops* should be read, partly because it has been brilliantly translated by Shelley, partly because it shows the powers of Euripides as a humorist. If one play only of each dramatist be read, the *Agamemnon*, the *Oedipus the King*, and perhaps the *Medea* or the *Trojan Women* should be selected.

Of the life of Aeschylus (525–456 : first dramatic victory, 484) we need know nothing except that he was middle-aged when the tiny Greek states beat back the great Persian Empire and made their liberty secure by one of those brilliant triumphs which wake men's imagination, that he himself fought at Salamis and Marathon, and valued this so much more than his literary successes, that his epitaph, ignoring his poetry, simply records that he fought the Persians. He is represented as a proud, fiery character, an aristocrat by temperament.

He stands in the dawn of drama, and his plays bear the mark of this. His earliest extant play, the *Suppliant Women*, is very primitive in construction. It has three characters besides the chorus, and requires only two actors ; the chorus takes up half the play and there is very little action. His late plays, culminating in the Trilogy, are more artistic, more like our idea of drama, but they are always simple, and in construction often clumsy ; and the chorus (he is the greatest lyrist of the Greek dramatists) plays a large part in them. His characters are simple ; we see one side of their nature, their great passion, whatever it may be, but do not get a complete picture of them, such as Shakespeare or even Euripides would give us. We feel their force, their personality, but we hardly can be said to know them.

Aeschylus' theology is inconsistent ; his conceptions of God are lofty, but a background of primitive polytheism continually reappears. His ideas too are often primitive. Four in particular recur, which were more important and convincing in a tribal society than in our own ; for in such a society (and the age of Aeschylus was but emerging from it) the family counts for more than the individual. The first of these ideas is that of a curse haunting certain families. A man sins, and from the first sin proceeds a hereditary taint that infects his descendants, leading them to sin and disaster (Ātē). ' The fathers have eaten sour grapes and the children's teeth are set on edge.' They plunge with a blind infatuation into courses that lead to ruin. Associated with this is the idea of blood revenge : a son inherits not only his father's goods, but the duty to avenge him. The dead man keeps a certain power over his family, and can punish neglect of his rights. If he is murdered, his son must kill the murderer, and then becomes in turn subject to the vengeance of the family of the man he has killed. Thirdly, Aeschylus has a theory of the origin of evil, of how men came to sin. It begins, he thinks, in prosperity. A man becomes rich and powerful ; this breeds Hūbris or Insolent Pride, for in prosperity men become arrogant and extreme in thought, word, and deed ; and on this Insolence retribution inevitably follows. How then can we be safe ? how save ourselves from Insolence and the Ate which is its consequences ? The remedy is Moderation or Sōphrosynē, the central idea of all Greek morality, ' the golden thread that runs through the virtues '. Avoid excess ; keep to the mean ; ' nothing too much '. These ideas—Ate, the law of blood revenge, Hubris, Sophrosyne, run throughout Greek Tragedy ; but the first two, the most primitive of them, are most fully realized and believed by Aeschylus. To Euripides blood revenge, the *lex talionis*, is as repulsive as to us.

With these primitive elements, it may be asked how it comes that Swinburne calls the *Oresteia* 'probably on the whole the greatest spiritual work of man ', that Shelley ranks the *Agamemnon* with *King Lear* ? The answer is not easy, for Aeschylus is the most impossible of poets to reproduce. Note, first, that most of his ideas are perfectly valid. They are the Greek way of expressing what most of us would accept, if they were translated into modern language. Hubris is almost equivalent to sin ; or rather, it is an attempt to go behind the fact of sin, to its cause and nature. We need not look far to see nations and individuals dazzled with success, and following with a blind infatuation the road to ruin. European history since 1800 might be written as an Aeschylean Trilogy. Hubris proceeding from prosperity, and issuing in Ate : how can we better describe the history of Napoleon or of Germany before the late war ? or what better counsel could have been given to Napoleon or to Germany, or could now be given to Britain and France than Sophrosyne, ' Nothing too much ' ? The idea of a curse haunting a family is equally modern, though to-day we call it the law of heredity ; and Aeschylus might find in the Stuarts, the Bourbons, and the family of Napoleon equivalents to the house of Atreus or Oedipus. The sins of the fathers are perpetuated and punished in the children.

If these ideas are still living, the idea of blood revenge is not. Within a few years of the appearance of the *Agamemnon* Euripides

was riddling it with a merciless criticism, and it clearly belongs
to a primitive stage of thought.   Yet from it Aeschylus draws
some of his greatest effects.   Imagine a young man—little more
than a boy—whose father has been killed by his mother and her
lover.   Religion, he believes, binds him to avenge his father, and
kill the murderess or be haunted by his father's spirit, yet he
knows that if he kills his mother he will be pursued by the hideous
monsters who punish matricide.   So the *Libation-Bearers* opens,
and its successive scenes are full of uncanny horror : the dead
Agamemnon restless, calling for blood, and sending his guilty
wife dreams of evil ; Orestes and his sister at their father's grave,
goading him to revenge by recital of his death, bribing him with
offerings, and reminding him that his children's interests are his
own ; Clytaemnestra pleading with her son for life, till he drives
her into the house to die ; the dead bodies before the palace,
and Orestes struggling, before madness descends on him, to
justify his act :

>   The boy
> With his white breast and brow and clustering curls
> Streaked with his mother's blood, but striving hard
> To tell his story ere his reason goes.

The human beings here are like ourselves : that is why their fate
is tragic.   But a background such as that against which they
move, can be found in no other poet.   Aeschylus lived on our
world and knew and could paint human beings ; but he was not
less at home in the world of gods and demi-gods.   Twice at least
in the Old Testament we are admitted to the courts of heaven ;
but in both cases the vision is dim ; we catch a half-glimpse of
the Deity, and He speaks as a man with men.   The gods and
giants and furies of Aeschylus wear no such mask ; they speak
as such beings might be supposed to speak.[1]   Nowhere else in
literature is such audacious and colossal imagination, nowhere
are we so constantly in the presence of the superhuman, nowhere
is that superhuman so boldly and nakedly portrayed.   Yet it
comes without effort to Aeschylus ; his unseen world must have
been as real to him as the streets of Athens.

   That world was an illusion, though we may be glad that he has
opened its doors to us.   Yet in one aspect it is not illusory.   We
do not believe in the deities and spirits in which he embodied
the moral and religious forces that were for him the ultimate

---

[1] Cp. *The Furies* ; and the giant Typhon ' whistling murder ', P. V. 355.

things in life ; but we may agree that such forces are ultimate, and be grateful to a poet who never forgets them. Men and women may be the actors in his plays ; but we are conscious that behind them and never absent from the scene

> The giant shades of Fate, silently flitting,
> Pile the dim outlines of the coming doom.

Aeschylus does not, so to speak, stop at the knob that turns on the electric light and the lamps that convey it; his imagination flies to the power-house and hears the purring dynamos from which it proceeds. It is in this consciousness of the background of life, this power of making us feel the great currents on which mankind is swept along, that Aeschylus has no rival. His sense of the unseen makes him a little unintelligible and uncongenial to our scientific and critical age, which easily forgets the mystery of nature because it has a superficial control over her. We prefer Euripides who is a rationalist like ourselves. But nature does not cease to be mysterious because men are dull to her mystery, and a poet has something to teach our generation who is penetrated by the sense of the unseen and sees the play of stupendous forces below the surface of the sensible world.

Aeschylus writes as a demi-god might write, and his language matches his subject. A play of Shakespeare may contain half a dozen lines of the quality of

> In the visitation of the winds,
> Who take the ruffian billows by the top,
> Curling their monstrous heads and hanging them
> With deafening clamour in the slippery clouds,
> That with the hurly death itself awakes.

But this exalted writing is the habitual style of Aeschylus. At times it degenerates into bombast : with any other writer, and on any other subjects, it would be tasteless. It exactly suits Aeschylus and his themes. A faint idea of his language may be gathered from some of the metaphors, which he uses as if things were too wonderful to be called by their real names, as if some odd likeness must be found, to make us feel their strangeness. A bonfire tosses in the air ' a great beard of flame ' ; war is ' a money-changer who deals in bodies ' (you give him men, and back comes dust) ; the full moon is ' the eldest of the stars, the eye of night ', a double image, which first carries the imagination back before the constellations were born, then makes us see the moon as the eye through which night looks at the world. Many of his metaphors are taken from the sea, and few poets show such imaginative sympathy with it. Ships in a storm ' butt each other, lashed by a wild shepherd ' (he sees them as cattle tormented by a demon herdsman) ; and after the storm the ' Aegean sea flowers with dead bodies ' (men floating on the waters, strange blossoms of the tide). ' A wave of warriors with nodding crests goes foaming, blown by the wind of war' round a beleaguered town (he sees the besiegers' army swell up to the walls and break on them like spray). When the drowned Persians after Salamis are eaten by the fishes, ' they are flayed by the silent children of the undefiled '. ' Aeschylus retaining the physical word " flayed ", paints the rest of the scene with a rich imagination. The children of earth, but now so clamorous, are at the mercy of the still children of that sea whose translucent purity they have harassed and distracted in vain.' [1] Yet with all these images of horror, Aeschylus wrote perhaps the finest description of the sea on a calm, sunny day, when he spoke of ' the unnumbered smile of the waves '.

But this poet of the colossal and the superhuman can paint the tenderer emotions with an unerring hand. Witness the portrait of the widowed husband in his palace, hating the statues that remind him of his lost wife and dreaming of her till the dream vanishes ' on wings that follow the pathways of sleep ' ; [2] or the sacrifice of Iphigenia gagged and struggling while her father stands by with the Greek chiefs, and thinks of her girl life at home.

HER 'Father, Father,' her sad cry that lingered,
Her virgin heart's breath they all held as naught,
Those bronze-clad witnesses and battle hungered ;
And there they prayed ; and when the prayer was wrought,
He charged the young men to uplift and bind her,
As ye lift a wild kid high above the altar,
Fierce huddling forward, fallen, clinging sore
To the robe that wrapt her ; yea he bids them hinder
The sweet mouth's utterance, the cries that falter,

   —His curse for evermore !—

---

[1] Morshead, *House of Atreus*, p. xxi   [2] Agamemnon, 423 f.

SOPHOCLES

With violence and a curb's voiceless wrath.
Her stole of saffron then to the ground she threw,
And her eye with an arrow of pity found its path
   To each man's heart that slew :
A face in a picture striving amazedly ;
The little maid who danced at her father's board,
The innocent voice man's love came never nigh,
Who joined to his her little paean cry
   When the third cup was poured. . . .[1]

It is impossible to appreciate Aeschylus in a translation, nor can the impression he creates be put into words. Some idea may be got from the epithets which critics use of him—sublime, grand, dithyrambic, colossal, elemental, titanic, superhuman. Milton at his grandest, Marlowe at moments, Shakespeare when he shows us the mad Lear in the storm on the moor, or Macbeth with the witches on the ' blasted heath ', Victor Hugo in certain passages of *La Légende des Siècles*, come nearest to him. But all these writers—and this is no criticism of their greatness—are further removed than Aeschylus from what they described. They speak at times with ' the large utterance of the early gods ' ; it is the habitual language of Aeschylus. They have imagined the supernatural world : Aeschylus seems to have lived in it.

If Aeschylus is unique, Sophocles (496–406), in everything but his genius, is ordinary. He was handsome, easy-tempered, popular. He held high political and military office, in which, as a contemporary tells us, he was ' neither particularly wise nor active, but like any sound Athenian '. While Aeschylus, though deeply religious, was boldly speculative, Sophocles never speculates, but is orthodox and devout. He hit popular taste, won the first prize in his first competition, and was more successful throughout his life than any other tragic poet. He lived to be ninety and was nearly that age when he wrote two of his best plays, the *Philoctetes* and the *Oedipus at Colonus*.

He is as unlike Aeschylus in his writings as in his temperament. *Par excellence* he is a great playwright, a master of stagecraft.

---

[1] *Agamemnon*, 238–58 (tr. Murray). The Greek fleet was windbound on its way to Troy. To secure its release Agamemnon sacrificed his daughter. A Greek banquet was followed by the pouring of libations—the third of them to Zeus the Saviour, accompanied by a Paean, or song to Apollo.

Of all the Greek dramatists, he *acts* best. The plot of *Oedipus the King* is so intricate that few persons even after reading it could retrace exactly the steps by which Oedipus is revealed as a parricide ; and yet the development in the play is perfectly natural and free from improbability. The following instance from the *Electra* may illustrate his technical skill. When Agamemnon was killed by Clytaemnestra and her lover Aegisthus, his son Orestes was sent abroad, his daughters Electra and Chrysothemis remained at home. In the course of time Orestes returned to avenge his father, and, to deceive Clytaemnestra, pretended that he was a stranger bringing home the ashes of Orestes who had been killed in an accident. How should we manage the recognition of Orestes by his sister ? To make him simply declare himself would be possible but inartistic. The method of Sophocles is as follows. Orestes originally intends to conceal his identity till vengeance is taken. But when he puts into Electra's hands the urn supposed to contain her brother's ashes, her sorrow is so moving that he can hide his feelings no longer, and, in spite of his intention, reveals himself. That is perfectly true to nature, and it is far more dramatic than if he had been recognized by a bystander, or had come in and said, ' I am Orestes.' The recognition is the more effective because Sophocles first reduces Electra to the depths of despair. Orestes, on whom all her hopes rested, is apparently dead ; her sister has refused to co-operate with her ; Aegisthus has threatened, when he returns, to bury her in a dungeon. She is at the nadir of her fortunes. This is the moment chosen by Sophocles to reveal Orestes, and by a sudden reversal to swing her to their zenith.

The dramatic power of the poet, shown in these instances, may be further illustrated from the close of the play. Orestes has killed his mother, and so partially avenged his father, but Aegisthus still remains. News arrives that he is approaching, and this scene follows :

Scene. In front of the palace at Mycenae. The Chorus and Electra are present. Enter Aegisthus.

Aeg. Which of you all knows of the Phōcian strangers,
        Who as I hear, came hither to announce
        Orestes slain amid the chariots wrecked ?
        (To Electra) You there, 'tis you shall tell me : you who were

So bold before : methinks it should concern
You most : you best should know, and tell me this.[1]

El. I know : assure thee. Else had I not heard
The dearest of all fortunes to my heart. 1450

Aeg. Then tell me where the strangers are.

El. In the house :
To the heart of their hostess they have found a way.

Aeg. Do they in very truth report him dead ?

El. Not only so. They showed him to our sight.

Aeg. And is he here that I may see him plain ?

El. You may indeed, and 'tis a sorry sight.

Aeg. Such joyful news you are not wont to give.

El. Much joy be thine, if this be joy to thee !

Aeg. Silence, I say. Wide let the gates be flung,
And let all Argos and Mycenae see, 1460
That whoso buoyed themselves with empty hopes,
May take my bit in their mouths, and not perforce
Learn wisdom, getting chastisement from me.

El. My lesson is already learnt : at length
I am schooled to labour with the stronger will.

(The palace doors are flung open and reveal a body on a bier covered with a shroud. Orestes and his friend Pylades, disguised as Phocians, stand by it.)

Aeg. Zeus, 'twas thy wrath whereby this sight befell ;
But be the word unsaid, if it offends.[2]
Take off the face-cloth from the face ; this life
Was near to mine, and claims some grief from me.

Or. Lift it thyself : thine office this, not mine, 1470
To look, and speak kind words to what lies here.

---

[1] Aegisthus' exultant brutality at once alienates what sympathy we may have for him, and forms a contrast to what he is soon to feel.
[2] Aegisthus affects to believe that Orestes' death was a judgement from heaven ; he then corrects himself, as if he said, ' but it is not for me to judge a fellow-mortal ' (Jebb).

Aeg. Well said, and as you say I'll do : meanwhile
          [*To an attendant*]
          Go call me Clytaemnestra from the house.
Or. She is beside thee : look not far off for her.

(*Aegisthus lifts the shroud, and sees, not Orestes, but his wife,
beneath it.*)

Aeg. What sight is this ?
Or.   So scared ?   Is the face strange ?
Aeg. Who are the men into whose midmost toils
          An ill hour brings me ?
Or.   So then ! knowest thou not
       Thou hast been taking living men for dead.[1]

A few lines later the play ends, Aegisthus being driven inside
the palace to die.

It need not be emphasized how effective on the stage this
scene would be. Again, as in the previous instances, we have the
element of abrupt and striking contrast, which is the essence of
the dramatic. Electra takes the urn to sorrow over its contents,
and lo ! her brother is before her. Aegisthus raises the covering
to see the body of Orestes, and lo ! the corpse of his wife.

The last passage contains several instances of another kind of
contrast, also highly dramatic and effective, which Sophocles
made so particularly his own, that it is often called 'Sophoclean
irony'. The Greek word means 'dissimulation', and this
dramatic 'irony' consists, like dissimulation, in an ambiguity
of meaning. It may take three forms, all of which are illustrated
in the passage quoted. Sometimes it is an ambiguity of *action* or
situation. A man does something, intending to produce a certain
result, and his action has a result totally opposite to his intention.
He supposes that he is standing on safe ground, and in a moment
hell opens at his feet. Thus Aegisthus prepares to gloat over his
dead enemy, and the corpse is his wife's. Thus Oedipus (and
the *Oedipus* is full of this irony) curses the unknown murderer
of King Laius, and the murderer is himself. Or 'irony' may be
an ambiguity of language. A speaker uses words that have
a double meaning and are taken in two senses. Sometimes this

[1] *Electra*, 1442 f.   Chiefly from the translations of Whitelaw and of
L. Campbell.)

ambiguity is deliberate. The speaker means one thing by the words, and intends some one else to take them in a different sense. Every sentence spoken above by Electra contains this irony. Her words mean one thing to herself and the Chorus, another to Aegisthus. Sometimes the ' irony ' is even subtler. It is unconscious, and the speaker uses phrases that express a truth unrealized by himself, but perceived by the audience. Thus when Aegisthus asks, ' Is he here that I may see him plain ? ' he means to ask whether he can see the ashes of his enemy ; but the words have another significance, patent to the bystanders who are in the secret, and soon to be realized by Aegisthus himself. Lines 1468–9 are another instance. The plays of Sophocles are full of this ingenious irony, characteristic of the keen-witted race to which he belonged ; most audiences would hardly take such subtle points. The other dramatists use it far less ; but its dramatic quality made it a favourite device with this master of stagecraft.

These few grains from a great storehouse must serve to indicate in what spirit the reader should approach Sophocles and to illustrate his mastery of technique and stagecraft. It is not surprising that this artist in drama is also an artist in words. He is often majestic, he is always highly wrought and finished ; but his peculiar gift is that of a haunting and delicate music, breaking from words generally simple in themselves. Something of his power has passed into Calverley's

> All strangest things the multitudinous years
> Bring forth, and shadow from us all we know.
> Falter alike great oath and steeled resolve ;
> And none shall say of aught, ' This may not be ',[1]

or into Professor Murray's

> Fair Aigeus' son, only to gods in heaven
> Comes no old age, nor death of anything.
> All else is turmoiled by our master Time.
> The earth's strength fades, and manhood's glory fades,
> Faith dies, and unfaith blossoms like a flower :
> And who shall find in open streets of men,
> Or secret places of his own heart's love,
> One wind blow true for ever ? [2]

[1] Ajax, 645 f.   [2] O. C. 607.

And again :

> Last peaks of the world, beyond all seas,
> Wellsprings of night, and gleams of opened heaven;
> The old garden of the sun.[1]

or :

> But my fate, on some throbbing wheel of God,
> Always must rise or fall, and change its being ;
> As the moon's image never two nights long
> May in one station rest ; out of the dark
> The young face grows, still lovelier, still more perfect,
> Then, at the noblest of her shining, back
> She melts and comes again to nothingness.[2]

So marked is the artistic power of Sophocles that there is a tendency at the present day to think of him as little more than an artist, with an admirable gift of poetry and sense of the dramatic, but, beside his great rivals, a little colourless and academic.

> All is silver grey,
> Placid and perfect with my art, the worse !

Such a view is false, though it is a compliment to Sophocles' dramatic skill that it should make us overlook his other qualities. But his portrayal of character and his sense of the tragic elements of life are worthy of his stagecraft. Even in the *Oedipus*, perhaps the best constructed play ever written, the interest is rather in the tragedy than in the plot; in the *Antigone* it is in a heroic character, in the *Philoctetes* in the study of a young man of honour whom an intriguing statesman tries to make his tool. The content, not the mere art, of these plays makes them great.

It is true that in passing from Aeschylus or Euripides to Sophocles we are conscious of a weakness from which they are free—a certain moral insensitiveness. Critics have often remarked that, in his *Electra*, Orestes and his sister after killing their mother settle down and live happily ever afterwards ; in the other dramatists Orestes goes mad. Sophocles conceives of ' matricide without tears ', a thing psychologically impossible, as Aeschylus and Euripides knew. That is a defect in him. He took the Homeric story and told it as Homer would have told it, not troubling the heroic legends with questionings from the age of thought in which he lived. It is almost true to say that he

---

[1] Fr. 870 (tr. G. Murray).   [2] Fr. 713 (tr. G. Murray).

never *thinks*. Euripides is always thinking. Aeschylus, though profoundly religious, is also a thinker, seeking for reasons with such light as he has, groping in the darkness, determined to understand the ways of God. Sophocles accepts the legends, softening them here and there, but more concerned to feel their poetry and tragedy than to criticize their meaning. The *Antigone* is the story of a woman who has to choose between obeying the moral law and the law of the state. Sophocles does not explain, discuss, or answer the problem raised; he merely shows a conflict of ideals and its tragic result. His plays may be less instructive as an essay in moral philosophy, but they are not less great as tragedies and as pictures of life. The *Oedipus* shows a great man, who has innocently committed the most terrible crimes, that rise out of the earth and overthrow him in the height of his power. Sophocles never questions or condemns the justice of a heaven which permits such things, he only sees in them the evidence of its power. But is his play the worse for that? Does it arouse our pity and fear the less? Does it the less give us a sense of the fragility of human happiness, of the treacherous bridge on which man crosses the river of Time?

If Sophocles does not think, he imagines and feels. For imaginative power it would be difficult to find anything in literature to surpass the close of the *Oedipus*. The poet's task was to show the demeanour and fate of the King after a disaster which made him an object of horror to his kind. Let the reader ask himself how he would treat such a situation. Obvious solutions suggest themselves—Christian resignation, stoical endurance, a revolt against an indifferent heaven. All these are possible, and all are tame beside the solution of Sophocles. When he learns the truth, the first instinct of Oedipus is to shut out for ever the world which saw his sin. He blinds himself. As reason begins to return, his instinct is still somehow to escape from the world. ' Hide me,' he cries, ' or kill me, or throw me into the sea, where no one will see me more.' It is a natural prayer, but one impossible to grant. What is left? A lesser poet would have made him either kill himself, or drag out his life in obscurity. Sophocles imagined an end more worthy of the great king that Oedipus had been. Oedipus is already isolated from the world of sight; if he had known how to destroy his hearing, he would, he says, have shut himself off entirely from the world of sense. His sufferings and offence have set him apart from men and in a sense, above them, in a world of his own. And he will have a world of his own to inhabit, wild, desolate, and, in a mysterious way, belonging to him—that mountain of Cithaeron where his parents cast him forth as a child to die. There he will live, like a leper of the Middle Ages, a homeless and solitary life, till in the appointed way and at the appointed hour his fate comes. No one but himself can bear his burden ; no disease or hostile agency can harm him. He follows a Fate, moving towards a fixed, but unknown, goal. So, as the play closes, he faces the future with the resolution and something of the calm of a man of destiny. So, in spite of his tragedy, he can bear to exist. Sophocles was over eighty when he returned to the story and wrote its sequel. Inferior in technique, the *Oedipus at Colonus* is in its presentment of the hero worthy of its predecessor.

Let us not then make the mistake of dismissing Sophocles as a mere artist. There are analogies between the fallen Oedipus and the rejected Lear. The conception of the one in Sophocles is not less imaginative and sublime than the conception of the other in Shakespeare. One cannot give it higher praise. It is true that Sophocles did not think. But he has, as any human being must have, his philosophy of life. If he had put it into words, it would have been not unlike the philosophy which Job learns in his sufferings. Sophocles is not an unthinking optimist, or he would not have shown a good and great man the victim of disaster through an involuntary error ; he is not a pessimist, or Oedipus would not have saved his soul when Fate broke his life. He combines belief in an ultimate—one can hardly call it righteousness—with a sense of the changes and chances of life, and neither ignores nor is embittered and overcome by the tragedy of life. He holds the view which the Bible and Shakespeare and most men (who are neither optimists nor pessimists) take of the world, and Matthew Arnold said of him with justice that he saw life steadily and saw it whole.

Euripides (480–406) was the youngest of the three dramatists. In character, fortunes, and genius he is the antithesis to his predecessor. He was unpopular and solitary, and won few victories. He was a student who took as little part in public life as an Athenian could. He was one of the first men in Athens to have a library, and he was a friend of Socrates and the ' Intellectuals ' of his day. He belonged to the next generation rather than to his own, and died in self-inflicted exile away from his home, in the wild kingdom of Thrace. But, disliked and suspected in his

EURIPIDES

lifetime, he was the favourite tragedian in succeeding ages. Aeschylus and Sophocles took their place on the shelf in the schoolroom as classics ; Euripides was read and acted by posterity as if he had been a contemporary poet.

Before speaking of his genius, we may note some peculiarities of his plays. The essence of drama is a conflict. In *Hamlet* or the *Oedipus* this is largely brought out in the course of the action ; the opposing parties do not make formal speeches setting out their respective points of view. But Euripides generally has something almost like a debate. The combatants expound their case in speeches, almost as if they were in the law courts ; indeed it is from the law court and the assembly, so prominent in Athenian life, that this habit of discussion has overflowed into the drama. The Athenian, with his keen intellect, loved these debates, and it is interesting to hear contrasted points of view expounded, differing states of mind analysed ; but it does not make for realism. Another peculiarity of Euripides is the prologue. Every play must begin by instructing the audience what is happening, where the scene is laid, and who are the actors. Shakespeare, and for the most part Sophocles, do this by means of a conversation between some of the characters. Euripides introduces a speaker, who frequently does not reappear, to give an outline of the story. A third peculiarity is the *deus ex machina*, or, as we may legitimately mistranslate it, ' god in the sky '. A play proceeds normally with its human characters till about a hundred lines from its end, when a god appears in the air and brings the story to its traditional conclusion. Divine intervention would seem natural to a Greek, and sometimes, as in the *Hippolytus*, the *deus* makes a beautiful ending. But often it is totally out of harmony with the spirit of the play. An atmosphere of religious rationalism worthy of the twentieth century passes into a stiff and unthinking orthodoxy of the kind which Euripides loves to criticize. There is no organic unity between the body of the play and its tail. Any reader of the *Ion* or the *Electra* (to mention no other plays) will see what I mean. Here we have a literary puzzle not yet certainly solved. Dr. Verrall supposed that Euripides permitted himself free criticism of traditional religion in the body of his plays, and added an orthodox close to satisfy the conservative Athenian. It is probable that public opinion demanded that the stories of the plays should have their traditional ending, and that Euripides used this method of satisfying his audience, treating the story as he liked, but closing

it as they expected. The method is not artistic. As a playwright
Euripides is inferior to Sophocles. This does not mean necessarily that his plays are less great. Their merits are different,
their maker's chief interests lay elsewhere.

Euripides is probably a better introduction to Greek Drama
than either of his rivals. It requires an effort of imagination
to rise into the superhuman world of Aeschylus. Sophocles is
a classic, and human perversity rebels against the unfaltering
perfection of classics. But Euripides is more than a great
dramatist ; he is interesting ; and he is astonishingly like ourselves. That is why he has come into his own in the last twenty
years : he was too modern for our fathers fully to understand,
as he was too modern for his contemporaries. He is the child of
an age of criticism and reason like our own. And he is the first
writer of ' problem plays '. Like his rivals, he took his plays
from Greek legend, but while they had treated them in good
faith, softening barbaric features but preserving the spirit of the
story, Euripides looked at legends with the eyes of a child of
reason, and mercilessly underlined the flaws in their morality.
He treats the Homeric legends as a modern playwright might
treat the primitive morality of the stories of Jael and Sisera, or
of Joseph's methods of enslaving the Egyptians to Pharaoh. He
brings the heroes of Homer into the daylight of fifth-century
Athens, and Menelaus becomes a coward, Agamemnon an egoist,
Odysseus a ruthless and cynical politician, like those whom
Euripides saw around him. He takes the gods of legend, and
a Christian apologist could not expose more mercilessly their
immoralities and abuse of power. He takes the siege of Troy,
and where Homer saw heroism and the delight of battle, shows
us savagery and embitterment, evil passions unchained, women
and children in slavery, ruined and bereaved homes alike among
the conquerors and the conquered, all the horror and evil of war.

He is a liberal in his attitude to religion, to war, to women, and
nearly all his plays centre round one of these three themes. If we
judge by his extant work, his main interest was in the last. It
would be difficult to find any poet who has thought more about
women or treated them with such insight and sympathy. A
woman is the centre of twelve of the eighteen extant plays that
are certainly his, and six of them are true heroines. They are not
all pleasant characters, and his enemies, very absurdly, called him
a misogynist. He is particularly fond of showing the effects of
ill treatment on women's character—Athens no doubt gave him

living examples—and we have several studies, ranging from women who are turned into demons by cruelty or oppression (Medea, Hecuba, Creüsa, Electra) to a finer type whose character stands the strain (Iphigenia).

In Euripides, then, we have a figure almost more modern than ourselves ; a critic, tapping the customs and ideas of his day for signs of hollowness or decay ; a realist, in the sense that he brings on the stage homely people and scenes, beggars and countrymen, children and nurses ; a sceptic, dissatisfied with the religion and ideals of his contemporaries, with a keen love and sensitiveness for the beautiful and the good, but without a clear and connected philosophy of his own. He is an Ibsen who writes heroic drama ; a Bernard Shaw who is a great poet and can paint virtue as well as satirize fools and unveil knaves. He was unfortunate enough to be born out of due time, to live in an uncongenial world, and to witness the moral and political decay of his country.

Criticism is negative. It may interest us to read problem plays, to see in the *Trojan Women* an attack on war, in the *Electra* to watch one woman made savage by ill treatment, and another who repents of her sin but cannot escape from its consequences. But it is by something positive that literature lives. The positive creations of Euripides are in poetry like that of the *Bacchae*, in character-studies like those of Medea and Phaedra, Alcestis and Iphigenia. Two special marks of his genius are indicated in an ancient and a modern criticism of him. Aristotle says, ' If a bad manager in all other points, Euripides is at least the most tragic of the poets,' and Mrs. Browning calls him ' Euripides the human '.

' The most tragic of the poets.' If we gave this title to a writer, we should presumably mean, not necessarily that he was the greatest of dramatists or poets, but that he gave us a sense of pain carried to the breaking-point, that, as Tennyson said of Scott's *Maid of Neidpath*, he was ' almost more pathetic than a man has a right to be '. A poet is tragic when he moves us so that we wish to shut the book or leave the theatre, as Shakespeare moves us in his portrait of Constance or of the death of Lear. The following instances may show what Aristotle meant. The first is Euripides' treatment of the sequel of the murder of Clytaemnestra. In the *Libation-Bearers* of Aeschylus Orestes comes out of the palace, spattered with his mother's blood, and tries to justify himself before the descent of the madness which he feels approaching.

His speech grows wilder and more incoherent, till he goes off pursued by grey figures, with serpents in their hair and eyes dripping blood, the Furies whose task it is to haunt the matricide. The version of Sophocles we have already seen. Orestes kills Aegisthus, and all ends in peace.[1] This account cannot be called tragic; the scene is effective and dramatic; it would act admirably. But it has no pain or pathos; we watch the fate of Aegisthus with mingled excitement and pleasure. The picture drawn by Aeschylus is tragic, but too remote from our world to give us pain; the impression left on the mind is rather one of terror and sublimity. Euripides takes the same story and treats it as follows. (To appreciate him, see the scene and the actors as if they were before you.) Electra is married to a peasant and living in a wretched cottage in the country. She traps her mother by sending a message that she has a child, and Clytaemnestra, in pity, comes to see what help she can give. (That detail obviously adds to the horror of what follows.) Clytaemnestra goes into the house, where Orestes is waiting. The Chorus are left on the stage. Then two cries are heard, in Clytaemnestra's voice; first: ' Children, in god's name, do not kill your mother;' and then, ' Oh, Oh ! ' A minute after the door opens, two bodies are seen on the ground, and Orestes and Electra come out. Both are covered with blood, and Orestes holds a bloody sword. They had prepared the murder, Orestes with misgivings, Electra with exultation : of their present mood we can judge from what follows :

Chorus. Lo, yonder, in their mother's new-spilt gore
　　　　Red-garmented and ghastly, from the door
　　　　They reel. . . . O horrible ! Was it agony
　　　　Like this she boded in her last wild cry ?
　　　　There lives no seed of man calamitous,
　　　　Nor hath lived, like this seed of Tantalus.
Orestes. 　　O Dark of the Earth, O God,
　　　　Thou to whom all is plain ;
　　　　Look on my sin, my blood,
　　　　This horror of dead things twain :

---

[1] Sophocles, adopting this treatment, skilfully ends with the death of Aegisthus, which in the heroic age would seem justifiable vengeance. Aeschylus and Euripides keep the death of Clytaemnestra, the real horror to the end.

Gathered as one, they lie
Slain ; and the slayer was I,
I, to pay for my pain !

Electra. Let tear rain upon tear,
Brother : but mine is the blame.
A fire stood over her,
And out of the fire I came,
I, in my misery. . . .
And I was the child at her knee.
' Mother,' I named her name. . . .

Or. Saw'st thou her raiment there,[1]
Sister, there in the blood ?
She drew it back as she stood,
She opened her bosom bare,
She bent her knees to the earth, . . .
And I . . . Oh, her hair, her hair. . . .

Cho. Oh, thou didst walk in agony,
Hearing thy mother's cry, the cry
Of wordless wailing, well know I.

El. She stretched her hand to my cheek,
And there brake from her lips a moan ;
Mercy, my child, my own ! '
Her hand clung to my cheek ;
Clung, and my arm was weak ;
And the sword fell, and was gone.

Cho. Unhappy woman, could thine eye
Look on the blood, and see her lie,
Thy mother, when she turned to die ?

Or. I lifted over mine eyes
My mantle : blinded I smote,
As one smiteth a sacrifice ;
And the sword found her throat.

El. I gave thee the sign and the word ;
I touched with mine hand thy sword.

---

[1] This and the following speeches let us see the details of what happened behind the closed doors.

Cho.	Dire is the grief ye have wrought.
Or.	Sister, touch her again ;
	Oh, veil the body of her ;
	Shed on her raiment fair,
	And close that death-red stain.
	—Mother ! And didst thou bear,
	Bear in thy bitter pain,
	To life, thy murderer ?
El.	On her that I loved of yore,
	Robe upon robe I cast :
	On her that I hated sore.
Cho.	O House that hath hated sore,
	Behold thy peace at the last.[1]

I do not think that any one could find this passage bearable if really well acted, or fail to see what Aristotle meant by calling Euripides 'most tragic'. Note how Euripides, who, according to Greek tradition, does not show the murder on the stage, lets us hear from the actor's lips every detail of what happened inside the house ; and note how he treats the story. The matricide, which Homer and Sophocles accept without misgivings, is to him a brutal murder ; he spares no detail that makes it detestable, and shows even the actors as horror-struck at what they have done. But what is their punishment ? Not a haunting by visible Furies, monsters crowned with snakes, but—a nervous breakdown. In the sequel play, the *Orestes*, the hero is mad, not with the supernatural madness imagined by Aeschylus, but with hallucinations, coming by fits, and sending him out of his mind with nervous terrors ; here he is obviously on the road to such a collapse. That is how Euripides, moralist and critic, read the story ; and surely his reading is true to life.[2]

'The human.' The older tragedy, stately, dignified, heroic,

> In sceptred pall comes sweeping by,
> Presenting Thebes or Pelops' line
> Or the tale of Troy divine.

[1] ll. 1172–1232 (with omissions), tr. Murray.
[2] Almost every play of Euripides has instances of this tragic power. The close of the *Bacchae*, the Messenger's speech in *Hercules Mad*, Medea and her children are good instances : the *Trojan Women* is full of it.

Euripides scandalized his contemporaries by mixing with it a flavour of the ordinary world—' intimate things which we know and live with '. Slaves and beggars, women and children played, they thought, an indecently prominent part in his pages ; heroes were seen in rags, and the dignity of tragedy was compromised. To us a poet seems no worse for these touches of nature, which bring tragedy down to earth. They are part of the greatness of Euripides, and we recognize him here as a forerunner of Shakespeare. This humanity is seen in the Athenian women of the *Ion*, on a visit to Delphi, wandering round the temple, looking at its treasures and gossiping like tourist sightseers : in Clytaemnestra bustling as she gets out of the carriage that has brought her to Aulis, handing out the sleeping baby, asking for help to dismount, remarking on the wild look in the horses' eyes. Typical of it is the part played by children in Euripides. There are none in Aeschylus ; but this bookish recluse loved and understood them. There are scenes in him which it seems impossible for a man to have written, such as that where the Athenian queen, now a middle-aged woman, is telling how as a girl she deserted her baby, the sign of her shame. Her confidant utters an exclamation of horror, ' How could you do it ? ' ' Yes, says the queen ; . . . and if you had seen the baby holding out its hands to me ! ' In this instance Euripides is equally ' tragic ' and ' human '. So he is in the *Hercules Mad*. The hero of that play is a man of giant strength who has spent his life civilizing the earth by cleansing it of monsters and pests. He comes back from one of his expeditions just in time to save his wife and young sons from being killed by his enemies. After he has rescued them, he calls them into the house. Still in a panic of fear, they keep crying and clinging to him, but will not move. So he pretends that they are ships which he is taking in tow, and thus playing with them distracts them from their terrors, till, holding his hands, they enter the palace. Such descents into familiar life disgusted Aristophanes, but we see in them an anticipation of the Mamilius or the young Macduff of Shakespeare.

Though no great practical achievement can be condensed into a few qualities, we may say that, for grandeur of conception and style, for his vision of the supernatural world, Aeschylus does not yield to Milton, while he has a wider range than the English poet ; that, for dramatic sense and mastery of stagecraft, Sophocles is unrivalled ; that in his human touch Euripides anticipates Shakespeare, in tragic quality and critical power (if this is a virtue in a dramatist) he goes beyond him. Individually, the Greek dramatists must be placed below Shakespeare, the most universal of men ; yet each of them is perhaps his superior in certain fields ; combined, they would make a poet such as the world has never seen.

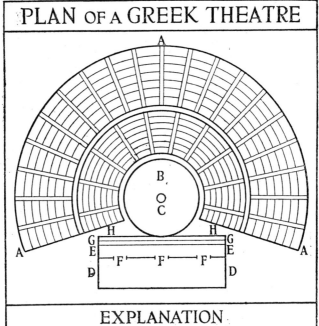

PLAN OF A GREEK THEATRE

EXPLANATION

AAA = Auditorium (θέατρον). B = Orchestra (ὀρχήστρα). C = Altar (θυμέλη).
DD = Dressing-hut (σκηνή). EE = Stage (λογεῖον). FFF = Doorways
GG = Steps to orchestra. HH = Entrances (πάροδοι).
This plan does not correspond exactly to any extant theatre, but represents the general plan of a Greek theatre.

V

COMEDY: ARISTOPHANES

As for comic Aristophanes,
The dog too witty and too profane is.—SWIFT.

He is not likely to be revived. He stands, like Shakespeare, an un-
approachable.—G. MEREDITH.

AT the Great Festival of Dionysus in early April, where tragedy
was acted, comedies were also performed. But in spite of its
name, the comedy of the fifth century, which flourished during
the great age of tragedy and by its side, bore no resemblance to
the comedies of Shakespeare, or to anything that treads, under
that title, the boards of the modern stage. Let us attend a performance which took place in the year 414 B.C. On the stage we
see actors dressed up as a raven, a jackdaw, a sandpiper, and
a hoopoe; shortly after, the Chorus enters, attired as birds.
Among the minor characters are a god and three demi-gods,
a poet, an astronomer, a priest, a parricide, and some disreputable
politicians. The play (the *Birds*) contains parodies of contemporary poets, some amazing profanity, and endless personal and
political satire, often mentioning by name persons in the audience.
In the middle of this come bursts of pure poetry. Again, as with
tragedy, the questions confront us: where does all this come from,
and what is its value?

It is a lineal descendant of a harvest festival that we have been
witnessing—not our own decorous fête, but the harvest of the
grapes—and it takes our thoughts back to the harvest home of
Greek country villages, when the country-side turned out to
thank the god, Dionysus, who had given the wine. Hearts were
lightened and tongues loosened by the new wine. Song, reckless
merriment, buffoonery, scurrilous humour were its fruits, all
inextricably mixed with the worship of the god. Among a stupid
people the feast would have remained a September revel: in
Attica it gave an occasion to poetic genius, and the religion and
laughter, song and satire, so strangely blended, took a literary
form as the Old Comedy.

It took this form in the years following the Persian Wars.

K

Three poets competed, but with one play each. There were three actors, wearing masks ; there was a chorus, but one composed of twenty-four persons, and there was song and dance. The metres were partly those of tragedy, treated with greater looseness, partly proper to comedy. The construction of the play was peculiar. The action was practically confined to its first half ; about the middle of the play the Chorus came forward and delivered what was called the *Parabasis* (Coming Forward), an elaborate choric piece, partly song, partly recitative, opening with a speech which often had nothing to do with the play, but aired its writer's views. Then followed a number of loosely connected scenes to the end of the play. As can be guessed, the form of comedy was partly taken from tragedy ; but some of its form and all its spirit is derived from its origin. Hence came the looseness of the plot ; hence the animal choruses (Wasps, Frogs, Goats, Storks) ; and, above all, hence came the wild buffoonery and licence of tongue that is its essence. It spares no one, not even the gods, and its profanity may be compared to that of a mediaeval mystery play. It is always personal. If we could bring one of its writers to life, and persuade him to compose a modern comedy on the old lines, we should expect to see eminent politicians, men of letters, journalists, bureaucrats, middlemen, bolsheviks, held up to our ridicule, together with any one else who had been in the popular eye as a knave, a fool, or an eccentric ; and the interest would be increased by the chance of hearing public attention called to our own or our next-door neighbour's peculiarities. It is often very coarse ; the Stage Society itself would not have the face to perform some of the plays. But the coarseness is the honest dung of a farmyard, not, as so often in modern farces, the nasty dirt of a chicken run.

We have eleven plays by one great comic writer, Aristophanes (446–385) ; his predecessors, and the rivals who often defeated him, survive only in fragments. He is perhaps the most difficult of Greek writers to appreciate : he takes us into the political, social, intellectual life of his day, and fully to understand him we should have to know as well as he did the streets and gossip and literature of Athens. But he would be the last writer in Greek literature whom his admirers would be willing to lose. Of his plays the *Frogs*, which recounts a journey to Hades to bring back a dead poet, and turns on a dispute whether he is to be Aeschylus or Euripides, is full of clever parody and acute criticism ; the *Clouds* ridicules Socrates and contemporary science ; the *Wasps* is a satire on the Athenian juryman and his passion for the law courts; the *Birds* shows two Athenians tired of Athens and seeking a home in the Country of the Birds; the *Knights* is an attack on the demagogues, the *Peace* and the *Acharnians* are anti-war plays (his best work was all done under the cloud of the Peloponnesian War); the *Lysistrata*, *Ecclēsiāzūsae*, and *Thesmophoriāzūsae* have women as their subject; the first shows how women put a stop to the war, the second shows them in parliament, the third shows their attempts to punish Euripides for maligning their sex. These three plays are exceedingly amusing, but are best read in an expurgated edition. The *Plutus* ('Wealth') is a late play in a different style from the rest. It was written after the war, when, as to-day, financial problems pressed hard, and money was in the hands of profiteers. An Athenian goes to inquire at Delphi if injustice is the road to Wealth; on the way he meets Wealth himself. Wealth is cured of his blindness, and we see the results that follow. The *Peace* and the *Plutus* are the least interesting of the plays; the *Knights* gives a good picture of Aristophanes' politics, but has more buffoonery than wit. The *Birds*, *Frogs*, *Clouds*, or *Acharnians* are perhaps the best plays to commence with.

Aristophanes' Comedy is founded on broad farcical buffoonery. It is written for acting and needs the stage; but even a reader can feel the admirable verve and gusto that give it life. Here is a specimen. The god Dionysus, attended by his slave Xanthias, goes to the Underworld dressed as Heracles. Heracles on a previous visit has stolen things and fought the local police, who now arrest Dionysus, mistaking him for the offender. Dionysus persuades Xanthias to assume the dress of Heracles, and himself dresses as a slave. Seized by the police, Xanthias turns the tables on Dionysus by offering to surrender him to be tortured. (Slaves at Athens might be thus 'put to the question' when their masters were accused at law.)

The Porter, Aeacus, comes out with several ferocious-looking Thracian or Scythian constables.

Aeacus. Here, seize this dog-stealer and lead him forth
To justice, quick.
Dionysus (*imitating Xanthias*). Here's fun for somebody.
Xanthias (*in a Herculean attitude*). Stop, zounds! Not one step!

Aea. What ? You want to fight ?
Ho, Ditylas, Skeblyas, and Pardokas,[1]
Forward ! Oblige this person with some fighting !
  Dio. (*while the constables gradually overpower Xanthias*).
How shocking to assault the constables—
And stealing other people's things !
  Aea. Unnatural,
That's what I call it.
  Dio. Quite a pain to see.
  Xan. (*now overpowered and disarmed*).
Now, by Lord Zeus, if ever I've been here
Or stol'n from you the value of one hair,
You may take and hang me on the nearest tree ! . . .
Now, listen : and I'll act quite fairly by you ;
                    [*Suddenly indicating Dionysus.*
Take this poor boy, and put him to the question !
And if you find me guilty, hang me straight.
  Aea. What tortures do you allow ?
  Xan. Use all you like.
Tie him in the ladder, hang him by the feet,
Whip off his skin with bristle-whips and rack him ;
You might well try some vinegar up his nose,
And bricks upon his chest, and so on.
  Aea. A most frank offer, most frank.—If my treatment
Disables him, the value shall be paid.
  Xan. Don't mention it. Remove him and begin.
  Aea. Thank you, we'll do it here, that you may witness
Exactly what he says. (*To Dionysus*) Put down your bundle,
And mind you tell the truth.
  Dio. (*who has hitherto been speechless with horror, now bursting out*).
                    I warn all present,
To torture me is an illegal act,
Being immortal ! And whoever does so
Must take the consequences.

---

[1] Barbarous names. The police at Athens were foreign slaves.

Aea.   Why, who *are* you ?

Dio. The immortal Dionysus, son of Zeus ;
And this my slave.

Aea. (to Xanthias). You hear his protest ?

Xan.   Yes ;
All the more reason, that, for whipping him ;
If he 's a real immortal he won't feel it.

Dio. Well, but you claim to be immortal too ;
They ought to give you just the same as me.

Xan. That 's fair enough. All right ; whichever of us
You first find crying, or the least bit minding
Your whip, you're free to say he 's no true god.

Aea. Sir, you behave like a true gentleman ;
You come to justice of yourself !—Now then,
Strip, both.

Xan.   How will you test us ?

Aea.   Easily :
You'll each take whack and whack about.

Xan.   All right.

Aea. (striking Xanthias). There.

Xan. (controlling himself with an effort).
                Watch now, if you see me even wince.

Aea. But I've already hit you !

Xan.   I think not.

Aea. Upon my word, it looks as if I hadn't.
Well, now I'll go and whack the other.   *[Strikes Dionysus.*

Dio. (also controlling himself).   When ?

Aea. I've done it.

Dio. (with an air of indifference). Odd, it didn't make me
sneeze !

Aea. It *is* odd !—Well, I'll try the first again.
                    [He crosses to Xanthias.

Xan. All right. Be quick. *(The blow falls)* Whe-ew !

Aea.   Ah, why 'whe-ew'?
It didn't hurt you ?

Xan. (recovering himself). No ; I just was thinking
When my Diomean Feast [1] would next be due.

    Aea. A holy thought !—I'll step across again.

                      [Strikes Dionysus, who howls.

    Dio. Ow-ow !

    Aea.   What 's that ?

    Dio. (recovering himself).   I saw some cavalry.

    Aea. What makes your eyes run ?

    Dio.   There 's a smell of onions !

    Aea. You're sure it didn't hurt you ?

    Dio.   Hurt ? Not it.

    Aea. I'll step across again then to the first one.

                   [Strikes Xanthias, who also howls.

    Xan. Hi-i !

    Aea.   What is it now ?

    Xan.   Take out that thorn.

                     [Pointing to his foot.

    Aea. What does it mean ?—Over we go again.

                     [Strikes Dionysus.

    Dio. (hurriedly turning his wail into a line of poetry).
O Lord ! . . . 'of Dēlos or of Pytho's rock.'

    Xan. (triumphantly). It hurts. You heard ?

    Dio.   It doesn't ! I was saying
A verse of old Hippōnax [2] to myself.

    Xan. You're making nothing of it. Hit him hard
Across the soft parts underneath the ribs.

    Aea. (to Xanthias). A good idea ! Turn over on your back !

                     [Strikes him.

    Xan. (as before). O Lord !

    Aea.   What 's that ?

    Xan. (as though continuing).   ' Poseidon ruler free
Of cliffs Aegean and the grey salt sea.' [3]

---

[1] A festival in honour of Heracles (whom Xanthias is now personating).
[2] A sixth-century poet.
[3] A line from Sophocles.

Aea. Now, by Dēmēter, it's beyond my powers
To tell which one of you's a god !—Come in ;
We'll ask my master.[1] He and Persephassa
Will easily know you, being gods themselves.

Dio. Most wisely said. Indeed I could have wished
You'd thought of that before you had me swished.[2]

This, especially on the stage, is excellent fooling. But there
are passages in modern humorists quite as amusing. What is
unique in Aristophanes is the building which rises from this
basis of farce. It has rooms of pure poetry ; it has rooms
stored with serious political, social, and literary ideals : and
parody, theory, poetry, buffoonery, pass into each other with
the gay irresponsibility of a dance. Other comic writers have had
wit, humour, and philosophy. But none perhaps except Aristophanes has had poetic genius. We can find something of him,
but a more savage temper, in Swift ; we can find something, but
a less keen brain, in Gilbert. But neither of these was, like Aristophanes, a great lyrical poet. Heine compares him to a grove full
of singing nightingales and chattering apes. Suddenly out of
a sea of bitter satire and political abuse rises a shining islet, full
of wood notes as clear and simple as a bird's and as impossible
to recapture. ' We may build up a conception of his powers if we
mount Rabelais upon Hudibras, lift him with the songfulness of
Shelley, give him a vein of Heinrich Heine, and cover him with
the mantle of the Anti-Jacobin, adding (that there may be some
Irish in him) a dash of Grattan.' [3]

Some extracts from the *Clouds* will illustrate the triple thread
of buffoonery, poetry, and seriousness which runs through the
comedy of Aristophanes. Roughly the plot is this. Strepsiades
has an unsatisfactory son Pheidippides, who has taken to racing
and is ruining him. To escape from his creditors he goes to the
' Thinking-Shop ' of Socrates, who is popularly supposed to be
able to make the worse the better reason. That is Aristophanes'
view of Socrates. He hated the intellectuals, because in teaching
young Athens to think and criticize they seemed to be educating
a generation sceptical, irreverent, shallow, good with their

[1] i. e. Pluto, King of the Underworld.
[2] Frogs, 605 f. (tr. G. Murray). Meredith says of this scene that ' nothing
in the world surpasses it in stormy fun '.
[3] G. Meredith, *Essay on Comedy*.

tongues, bad at everything else, pallid students, grubbers in the dunghills of human nature, intellectual fops. So he thought. So perhaps ten years ago a modern Aristophanes might have thought of Shaw and Wells and Galsworthy. Here Socrates is shown as occupied, among other things, with science, a study which he followed in youth, but of which there is no trace in the Socrates we know. For convenience' sake Aristophanes attributes to Socrates traits that belong to the Sophists (p. 252 f.), and uses him as a general butt for his ridicule of contemporary science and philosophy.

Strepsiades and his son are discovered outside a house.

Strepsiades. See you that wicket and the lodge beyond ?

Pheidippides. I see : and prithee what is that, my father ?

Strep. That is the thinking-house of sapient souls.
There dwell the men who teach—aye, who persuade us,
That Heaven is one vast fire-extinguisher
Placed round about us, and that we're the cinders.
Aye, and they'll teach (only they'll want some money)
How one may speak and conquer, right or wrong.

Phei. Come, tell their names.

Strep.   Well, I can't quite remember,
But they're deep thinkers, and true gentlemen.

Phei. Out on the rogues ! I know them. Those rank pedants,
Those pale-faced, barefoot vagabonds you mean :
That Socrates, poor wretch, and Chaerephon.[1]

They kick the door.

Student. [*Within.*] O, hang it all ! who 's knocking at the door ?

Strep. Me ! Pheidon's son : Strepsiades of Cicynna.

Stu. Why, what a clown you are ! to kick our door,
In such a thoughtless inconsiderate way !
You've made my cogitation to miscarry.

Strep. Forgive me : I'm an awkward country fool.
But tell me, what was that I made miscarry ?

Stu. 'Tis not allowed : students alone may hear.

[1] A pupil and friend of S. For Socrates see p. 252 f.

Strep. O that's all right : you may tell *me* : I'm come
To be a student in your thinking-house.

Stu. Come then. But they're high mysteries, remember.
'Twas Socrates was asking Chaerephon,
How many feet of its own a flea could jump.
For one first bit the brow of Chaerephon,
Then bounded off to Socrates's head.

Strep. How did he measure this ?

Stu. Most cleverly.
He warmed some wax, and then he caught the flea,
And dipped its feet into the wax he'd melted :
Then let it cool, and there were Persian slippers !
These he took off, and so he found the distance.

Strep. O Zeus and king, what subtle intellects !

Stu. What would you say then if you heard another,
Our Master's own ?

Strep. O come, do tell me that.

Stu. Why, Chaerephon was asking him in turn,
Which theory did he sanction ; that the gnats
Hummed through their mouth, or backwards, through the tail ?

Strep. Aye, and what said your Master of the gnat ?

Stu. He answered thus : the entrail of the gnat
Is small : and through this narrow pipe the wind
Rushes with violence straight towards the tail ;
There, close against the pipe, the hollow rump
Receives the wind, and whistles to the blast.

Strep. So then the rump is trumpet to the gnats !
O happy, happy in your entrail-learning ;
Full surely need he fear, nor debts, nor duns,
Who knows about the entrails of the gnats.

Stu. Then yesterday, poor we, we'd got no dinner.

Strep. Hah ! what did he devise to do for barley ?

Stu. He sprinkled on the table—some fine ash—
He bent a spit—he grasped it compass-wise—
And—filched a mantle from the Wrestling School.

Strep. Good heavens ! Why, Thales[1] was a fool to this !
O open, open, wide the study door,
And show me, show me, show me, Socrates.
I die to be a student. Open, open !

> [*The door opens and a number of students are seen
> bowed over their calculations.*

O Heracles, what kind of beasts are these !
What makes them fix their eyes so on the ground ?
   Stu. They seek things underground.
   Strep.   O ! to be sure,
Truffles ! You there, don't trouble about that !
I'll tell you where the best and finest grow.
Look ! why do those stoop down so very much ?
   Stu. They're diving deep into the deepest secrets.
   Strep. Then why 's their rump turned up towards the sky ?
   Stu. It 's taking private lessons on the stars.

> [*To the other Students.*

Come, come : get in : HE'll catch us presently.
   Strep. Not yet ! not yet ! just let them stop one moment,
While I impart a little matter to them.
   Stu. No, no : they must go in : 'twould never do
To expose themselves too long to the open air.[2]
   Strep. [*Pointing to different groups*].
O ! by the Gods, now, what are these ? do tell me.
   Stu. This is Astronomy.
   Strep.   And what is this ?
   Stu. Geometry.
   Strep.   Well, what 's the use of that ?
   Stu. To mete out lands.
   Strep.   What, for allotment grounds ?[3]

---

[1] See p. 409. Socrates, pretending to draw a geometrical figure in the ashes with a spit, uses the latter to steal a cloak—to be converted into money. The Wrestling School was one of his haunts.

[2] The fresh air would blow away their fancies.

[3] The only use for science which the Philistine Strepsiades can conceive is a practical one.

Stu. No, but all lands.

Strep.   A choice idea, truly.
Then every man may take his choice, you mean.

Stu. Look ; here's a chart of the whole world. Do you see ?
This city 's Athens.

Strep.   Athens ? I like that.
I see no juries [1] sitting. That 's not Athens.

Stu. In very truth, this is the Attic ground.

Strep. But now, where 's Sparta ?

Stu.   Let me see : O, here.

Strep. Heavens ! how near us. O do please manage this
To shove her off from us, a long way further.[2]

Stu. We can't do that, by Zeus.

Strep.   The worse for you.
[*Pointing to a man sitting in a swinging basket, deep in thought*].
Hallo ! who 's that ? that fellow in the basket ?

Stu. That 's HE.

Strep.   Who 's HE ?

Stu.   Socrates !

Strep.   Socrates !
[*To a student*] You, sir, call out to him as loud as you can.

Stu. Call him yourself : I have not leisure now.

Strep.   Socrates ! Socrates !
Sweet Socrates !

Soc. [*Gradually emerging from his meditation*].
                    Mortal ! why call'st thou me ?

Strep. O, first of all, please tell me what you are doing.

Soc. I walk on air, and contem-plate the Sun.

Strep. O then from a basket you contemn the Gods,
And not from the earth, at any rate ?

Soc.   Most true.
I could not have searched out celestial matters
Without suspending judgement, and infusing

---

[1] A hit at the Athenian fondness for litigation.
[2] The play was produced during the war with Sparta.

My subtle spirit with the kindred air.
If from the ground I were to seek these things,
I could not find : so surely doth the earth
Draw to herself the essence of our thought.
The same too is the case with water-cress.[1]

   Strep.   Hillo ! what 's that ?
Thought draws the essence into water-cress ?
Come down, sweet Socrates, more near my level,
And teach the lessons which I come to learn.

                               [*Socrates comes to the ground.*

   Soc. And wherefore art thou come ?
   Strep.   To learn to speak.
For, owing to my horrid debts and duns,
My goods are seized, I'm robbed, and mobbed, and plundered.
   Soc. How did you get involved with your eyes open ?
   Strep. A galloping consumption seized my money.
Come now : do let me learn the unjust Logic
That can shirk debts : now do just let me learn it.
Name your own price, by all the Gods I'll pay it.
   Soc. The Gods ! why you must know the Gods with us
Don't pass for current coin.
Come, would you like to learn celestial matters,
How their truth stands ?
   Strep.   Yes, if there 's any truth.
   Soc. And to hold intercourse with yon bright Clouds,
Our virgin Goddesses ?
   Strep.   Yes, that I should.
   Soc. Then sit you down upon that sacred bed.
   Strep. Well, I am sitting.
   Soc. [*Handing him a garland*].   Here then, take this chaplet.
   Strep. Chaplet ? why ? why ? now, never, Socrates :
Don't sacrifice poor me.[2]

   [1] A parody of Socrates' habit of illustrating his meaning by examples
from everyday life.
   [2] Animals for sacrifice were crowned. All this is a parody of a religious
service.

Soc. Fear not : our entrance-services require
All to do this.
    Strep.   But what am I to gain ?
    Soc. [*Sprinkling grain on his head*].
You'll be the flower of talkers, prattlers, gossips :
Only keep quiet.
    Strep.   Zeus ! your words come true !
I shall be flour indeed with all this peppering.[1]

The Clouds, the chorus of the play, then enter and sing a magnificent piece of poetry. The first stanza takes us from their birthplace in the sea to the forest-clad mountains, past whose watch-towers they drift, looking out on the plains below. Then characteristically comes a piece of coarse buffoonery, here omitted; and in the second stanza the Clouds descend to their chosen land of Attica.

            Clouds of all hue,
Rise we aloft with our garments of dew.
Come from old Ocean's unchangeable bed,
Come, till the mountain's green summits we tread,
Come to the peaks with their landscapes untold,
Gaze on the Earth with her harvests of gold,
Gaze on the rivers in majesty streaming,
   Gaze on the lordly, invincible Sea,
Come, for the Eye of the Ether is beaming,
   Come, for all Nature is flashing and free.
      Let us shake off this close-clinging dew
      From our members eternally new,
      And sail upwards the wide world to view.
          Come away ! Come away !
              Come then with me,
Daughters of Mist, to the land of the free.
Come to the people whom Pallas hath blest,
Come to the soil where the Mysteries rest ;
Come, where the glorified Temple invites

[1] *Clouds*, 92 f. (tr. Rogers).

The pure to partake of its mystical rites :
Holy the gifts that are brought to the Gods,
   Shrines with festoons and with garlands are crowned,
Pilgrims resort to the sacred abodes,
   Gorgeous the festivals all the year round.
      And the Bromian rejoicings in Spring,
      When the flutes with their deep music ring,
      And the sweetly-toned Choruses sing
           Come away ! Come away ![1]

The following scene, in which Socrates tries to educate the invincibly stupid Strepsiades, is full of satire on the thought of the day, and less amusing to us than to a contemporary. Finally the Right Logic and the Wrong Logic make their appeal to Pheidippides. (So a Victorian and an extreme follower of Bernard Shaw might contend for the sympathies of a modern undergraduate.) The Wrong Logic represents Aristophanes' idea of the Sophists (and of Socrates), who seemed to him to think only of sharpening their pupil's wits and to breed a cynical and unhealthy type.[2] The serious ideals of Aristophanes break through in this passage. Its close illustrates the Sophists' supposed habit of using clever quibbles to make the worse reason appear the better.

> *Right Logic.* To hear then prepare of the Discipline rare which
>   flourished in Athens of yore
> When Honour and Truth were in fashion with youth and Sobriety
>   bloomed on our shore ;
> First of all the old rule was preserved in our school that ' boys
>   should be seen and not heard ' :
> And then to the home of the Harpist [3] would come decorous in
>   action and word

---

[1] Clouds, 275 f. (tr. Rogers). The allusions are to the famous religious mysteries at Eleusis and to the spring festival of Dionysus (Bromios), at which the dramas were acted.

[2] As we see from the *Frogs*, he brought the same charge against Euripides, whose morbid influence he contrasts with the healthy atmosphere of Aeschylus.

[3] Music was an essential part of Greek education.

All the lads of one town, though the snow peppered down, in
    spite of all wind and all weather :

And they sung an old song as they paced it along, not shambling
    with thighs glued together :

'O the dread shout of War how it peals from afar', or *'Pallas the
    Stormer adore'*,

To some manly old air all simple and bare which their fathers
    had chanted before.

And should any one dare the tune to impair and with intricate
    twistings to fill,

Such as Phrynis is fain, and his long-winded train, perversely to
    quaver and trill,

Many stripes would he feel in return for his zeal, as to genuine
    Music a foe.

    Wrong Logic. Faugh ! this smells very strong of some musty
    old song, and Chirrupers mounted in gold ;[1]

And Slaughter of beasts,[2] and old-fashioned feasts.

    R. L.   Yet these are the precepts which taught

The heroes of old to be hardy and bold, and the Men who at
    Marathon fought !

But now must the lad from his boyhood be clad in a Man's all-
    enveloping cloke :

So that, oft as the Panathenaea[3] returns, I feel myself ready to
    choke

When the dancers go by with their shields to their thigh, not
    caring for Pallas a jot.

You therefore young man, choose me while you can ; cast in
    with my Method your lot ;

And rise from your chair if an elder be there, and respectfully
    give him your place,

And with love and with fear your parents revere, and shrink
    from the brand of Disgrace,

---

[1] Old-fashioned Athenians had their hair fastened up with brooches in
the form of cicadas.   [2] Refers to an old-fashioned festival.

[3] A feature of this festival was the dance in armour. The effeminate
young Athenians did not know how to manage their shields.

And deep in your breast be the Image imprest of Modesty,
  simple and true,

Nor dare to reply when your Father is nigh, nor ' musty old
  Japhet ' to call

In your malice and rage that Sacred Old Age which lovingly
  cherished your youth.

  W. L. Yes, Yes, my young friend, if to him you attend, by
  Bacchus I swear of a truth

You will scarce with the sty of Hippocrates [1] vie, as a mammy-
  suck known even there !

  R. L. But then you'll excel in the games you love well, all
  blooming, athletic and fair :

Not learning to prate as your idlers debate with marvellous prickly
  dispute,

Nor dragged into Court day by day to make sport in some small
  disagreeable suit :

But you will below to the Academe [2] go, and under the olives
  contend

With your chaplet of reed, in a contest of speed with some
  excellent rival and friend :

All fragrant with woodbine and peaceful content, and the leaf
  which the lime blossoms fling,

When the plane whispers love to the elm in the grove in the
  beautiful season of Spring.

If then you'll obey and do what I say

And follow with me the more excellent way,

Your chest shall be white, your skin shall be bright,

Your arms shall be tight, your tongue shall be slight,

And everything else shall be proper and right.

But if you pursue what men nowadays do,

You will have, to begin, a cold pallid skin,

Arms small and chest weak, tongue practised to speak,

Special laws very long,[3] and the symptoms all strong

[1] H. was a well-knnown general whose sons were famous for bad manners.
[2] Where was a famous open-air gymnasium.
[3] An allusion to political activities, which A. does not favour in young
men.

Which show that your life is licentious and wrong.
And your mind he'll prepare so that foul to be fair
And fair to be foul you shall always declare.
   Chorus. O glorious Sage ! with loveliest Wisdom teeming !
   Sweet on thy words does ancient Virtue rest !
Thrice happy they who watched thy Youth's bright beaming !
     Thou of the vaunted genius, do thy best ;
   This man has gained applause : his Wisdom stands confest,
And you with clever words and thoughts must needs your case
     adorn,
Else he will surely win the day, and you retreat with scorn.
   W. L. Aye, say you so ? why I have been half-burst ; I do so
     long
To overthrow his arguments with arguments more strong.
I am the Lesser Logic ? True : these Schoolmen call me so,
Simply because I was the first of all mankind to show
How old established rules and laws might contradicted be :
And this, as you may guess, is worth a thousand pounds to me,
To take the feebler cause, and yet to win the disputation.
And mark me now, how I'll confute his boasted Education !
You said that always from warm baths the stripling must
     abstain :
Why must he ? on what grounds do you of these warm baths
     complain ?
   R. L. Why it 's the worst thing possible, it quite unstrings
   a man.
   W. L. Hold there : I've got you round the waist : escape
   me if you can.
And first : of all the sons of Zeus which think you was the best ?
Which was the manliest ? which endured more toils than all the
     rest ?
   R. L. Well, I suppose that Heracles was bravest and most bold.
   W. L. And are the baths of Heracles [1] so wonderfully cold ?
Aha ! you blame warm baths, I think.

   [1] The famous hot springs of Thermopylae were said to have burst out
to refresh Heracles.

R. L.   This, this is what they say :
This is the stuff our precious youths are chattering all the day !
This is what makes them haunt the baths, and shun the manlier
    Games !
    W. L. Well, then, we'll take the Forum next : I praise it, and
    he blames.
But if it *was* so bad, do you think old Homer would have made
Nestor and all his worthies ply a real forensic trade ?
Well : then he says a stripling's tongue should always idle be :
I say it should be used of course : so there we disagree.[1]

These passages have revealed something of Aristophanes'
views. With all his buffoonery no poet ever had stronger likes
and dislikes. He is anything but a *gamin de génie.* He is a conservative and is of those who are conservative, not because they
do not understand the new, but because they detest the humbug,
follies, and extravagancies that accompany it, and because they
would rather spend their time in enjoying the undoubted good
things of life than in criticisms and reforms which, they suspect,
will upset the world and finally leave it much the same as before.
Aristophanes is the incarnation of robust human nature genially
enjoying life.[2] Men of this type are rarely reformers. Yet, as his
hates and loves show, he is not a mere conservative.
    He hated, not democracy (for he is severe on the aristocrats),
but the politicians of the democracy. The People he personifies
as a good-natured, stupid, indolent, and rather greedy old man,
good enough but for his leaders, who excite his cupidity, bribe and
delude him, in order to keep themselves in power and money.
Aristophanes has no words bad enough for the leader of the
democracy, Cleon : yet he is severe on the conservatives too.
The following conversation gives his view of the politicians'
methods of appealing to the electorate. (They are supposed to
be addressing the Democracy.)
    Democrat. Dear Demos, wipe your nose on me.
    Conservative. Oh, no, on me, please.
The metaphor is coarse, but not coarser than the methods of

    [1] Clouds, 961 f. (tr. Rogers).
    [2] See Browning, *Aristophanes' Apology*, which is good on Euripides,
and, with Meredith's few pages, the best study of Aristophanes ever
written.

which we see something at election times. He hated the war, partly because he did not hate Sparta, and conceived a nobler ideal for Greece than internecine quarrels between its inhabitants, partly because war was the policy of the democratic party who were safe inside the city walls and had no farms, as had Aristophanes' friends, to be burnt by yearly incursions of the enemy. He hated the intellectuals, the sophists and Socrates and Euripides. This is the stranger, because in a sense he was an intellectual himself. Mixed up with much buffoonery, he gives sound arguments for the admission of women to political power, and clearly understood feminism, if he did not sympathize with it. He must have known Euripides by heart, for almost every play abounds in parodies of him. He met and discussed with Socrates at the dinner-table, as Plato's *Symposium* shows (p. 261) ; and as the *Clouds* shows, he was intimate with current science and philosophy. But he hated the intellectuals, for the reasons we have already given. He disliked the type they bred, forgetting that it is among the inconveniences of an age of reason, whether five centuries before Christ or nineteen centuries after him, that it will produce a certain number of silly and tiresome young men.

We have seen what Aristophanes hated. The speech of Right Logic reveals some of the things he loved—healthy young men, the great spacious days of Marathon, the Athenians of those days, genial, jovial and robust, fighters, drinkers and good comrades. He loved his country. The following passage contains, with much else, his ideal for her policy. The play was acted in the spring of 411, shortly after the crushing disaster in Sicily. Since 1914 we can better appreciate this picture of a people under the shadow of war. Note the remarkable sympathy shown by the poet for the women's point of view. The scene is below the Acropolis, where an Athenian magistrate discovers a meeting of Greek women discussing how to end the war.

MAGISTRATE. Fools ! what on earth can possess you to meddle with
        matters of war, and matters of peace ?
LYSISTRATA (an Athenian woman). Well, I will tell you the
        reason. MAG. And speedily,
        else you will rue it. LYS. Then listen, and cease
Clutching and clenching your fingers so angrily ;
        keep yourself peaceable. MAG. Hanged if I can ;
Such is the rage that I feel at your impudence.

STRATYLLIS (leader of the Women's Chorus). Then it is *you* that
will rue it, my man.

MAG. Croak your own fate, you ill-omened antiquity.

(*To Lysistrata.*) *You* be the spokeswoman, lady.   LYS. I will.
    Think of our old moderation and gentleness,
                think how we bore with your pranks, and were
                    still,
    All through the days of your former pugnacity,
                all through the war that is over and spent :
    Not that (be sure) we approved of your policy ;
                never our griefs you allowed us to vent.
    Well we perceived your mistakes and mismanagement.
                Often at home on our housekeeping cares,
    Often we heard of some foolish proposal you
                made for conducting the public affairs.
    Then would we question you mildly and pleasantly,
                inwardly grieving, but outwardly gay ;
    Husband, how goes it abroad ? we would ask of him ;
                what have ye done in Assembly to-day ?
    What would ye write on the side of the Treaty stone ? [1]
                Husband says angrily, *What 's that to you ?*
    You, hold your tongue ! And I held it accordingly.
    STRAT. That is a thing which I NEVER would do !

MAG. Ma'am, if you hadn't, you'd soon have repented it.
    LYS. Therefore I held it, and spake not a word.
    Soon of another tremendous absurdity,
                wilder and worse than the former we heard.
    Husband, I say, with a tender solicitude,
                Why have ye passed such a foolish decree ?
    Viciously, moodily, glaring askance at me,
                Stick to your spinning, my mistress, says he,
    Else you will speedily find it the worse for you,
                WAR IS THE CARE AND THE BUSINESS OF MEN ! [2]

---

[1] Treaties were inscribed on stone.
[2] From the speech of Hector to Andromache (p. 30).

MAG. Zeus ! 'twas a worthy reply, and an excellent !

    LYS. What ! you unfortunate, shall we not then,

Then, when we see you perplexed and incompetent,
    shall we not tender advice to the State ?

So when aloud in the streets and the thoroughfares
    sadly we heard you bewailing of late,

Is there a Man to defend and deliver us ?
    No, says another, *there's none in the land ;*

Then by the Women assembled in conference
    jointly a great Revolution was planned,

Hellas to save from her grief and perplexity.
    Where is the use of a longer delay ?

Shift for the future our parts and our characters ;
    you, as the women, in silence obey ;

We, as the men, will harangue and provide for you ;
    then shall the State be triumphant again,

Then shall we do what is best for the citizens.

    MAG. Women to do what is best for the men !

That were a shameful reproach and unbearable !

    LYS. Silence,[1] old gentleman. MAG. Silence for YOU ?

Stop for a wench with a wimple enfolding her ?
    No, by the Powers, may I DIE if I do !

LYS.   Do not, my pretty one, do not, I pray,

    Suffer my wimple to stand in the way.

    Here, take it, and wear it, and gracefully tie it,

    Enfolding it over your head, and be quiet.

    Now to your task.

A WOMAN. Here is an excellent spindle to pull.

ANOTHER. Here is a basket for carding the wool.

LYS.   Now to your task.

    Haricots chawing up, petticoats drawing up,

---

[1] Lysistrata is putting her system into immediate practice, and therefore addresses the same language and assigns the same duties to the Magistrate, as the Men had been accustomed aforetime to address and assign to the Women.

Off to your carding, your combing, your trimming,
WAR IS THE CARE AND THE BUSINESS OF WOMEN.

During the foregoing lines the women have been arraying the Magistrate in the garb and with the apparatus of a spinning-woman: just as below they bedeck him in the habiliments of a corpse.)

WOMEN'S CHORUS. Up, up, and leave the pitchers there,
and on, resolved and eager,
Our own allotted part to bear
in this illustrious leaguer.
Children of stiff and intractable grandmothers,
heirs of the stinging viragoes that bore you,
On, with an eager, unyielding tenacity,
wind in your sails, and the haven before you.

LYS. Only let Love, the entrancing, the fanciful,
only let Queen Aphrodite to-day
Breathe on our persons a charm and a tenderness,
lend us their own irresistible sway,
Drawing the men to admire us and long for us ;
then shall the war everlastingly cease,
Then shall the people revere us and honour us,
givers of Joy, and givers of Peace.

MAG. Tell us the mode and the means of your doing it.
LYS. First we will stop the disorderly crew,
Soldiers in arms promenading and marketing.
STRAT. Yea, by divine Aphrodite, 'tis true.

LYS. Now in the market you see them like Corybants,[1]
jangling about with their armour of mail.
Fiercely they stalk in the midst of the crockery,
sternly parade by the cabbage and kail.

MAG. Right, for a soldier should always be soldierly !
LYS. Troth, 'tis a mighty ridiculous jest,
Watching them haggle for shrimps in the market-place,
grimly accoutred with shield and with crest.

---

[1] Priests of Cybele, who wore armour. The whole population of Attica were now, after the Sicilian disaster, called up for military service.

STRAT. Lately I witnessed a captain of cavalry,
    proudly the while on his charger he sat,
  Witnessed him, soldierly, buying an omelet,
    stowing it all in his cavalry hat.
  Comes, like a Tereus,[1] a Thracian irregular,
    shaking his dart and his target to boot ;
  Off runs a shop-girl, appalled at the sight of him,
    down he sits soldierly, gobbles her fruit.

MAG. You, I presume, could adroitly and gingerly
    settle this intricate, tangled concern :
  You in a trice could relieve our perplexities.
    LYS. Certainly. MAG. How ? permit me to learn.

LYS. Just as a woman, with nimble dexterity,
    thus with her hands disentangles a skein,
  Hither and thither her spindles unravel it,
    drawing it out, and pulling it plain.
  So would this weary Hellenic entanglement
    soon be resolved by our womanly care,
  So would our embassies neatly unravel it,
    drawing it here and pulling it there.

MAG. Wonderful, marvellous feats, not a doubt of it,
    you with your skeins and your spindles can show ;
  Fools ! do you really expect to unravel a
    terrible war like a bundle of tow ?

LYS. Ah, if you only could manage your politics
    just in the way that we deal with a fleece !

MAG. Tell us the recipe. LYS. First, in the washing-tub
    plunge it, and scour it, and cleanse it from grease,
  Purging away all the filth and the nastiness ;
    then on the table expand it and lay,
  Beating out all that is worthless and mischievous,
    picking the burrs and the thistles away.
  Next, for the clubs, the cabals, and the coteries,
    banding unrighteously, office to win,

---

[1] A Thracian king of legend. This man would be one of the wild mercenaries employed by Athens.

Treat them as clots in the wool, and dissever them,
      lopping the heads that are forming therein.
Then you should card it, and comb it, and mingle it,
      all in one Basket of love and of unity,
Citizens, visitors, strangers, and sojourners,
      all the entire, undivided community.
Know you a fellow in debt to the Treasury ? [1]
      Mingle him merrily in with the rest.
Also remember the cities, our colonies,
      outlying states in the east and the west,
Scattered about to a distance surrounding us,
      these are our shreds and our fragments of wool ;
These to one mighty political aggregate
      tenderly, carefully, gather and pull,
Twining them all in one thread of good fellowship ;
      thence a magnificent bobbin to spin,
Weaving a garment of comfort and dignity,
      worthily wrapping the People therein.[2]
MAG. Heard any ever the like of their impudence,
      these who have nothing to do with the war,
Preaching of bobbins, and beatings, and washing-tubs ?
   LYS. Nothing to do with it, wretch that you are !
We are the people who feel it the keenliest,
      doubly on us the affliction is cast :
Where are the sons that we sent to your battle-fields ?
   MAG. Silence ! a truce to the ills that are past.
LYS. Then in the glory and grace of our womanhood,
      all in the May and the morning of life,
Lo, we are sitting forlorn and disconsolate,
      what has a soldier to do with a wife ?
We might endure it, but ah ! for the younger ones,
      still in their maiden apartments they stay,

[1] Such debtors were disfranchised. Aristophanes, however, urges a general amnesty.
[2] This magnificent passage illustrates Meredith's remark that the idea of Aristophanes' comedies is the Idea of Good Citizenship.

Waiting the husband that never approaches them,
  watching the years that are gliding away.
MAG. Men, I suppose, have their youth everlastingly.
  LYS. Nay, but it isn't the same with a man :
Grey though he be when he comes from the battle-field,
  still if he wishes to marry, he can.
Brief is the spring and the flower of our womanhood,
  once let it slip, and it comes not again ;
Sit as we may with our spells and our auguries,
  never a husband will marry us then.
MAG. Truly whoever is able to wed—[1]
LYS. Truly, old fellow, 'tis time you were dead.
  So a pig shall be sought, and an urn shall be bought,
  And I'll bake you and make you a funeral cake.
   Take it and go.
CAL. Here are the fillets all ready to wear.
MYRR. Here is the chaplet to bind in your hair.
   Take it and go.
  What are you prating for ? What are you waiting for ?
  Charon [2] is staying, delaying his crew,
  Charon is calling and bawling for you.[3]

Perhaps as much as anything Aristophanes loved the farm,
where he lived the country life with Greek simplicity and homely
neighbourliness.

AH, there 's nothing half so sweet as when the seed is in the
  ground,
  God a gracious rain is sending, and a neighbour saunters
  round.
' O Comarchides,' he hails me, ' how shall we enjoy the hours ? '
' Drinking seems to suit my fancy, what with these benignant
  showers.

---

[1] Apparently he was about to add ' will soon find a wife ', but Lysistrata
interrupts him, and she and her companions dress him up like a corpse.
[2] The ferryman of the dead.
[3] Lysistrata, 502 f. (tr. Rogers).

Therefore let three quarts, my mistress, of your kidney-beans be
    fried,
Mix them nicely up with barley, and your choicest figs provide ;
Syra,[1] run and shout to Manes,[2] call him in without delay,
'Tis no time to stand and dawdle pruning out the vines to-day,
Nor to break the clods about them, now the ground is soaking
    through,
Bring me out from home the fieldfare, bring me out the siskins
    two,
Then there ought to be some beestings, four good plates of hare
    beside
(Hah ! unless the cat purloined them yesterday at eventide ;
Something scuffled in the pantry, something made a noise and
    fuss) ;
If you find them, one's for father, bring the other three to us.
Ask Aeschīnades to send us myrtle branches green and strong,[3]
Bid Charīnades attend us, shouting as you pass along.

> Then we'll sit and drink together,
> God the while refreshing, blessing
> All the labour of our hands.[4]

We may end with a passage whose poetic fancies show how
unlike Aristophanes is to humorists of the various types of
Swift, Dickens, Rabelais, or Molière. Any one watching the free
life of birds between earth and heaven will feel how these fancies
came to Aristophanes. Birds seem to stand so entirely apart
from creation, that he fancies them existing before all created
things, even before the gods. He imagines the contempt with
which they might be supposed to look on the younger race of
man : then, playing with Greek stories of creation, he makes
them describe how they came to be, whose children they are,
whence came their wings—they know much more of the origin of
the world than the philosophers. Next he lets his humour play
on what they do for men, and might do for them, and on the
advantages of having wings.

---

[1] The maid.   [2] The farm labourer.
[3] To be passed from hand to hand as they sang after dinner.
[4] Peace, 1140 f. (tr. Frere).

YE Children of Man ! whose life is a span,
    Protracted with sorrow from day to day,
    Naked and featherless, feeble and querulous,
Sickly, calamitous, creatures of clay !
Attend to the words of the Sovereign Birds,
(Immortal, illustrious, lords of the air)
Who survey from on high, with a merciful eye,
Your struggles of misery, labour, and care.
Whence you may learn and clearly discern
Such truths as attract your inquisitive turn ;
Which is busied of late, with a mighty debate,
A profound speculation about the creation,
And organical life, and chaotical strife,
With various notions of heavenly motions,
And rivers and oceans, and valleys and mountains,
And sources of fountains, and meteors on high,
And stars in the sky. We propose by-and-by
(If you'll listen and hear) to make it all clear.
And Prodicus[1] henceforth shall pass for a dunce,
When his doubts are explained and expounded at once.

    Before the creation of Aether and Light,
Chaos and Night together were plight,
In the dungeon of Erebus foully bedight.
Nor Ocean, or Air, or substance was there,
Or solid or rare, or figure or form,
But horrible Tartarus ruled in the storm :
    At length, in the dreary chaotical closet
Of Erebus old, was a privy deposit
By Night the primaeval in secrecy laid ;
A Mystical Egg, that in silence and shade
Was brooded and hatched ; till time came about :
And Love, the delightful, in glory flew out,
In rapture and light, exulting and bright,

---

[1] The reference is to current scientific speculations. Prodicus was a famous sophist (p. 258)

Sparkling and florid, with stars in his forehead,
His forehead and hair, and a flutter and flare,
As he rose in the air, triumphantly furnished
To range his dominions, on glittering pinions,
All golden and azure, and blooming and burnished :
    He soon, in the murky Tartarean recesses,
With a hurricane's might, in his fiery caresses
Impregnated Chaos ; and hastily snatched
To being and life, begotten and hatched,
The primitive Birds : but the Deities all,
The celestial Lights, the terrestrial Ball,
Were later of birth, with the dwellers on earth,
More tamely combined, of a temperate kind.
    Our antiquity proved, it remains to be shown,
That Love is our author, and master alone,
Like him, we can ramble, and gambol and fly
O'er ocean and earth, and aloft to the sky :
And all the world over we're friends to the lover,
And when other means fail, we are found to prevail,
When a peacock or pheasant is sent as a present.
    All lessons of primary daily concern,
You have learnt from the Birds, and continue to learn
Your best benefactors and early instructors ;
We give you the warning of seasons returning.
    When the cranes are arranged, and muster afloat
In the middle air, with a creaking note,
Steering away to the Lybian sands,
Then careful farmers sow their lands ;
The crazy vessel is hauled ashore,
The sail, the ropes, the rudder and oar
Are all unshipped, and housed in store.
    The shepherd is warned, by the kite reappearing,
To muster his flock, and be ready for shearing.
    You quit your old cloak, at the swallow's behest,
In assurance of summer, and purchase a vest.

MENANDER

Then take us as gods, and you'll soon find the odds,
We'll serve for all uses, as Prophets and Muses ;
We'll give ye fine weather, we'll live here together ;
We'll not keep away, scornful and proud, a-top of a cloud,
(In Jupiter's way) ; but attend every day,
To prosper and bless, all you possess,
And all your affairs, for yourselves and your heirs.

   And as long as you live, we shall give
   You wealth and health, and pleasure and treasure,
   In ample measure ;
   And never bilk you of pigeon's milk,[1]
   Or potable gold ; you shall live to grow old,
   In laughter and mirth, on the face of the earth,
   Laughing, quaffing, carousing, bousing,
    Your only distress, shall be the excess
    Of ease and abundance and happiness.

Nothing can be more delightful than the having wings to wear !
A spectator sitting here, accommodated with a pair,
Might for instance (if he found a tragic chorus dull and heavy)
Take his flight, and dine at home ; and if he did not choose to
  leave ye,
Might return in better humour, when the weary drawl was ended.
Introduce then wings in use—believe me, matters will be mended.[2]

Modern comedy obviously owes nothing to Aristophanes :
but the comedy of Molière descends, through Latin imitators,
from a group of writers who lived in the late fourth century.[3]
This New Comedy, as the Greeks called it, was a comedy of
manners and took its subjects from everyday life. Large fragments of its greatest writer, Menander (343–291), have lately
been recovered from the rubbish heaps of Egypt. Naturalness,
mastery of plot-making and character, and an exquisite style
(which translation murders) are the chief elements of his genius.
Julius Caesar praises the latter in an enthusiastic epigram,

[1] ' Bird's milk ' was an expression for anything rare and precious.
[2] Birds, 685 f. (tr. Frere).
[3] The plot of *The Comedy of Errors* comes from one of these writers.

and took the decisive and most dangerous step of his life with
a line of Menander on his lips. Meredith speaks of his ' beautiful
translucency of language', and says that ' Menander and
Molière stand alone specially as comic poets of the feeling and the
idea '. The following phrases are characteristic of his art and
philosophy.

Whom the gods love die young.

I hold him happiest
Who, before going quickly whence he came,
Hath looked ungrieving on these majesties,
The world-wide sun, the stars, waters and clouds
And fire. Live, Parmeno, a hundred years
Or a few weeks, these thou wilt always see,
And never, never, any greater thing.[1]

Are life and sorrow kinsmen ? Surely sorrow
Is wealth's attendant, fame's familiar,
And walks with poverty the path to age.

As in a chorus
Not all are singers, but some two or three,
Behind the rest, to make the sum complete,
Stand and say nothing—so on this world's stage.
'Tis livelihood gives life : those without money
But fill a place.

[1] Quoted in Morley, *Recollections*, ii .136.

VI

HISTORY: HERODOTUS

THE study of Greek prose and poetry is the study of the origin, one after another, of the various branches of European literature. We now come to the Father of history, Herodotus. To-day history is a branch of literature with well-defined objects, scope, and methods, and a modern historian knows exactly what is expected of him. Not so Herodotus. Though he calls his work a ' history ' (the Greek word simply means ' inquiry '), his object in writing was ' that the great and wonderful deeds done by Greeks and Persians should not lack renown ' (notice that he does not ignore the latter because they were his country's enemies). We must admire the genius of the men who by instinct, without pattern or precedent, divined the nature and laws of what has become one of the great branches of literature ; but we must expect some differences between their conception of its nature and methods, and our own. One difference is that Greek histories are less full than ours. A modern historian considers it his task to give a complete account of the period with which he deals, including its literature, social life, religious movements, &c., as well as its outstanding events and men. Herodotus and Thucydides had no such idea of completeness ; they never treat directly of religion or literature or many other things. Their way of writing too is different from ours. A modern historian tells his story, but draws out its lessons, discusses them, and makes his personal comments. A Greek writer tends simply to describe what happened and leaves the story to convey its own meaning. The facts tell their own tale and carry with them the feeling they should evoke without any comment from him. Indeed the Greeks wrote their histories as they wrote plays or epics, allowing the characters and events to speak for themselves. A modern reader, accustomed to have conclusions pointed out to him, will at first miss them, but he may come to prefer a method which is not only highly dramatic but leads to good writing, since, if the facts are to convey their own lesson, they must be well described.

Born in 484, at Halicarnassus, in Asia Minor, an Ionian, and writing in an Ionian dialect, Herodotus before the age of twenty rebelled against the local prince ; he was exiled, returned, was driven out again by the 'intolerable criticism' of the citizens, travelled northwards as far as the Crimea, southward to Assouan, eastward to Persia, westward to Sicily, and spent the rest of his life between Athens and the colony of Thurii in Italy, which he had helped to found and where he died about the age of sixty. His was a full life and a good training for an historian. It is difficult to define the subject of the nine books of his history, which rises in sixth-century Lydia, when Croesus is king, flows with infinite meanders and digressions through Persia, Egypt, Asia Minor, South Russia, culminating with the Persian invasions of Greece and ending with their defeat at Plataea in 479. Perhaps we may give it the sub-title of 'The Story of the Greeks and Foreign Peoples '.

At first Herodotus seems to be in life what Odysseus is in fiction, the ideal traveller ; he has something of the credulity and superficiality of a tourist, conducted round Egyptian temples by the priests, and fed with travellers' tales by Babylonian guides, but he is intensely interested in the ways and character of all manner of men and he knows how to record them. But he is historian as well as traveller, and here his standards are not ours. He does not know the language of the peoples he visited, he believes in oracles and miracles, he relates conversations that he could never have heard, and stories that are clearly untrue ; though some of these are excused by his statement, ' I am bound to report all that is said, but I am not bound to believe it.' All these things should make him a bad historian : against them we must set certain great virtues. First, he has an infinite curiosity about every kind of fact, incident, and human being, from the revenues of Persia to the Scythian methods of milking, from the Great King to Spartan muledrivers, from Egyptian cats to Greek children. This fills his pages with a life, variety, and movement, unrivalled perhaps by any other historian, and re-creates, as no amount of research or documentation could do, the world of his day. The following extracts will give an idea of the width of his interests. Incidentally they will reveal his second great quality. He is a prince of story-tellers, equally at home with a fairy tale or romance, and (as his account of Thermopylae shows) with the emotions and issues of a great war.

Babylonian Customs

I WILL now show what seems to me to be the most marvellous thing in the country, next to the city itself. Their boats which ply on the river and go to Babylon are all of skins, and round. They make these in Armenia, higher up the stream than Assyria. First they cut frames of willow, then they stretch hides over these for a covering, making as it were a hold; they neither broaden the stern nor narrow the prow, but the boat is round, like a shield. They then fill it with reeds and send it floating down the river with a cargo; and it is for the most part palm-wood casks of wine that they carry down. Two men standing upright steer the boat, each with a paddle, one drawing it to him, the other thrusting it from him. These boats are of all sizes, some small, some very great; the greatest of them are even of five thousand talents [1] burden. There is a live ass in each boat, or more than one in the larger. So when they have floated down to Babylon and disposed of their cargo, they sell the framework of the boat and all the reeds; the hides are set on the backs of asses, which are then driven back to Armenia, for it is not by any means possible to go up stream by water, by reason of the swiftness of the current; it is for this reason that they make their boats of hides and not of wood. When they have driven their asses back into Armenia they make more boats in the same way.

Such then are their boats. For clothing, they wear a linen tunic, reaching to the feet; over this the Babylonian puts on another tunic, of wool, and wraps himself in a white mantle; he wears the shoes of his country, which are like Boeotian sandals. Their hair is worn long, and covered by caps; the whole body is perfumed. Every man has a seal and a carven staff, and on

[1] Either 125 or 175 tons. (The Attic and the Aeginetan talent differ.) These boats are still used.

every staff is some image, such as that of an apple or a rose or a lily or an eagle : no one carries a staff without a device.

Such is the equipment of their persons. I will now speak of their established customs. The wisest of these, in my judgement, is this : once a year in every village all the maidens as they came to marriageable age were collected and brought together into one place, with a crowd of men standing round. Then a crier would stand up and offer them for sale one by one, first the fairest of all ; and then when she had fetched a great price he put up for sale the next comeliest, selling all the maidens as lawful wives. Rich men of Assyria who desired to marry would outbid each other for the fairest ; the commonalty, who desired to marry and cared nothing for beauty, could take the ill-favoured damsels and money therewith ; for when the crier had sold all the comeliest, he would put up her that was least beautiful, or crippled, and offer her to whosoever would take her to wife for the least sum, till she fell to him who promised to accept least ; the money came from the sale of the comely damsels, and so they paid the dowry of the ill-favoured and the cripples. But a man might not give his daughter in marriage to whomsoever he would, nor might he that bought the girl take her away without giving security that he would indeed make her his wife. And if the two could not agree, it was a law that the money be returned. Men might also come from other villages to buy if they so desired.

I come now to the next wisest of their customs : having no use for physicians, they carry the sick into the market-place ; then those who have been afflicted themselves by the same ill as the sick man's, or seen others in like case, come near and advise him about his disease and comfort him, telling him by what means they have themselves recovered of it or seen others so recover. None may pass by the sick man without speaking and asking what is his sickness.[1]

[1] I. 194 f. The translations from Bks. I–IV are taken from Dr. Godley's version (Loeb).

Story of the Babylonian Queen Nitōcris

THERE was a trick, moreover, which this same queen contrived. She had a tomb made for herself and set high over the very gate of that entrance of the city which was most used, with a writing graven on the tomb, which was this: ' If any king of Babylon in future time lack money, let him open this tomb and take whatso money he desires: but let him not open it except he lack ; for it will be the worse for him.' This tomb remained untouched till the kingship fell to Darīus. He thought it a very strange thing that he should never use this gate, nor take the money when it lay there and the writing itself invited him to the deed. The cause of his not using the gate was that the dead body must be over his head as he passed through. Having opened the tomb, he found there no money, but only the dead body, with this writing : ' Wert thou not insatiate of wealth and basely desirous of gain, thou hadst not opened the coffins of the dead.' [1]

Scythian Burial Customs

THE burial-places of the kings are in the land which is the end of the navigation of the Borysthenes.[2] There, whenever their king has died, the Scythians dig a great four-cornered pit in the ground ; when this is ready they take up the dead man—his body enclosed in wax, his belly cut open and cleansed and filled with cut marsh-plants and frankincense and parsley and anise seed, and sewn up again—and carry him on a wagon to another tribe. Then those that receive the dead man cut off a part of their ears, shave their heads, make cuts round their arms, tear their foreheads and noses, and pierce their left hands with arrows. Thence the bearers carry the king's body on the wagon to another of the tribes which they rule, and those to whom they have already come follow them ; and having carried the dead

[1] I. 187.
[2] The Dnieper. Excavations of tombs in S. Russia have confirmed H.'s account. Servants, &c., are buried with the dead king that he may have them for use in the next world.

man to all in turn, they are in the country of the Gerrhi, the farthest distant of all tribes under their rule, and at the place of burial. Then, having laid the dead in the tomb on a couch, they plant spears all round the body and lay across them wooden planks, which they then roof over with hides ; in the open space which is left in the tomb they bury, after strangling, one of the king's wives, his cupbearer, his cook, his groom, his squire, and his messenger, besides horses, and first-fruits of all else, and golden cups ; for the Scythians make no use of silver or bronze. Having done this they all build a great barrow of earth, vying zealously with one another to make this as great as may be.

With the completion of a year they begin a fresh practice. Taking the trustiest of the rest of the king's servants they strangle fifty of these squires and fifty of their best horses and empty and cleanse the bellies of all and fill them with chaff. Then they make fast the half of a wheel to two posts, so that it hangs down, and the other half to another pair of posts, till many posts thus furnished are planted in the ground, and, presently, driving thick stakes lengthways through the horses' bodies to their necks, they lay the horses aloft on the wheels so that the wheel in front supports the horse's shoulders and the wheel behind takes the weight of the belly by the hindquarters, and the forelegs and hindlegs hang free ; and putting bridles and bits in the horses' mouths they stretch the bridles to the front and make them fast with pegs. Then they take each one of the fifty strangled young men and mount him on the horse ; their way of doing it is to drive an upright stake through each body passing up by the spine to the neck, and enough of the stake projects below to be fixed in a hole made in the other stake, that which passes through the horse. So having set horsemen of this fashion round about the tomb they ride away.

Such is their way of burying their kings. All other Scythians when they die, are laid in wagons and carried about among their friends by their nearest of kin ; each receives them and entertains the retinue hospitably, setting before the dead man about as much of the fare as he serves to the rest. All but the kings are thus borne about for forty days and then buried. After the burial the Scythians cleanse themselves as I will show : they anoint and wash their heads ; as for their bodies, they set up three poles leaning together to a point and cover these over with woollen rugs ; then, in the place so enclosed to the best of their power, they make a pit in the centre beneath the poles and the rugs and throw red-hot stones into it.

They have hemp growing in their country, very like flax, save that the hemp is by much the thicker and taller. This grows both of itself and also by their sowing, and of it the Thracians even make garments which are very like linen ; nor could any, save he were a past master in hemp, know whether they be hempen or linen ; whoever has never yet seen hemp will think the garment to be linen.

The Scythians then take the seed of this hemp and, creeping under the rugs, they throw it on the red-hot stones ; and, being so thrown, it smoulders and sends forth so much steam that no Greek vapour-bath could surpass it. The Scythians howl in joy for the vapour-bath. This serves them instead of bathing, for scarce ever do they wash their bodies with water.[1]

A Thracian Custom

WHEN a child is born its relations sit round and lament all the misfortunes which it is destined to undergo, recounting all the sufferings of humanity. But when a man dies they bury him with jest and rejoicing, considering him delivered from many sorrows and completely happy.[2]

Persian Customs

AS to the usages of the Persians, I know them to be these. It is not their custom to make and set up statues and temples and altars, but those who make such they deem foolish, as I suppose, because they never believed the gods, as do the Greeks, to

[1] IV. 71 f.   [2] V. 4.

be in the likeness of men ; but they call the whole circle of heaven
Zeus, and to him they offer sacrifice on the highest peaks of the
mountains ; they sacrifice also to the sun and moon and earth
and fire and water and winds. These are the only gods to whom
they have ever sacrificed from the beginning.

And this is their fashion of sacrifice to the aforesaid gods :
when about to sacrifice they neither build altars nor kindle fire,
they use no libations, nor music, nor garlands, nor barley meal ; [1]
but to whomsoever of the gods a man will sacrifice, he leads the
beast to an open space and then calls on the god, himself wearing
a crown on his cap, of myrtle for choice. To pray for blessings
for himself alone is not lawful for the sacrificer ; rather he prays
that it may be well with the king and all the Persians ; for he
reckons himself among them. He then cuts the victim limb
from limb into portions, and having roasted the flesh spreads
the softest grass, trefoil by choice, and places all of it on this.
When he has so disposed it a Magian [2] comes near and chants over
it the song of the birth of the gods, as the Persian tradition relates
it ; for no sacrifice can be offered without a Magian. Then after
a little while the sacrificer carries away the flesh and uses it as he
pleases.

The day which every man most honours is his own birthday.
On this he thinks it right to serve a more abundant meal than on
other days ; before the rich are set oxen or horses or camels or
asses, roasted whole in ovens ; the poorer serve up the lesser
kinds of cattle. Their courses are few, the dainties that follow
are many and not all served together.[3] This is why the Persians
say of the Greeks, that they rise from table still hungry, because
not much dessert is set before them : were this too given to the
Greek (say the Persians) he would never cease eating. They are
greatly given to wine. Moreover it is their custom to deliberate
about the gravest matters when they are drunk ; and what they

[1] All these were usual in Greek sacrifices.
[2] A Persian priest.
[3] The Greeks had their dessert at the end of the meal, the Persians had
it served several times during it.

approve in their counsels is proposed to them the next day by the master of the house where they deliberate, when they are now sober ; and if being sober they still approve it, they act thereon, but if not, they cast it aside. And when they have taken counsel about a matter when sober, they decide upon it when they are drunk.[1]

When one man meets another in the way, it is easy to see if the two are equals ; for then without speaking they kiss each other on the lips ; if the difference in rank be but little, it is the cheek that is kissed ; if it be great, the humbler bows down and does obeisance to the other. They honour most of all those who dwell nearest them, next those who are next farthest removed, and so going ever onwards they assign honour by this rule ; those who dwell farthest off they hold least honourable of all ; for they deem themselves to be in all regards by far the best of all men, the rest to have but a proportionate claim to merit, till those who dwell farthest away have least merit of all.

But of all men the Persians most welcome foreign customs. They wear the Median dress, deeming it more beautiful than their own, and the Egyptian cuirass in war. Their luxurious practices are of all kinds, and all borrowed. Every Persian marries many lawful wives.

After valour in battle it is most reckoned as manly merit to show the greatest number of sons : the king sends gifts yearly to him who can show most. Numbers, they hold, are strength. They educate their boys from five to twenty years old, and teach them three things only, riding and archery and truth-telling. A boy is not seen by his father before he is five years old, but lives with the women : the reason of this is that, if the boy should die in the time of his rearing, the father may suffer no grief.

This is a law which I praise ; and it is a praiseworthy law too which suffers not the king himself to slay any man for one offence, nor any other Persian for one offence to do incurable hurt to one of his servants. Not till reckoning shows that the offender's

[1] The idea is, Wine in, Truth out. The Persians are still famous drinkers.

wrongful acts are more and greater than his services may a man give vent to his anger. They say that none has ever yet killed his father or mother ; for it is not to be believed (say they) that a son should kill his true parent.

Moreover of what they may not do neither may they speak. They hold lying to be foulest of all, and next to that debt ; for which they have many other reasons, but this in especial, that the debtor must needs (so they say) speak some falsehood. The citizen who has leprosy or the white sickness may not come into a town or consort with other Persians. They say that he is so afflicted because he has sinned in some wise against the sun. Many drive every stranger, who takes such a disease, out of the country ; and so they do to white doves, for the reason aforesaid. Rivers they chiefly reverence ; they will neither spit nor wash their hands therein, nor suffer any one so to do.[1]

Here follow some incidents of the Persian march to Greece. True or not, they illustrated to Herodotus the unrestrained presumption and despotic cruelty of the Persian character, vices which revolted the Greeks.

Xerxes crossed the Dardanelles by a bridge, which was broken in a storm.

HEARING this and being angry with the Dardanelles, he ordered that the sea should receive 300 hundred lashes and that a pair of fetters should be thrown into it. I have been told that at the same time he sent men to brand it. At any rate he told those who administered the lashes to use the following barbarous and presumptuous words : ' O bitter water, your master inflicts this punishment on you, because you have done him injury, though he did you none. King Xerxes will cross you, whether you like it or not. No man sacrifices to you, and rightly, for you are a turbid and salt stream.' Such were the punishments Xerxes imposed on the sea ; and he ordered that the officers in charge of the bridge should be beheaded.[2]

[1] I. 131 f.   [2] VII. 34.

A rich Lydian, Pythius, who had hospitably entertained Xerxes, asked the following favour. ' Master, I should like to make a request, which means much to me and is easy for you to grant.' Xerxes, thinking that he would ask anything but what he did, promised to comply and told him to say what he wanted. Pythius was encouraged and said: ' Master, I have five sons, and you are taking all on your expedition. King, pity me, for I am old ; take my other four sons with you, but release my eldest son, to take care of me and my business : and may you accomplish your purpose and return.' Xerxes was enraged and answered : ' Villain, I am marching against Greece and taking my children, brothers, kinsmen and friends ; and you, my slave, who ought to be following with your wife and all your house, have the audacity to think of your son. Though your former conduct was good and though your promises are good, you will not assert that you were more liberal than your king : now you have lost all sense of shame, and you shall be punished, though much less than you deserve. Your hospitality saves you and your four sons : you shall be requited by the death of one, your darling.' With this answer, he directed the proper officers to find the eldest son of Pythius, cut him in half, and place the two halves to right and left of the road, so that the army marched between them.[1]

Herodotus recounts this brutality without condemning it. That is his way. But what he felt about it, what any Greek would have felt, may be guessed from the following story.

After the defeat of the Persians at Plataea, a Greek from Aegīna went to the Greek commander Pausanias and said :

' WHEN Leonidas was killed at Thermopylae, Mardonius [2] and Xerxes cut off his head and crucified him. Pay Mardonius back in his own coin, and you will win the approval of Sparta and of the rest of Greece. Crucify him, and you will avenge your uncle Leonidas.' This he said thinking to

[1] VII. 38 f.
[2] Left in command of the Persians, when Xerxes returned home. He was killed at Plataea.

please him : but Pausanias answered: ' My Aeginetan friend, I admire your forethought and your good intentions, but your proposal is mistaken and wrong. You have highly extolled my country, my achievement and myself, and now you degrade them to the dust by recommending me to outrage the dead and telling me that this will bring me credit. That is conduct more suitable to foreigners than to Greeks ; and we blame it even in foreigners. In this I would rather not please the Aeginetans or those who approve such conduct : I am satisfied to do and say what is right, and to have the approval of Sparta. Leonidas, whom you tell me to avenge, has already been amply avenged : unnumbered Persian dead have paid for him and for those who fell at Thermopylae. If you remain of the same opinion, spare me your presence and your advice, and be thankful that I do you no harm.' [1]

An Egyptian Story

THE next to reign (they said) was Rhampsinitus. The memorial of his name left by him was the western forecourt of the temple of Hephaestus ; before this he set two statues of twenty-five cubits' height ; the northernmost of these is called by the Egyptians Summer, and the southernmost Winter ; that one which they call Summer they worship and entreat well, but do contrariwise to the statue called Winter. This king (they told me) had great wealth of silver, so great that none of the later-born kings could surpass or nearly match it. That he might store his treasure safely, he made to be built a stone chamber, one of its walls abutting on the outer side of his palace. But the builder of it craftily contrived that one stone should be so placed as to be easily removed by two men or even by one. So when the chamber was finished, the king stored his treasure in it. But as time went on, the builder, being now near his end, called to him his two sons and told them how he had provided an ample livelihood for them by the art with which he had built the king's treasure-house ; he made them clearly to understand concerning

[1] IX. 78 f.

the removal of the stone, and gave the measurements which would find it ; saying that if they kept these in mind they would be stewards of the king's riches. So when he was dead, his sons set to work with no long delay : coming to the palace by night, they easily found and handled the stone in the building, and took away much of the treasure. When the king opened the building, he was amazed to see the vessels lacking their full tale of treasure ; yet he knew not whom to accuse, seeing that the seals were unbroken and the chamber fast shut. But when at the second and third opening of the chamber he saw the treasure grown ever less (for the thieves ceased not from plundering), he bid traps to be made and set about the vessels in which his riches lay. The thieves came as they had done before, and one of them crept in ; when he came near the vessel, at once he was caught and held in the trap. Seeing his evil plight, he straightway called to his brother, and, showing him how matters stood, ' Creep in quickly,' said he, ' and cut off my head, lest I be seen and recognized and so bring you too to ruin.' The brother consented and did this, thinking the counsel good. Then he set the stone in place again, and went away home, carrying his brother's head. When it was morning the king came to the chamber, and was amazed to see the thief's headless body in the trap, yet the chamber unbroken, with no way of passing in or out ; and he knew not what to do. But presently he hung the thief's dead body on the outer wall, and set guards over it, charging them to seize and bring before him whomsoever they should see weeping or making lamentation.

But the thief's mother, when the body had been so hung, was greatly moved : she talked with her surviving son, and bade him contrive by whatever means to loose and bring her his brother's body, threatening that if he would not obey her she would go to the king and lay an information that he had the treasure. So when she bitterly reproached him and for all he said he could not overpersuade her, the brother devised a plot : he got his asses and loaded them with skins full of wine and then

drove them before him till he came near those who guarded the
hanging body ; then he pulled at the feet of two or three of the
skins and loosed their fastenings ; and the wine so running out,
he cried aloud and beat his head like one that knew not which
of his asses he should deal with first. The guards, seeing the
wine running freely, all took vessels and ran into the highway,
where they caught the spilt wine, and thought themselves lucky ;
the man pretended to be angry and reviled each and all of them ;
but the guards speaking peaceably to him, he presently made as
if he were comforted and appeased, till at last he drove his asses
aside from the highway and put his gear in order. So the guards
and he fell into talk, and one of them jesting with him, so that
there was laughter, he gave them one of the skins : whereupon
without more ado they sat down and began to drink, making
him one of their company and bidding him stay and drink with
them ; and he consented and stayed. They drank to him merrily,
and he gave them yet another of the skins, till the guards grew
very drunk with the abundance of liquor, and at last being over-
mastered by sleep lay down in the place where they had been
drinking. When the night was far spent, the thief cut down his
brother's body and then (first shaving the guards' right cheeks
by way of insult) laid it on his asses and drove them home,
having so fulfilled his mother's commands for her.

When the king was told of the stealing away of the dead thief's
body he was very angry, and resolved by all means to find who
it was that had plotted the deed. So he bade his daughter (such
is the story, but I myself do not believe it) to sit in a certain
room and receive alike all who came ; she should compel them
to tell her what was the cleverest trick and the greatest crime of
their life ; then if any told her the story of the thief she must
seize him and not suffer him to pass out. The girl did as her
father bade her. The thief, learning the purpose of the king's
act, was minded to get the better of him by ready cunning. He
therefore cut off the arm of a man newly dead at the shoulder,
and went to the king's daughter, carrying it under his cloak,

and when asked the same question as the rest, he told her that his greatest crime was the cutting off of his brother's head when the brother was caught in a trap in the king's treasury, and his cleverest trick the release of his brother's hanging body by making the guards drunk. Hearing this, the princess would have laid hands on him, but the thief in the darkness giving her the dead man's arm, she seized that, thinking that she was grasping the arm of the thief, who, having given it to her, made his escape by way of the door.

When this also came to the king's ears, he was astonished at the man's ingenuity and daring, and in the end, he sent a proclamation to every town, promising the thief impunity and a great reward if he would come into the king's presence. The thief trusted the king and came before him ; Rhampsinitus admired him greatly and gave him his daughter to wife for his surpassing cleverness, for as the Egyptians (said he) excelled all others in craft, so did he excel the Egyptians.[1]

The last story brings us into a world of mere romance ; but Herodotus is perhaps at his most fabulous in India and Arabia— the latter now as then a land of mystery.

OTHER Indians dwell near the town of Caspatyrus,[2] northward of the rest of India ; they are of all Indians the most warlike, and it is they who are charged with the getting of the gold ; for in these parts all is desert by reason of the sand. There are found in this sandy desert ants[3] not so big as dogs but bigger than foxes ; the Persian king has some of these, which have been caught there. These ants make their dwellings underground, digging out the sand in the same manner as do the ants in Greece, to which they are very like in shape, and the sand which they carry forth from the holes is full of

[1] II. 121.
[2] NE. Afghanistan. Caspatyrus (or Caspapyrus) is said to be probably Cabul.
[3] It is suggested that the ' ants ' may have been really marmots. But even this does not seem to make the story much more probable.

gold. It is for this sand that the Indians set forth into the desert.
They harness three camels apiece, a male led camel on either side
to help in draught, and a female in the middle : the man himself
rides on the female, careful that when harnessed she has been
taken away from as young an offspring as may be. Their camels
are as swift as horses, and much better able to bear burdens
besides.

Thus and with teams so harnessed the Indians ride after the
gold, using all diligence that they shall be about the business of
taking it when the heat is greatest ; for the ants are then out of
sight underground. Now in these parts the sun is hottest in the
morning, not at midday as elsewhere, but from sunrise to the
hour of market-closing. Through these hours it is hotter by
much than in Hellas at noon, so that men are said to sprinkle
themselves with water at this time. At midday the sun's heat
is wellnigh the same in India and elsewhere. As it grows to
afternoon, the sun of India has the power of the morning sun in
other lands ; with its sinking the day becomes ever cooler, till
at sunset it is exceeding cold.

So when the Indians come to the place with their sacks, they
fill these with the sand and ride away back with all speed ; for,
as the Persians say, the ants forthwith scent them out and give
chase, being, it would seem, so much swifter than all other
creatures that if the Indians made not haste on their way while
the ants are mustering, not one of them would escape. So they
loose the male trace-camels that they lead, one at a time (these
being slower than the females) ; the mares never tire, for they
remember the young that they have left. Such is the tale.[1]

T HE Arabians get their frankincense as I have shown ;
for the winning of casia, when they seek it they bind
ox-hides and other skins over all their bodies and faces,
leaving only the eyes. Casia grows in a shallow lake ; round
this and in it are encamped certain winged creatures, very like

----

[1] III. 102 f.

bats, that squeak shrilly and make a stout resistance ; these must be kept from the men's eyes if the casia is to be plucked.

As for cinnamon, they gather it in a fashion even stranger. Where it grows and what kind of land nurtures it they cannot say, save that it is reported, reasonably enough, to grow in the places where Dionysus was reared. There are great birds, it is said, that take these sticks which the Phoenicians have taught us to call cinnamon, and carry them off to nests built of mud on the mountain crags, where no man can approach. The Arabian device for defeating the birds is to cut into very large pieces dead oxen and asses and other beasts of burden, then to set these near the aeries, withdrawing themselves far off. The birds then fly down (it is said) and carry the morsels of the beasts up to their nests ; which not being able to bear the weight break and fall down the mountain-side ; and then the Arabians come up and gather what they seek.[1]

I HAVE said enough of the spices of Arabia ; airs wondrous sweet blow from that land. They have moreover two marvellous kinds of sheep, nowhere else found. One of these has tails no less than three cubits long. Were the sheep to trail these after them, they would suffer hurt by the rubbing of the tails on the ground ; but as it is every shepherd there knows enough of carpentry to make little carts which they fix under the tails, binding the tail of each several sheep on its own cart. The other kind of sheep has tails a full cubit broad.

Where south inclines westwards, the part of the world stretching farthest towards the sunset is Ethiopia ; here is great plenty of gold, and abundance of elephants, and all woodland trees, and ebony ; and the people are the tallest and fairest and longest-lived of all men.

This is plain, that to the north of Europe there is by far more gold than elsewhere. I cannot with certainty say how the gold is got ; some will have it that one-eyed men called Arimaspians

[1] Ib. 110 f. Casia is a spice.

steal it from griffins. But this too I hold incredible, that there can be men in all else like other men, yet having but one eye. Suffice it that it is but reasonable that the most distant parts of the world, as they enclose and wholly surround all other lands, should have those things which we deem best and rarest.[1]

Three stories about Children

No history contains so many stories about children as that of Herodotus.

NOW before Psammetichus became king of Egypt,[2] the Egyptians deemed themselves to be the oldest nation on earth. But ever since he desired to learn, on becoming king, what nation was oldest, they have considered that, though they came before all other nations, the Phrygians are older still. Psammetichus, being nowise able to discover by inquiry what men had first come into being, devised a plan whereby he took two newborn children of common men and gave them to a shepherd to bring up among his flocks. He gave charge that none should speak any word in their hearing ; they were to lie by themselves in a lonely hut, and in due season the shepherd was to bring goats and give the children their milk and do all else needful. Psammetichus did this, and gave this charge, because he desired to hear what speech would first break from the children, when they were past the age of indistinct babbling. And he had his wish ; for when the shepherd had done as he was bidden for two years, one day as he opened the door and entered both the children ran to him stretching out their hands and calling ' Bekos '. When he first heard this he said nothing of it ; but coming often and taking careful note, he was ever hearing this same word, till at last he told the matter to his master, and on command brought the children into the king's presence. Psammetichus heard them himself, and inquired to what language this word Bekos might belong ; he found it to be a Phrygian

[1] III. 113 f.   [2] In 664 B.C., probably.

word signifying bread. Reasoning from this fact the Egyptians confessed that the Phrygians were older than they. This is the story which I have heard from the priests of Hēphaestus'[1] temple at Memphis.[2]

An oracle had warned the Corinthians to beware of a child who was to be born to one Ēëtion and his wife Labda.

A S soon as the child of Labda was born, the Corinthians sent ten of their number to the village where Eetion lived with the purpose of killing the child. They duly reached Petra, and going into the court of Eetion's house asked for the baby. Labda had no idea of their intentions, and thinking that they were acting from goodwill to its father brought the child and put it into the arms of one of them. Now they had agreed on the road that the one who first received the child should dash it to the ground. But it happened by a divine chance that the child smiled at the man who took it ; and he, noticing it, was overcome by pity and could not bring himself to destroy it. So he gave it to the second, and he to the third, till it passed through the hands of all the ten, and none of them would destroy it. Then they gave the child back to its mother and went outside. There they stopped at the gate and began to blame and reproach each other, particularly the one to whom the child had been first given.[3]

The Ionian Aristagoras tried to persuade the Spartan king Cleomenes to attack Persia.

H E took an olive branch[4] and going to the house of Cleomenes entered, and requested the king to hear him, after sending his child away : for Cleomenes' daughter was with him : her name was Gorgo, she was his only child and about eight or nine years old. Cleomenes told him to say what

---

[1] Identified by the Greeks with the Egyptian Ptah.
[2] II. 2.   [3] V. 92.
[4] As a sign that he was suppliant, which gave him a better chance of a hearing.

he wished and not mind the girl. So Aristagoras began promising him ten talents, if he would do what he wished. Cleomenes refused, and Aristagoras increased his offers to fifty talents, upon which the child cried, ' Father, unless you go away, the stranger will corrupt you.' Cleomenes was pleased with the child's advice and went into another room. Aristagoras could not get another audience with him and left Sparta for good.[1]

Stories of some Greeks

The following is the legend of how Alcmaeon, the founder of the great Athenian family to which Pericles belonged, acquired his wealth. Croesus, the King of Lydia, presented him with as much gold as he could carry.

DRESSING himself in a large tunic, which he arranged with a deep fold, and putting on the biggest boots he could find, Alcmaeon followed his guide to the treasury. There throwing himself on a heap of gold dust, he filled his boots with as much gold as they would contain, then he completely filled the fold in his shirt, poured gold dust over his hair and put some more into his mouth. In this condition he came out of the treasury, dragging his feet with difficulty and looking like anything rather than a human being. His mouth was stuffed full and he was distended all over. Croesus burst into laughter when he saw him, and made him a present of all he had taken and as much again.[2]

THERE is a story that Sōphanes wore an iron anchor fastened by a bronze chain to his belt. Whenever he got near the enemy he used to throw this down to prevent their attack dislodging him from his position ; and when they fled it was his method to pick up the anchor and pursue them.[3]

These last stories have introduced us to the Greeks. We see them, amid wild peoples and ruthless despots, naïve, clever, inquiring. Compared with the savage tribes and oriental despotisms around them, they sometimes have the air of children.

[1] V. 51.   [2] VI. 125.   [3] IX. 74.

Yet these children beat Persia, and they carry the seed of an intellectual and moral life, of which there is no sign in the barren ocean of barbarism that surrounded them. In particular they possessed two things, unknown to their neighbours but of infinite importance for the future of the world, liberty and that respect for law, without which liberty perishes. Herodotus says something of each in the following passages. His interesting argument for democracy may be illustrated by the fact that, of the nations engaged in the recent war, Russia did worst, and England and France did best.

THE power of Athens grew; and here is evidence—and there is proof of it everywhere—that liberty is a good thing. While the Athenians were despotically governed, they were not superior in war to any of their neighbours, but when they got rid of their despots, they far surpassed them. This shows that in subjection they did not exert themselves, because they were working for a master, but when they became free each individual keenly did his best on his own account.[1]

Before his final advance Xerxes reviewed his army. He then asked a Spartan exile, Dēmarātus, who was with him, whether the Greeks would presume to resist so enormous a host. Demaratus replied that they would.

'POVERTY, prince, has always been indigenous in Greece, but virtue is an imported growth, the achievement of wisdom and of strict law. It is by her virtue that Greece protects herself against poverty and despotism. This is true of all the Dorians, but at present I am going to speak only about the Spartans. They will never accept your proposals which would make the Greeks slaves, and they will face you in the field, even if the rest of Greece supports you. Do not ask their numbers or how many men they have to do this. They will fight you, whether they have a thousand men under arms, or whether they have more or less.' Xerxes laughed and replied: How could a thousand or ten thousand or even fifty thousand

[1] V. 78. The Greek word here translated 'liberty' means the right of free speech for all.

men, who are all equally free and not under a single ruler, face
my great army. If they were 5,000, we should still be a thousand
to one. An army, which like mine is under a single ruler, would
be afraid of him and be brave in spite of themselves, and under
the compulsion of flogging would attack an enemy more numerous
than themselves : but if they were left free, they would do nothing
of the sort. You know nothing about it and are talking rubbish.'

After some polite remarks, Demaratus replies that the king
is wrong :

When they fight individually, the Spartans are inferior to
none, *en masse* they are unrivalled. For they are free men,
yet not entirely free : Law is the master set over them, and
they fear this master far more than the Persians fear you.
They obey his commands, and his commands are always the
same—that they are not to turn their backs, however many the
enemy, but are to stay in their ranks and either conquer or die.' [1]

That these are not mere words, the story of Thermopylae
shows. The scene of the following battle is a narrow pass, which
was the key to central Greece. The Persians had on their left
the sea, on their right precipitous cliffs running up to 3,000 feet.
Between sea and mountain was a narrow strip of land along which
the road ran. It was blocked by a wall held by some 6,000
Greeks ; though in the final fighting only 300 Spartans and 700
Thespians took part. There was a difficult way through the
mountains, by which the Greek flank could be turned. This was
held by 1,000 Phōcians.

FINDING the pass held, Xerxes sent a spy on horseback to
observe the number and proceedings of the defenders ;
for he had been told that there was a little body of men
gathered together at this place, with certain Spartans at their
head under the captaincy of one Leōnidas. Spurring to the camp,
the rider gazed about him and saw something less than all the
army, as the men on the inner side of the wall were invisible—
they had rebuilt and were guarding it. However, he saw the

[1] VII. 102 f.

troops stationed in front of the rampart—a post, as it happened, at that time occupied by the Spartans, some of whom were taking exercise and some combing their hair. The sight amazed him, but he counted the number of the men and returned unmolested : for no one pursued or indeed paid any attention to him. On his return he acquainted Xerxes with all he had seen.

On receipt of his report, the king failed to fathom the truth —which was that they were preparing to use their utmost endeavours and either do or die. Indeed their conduct seemed to him so ridiculous that he sent to Demaratus, an exiled Spartan who was in his army, and questioned him. ' King,' replied Demaratus, ' before the expedition started, I spoke to you about these men, but you laughed at me, though I told you faithfully what would happen : for it is my chief study to tell you the truth. But hear me once again. These men are come to dispute our passage with arms, and they are preparing to that end. For they have the following custom : when about to risk their lives, they beautify their heads. Know, also, that if you conquer this force and their countrymen in Sparta, no other nation on earth will face you. You are now dealing with the goodliest kingdom and city in Greece, and with the bravest of her sons.'

His words seemed entirely incredible to Xerxes, who demanded yet again how such a handful would do battle with his host : to which Demaratus replied : ' O King, treat me as a liar if what I say does not happen.' But for all that he persuaded not the king, who accordingly allowed four days to pass, in the expectation that the enemy would retreat. On the fifth, however, as they made no movement, but remained (as he conceived) through sheer impudence and folly, he grew angry and sent against them the Medes and Cissians, with orders to take them alive and bring them before his face. The Medes charged the Greeks and lost heavily : others took their place, but could not drive them back in spite of their vigorous attack : which made it clear to all beholders and especially to the king that he could command many men but little manhood.

The Medes after being very roughly handled withdrew, and the band of Persians, which the king called his Immortals, took their place under Hȳdarnes. These, it was supposed, would succeed without difficulty. They commenced the attack, but made no greater impression than the Medes : their spears were shorter than those of the Greeks and they had no room to employ their numbers. Finally, as none of their efforts won them an inch of the pass whether they attacked in divisions or in any other way, the Immortals drew off. It is said that, during these assaults, Xerxes, who sat watching, leapt three times from his throne in terror for his army.

On the following day the Persians succeeded no better. They came to grips again, imagining that as their enemies were so few, they must be surely disabled by their wounds and unable to meet them. But the Greeks had marshalled themselves in companies by their nations, and took it in turns to fight—excepting the Phocians who had been posted on the mountain to defend the pass. The Persians, finding things as they had been on the previous day, retired.

While the king was exceedingly perplexed what to do, a Mēlian called Ephialtes asked for an audience. Expecting to receive a great reward, he disclosed the pass leading to Thermopylae across the mountains, and doomed to death the Greeks who stood firm in the defile. Xerxes accepted the proposals of Ephialtes, and highly pleased sent off Hydarnes and his troop, who left the camp at the hour of lamp-lighting. Following the track, they marched all night, with the Oetaean hills on their right and the heights of Trāchis on their left, and at the first glimmer of dawn they found themselves on the summit. Here a thousand Phocians were stationed, to defend their own country and the pass. Now so long as they were climbing the mountain, which was covered with oaks, the Persians were invisible. It was a windless night, and as they were trampling over fallen leaves, they made a great rustling, at the noise of which the Phocians ran to arms. In a moment the Persians appeared, and were astonished to find men arming themselves. For they had expected to find not a soul in the way, and they had fallen on an army. Hydarnes, apprehending that they might prove to be Spartans, asked Ephialtes who they were : and when he learnt the truth, drew his men up to battle. However, the Phocians, assaulted with thick volleys of arrows and supposing themselves to be the chief object of attack, fled to the crest of the hill and prepared for death. But the Persians paid no attention to them and rapidly descended the mountain.

The Greeks in Thermopylae were first apprised of the death awaiting them at daybreak by the seer Megistias, who had inspected the entrails of the victims.[1] Some deserters also informed them of the outflanking Persian movement. These tidings were confirmed by their sentinels running down from the hills as dawn appeared. They then held a council, where opinions were divided ; some were for holding their post, others disagreed. After this they broke up, some going away and scattering to their several cities, and a part preparing to remain with Leonidas. It is said that the prince dismissed them of his own accord, through solicitude for their lives ; whereas it was not consistent with his own honour or with that of the Spartans in his company to forsake the post they had come to defend. To this view I am myself strongly inclined. Leonidas, I judge, perceiving his allies to have little will to see the danger out at his side, told them to go their ways. He thought it dishonourable to retreat himself : if he stayed, there was great fame in store for him, and the felicity of Sparta was not blotted out. For at the first stirring of this war his countrymen consulted the oracle about the campaign and were told by the priestess at Delphi that either Sparta must be destroyed by the foreigner or that a king of Sparta must die. I find strong evidence of the truth of this view from the case of the prophet Megistias, who followed the army. After he foretold their fate from the burnt offerings, Leonidas dismissed him, lest he should perish with the rest. But he refused

[1] The future was inferred by examining the entrails of animals sacrificed.

to forsake his friends, merely sending away his only son, who was serving with him.

The allies who were dismissed went their way as Leonidas had told them, and only the Thespians and Thebans remained with the Spartans—the Thebans by no wish of their own, but because Leonidas kept them as hostages, the Thespians wholly at their own desire ; they refused to leave Leonidas and his company, and stayed and died with him. Their captain was Dēmophilus, the son of Diadromes.

At sunrise Xerxes performed a number of libations : he then waited till the forenoon and attacked. The Greeks under Leonidas, knowing well that they were going to meet death, advanced much further than they had hitherto done to the broader part of the pass. Till now they had defended themselves behind their wall, and fought in the narrows : but now they joined battle outside the defile, and many of the Persians fell. Behind them were the captains of companies with whips, flogging and driving them continually forward. Many fell into the sea and perished, many more were trampled alive under foot by their own friends : and no one cared for the dying. The Greeks, knowing that death was coming from the Persians who were crossing the hill, put forth all their strength and fought like men reckless and possessed. By now their spears were mostly broken, and they used their swords against the Persians. In this struggle fell Leonidas, having greatly approved himself, and with him many Spartans of renown. Their names (as indeed those of all the 300) I have been at pains to discover. Many famous Persians also fell, among them two brothers of Xerxes.

There was a violent struggle between Spartans and Persians over the body of Leonidas, till the Greeks by their courage pulled his body away and four times routed their enemies. This fighting lasted till the coming of the party with Ephialtes. When the Greeks perceived their arrival, the battle wore another colour : they fell back on the narrows, crossed the wall, and posted themselves on the hillock in the mouth of the pass, where to-day the stone lion stands in honour of Leonidas. Here those with swords used them, and those who had none fought with hands and teeth, till they were buried under the volleys of the Persians, some of whom had thrown down the wall and attacked them in front, while others surrounded and shot at them from every side.

Such was the conduct of the Spartans and Thespians, but none distinguished themselves like Dieneces the Spartan. A certain Trachinian told him that when the Persians shot off their bows, the quantity of the arrows obscured the sun. Nothing daunted, he replied that this was good news, for if the Persians obscured the sun, the Greeks would fight them in the shade.

The slain were buried where they fell; and over them and over those who died before Leonidas dismissed his allies is an inscription:

> Go, tell to Sparta, thou that passest by,
> That here obedient to their words we lie.

The prophet has his own epitaph:

> Here famed Megistias lies, whom once the Mede
> Slew, when he left behind Spercheius' ford.
> The book of doom well did the prophet read,
> Yet brooked not to abandon Sparta's lord.

There is a story of two of the Three Hundred—Eurytus and Aristodemus—who were suffering from very bad ophthalmia and had been released from the army by Leonidas. Eurytus, on discovering that the Persians had turned the hill, called for his arms and, putting them on, told his slave to take him to the field of battle. The slave did this and then ran away, while his master entered the fray and fell. Aristodemus lacked spirit and stayed behind. Another story of Aristodemus' escape is that he was sent on a message from the army and might well have been in time for the battle, but that he deliberately lingered on the way and saved himself, whereas his fellow messenger returned and fell. On his return to Sparta he fell into public and private disgrace : no one would speak to him ; no one would give him fire ; and he received the abusive nickname of ' The Trembler '.[1]

The passages already quoted show how wide are the interests of Herodotus, how well he tells a story, and, we must add, how far he is from modern standards of historical truth. Yet, unscientific as he is, he has the greatest and rarest virtue of an historian, openmindedness. He describes the struggle in which Persia all but conquered Greece, and he is an ardent patriot. Yet he writes of the Persians without bitterness, and continually calls attention to their virtues. Will the English or German historians of the Great War be as just to their enemy ? Herodotus has that peculiar gift of sinking himself and his personal feelings, becoming interested by things for their own sake, and looking at foe and friend with equal disinterestedness. The following passage, with its quaint moralizing, partly explains his attitude. He has been describing how Cambÿses, King of Persia, profaned the Egyptian temples.

I HOLD it then in every way proved that Cambyses was very mad ; else he would never have set himself to deride religion and custom. For if it were proposed to all nations to choose which seemed best of all customs, each, after examination made, would place its own first ; so well is each persuaded that its own are by far the best. It is not therefore to be supposed that any, save a madman, would turn such things to ridicule. I will give this one proof among many from which it may be inferred that all men hold this belief about their customs :—When Darius was king, he summoned the Greeks who were with him and asked them what price would persuade them to eat their fathers' dead bodies. They answered that there was no price for which they would do it. Then he summoned those Indians who are called Callatiae, who eat their parents, and asked them (the Greeks being present and understanding by interpretation what was said) what would make them willing to burn their fathers at

---

[1] VII. 208 f. In this passage I have had the advantage of consulting an unpublished translation by Mr. J. Jackson, of which I have made considerable use. Aristodemus redeemed his disgrace at the battle of Plataea, where he fell.

death.[1] The Indians cried aloud, that he should not speak of so
horrid an act. So firmly rooted are these beliefs ; and it is,
I think, rightly said in Pindar's poem that use and wont is lord
of all.

  As this passage shows, Herodotus had a philosophy of life.
We may now glance at it. He has one foot in the coming age of
reason, but, unlike his great successor, he really belongs to the
unscientific age that was passing away. His views, which are
largely those of the ordinary Greek, are naïve, but strikingly
clear-sighted. Thus he thinks that a nation's history has three
stages : success ; then, as a consequence of success, arrogance
and injustice ; then, as a consequence of these, downfall. That,
he thought, was the moral of the defeat of Persia, and it would
be difficult to find any concise philosophy of history in general
to which facts give more support.
  The fortunes of Europe and of most of its inhabitants since
1914 might be taken to illustrate the philosophy of life which
my concluding extracts put forward. The first passage is typical
of the Greek view of life, gloomy, yet too courageous to be called
pessimistic. The speakers are Persians discussing their prospects
before their great expedition, but the conversation is imaginary
and the voice is that of Herodotus.

WHEN they reached Abȳdos, Xerxes wished to survey
his whole army. The inhabitants, at his request, had
expressly constructed for him on a hill there a throne
of white marble. Here he sat and watched his army and fleet
below. And seeing the whole of the Dardanelles covered with
ships, and the whole beach and the plain of Abydos crowded
with men, Xerxes congratulated himself : and afterwards he
broke into tears. His uncle Artabanus noticed him and asked
him the reason of his change of feeling. And Xerxes answered :
' Pity came over me as I reflected on the shortness of human life,
and thought that in a hundred years none of this great multitude
will be alive.' Artabanus answered : ' There are things more
melancholy than this in our life. Short as it is, no human being

---

[1] The Greeks cremated their dead.

in this host or in the whole world is so happy, that he will not many times wish that he was dead rather than alive. Misfortunes befall us, diseases harass us, and make life, in spite of its shortness, seem long. So bad is life that death becomes a delightful refuge, and the jealousy[1] of God is revealed by the taste he gives us of the sweetness of the world.' Xerxes replied : ' Life is as you describe it, Artabanus, but let us say no more, nor remember its evils, while we are possessed of its good.' (Xerxes then asks Artabanus what he thinks of the Persian chances of victory, and, receiving a pessimistic answer, replies :) ' There is reason in what you say, but you ought not to see danger everywhere or to reckon every risk. If, whatever comes up, you are going to weigh everything alike, you will never do anything. It is better to be always an optimist and to suffer half the amount of evil, than always to be full of gloomy anticipations and never suffer any-thing at all. If you attack every proposal made without showing us the right course to follow, you will come to grief as much as those whom you oppose. The scales are evenly balanced : how can a human being know certainly which way they will incline ? He cannot. But success generally attends those who wish to act ; and it does not attend those who are timid and balance every-thing. You see the great power which Persia has attained. If my predecessors on the throne had held your views, or without holding them had had counsellors like you, you would have never seen our kingdom become so great. It is by taking risks that they made us what we are. Great things are achieved through great dangers.'[2]

There is a Shakespearian ripeness of wisdom in these words, tinged with melancholy, full of courage and springing from profound experience of life.

If life is as Herodotus thought it, what is happiness ? Croesus, the great king of Lydia, at the height of his power put some such question to the Athenian law-giver Sōlon, expecting to be told

---

[1] This doctrine of God's jealousy of human happiness is found elsewhere in early Greek literature.
[2] VII. 44 f.

that he, Croesus, was the happy man. The conversation no doubt is imaginary, but the story illustrates Herodotus' narrative power, his dramatic sense, and his view of life. The phrase ' Call no man happy till he is dead ' is characteristic of an age of insecurity, but Solon's conception of happiness is still more worthy of note. The story may be regarded as a play in three acts.

Act I:

THERE came to the city [1] all the teachers from Hellas who then lived, in this or that manner ; and among them came Solon of Athens : he, having made laws for the Athenians at their request, left his home for ten years and set out on a voyage to see the world, as he said. This he did, lest he should be compelled to repeal any of the laws he had made, since the Athenians themselves could not repeal them, for they were bound by solemn oaths to abide for ten years by such laws as Solon should make.

For this reason, and to see the world, Solon left Athens and visited Amāsis in Egypt and Croesus at Sardis : and when he had come, Croesus entertained him in his palace. Now on the third or fourth day after his coming Croesus bade his servants lead Solon round among his treasures, and they showed him all that was there, the greatness and the prosperous state of it ; and when he had seen and considered all, Croesus when occasion served thus questioned him : ' Our Athenian guest, we have heard much of you, by reason of your wisdom and your wanderings, how that you have travelled far to seek knowledge and to see the world. Now therefore I am fain to ask you, if you have ever seen a man more blest than all his fellows.' So Croesus inquired, supposing himself to be blest beyond all men. But Solon spoke the truth without flattery : ' Such an one, O King,' he said, ' I have seen—Tellus of Athens.' Croesus wondered at this, and sharply asked Solon, ' How do you judge Tellus to be most blest ? ' Solon replied : ' Tellus' city was prosperous, and he was the father of noble sons, and he saw children born to all

[1] Sardis, the capital of Croesus.

of them and their state well stablished ; moreover, having then as much wealth as a man may among us, he crowned his life with a most glorious death : for in a battle between the Athenians and their neighbours at Eleusis he attacked and routed the enemy and most nobly there died ; and the Athenians gave him public burial where he fell and paid him great honour.'

Now when Solon had admonished Croesus by recounting the many ways in which Tellus was blest, the king further asked him whom he placed second after Tellus, thinking that assuredly the second prize at least would be his. Solon answered : ' Cleobis and Biton. These were Argives, and besides sufficient wealth they had such strength of body as I will show. Both were prize-winners ; and this story too is related of them. There was a festival of Hēre toward among the Argives, and their mother must by all means be drawn to the temple by a yoke of oxen. But the oxen did not come in time from the fields ; so the young men, being thus thwarted by lack of time, put themselves to the yoke and drew the carriage with their mother sitting thereon : for five-and-forty furlongs they drew it till they came to the temple. Having done this, and been seen by the assembly, they made a most excellent end of their lives, and the gods showed by these men how that it was better for a man to die than to live. For the men of Argos came round and gave the youths joy of their strength, and so likewise did the women to their mother, for the excellence of her sons. She then in her joy at what was done and said, came before the image of the goddess and prayed that her sons Cleobis and Biton, who had done such great honour to the goddess, should be given the best boon that a man may receive. After the prayer the young men sacrificed and ate of the feast ; then they lay down to sleep in the temple itself and never rose up more, but here ended their lives. Then the Argives made and set up at Delphi images of them because of their excellence.'

So Solon gave to Cleobis and Biton the second prize of happiness. But Croesus said in anger, ' Guest from Athens ! is our prosperity, then, held by you so worthless that you match us not even with common men ? ' ' Croesus,' said Solon, ' you ask me concerning the lot of man ; well I know how jealous is Heaven and how it loves to trouble us. In a man's length of days he may see and suffer many things that he much mislikes. For I set the limit of man's life at seventy years ; in these seventy are days twenty-five thousand and two hundred, and one may well say that no one of all these days is like another in that which it brings. Thus then, Croesus, the whole of man is but chance. Now if I am to speak of you, I say that I see you very rich and the king of many men. But I cannot yet answer your question, before I hear that you have ended your life well. For he who is very rich is not more blest than he who has but enough for the day, unless fortune so attend him that he ends his life well, having all good things about him. Many men of great wealth are unblest, and many that have no great substance are fortunate. Now the very rich man who is yet unblest has but two advantages over the fortunate man, but the fortunate man has many advantages over the rich but unblest : for this latter is the stronger to accomplish his desire and to bear the stroke of great calamity ; but these are the advantages of the fortunate man, that though he be not so strong as the other to deal with calamity and desire, yet these are kept far from him by his good fortune, and he is free from deformity, sickness, and all evil, and happy in his children and his comeliness. If then such a man besides all this shall also end his life well, then he is the man whom you seek, and is worthy to be called blest ; but we must wait till he be dead, and call him not yet blest, but fortunate. Now no one (who is but man) can have all these good things together, just as no land is altogether self-sufficing in what it produces : one thing it has, another it lacks, and the best land is that which has most ; so too no single person is sufficient for himself : one thing he has, another he lacks ; but whoever continues in the possession of most things, and at last makes a gracious end of his life, such a man, O King, I deem worthy of this title. We must look to the conclusion of every matter, and see how it shall end, for there are many to whom Heaven has given a vision of blessedness, and yet afterwards brought them to utter ruin.'

So spoke Solon : Croesus therefore gave him no largess, but sent him away as a man of no account, for he thought that man to be very foolish who disregarded present prosperity and bade him look rather to the end of every matter.[1]

Act II :

BUT after Solon's departure, the divine anger fell heavily on Croesus : as I guess, because he supposed himself to be blest beyond all other men. Presently, as he slept, he was visited by a dream, which foretold truly to him the evil which should befall his son. He had two sons, one of whom was wholly undone, for he was deaf and dumb, but the other, whose name was Atys, was in every way far pre-eminent over all of his years. The dream then showed to Croesus that Atys should be smitten and killed by a spear of iron. So Croesus, when he woke and considered the dream with himself, was greatly affrighted by it ; and first he made a marriage for his son, and moreover, whereas Atys was wont to lead the Lydian armies, Croesus now would not suffer him to go out on any such enterprise, while he took the javelins and spears and all such instruments of war from the men's apartments and piled them up in his storehouse, lest any of them should fall upon his son from where it hung.

Now while Croesus was busied about the marriage of his son, there came to Sardis a Phrygian of the royal house, in great distress and with hands unclean. This man came to Croesus' house, and entreated that he might be purified after the custom of the country ; so Croesus purified him (the Lydians use the same manner of purification as do the Greeks), and when he had done all according to usage, he inquired of the Phrygian whence he came and who he was : ' Friend,' said he, ' who are you, and from what place in Phrygia do you come to be my suppliant ?

[1] I. 29 f.

and what man or woman have you slain ? ' ' O King,' the man answered, ' I am the son of Gordias the son of Mĭdas, and my name is Adrastus ; by no will of mine, I slew my brother, and hither I am come, banished by my father and bereft of all.' Croesus answered, ' All of your family are my friends, and to friends you have come, among whom you shall lack nothing but abide in my house. And for your misfortune, bear it as lightly as may be and you will be the more profited.'

So Adrastus lived in Croesus' house. About this same time there appeared on the Mysian Olympus a great monster of a boar, who would issue out from that mountain and ravage the fields of the Mysians. Often had the Mysians gone out against him : but they never did him any harm and rather were themselves hurt thereby. At last they sent messengers to Croesus, with this message : ' King, a great monster of a boar has appeared in the land, who destroys our fields ; for all our attempts, we cannot kill him ; now therefore, we beseech you, send with us your son, and chosen young men and dogs, that we may rid the country of him.' Such was their entreaty, but Croesus remembered the prophecy of his dream and thus answered them : ' Say no more about my son : I will not send him with you : he is newly married, and that is his present business. But I will send chosen men of the Lydians, and all the hunt, and I will bid those who go to use all zeal in aiding you to rid the country of this beast.'

So he replied, and the Mysians were satisfied with this. But the son of Croesus now came in, who had heard the request of the Mysians ; and when Croesus refused to send his son with them, ' Father,' said the young man, ' it was formerly held fairest and noblest that we princes should go constantly to war and the chase and win thereby renown ; but now you have barred me from both of these, not for any sign that you have seen in me of a coward or craven spirit. With what face can I thus show myself whenever I go to and from the market-place ? What will the men of the city think of me, and what my new-wedded

wife ? With what manner of man will she think that she dwells ?
Nay, do you either let me go to this hunt, or show me by reason
good that what you are doing is best for me.'

' My son,' answered Croesus, ' if I do this, it is not that I have
seen cowardice or aught unseemly in you ; no, but the vision
of a dream stood over me in my sleep, and told me that your
life should be short, for you should be slain by a spear of iron. It
is for that vision that I was careful to make your marriage, and
send you on no enterprise that I have in hand, but keep guard
over you, so that haply I may trick death of you through my
lifetime. You are my only son : for that other, since his hearing
is lost to him, I count no son of mine.'

' Father,' the youth replied, ' none can blame you for keeping
guard over me, when you have seen such a vision ; but it is my
right to show you this which you do not perceive, and wherein
you mistake the meaning of the dream. You say that the dream
told you that I should be killed by a spear of iron ; but has a boar
hands ?   Has it that iron spear which you dread ?   Had the
dream said I should be slain by a tusk or some other thing belonging to a boar, you had been right in acting as you act ; but no,
it was to be a spear. Therefore, since it is not against men that
we are to fight, suffer me to go.'

Croesus answered, ' My son, your judgement concerning the
dream does somewhat overpersuade me ; and being so convinced
by you I change my purpose and permit you to go to the
chase.'

Having said this, Croesus sent for Adrastus the Phrygian and
when he came thus addressed him : ' Adrastus, when you were
smitten by grievous misfortune, for which I blame you not, it
was I who cleansed you, and received and still keep you in my
house, defraying all your charges. Now therefore (as you owe
me a return of good service for the benefits which I have done
you) I ask you to watch over my son as he goes out to the chase.
See to it that no ruffian robbers meet you on the way, to do you
harm. Moreover it is but right that you too should go where

you can win renown by your deeds. That is fitting for your
father's son ; and you are strong enough withal.'

' O King,' Adrastus answered, ' had it been otherwise, I would
not have gone forth on this enterprise. One so unfortunate as
I should not consort with the prosperous among his peers ; nor
have I the wish so to do, and for many reasons I would have
held back. But now, since you so desire and I must do your
pleasure (owing you as I do a requital of good service), I am
ready to obey you in this ; and for your son, in so far as I can
protect him, look for his coming back unharmed.'

So when Adrastus had thus answered Croesus they went out
presently equipped with a company of chosen young men and
dogs. When they had come to Mount Olympus they hunted for
the beast, and having found him they made a ring and threw
their spears at him : then the guest called Adrastus, the man
who had been cleansed of the deed of blood, missed the boar
with his spear and hit the son of Croesus. So Atys was smitten
by the spear and fulfilled the utterance of the dream. One ran
to bring Croesus word of what had been done, and came to
Sardis, where he told the king of the fight and the manner of
his son's end.

Croesus, distraught by the death of his son, cried out the more
vehemently because the slayer was one whom he himself had
cleansed of a bloody deed, and in his great and terrible grief at
this mischance he called on Zeus by three names—Zeus the
Purifier, Zeus of the Hearth, Zeus of Comrades : the first,
because he would have the god know what evil his guest had
wrought him ; the second, because he had received the guest
into his house and thus unwittingly entertained the slayer of
his son ; and the third, because he had found his worst foe in
the man whom he sent as a protector.

Soon came the Lydians, bearing the dead corpse, with the
slayer following after. He then came and stood before the body
and gave himself wholly into Croesus' power, holding out his
hands and praying the king to slay him where he stood by the

dead man : ' Remember,' he said, ' my former mischance, and see how besides that I have undone him who purified me ; indeed, it is not fit that I should live.' On hearing this Croesus, though his own sorrow was so great, took pity on Adrastus and said to him, ' Friend, I have from you all that justice asks, since you deem yourself worthy of death. But it is not you that I hold the cause of this evil, save in so far as you were the unwilling doer of it : rather it is the work of a god, the same who told me long ago what was to be.' So Croesus buried his own son in such manner as was fitting. But Adrastus, son of Gordias who was son of Midas, this Adrastus, the slayer of his own brother and of the man who purified him, when the tomb was undisturbed by the presence of men, slew himself there by the sepulchre, seeing now clearly that he was the most ill-fated wretch of all men whom he knew.[1]

Act III. Alarmed by the growing power of Persia, Croesus determined to destroy it betimes. But he was defeated by Cyrus,[2] the Persian king, and his capital taken.

I WILL now tell what befell Croesus himself. He had a son, of whom I have already spoken, a likely youth enough save that he was dumb. Now in his past days of prosperity Croesus had done all that he could for his son ; and besides resorting to other plans he had sent to Delphi to inquire of the oracle concerning him. The Pythian priestess thus answered him :

' Lydian, of many the lord, thou know'st not the boon that thou
     askest.
Wish not nor pray that the voice of thy son may be heard in the
     palace ;
Better it were for thee that dumb he abide as aforetime ;
Luckless that day shall be when first thou hearest him speaking.'

So at the taking of the fortress a certain Persian, not knowing who Croesus was, came at him with intent to kill him. Croesus

---

[1] I. 34 f.   [2] The Cyrus of the Bible.

saw him coming, but by stress of misfortune he was past caring, and would as soon be smitten to death as not ; but his dumb son, seeing the Persian coming, in his fear and his grief broke into speech and cried, ' Man, do not kill Croesus ! ' This was the first word he uttered ; and after that for all the days of his life he had power of speech.

So the Persians took Sardis and made Croesus himself prisoner, he having reigned fourteen years and been besieged fourteen days, and, as the oracle foretold, brought his own great empire to an end. Having then taken him they led him to Cyrus. Cyrus had a great pyre built, on which he set Croesus, bound in chains, and twice seven Lydian boys beside him : either his intent was to sacrifice these firstfruits to some one of his gods, or he desired to fulfil a vow, or it may be that, learning that Croesus was a god-fearing man, he set him for this cause on the pyre, because he would fain know if any deity would save him from being burnt alive. It is related then that he did this ; but Croesus, as he stood on the pyre, remembered even in his evil plight how divinely inspired was that saying of Solon, that no living man was blest. When this came to his mind, having till now spoken no word, he sighed deeply and groaned, and thrice uttered the name of Solon. Cyrus heard it, and bade his inter-preters ask Croesus who was this on whom he called ; they came near and asked him ; Croesus at first would say nothing in answer, but presently, being compelled, he said, ' It is one with whom I would have given much wealth that all sovereigns should hold converse.' This was a dark saying to them, and again they questioned him of the words which he spoke. As they were instant, and troubled him, he told them how Solon, an Athenian, had first come, and how he had seen all his royal state and made light of it (saying thus and thus), and how all had happened to Croesus as Solon said, though he spoke with less regard to Croesus than to mankind in general and chiefly those who deemed them-selves blest. While Croesus thus told his story, the pyre had already been kindled and the outer parts of it were burning.

Then Cyrus, when he heard from the interpreters what Croesus said, repented of his purpose. He bethought him that he, being also a man, was burning alive another man who had once been as fortunate as himself; moreover, he feared the retribution, and it came to his mind that there was no stability in human affairs : wherefore he gave command to quench the burning fire with all speed and bring Croesus and those with him down from the pyre. But his servants could not for all their endeavour now master the fire.

Then (so the Lydians relate), when Croesus was aware of Cyrus' repentance and saw all men striving to quench the fire but no longer able to check it, he cried aloud to Apollo, praying that if the god had ever been pleased with any gift of his offering he would now come to his aid and save him from present destruction. Thus with weeping he invoked the god ; and suddenly in a clear and windless sky clouds gathered and a storm burst and there was a most violent rain, so that the pyre was quenched. Then indeed Cyrus perceived that Croesus was a good man and one beloved of the gods ; and bringing him down from the pyre, he questioned him, saying, ' What man persuaded you, Croesus, to attack my country with an army, and be my enemy instead of my friend ? ' ' O King,' said Croesus, ' it was I who did it, and brought thereby good fortune to you and ill to myself ; but the cause of all was the god of the Greeks, in that he encouraged me to send my army. No man is so foolish as to desire war more than peace : for in peace sons bury their fathers, but in war fathers bury their sons. But I must believe that heaven willed all this so to be.' [1]

[1] I. 85 f.

THUCYDIDES

VII

HISTORY : THUCYDIDES

Of what historian, then, do you say that he best knew the art of telling things as they really happened ? Bare chronicles apart, I suppose Thucydides.—JOHN MORLEY.

This day I finished Thucydides, after reading him with inexpressible interest and admiration. He is the greatest historian that ever lived.—MACAULAY. 27 Feb. 1835.

I am still of the same mind.—ID. 30 May 1836.

THŪCYDIDES was born about 471 B.C. ; related to some of the great families in Athens, he was a rich man with mining interests in North Greece, where he commanded the Athenian fleet in 424. Banished in that year for failing to prevent loss of the important town of Amphipolis, he was not allowed to return to Athens till the end of the war in 404. It is to this accident perhaps that we owe his History, and, in part, its impartiality : for he travelled, and saw the war from the side of the enemies of Athens. He died in the early years of the fourth century. Like Herodotus, he is not a study-historian, but a man of action who knew the world. His history traces the origins of the great war between the Athenian Empire and Sparta and her allies, and its course to 411 B.C., ending in a broken sentence.

In passing from Herodotus to Thucydides, history suffers a contraction from the known universe to a war between two leagues of small Greek states. The countless figures that pass across the stage of the older historian are gone : few faces meet us in Thucydides. It is not even a complete history of the brief period which it covers ; we hear hardly anything of commerce, religion, home politics, social life, literature, or art, and though it is the history of a war, the descriptions of the battles, with a few exceptions, are not minute. ' It was the phenomenon of the empire of Athens—an empire governed by a democracy—a new thing in the history of the world—that captured the interest of Thucydides. He did not take his pen to celebrate ; his aim was to understand—to observe critically how the empire behaved in the struggle which was to test its powers.' [1] In style, as

[1] Bury, *Ancient Greek Historians*, p. 78.

in subject and attitude, he is a contrast to Herodotus. In narrative Thucydides is for the most part lucid and direct, though he has not the fluent simplicity of his predecessor ; but in the speeches and political disquisitions the style is often artificial, obscure, and even ungrammatical, though deriving a singular power from the giant intellect that here wrestles with new methods of expression. The power of his narrative may be judged from the following vivid and tragic story, told with characteristic restraint. Some Thracian mercenaries, who had come too late for the Athenian expedition to Syracuse, were sent home. On their way their commander led them against a small Boeotian town.

HE passed the night unperceived at the temple of Hermes, which is distant from Mycalessus about two miles, and at the dawn of day he assaulted and captured the city, which is not large. The inhabitants were taken off their guard ; for they never imagined that an enemy would come and attack them at so great a distance from the sea. The walls were weak, and in some places had fallen down ; in others they were built low ; while the citizens, in their sense of security, had left their gates open. The Thracians dashed into the town, sacked the houses and temples, and slaughtered the inhabitants. They spared neither old nor young, but cut down, one after another, all whom they met, the women and children, the very beasts of burden, and every living thing which they saw. For the Thracians, when they dare, can be as bloody as the worst barbarians. There in Mycalessus the wildest panic ensued, and destruction in every form was rife. They even fell upon a boys' school, the largest in the place, which the children had just entered, and massacred them every one. No calamity could be worse than this, touching as it did the whole city, none was ever so sudden or so terrible.[1]

Macaulay thought Thucydides the greatest historian of the world, and he is certainly one of the most powerful thinkers in Greek literature. Though a younger contemporary of Herodotus,

[1] VII. 29. The quotations, with the exception of the Funeral Speech, are from Jowett's translation.

as a thinker he is ages in advance of him, and we can measure by the difference between the two men the astounding development of Athenian thought under the influence of the sophists. He is almost more modern than ourselves. What qualities have won him the praise of historians and thinkers ? Not only (unlike Herodotus) is he very accurate, but he has the detached impartiality which we have noticed in Herodotus, carried to an even higher power. It is almost incredible that contemporary history should be unbiased. Yet, though the microscope of criticism has tested Thucydides, there are not more than one or two instances where he has been suspected of unfairness, and there are none where the charge has been certainly proved. He was an Athenian patriot, but the reader could hardly guess from his History whether he was Athenian or Spartan ; not only is he fair to both sides, but he knows and brings out the strong and weak points of both (p. 203 f.). He is equally detached where he is personally concerned, as we have already seen (p. 11).

Then he is the first scientific historian ; his aim is truth. The spirit of the sentences in which he sums up his methods could not be bettered.

OF the events of the war I have not ventured to speak from any chance information nor according to any notion of my own : I have described nothing but what I either saw myself, or learned from others of whom I made the most careful and particular inquiry. The task was laborious, because eye-witnesses of the same occurrences gave different accounts of them, as they remembered or were interested in one side or the other. And very likely the strictly historical character of my narrative may be disappointing to the ear. But if he who desires to have before his eyes a true picture of the events which have happened, shall pronounce what I have written useful, then I shall be satisfied. My history is an everlasting possession, not a prize composition which is heard and forgotten.[1]

And he is scientific in a further sense. His opening chapters have won the admiration of historians for their anticipation of the sciences ancillary to history. ' Let those who deny that Thucydides was a sociologist . . . re-read his account of the evolution of

[1] I. 22.

Greek society from the earliest times to his own day. Let those who cry up anthropology examine into his treatment of legend and custom, and his power, untrained in Seminar or Institute, to use it as sociological evidence. Let the geographers . . . refresh their minds by recalling those brilliant sallies in geographical thinking, in which he explains some of the features of early Greek settlement and city-building. It is not only orthodox history, of the school of Ranke, of which Thucydides is the father and inspirer : there is not one of the many movements which have sought to broaden out historical study in recent years, from Buckle and Leplay and Vidal Lablache down to the psycho-analysts of our own day and of to-morrow, who will not find in Thucydides some gleaming anticipation along the path of their own thought.' [1]

For history to be history at all, it must be accurate, scientific, impartial, and these qualities are possessed by a number of modern historians. For it to be great history it must be written with imagination. Events and scenes must be pictured, personalities brought to life, till we seem to live in the world which the historian describes. Whether Thucydides has this power can be judged from the passages quoted below. But the historian must also have something of the tragic poet's power. In the scenes and figures that hurry across the stage, he must divine the clash of ideals, the working of inexorable laws, the ironies and tragedies of life. If he does this and conveys it to us, if his imagination perceives and his art renders the underlying significance of the whole, and yet never ignores or distorts facts, then, and then only, he ceases to be a mere chronicler, and becomes a great historian. This power of imagination is the fourth quality of Thucydides. He feels the tragedy of his story, and divines beneath the hard facts of it the ideas that give them life and meaning. Yet he remains accurate, scientific, impartial. Such a union of truth and imagination is not to be found in Gibbon, Macaulay, Froude, or any other English historian. It is found in Thucydides, and that, no doubt, is why he has been called the greatest of historians. His History has the tragic quality of Shakespeare or Aeschylus, yet the veracity of scientific work.

Finally, Thucydides is the first political thinker of Greece, and, in the opinion of some judges, the greatest. E. A. Freeman could say of him—it is an exaggeration—' There is hardly a problem in the science of government, which the statesman will not

[1] A. E. Zimmern, *The Greek Legacy*, p. 341 f.

find handled, if not solved, in the pages of this universal master.'[1] A politician and soldier, he is in closer touch with facts of life than either Plato or Aristotle. He had lived with the philosophers of his day ; he had mixed with men and had played a part in politics ; and his exile enlarged his experience and brought him in contact with foreign peoples. His political thinking is largely to be found in the imaginary speeches which he inserts in his History, the one unscientific thing in it. For though he professes to have given the speaker's sentiments as far as he could, it is impossible to doubt that the thoughts are often those of Thucydides.

A double thread runs through the History of Thucydides : the destruction of the Athenian empire by Sparta and her allies ; and by the side of this destruction and partly responsible for it, the decline of that empire from a liberal and idealistic democracy into a tyrannical state. It is characteristic of the dramatic method of Thucydides that he never calls our attention to this double plot, but makes us aware of it by simply telling the story. The following extracts are chosen to show the development of the twofold tragedy. The first shows Athenian and Spartan characters as seen by an outsider. The speaker is a Corinthian urging the Spartans to declare war on Athens.

'YOU have never considered what manner of men are these Athenians with whom you will have to fight, and how utterly unlike yourselves. They are revolutionary, equally quick in the conception and in the execution of every new plan ; while you are conservative—careful only to keep what you have, originating nothing, and not acting even when action is most urgent. They are bold beyond their strength ; they run risks which prudence would condemn ; and in the midst of misfortune they are full of hope. Whereas it is your nature, though strong, to act feebly ; when your plans are most prudent, to distrust them ; and when calamities come upon you, to think that you will never be delivered from them. They are impetuous, and you are dilatory ; they are always abroad, and you are always at home. For they hope to gain something by leaving their homes ; but you are afraid that any new enterprise may

[1] *Hist. Essays*, 2nd series, iii.

imperil what you have already. When conquerors, they pursue their victory to the utmost; when defeated, they fall back the least. Their bodies they devote to their country as though they belonged to other men; their true self is their mind, which is most truly their own when employed in her service. When they do not carry out an intention which they have formed, they seem to themselves to have sustained a personal bereavement; when an enterprise succeeds, they have gained a mere instalment of what is to come; but if they fail, they at once conceive new hopes and so fill up the void. With them alone to hope is to have, for they lose not a moment in the execution of an idea. This is the lifelong task, full of danger and toil, which they are always imposing upon themselves. None enjoy their good things less, because they are always seeking for more. To do their duty is their only holiday, and they deem the quiet of inaction to be as disagreeable as the most tiresome business. If a man should say of them, in a word, that they were born neither to have peace themselves nor to allow peace to other men, he would simply speak the truth.

' In the face of such an enemy, Lacedaemonians, you persist in doing nothing. You do not see that peace is best secured by those who use their strength justly, but whose attitude shows that they have no intention of submitting to wrong. Justice with you seems to consist in giving no annoyance to others and in defending yourselves only against positive injury. But this policy would hardly be successful, even if your neighbours were like yourselves; and in the present case, as we pointed out just now, your ways compared with theirs are old-fashioned. And, as in the arts, so also in politics, the new must always prevail over the old. In settled times the traditions of government should be observed: but when circumstances are changing and men are compelled to meet them, much originality is required.'[1]

This extract gives an idea of the Athenian as he was. The following speech by Pericles, made in the winter of 431 B.C.,

[1] I. 70 f.

describes the national ideal as that statesman conceived it, and might be entitled ' What Athens stood for '. The opening paragraphs explain its occasion ; the rest represents the ideals of Pericles, though not necessarily reproducing his words. The speech brings the mind of a fifth-century Athenian before us, and is as closely packed with thought as an essay of Bacon. In the first half of c. 40, for instance, Thucydides touches on the enjoyment of literary and artistic pleasures without great wealth, on their consistency with sturdiness of character, on the use of money, on the right attitude to poverty, on the part of politics in a citizen's life, on the question whether thought impairs a man's power to act. Note especially the definition of democracy (37), the splendid description of patriotism, its motives and its fruits (42–3), and the way in which Pericles and his age, with no definite hope of a future life, face the bereavements of a great war (44). In certain points the contrast between the austere discipline of Sparta and the freer life of Athens (39) reads like a comparison between pre-war Prussia and Britain. Fully to appreciate the speech let the reader think : (1) How a speech by a modern statesman on the dead of 1914–18 would differ from it ; (2) Whether our ideal of a state is that which Pericles propounds, and whether we fall short or have gone beyond it.

(34) IN the same winter, following the law of their fathers, the Athenians held the first public funeral of those who had fallen in the war. The ceremony is as follows. The bones of the dead are exposed on a covered platform for three days, during which any one may place his personal offerings at their side. On the third day they are laid in ten coffins of cypress wood, one for each tribe, every man's bones in the coffin of his tribe ; these are put on carriages and driven to the grave. One empty bed covered with a winding sheet is also borne for the missing whose bodies were not recovered for burning. All who so desire, whether citizens or strangers, may join in the procession, and the women folk of the dead are at the graveside bewailing them. The interment takes place in the State burial ground, which is situated in the most beautiful suburb of the city. All Athenians who have died in war lie buried there, except those who fell at Marathon ; their valour was adjudged so conspicuous that the

funeral was held on the field of battle. When the coffins have been laid in the earth some speaker elected by the city for his wisdom and public estimation delivers an appropriate speech ; after this the gathering disperses. This is the customary ceremonial, and it was adhered to throughout the war whenever occasion arose. It was at the funeral of this first group of fallen that Pericles the son of Xanthippus was elected to speak. When the moment came, he stepped forward from the graveside on to a high platform made for the occasion, so that his voice might carry as far as possible over the crowd, and spoke as follows :

(35) Most of those who have stood in this place before me have commended the institution of this closing address. It is good, they have felt, that solemn words should be spoken over our fallen soldiers. I do not share this feeling. Acts deserve acts, not words, in their honour, and to me a burial at the State's charges, such as you see before you, would have appeared sufficient. But since the wisdom of our ancestors enacted this law I too must submit and try to suit as best I can the wishes and feelings of every member of this gathering.

(36) My first words shall be for our ancestors ; it is both just to them and seemly that on an occasion such as this our tribute of memory should be paid them. For, dwelling always in this country, generation after generation in unchanging and unbroken succession, they have handed it down to us free by their exertions. So they are worthy of our praises ; and still more so are our fathers. For they enlarged the ancestral patrimony by the Empire which we hold to-day and delivered it, not without labour, into the hands of our own generation ; while it is we ourselves, those of us who are now in middle life, who consolidated our power throughout the greater part of the Empire and secured the city's complete independence both in war and peace. Of the battles which we and our fathers fought, whether in the winning of our power abroad or in bravely withstanding the warfare of foreigner or Greek at home, I do not wish to say more : they are too familiar to you all. I wish rather to set forth the spirit in which

we faced them, and the constitution and manners with which we rose to greatness, and to pass from them to the dead.

(37) Our government is not copied from those of our neighbours : [1] we are an example to them rather than they to us. Our constitution is named a democracy, because it is in the hands not of the few but of the many. But our laws secure equal justice for all in their private disputes, and our public opinion welcomes and honours talent in every branch of achievement, not for any sectional reason but on grounds of excellence alone. And as we give free play to all in our public life, so we carry the same spirit into our daily relations with one another. We have no black looks or angry words for our neighbour if he enjoys himself in his own way, and we abstain from the little acts of churlishness which, though they leave no mark, yet cause annoyance to whoso notes them. Open and friendly in our private intercourse, in our public acts we keep strictly within the control of law. We acknowledge the restraint of reverence ; we are obedient to those in authority, and to the laws, more especially to those which offer protection to the oppressed and those unwritten ordinances whose transgression brings admitted shame. (38) Yet ours is no workaday city only. No other provides so many recreations for the spirit— games and sacrifices all the year round, and beauty in our public buildings to cheer the heart and delight the eye day by day.[2]

(39) Our military training too is different from our opponents'. The gates of our city are flung open to the world. We practise no periodical deportations, nor do we prevent our visitors from observing or discovering what an enemy might usefully apply to his own purposes. For our trust is not in the devices of material equipment, but in our own good spirits for battle.

So too with education. They toil from early boyhood in

[1] *Not copied from those of our neighbours* : a reference to the Spartans. The next few chapters are full of covert references to Sparta, the home of Discipline, where men were afraid of Freedom and Originality, and to Corinth, the home of Licence, where men cared only for Riches.

[2] This paragraph contains the only mention of official religion in the whole speech. Note how it is sandwiched in amongst athletics, architecture, and commerce.

a laborious pursuit after courage, while we, free to live and wander as we please, march out none the less to face the self-same dangers. Indeed, if we choose to face danger with an easy mind rather than after a rigorous training, and to trust rather in native manliness than in state-made courage, the advantage lies with us ; for we are spared all the weariness of practising for future hardships, and when we find ourselves amongst them we are as brave as our plodding rivals. Here as elsewhere, then, the city sets an example which is deserving of admiration. (40) We are lovers of beauty without extravagance, and lovers of wisdom without unmanliness. Wealth to us is not mere means for display but an opportunity for achievement ; and poverty we think it no disgrace to acknowledge, but a real degradation to make no effort to overcome. Our citizens attend both to public and private duties, and do not allow absorption in their own various affairs to interfere with their knowledge of the city's. We differ from other states in regarding the man who holds aloof from public life not as 'quiet' but as useless ; [1] we decide or debate, carefully and in person, all matters of policy, holding, not that words and deeds go ill together, but that acts are foredoomed to failure when undertaken undiscussed. For we are noted for being at once most adventurous in action and most reflective beforehand. Other men are bold in ignorance, while reflection will stop their onset. But the bravest are surely those who have the clearest vision of what is before them, glory and danger alike, and yet notwithstanding go out to meet it. (41) In a word I claim that our city as a whole is an education to Greece, and that her members yield to none, man by man, for independence of spirit, manysidedness of attainment, and complete self-reliance in limbs and brain.

That this is no vainglorious phrase but actual fact, the supremacy which our manners have won us itself bears testi-

[1] *Not as 'quiet' but as useless* : these are the Mugwumps or small minority of Athenians who undertake no public service. 'Quiet' is what they like to call themselves as opposed to political 'busybodies'. But the fifth-century Athenians were proud of being busybodies.

mony. No other city of the present day goes out to her ordeal greater than ever men dreamed ; no other is so powerful that the invader feels no bitterness when he suffers at her hands, and her subjects no shame at the indignity of their dependence.[1] Great indeed are the symbols and witnesses of our supremacy, at which posterity, as all mankind to-day, will be astonished. We need no Homer or other man of words to praise us ; for such give pleasure for a moment, but the truth will put to shame their imaginings of our deeds. For our pioneers have forced a way into every sea and every land, establishing among all mankind, in punishment or beneficence, eternal memorials of their settlement.

Such then is the city for whom, lest they should lose her, the men whom we celebrate died a soldier's death : and it is but natural that all of us, who survive them, should wish to spend ourselves in her service. (42) That, indeed, is why I have spent many words upon the city. I wished to show that we have more at stake than men who have no such inheritance, and to support my praise of the dead by making clear to you what they have done. For if I have chanted the glories of the city it was these men and their like who made Athens great. With them, as with few among Greeks, words cannot exaggerate the deeds that they have done. Such an end as we have here seems indeed to show us what a good life is, from its first signs of power to its final consummation.[2] For even where life's previous record showed faults and failures it is just to weigh the last brave hour of devotion against them all.[3] There they wiped out evil with good and did the city more service as soldiers than they did

---

[1] *Her subjects no shame at the indignity of their dependence.* This is Pericles' theory of imperialism. The Empire is based, not on justice (as between equals) but on sentiment ; not on rights secured to the other cities, but on the admiring loyalty they ought to feel. If they do not happen to feel it, he has nothing to fall back upon but naked force.

[2] *What a good life is.* This is the subject of Aristotle's *Ethics*, which is often taken as giving the standard Greek view on Virtue or the good life. But of course Thucydides is a much better authority for the fifth-century Greeks.

[3] *The last brave hour* : compare the parable of the Labourers in the Vineyard.

her harm in private life. There no hearts grew faint because they loved riches more than honour ; none shirked the issue in the poor man's dream of wealth. All these they put aside to strike a blow for the city. Counting the quest to avenge her honour as the most glorious of all ventures, and leaving Hope, the uncertain goddess, to send them what she would, they faced the foe as they drew near him in the strength of their own manhood ; and when the shock of battle came, they chose rather to suffer the uttermost than to win life by weakness.[1] So their memory has escaped the reproaches of men's lips, but they bore instead on their bodies the marks of men's hands, and in a moment of time, at the climax of their lives, were rapt away from a world filled, for their dying eyes, not with terror but with glory.

(43) Such were the men who lie here and such the city that inspired them. We survivors may pray to be spared their bitter hour, but must disdain to meet the foe with a spirit less triumphant. Let us draw strength, not merely from twice-told arguments—how fair and noble a thing it is to show courage in battle—but from the busy spectacle of our great city's life as we have it before us day by day, falling in love with her as we see her, and remembering that all this greatness she owes to men with the fighter's daring, the wise man's understanding of his duty, and the good man's self-discipline in its performance—to men who sacrificed their lives as the best offerings on her behalf. So they gave their bodies to the commonwealth and received, each for his own memory, praise that will never die, and with it the grandest of all sepulchres, not that in which their mortal bones are laid, but a home in the minds of men, where their glory remains fresh to stir to speech or action as the occasion comes by. For the whole earth is the sepulchre of famous men ; and their story is not graven only on stone over their native earth, but lives

---

[1] *Rather to suffer the uttermost than to win life by weakness* : he does not pretend that, like the Christian martyrs, they died joyfully : only they feel that they could not die at a better moment or in a better way.

on far away, without visible symbol, woven into the stuff of other men's lives. For you now it remains to rival what they have done.

(44) Therefore I do not mourn with the parents of the dead who are here with us. I will rather comfort them. For they know that they have been born into a world of manifold chances and that he is to be accounted happy to whom the best lot falls— the best sorrow, such as is yours to-day, or the best death, such as fell to these, for whom life and happiness were cut to the self-same measure. I know it is not easy to give you comfort. I know how often in the joy of others you will have reminders of what was once your own, and how men feel sorrow, not for the loss of what they have never tested, but when something that has grown dear to them has been snatched away. But you must keep a brave heart in the hope of other children, those who are still of age to bear them. For the newcomers will help you to forget the gap in your own circle, and will help the city to fill up the ranks of its workers and its soldiers. For no man is fitted to give fair and honest advice in council if he has not, like his fellows, a family at stake in the hour of the city's danger. To you who are past the age of vigour I would say : count the long years of happiness so much gain to set off against the brief space that yet remains, and let your burden be lightened by the glory of the dead. For the love of honour alone is not staled by age, and it is by honour, not, as some say, by gold, that the helpless end of life is cheered.

(46) I have spoken such words as I had to say according as the law prescribes, and the graveside offerings to the dead have been duly made. Henceforward the city will take charge of their children till manhood : such is the crown and benefit she holds out to the dead and to their kin for the trials they have under-gone for her. For where the prize is highest, there, too, are the best citizens to contend for it.

And now, when you have finished your lamentation, let each of you depart.[1]

[1] II. 34 f. Translation and notes by A. E. Zimmern.

The following passage gives the character of Pericles, and, incidentally, shows the type of leader under which democracy is safe, and the type under which it is not.

DURING the peace while he was at the head of affairs he ruled with prudence ; under his guidance Athens was safe, and reached the height of her greatness in his time. When the war began he showed that here too he had formed a true estimate of the Athenian power. He survived the commencement of hostilities two years and six months ; and, after his death, his foresight was even better appreciated than during his life. For he had told the Athenians that if they would be patient and would attend to their navy, and not seek to enlarge their dominion while the war was going on, nor imperil the existence of the city, they would be victorious ; but they did all that he told them not to do, and in matters which seemingly had nothing to do with the war, from motives of private ambition and private interest they adopted a policy which had disastrous effects in respect both of themselves and of their allies ; their measures, had they been successful, would only have brought honour and profit to individuals, and, when unsuccessful, crippled the city in the conduct of the war. The reason of the difference was that he, deriving authority from his capacity and acknowledged worth, being also a man of transparent integrity, was able to control the multitude in a free spirit ; he led them rather than was led by them ; for, not seeking power by dishonest arts, he had no need to say pleasant things, but, on the strength of his own high character, could venture to oppose and even to anger them. When he saw them unseasonably elated and arrogant, his words humbled and awed them ; and, when they were depressed by groundless fears, he sought to reanimate their confidence. Thus Athens, though still in name a democracy, was in fact ruled by her greatest citizen. But his successors were more on an equality with one another, and, each one struggling to be first himself, they were ready to sacrifice the whole conduct of affairs to the whims of the people.[1]

[1] II. 65. For a story of Pericles see p. 396.

What hindered the ideas of Pericles from being realized ? First, as a minor cause, supervening on the war, the plague, which not only killed Pericles, and seriously impaired the strength of Athens, but brought demoralization with it. The passage illustrates Thucydides' exact observation, not only of medical details. He traces clearly the effect of physical conditions on character. I have omitted most of the physical symptoms, which are noted with great precision.

THE disease is said to have begun south of Egypt in Aethiopia ; thence it descended into Egypt and Libya, and after spreading over the greater part of the Persian Empire, suddenly fell upon Athens. It first attacked the inhabitants of the Piraeus,[1] and it was supposed that the Peloponnesians had poisoned the cisterns, no conduits having as yet been made there. It afterwards reached the upper city, and then the mortality became far greater. As to its probable origin or the causes which might or could have produced such a disturbance of nature, every man, whether a physician or not, will give his own opinion. But I shall describe its actual course, and the symptoms by which any one who knows them beforehand may recognize the disorder should it ever reappear. For I was myself attacked, and witnessed the sufferings of others.

The season was admitted to have been remarkably free from ordinary sickness ; and if anybody was already ill of any other disease, it was absorbed in this. Many who were in perfect health, all in a moment, and without any apparent reason, were seized with violent heats in the head and with redness and inflammation of the eyes. But the internal fever was intense ; the sufferers could not bear to have on them even the finest linen garment ; they insisted on being naked, and there was nothing which they longed for more eagerly than to throw themselves into cold water. And many of those who had no one to look after them actually plunged into the cisterns, for they were tormented by unceasing thirst, which was not in the least assuaged whether they drank little or much. They could not sleep ; a restlessness

[1] The harbour of Athens.

which was intolerable never left them. While the disease was at its height the body, instead of wasting away, held out amid these sufferings in a marvellous manner, and either they died on the seventh or ninth day, not of weakness, for their strength was not exhausted, but of internal fever, which was the end of most ; or if they survived, other complications set in : for the disorder which had originally settled in the head passed gradually through the whole body, and, if a person got over the worst, would often seize the extremities and leave its mark, attacking the fingers and the toes ; and some escaped with the loss of these, some with the loss of their eyes. Some again had no sooner recovered than they were seized with a forgetfulness of all things and knew neither themselves nor their friends.

The general character of the malady no words can describe, and the fury with which it fastened upon each sufferer was too much for human nature to endure. There was one circumstance in particular which distinguished it from ordinary diseases. The birds and animals which feed on human flesh, although so many bodies were lying unburied, either never came near them, or died if they touched them. This was proved by a remarkable disappearance of the birds of prey, which were not to be seen either about the bodies or anywhere else ; while in the case of the dogs the result was even more obvious, because they live with man.

Such was the general nature of the disease : I omit many strange peculiarities which characterized individual cases. None of the ordinary sicknesses attacked any one while it lasted, or, if they did, they ended in the plague. Some of the sufferers died from want of care, others equally who were receiving the greatest attention. No single remedy could be deemed a specific ; for that which did good to one did harm to another. No constitution was of itself strong enough to resist or weak enough to escape the attacks ; the disease carried off all alike and defied every mode of treatment. Most appalling was the despondency which seized upon any one who felt himself sickening ; for he instantly abandoned his mind to despair and, instead of holding out, absolutely threw away his chance of life. Appalling too was the rapidity with which men caught the infection, dying like sheep if they attended on one another; and this was the principal cause of mortality. When they were afraid to visit one another, the sufferers died in their solitude, so that many houses were empty because there had been no one left to take care of the sick; or if they ventured they perished, especially those who aspired to heroism. For they went to see their friends without thought of themselves and were ashamed to leave them, at a time when the very relations of the dying were at last growing weary and ceased even to make lamentations, overwhelmed by the vastness of the calamity. But whatever instances there may have been of such devotion, more often the sick and the dying were tended by the pitying care of those who had recovered, because they knew the course of the disease and were themselves free from apprehension. For no one was ever attacked a second time, or not with a fatal result. All men congratulated them, and they themselves, in the excess of their joy at the moment, had an innocent fancy that they could not die of any other sickness.

The crowding of the people out of the country into the city [1] aggravated the misery; and the newly-arrived suffered most. For, having no houses of their own, but inhabiting in the height of summer stifling huts, the mortality among them was dreadful, and they perished in wild disorder. The dead lay as they had died, one upon another, while others hardly alive wallowed in the streets and crawled about every fountain craving for water. The temples in which they lodged were full of corpses of those who died in them; for the violence of the calamity was such that men, not knowing where to turn, grew reckless of all law, human and divine. The customs which had hitherto been observed at funerals were universally violated, and they buried their dead each one as best he could. Many, having no proper appliances, because the deaths in their household had been so numerous already, lost all shame in the burial of the dead. When one man

---

[1] Owing to the invasion of Attica by the Peloponnesians.

had raised a funeral pile, others would come, and throwing on their dead first, set fire to it ; or when some other corpse was already burning, before they could be stopped, would throw their own dead upon it and depart.

There were other and worse forms of lawlessness which the plague introduced at Athens. Men who had hitherto concealed what they took pleasure in, now grew bolder. For, seeing the sudden change—how the rich died in a moment, and those who had nothing immediately inherited their property—they reflected that life and riches were alike transitory, and they resolved to enjoy themselves while they could, and to think only of pleasure. Who would be willing to sacrifice himself to the law of honour when he knew not whether he would ever live to be held in honour ? The pleasure of the moment and any sort of thing which conduced to it took the place both of honour and of expediency. No fear of Gods or law of man deterred a criminal. Those who saw all perishing alike, thought that the worship or neglect of the Gods made no difference. For offences against human law no punishment was to be feared ; no one would live long enough to be called to account. Already a far heavier sentence had been passed and was hanging over a man's head ; before that fell, why should he not take a little pleasure ? [1]

But the real ruin of Athenian ideals came through the war itself. The following analysis of the ' war-spirit ' is a fine example of the political thinking of Thucydides, and is more intelligible to Europe since 1914. Englishmen behave with more restraint than the excitable southerner. But mediaeval Italy and the French and the Russian Revolutions furnish illustrations of what Thucydides describes.

REVOLUTION brought upon the cities of Hellas many terrible calamities, such as have been and always will be while human nature remains the same, but which are more or less aggravated and differ in character with every new combination of circumstances. In peace and prosperity both

[1] II. 48 f.

states and individuals are actuated by higher motives, because
they do not fall under the dominion of imperious necessities ;
but war, which takes away the comfortable provision of daily
life, is a hard master and tends to assimilate men's characters
to their conditions.

When troubles had once begun in the cities, those who followed
carried the revolutionary spirit further and further, and determined to outdo the report of all who had preceded them by the
ingenuity of their enterprises and the atrocity of their revenges.
The meaning of words had no longer the same relation to things,
but was changed by them as they thought proper. Reckless
daring was held to be loyal courage ; prudent delay was the
excuse of a coward ; moderation was the disguise of unmanly
weakness ; to know everything was to do nothing. Frantic
energy was the true quality of a man. A conspirator who wanted
to be safe was a recreant in disguise. The lover of violence was
always trusted, and his opponent suspected. He who plotted
from the first to have nothing to do with plots was a breaker-up of
parties and a poltroon who was afraid of the enemy. In a word,
he who could outstrip another in a bad action was applauded,
and so was he who encouraged to evil one who had no idea of it.
The tie of party was stronger than the tie of blood, because
a partisan was more ready to dare without asking why. (For
party associations are not based upon any established law, nor
do they seek the public good ; they are formed in defiance of the
laws and from self-interest.) The seal of good faith was not
divine law, but fellowship in crime. If an enemy when he was
in the ascendant offered fair words, the opposite party received
them not in a generous spirit, but by a jealous watchfulness of his
actions. Revenge was dearer than self-preservation. Any agree-
ments sworn to by either party, when they could do nothing else,
were binding as long as both were powerless. But he who on
a favourable opportunity first took courage, and struck at his
enemy when he saw him off his guard, had greater pleasure in
a perfidious than he would have had in an open act of revenge ;

he congratulated himself that he had taken the safer course, and also that he had overreached his enemy and gained the prize of superior ability.

The cause of all these evils was the love of power, originating in avarice and ambition, and the party-spirit which is engendered by them when men are fairly embarked in a contest. For the leaders on either side used specious names, the one party professing to uphold the constitutional equality of the many, the other the wisdom of an aristocracy, while they made the public interests, to which in name they were devoted, in reality their prize. Striving in every way to overcome each other, they committed the most monstrous crimes; yet even these were surpassed by the magnitude of their revenges which they pursued to the very utmost, neither party observing any definite limits either of justice or public expediency, but both alike making the caprice of the moment their law. Either by the help of an unrighteous sentence, or grasping power with the strong hand, they were eager to satiate the impatience of party-spirit. Neither faction cared for religion; but any fair pretence which succeeded in effecting some odious purpose was greatly lauded. And the citizens who were of neither party fell a prey to both; either they were disliked because they held aloof, or men were jealous of their surviving.

Thus revolution gave birth to every form of wickedness in Hellas. The simplicity which is so large an element in a noble nature was laughed to scorn and disappeared. An attitude of perfidious antagonism everywhere prevailed; for there was no word binding enough, nor oath terrible enough to reconcile enemies. Each man was strong only in the conviction that nothing was secure; he must look to his own safety, and could not afford to trust others. Inferior intellects generally succeeded best. For, aware of their own deficiencies, and fearing the capacity of their opponents, for whom they were no match in powers of speech, and whose subtle wits were likely to anticipate them in contriving evil, they struck boldly and at once. But the cleverer sort, presuming in their arrogance that they would be aware in time, and disdaining to act when they could think, were taken off their guard and easily destroyed.

Now in Corcȳra most of these deeds were perpetrated, and for the first time. There was every crime which men could commit in revenge who had been governed not wisely, but tyrannically, and now had the oppressor at their mercy. There were the dishonest designs of others who were longing to be relieved from their habitual poverty, and were naturally animated by a passionate desire for their neighbour's goods ; and there were crimes of another class which men commit, not from covetousness, but from the enmity which equals foster towards one another until they are carried away by their blind rage into the extremes of pitiless cruelty. At such a time the life of the city was all in disorder, and human nature, which is always ready to transgress the laws, having now trampled them under foot, delighted to show that her passions were ungovernable, that she was stronger than justice, and the enemy of everything above her. If malignity had not exercised a fatal power, how could any one have preferred revenge to piety, and gain to innocence ? But, when men are retaliating upon others, they are reckless of the future, and do not hesitate to annul those common laws of humanity to which every individual trusts for his own hope of deliverance should he ever be overtaken by calamity ; they forget that in their own hour of need they will look for them in vain.[1]

The events which gave rise to and which illustrate these reflections were a struggle between the democratic and antidemocratic parties in the island of Corcyra. It is a fine example of Thucydides' descriptive writing—vivid, intense, restrained.

ON the following day they skirmished a little, and both parties sent messengers round the country inviting the slaves to join them, and promising them liberty ; the greater number came to the aid of the people, while the other

[1] III. 82 f.

faction was reinforced by eight hundred auxiliaries from the mainland.

After resting a day they fought again, and the people, who had the advantage in numbers and in the strength of their positions, gained the victory. Their women joined vigorously in the fray, hurling tiles from the housetops, and showing amid the uproar a fortitude beyond their sex. The conflict was decided towards evening; the oligarchy, fearing lest the people should take the arsenal with a sudden rush and so make an end of them, set fire to the private houses which surrounded the Market, as well as to the larger blocks of buildings, sparing neither their own property nor that of any one else in their determination to stop them. Much merchandise was burnt, and the whole city would have been destroyed if the wind had carried the flame in that direction. Both parties now left off fighting, and kept watch in their own positions during the night.[1]

The aristocrats were defeated. An Athenian fleet which arrived tried to make peace between the two parties, and took some of the aristocrats on board. But the democrats

DISEMBARKED those whom they had induced to go on board, and dispatched them; they also went to the temple of Here, and persuading about fifty of the suppliants to stand their trial condemned them all to death. The majority would not come out, and, when they saw what was going on, destroyed one another in the enclosure of the temple where they were, except a few who hung themselves on trees, or put an end to their own lives in any other way which they could. And, during the seven days which Eurymedon after his arrival remained with his sixty ships, the Corcyraeans continued slaughtering those of their fellow citizens whom they deemed their enemies; they professed to punish them for their designs against the democracy, but in fact some were killed from motives of personal enmity, and some by the hands of debtors who owed money to them. Every

[1] III. 73 f.

form of death was to be seen ; and everything, and more than everything, that commonly happens in revolutions, happened then. The father slew the son, and the suppliants were torn from the temples and slain near them ; some of them were even walled up in the temple of Dionȳsus, and there perished.[1]

We see from a speech by Cleon, who succeeded Pericles in the leadership of the democracy, the change in Athenian ideals that took place under pressure of the war. Mitylēne, a state in the Athenian Empire, had revolted and been reduced. It had been decided to put the male population to death : then a proposal was made to rescind the decision. In the Athenian assembly which decided its fate, Cleon argued for severity. His speech is interesting as a portrait of the man, and as a perfect expression of what we have learnt to call *Real-Politik*, though it has its representatives in every country, including our own. Certain passages might come straight from the *Morning Post*. His position is clear and plausible : ' Empires, whatever we may wish, must be founded on force ; generosity and clemency are only wasted on an enemy.' Note Cleon's curious argument on the advantages of stupidity and his picture of the weaknesses of the Athenian democracy—over-clever, unstable, the prey of a good speaker. Note too how fair Thucydides is to Cleon and his point of view : he makes clear that he possessed the greatest and rarest of virtues in a democratic statesman, courage in opposing his audience.

' I HAVE remarked again and again that a democracy cannot manage an empire, but never more than now, when I see you regretting your condemnation of the Mytilenaeans. Having no fear or suspicion of one another in daily life, you deal with your allies upon the same principle, and you do not consider that whenever you yield to them out of pity or are misled by their specious tales, you are guilty of a weakness dangerous to yourselves, and receive no thanks from them. You should remember that your empire is a despotism exercised over unwilling subjects, who are always conspiring against you ; they do not obey in return for any kindness which you do them to your own injury, but in so far as you are their masters ; they have no love of you,

[1] III. 81.

but they are held down by force. Besides, what can be more
detestable than to be perpetually changing our minds ?   We
forget that a state in which the laws, though imperfect, are
inviolable, is better off than one in which the laws are good but
ineffective.   Dullness and modesty are a more useful combination
than cleverness and licence ;   and the more simple sort generally
make better citizens than the more astute.   For the latter desire
to be thought wiser than the laws; they want to be always getting
their own way in public discussions ;   they think that they can
nowhere have a finer opportunity of displaying their intelligence,
and their folly generally ends in the ruin of their country ;
whereas the others, mistrusting their own capacity, admit that
the laws are wiser than themselves :   they do not pretend to
criticize the arguments of a great speaker ;   and being impartial
judges, not ambitious rivals, they hit the mark.   That is the
spirit in which we should act ;   not suffering ourselves to be so
excited by our own cleverness in a war of wits as to advise the
Athenian people contrary to our own better judgement.

' And you are to blame.   No men are better dupes, sooner
deceived by novel notions, or slower to follow approved advice.
You despise what is familiar, while you are worshippers of every
new extravagance.   You are always hankering after an ideal state,
but you do not give your minds even to what is straight before
you.   In a word, you are at the mercy of your own ears, and sit
like spectators attending a lecture, but very unlike counsellors
of a state.' [1]

Cleon then points out how abominably Mitylene has behaved :
mercy will encourage others to follow her bad example.

' I STILL maintain that you should abide by your former decision,
and not be misled either by pity, or by the charm of words, or
by a too forgiving temper.   There are no three things more
prejudicial   to   empire.   Mercy   should   be   reserved   for   the
merciful, and not thrown away upon those who will have no

[1] III. 37 f.

compassion on us, and who must by the force of circumstances always be our enemies. Our charming orators will still have an arena, but one in which the questions at stake will not be so grave, and the city will not pay so dearly for her brief pleasure in listening to them, while they for a good speech get a good fee. Lastly, forgiveness is naturally shown to those who, being reconciled, will continue friends, and not to those who will always remain what they were, and will abate nothing of their enmity. In one word, if you do as I say, you will do what is just to the Mytilenaeans, and also what is expedient for yourselves ; but, if you take the opposite course, they will not be grateful to you, and you will be self-condemned. For, if they were right in revolting, you must be wrong in maintaining your empire. But if, right or wrong, you are resolved to rule, then rightly or wrongly they must be chastised for your good. Otherwise you must give up your empire, and, when virtue is no longer dangerous, you may be as virtuous as you please. Punish them as they would have punished you. Be true then to yourselves, and recall as vividly as you can what you felt at the time ; think how you would have given the world to crush your enemies, and now take your revenge. Do not be soft-hearted at the sight of their distress, but remember the danger which was once hanging over your heads. Chastise them as they deserve, and prove by an example to your other allies that rebellion will be punished with death. If this is made quite clear to them, your attention will no longer be diverted from your enemies by wars against your own allies.' [1]

We pass on to see this theory full-grown and in practice. The small Dorian island of Mēlos wished to remain neutral in the war. The Athenians decided that they could not allow this. Thucydides gives the views of the two parties in the form of a dialogue, which is an example of *Real-Politik* at its extreme. A few sentences will show how far we have come from the ideals of Pericles.

Ath. ' We Athenians will use no fine words; we will not go

[1] III. 40.

out of our way to prove at length that we have a right to rule, or that we attack you now because we are suffering any injury at your hands. We should not convince you if we did ; nor must you expect to convince us by arguing that, although a colony of the Spartans, you have taken no part in their expeditions, or that you have never done us any wrong. But you and we should say what we really think, and aim only at what is possible, for we both alike know that into the discussion of human affairs the question of justice only enters where there is equal power to enforce it, and that the powerful exact what they can, and the weak grant what they must.'

Mel. ' Well, then, since you set aside justice and invite us to speak of expediency, in our judgement it is certainly expedient that you should respect a principle which is for the common good ; that to every man when in peril a reasonable claim should be accounted a claim of right. Your interest in this principle is quite as great as ours, inasmuch as you, if you fall, will incur the heaviest vengeance, and will be the most terrible example to mankind.'

Ath. ' The fall of our empire, if it should fall, is not an event to which we look forward with dismay ; for ruling states such as Sparta are not cruel to their vanquished enemies. With the Spartans, however, we are not now contending ; the real danger is from our many subject states, who may of their own motion rise up and overcome their masters. But this is a danger which you may leave to us. And we will now endeavour to show that we have come in the interests of our empire, and that in what we are about to say we are only seeking the preservation of your city. For we want to make you ours with the least trouble to ourselves, and it is for the interests of us both that you should not be destroyed.'

Mel. ' It may be your interest to be our masters, but how can it be ours to be your slaves ? '

Ath. ' To you the gain will be that by submission you will avert the worst; and we shall be all the richer for your preservation.' [1]

The Melians conclude by asserting their confidence in the help of heaven:

Ath. ' As for the Gods, we expect to have quite as much of their favour as you : for we are not doing or claiming anything which goes beyond common opinion about divine or men's desires about human things. For of the Gods we believe, and of men we know, that by a law of their nature, wherever they can rule, they will. This law was not made by us, and we are not the first who have acted upon it ; we did but inherit it, and shall bequeath it to all time, and we know that you and all mankind, if you were as strong as we are, would do as we do.' [2]

After a desperate resistance Melos was reduced, and its males put to death, the Athenians colonizing the island. The very next words of Thucydides deal with the plans of the Athenians to acquire control of Sicily—the origin of the great expedition, which overtaxed their strength and delivered them into their enemies' hands. First Melos, then, with a magnificent dramatic appropriateness, Syracuse. The whole of Books VI and VII should be read. They contain perhaps the finest piece of historical writing in existence. We see the confidence with which the fleet started, the first faint presages of failure, the courage and determination with which the Athenians pushed their ill-starred attempt, the combination of mistakes and ill luck through which it miscarried, the completeness of the final ruin. All this unrolls itself for us as it did for the hapless actors in the tragedy, step by step : the mind has a sense of impending disaster, but is unaware of its extent and meaning till it is complete. Here only the opening and the close of the story can be given. This is the account of the start from Athens in 415 B.C. :

EARLY in the morning of the day appointed for their departure, the Athenian forces and such of their allies as had already joined them went down to the Piraeus and began to man the ships. Almost the entire population of Athens accom-

---

[1] V. 89 f.   [2] V. 105.

panied them, citizens and strangers alike. The citizens came to take
farewell, one of an acquaintance, another of a kinsman, another of
a son, and as they passed along were full of hope and full of tears ;
hope of conquering Sicily, tears because they doubted whether
they would ever see their friends again, when they thought of the
long voyage on which they were going away. At the last moment
of parting the danger was nearer ; and terrors which had never
occurred to them when they were voting the expedition now
entered into their souls. Nevertheless their spirits revived at the
sight of the armament in all its strength and of the abundant
provision which they had made. The strangers and the rest of
the multitude came out of curiosity, desiring to witness an enterprise of which the greatness exceeded belief. Never had a greater
expedition been sent to a foreign land ; never was there an enterprise in which the hope of future success seemed to be better
justified by actual power.

When the ships were manned and everything required for the
voyage had been placed on board, silence was proclaimed by the
sound of the trumpet, and all with one voice before setting sail
offered up the customary prayers ; these were recited, not in each
ship separately, but by a single herald, the whole fleet accompany-
ing him. On every deck both the officers and the marines,
mingling wine in bowls, made libations from vessels of gold and
silver. The multitude of citizens and other well-wishers who were
looking on from the land joined in the prayer. The crews raised
the paean and, when the libations were completed, put to sea.
After sailing out some distance in single file, the ships raced with
one another as far as Aegīna ; thence they hastened onwards to
Corcyra, where the allies who formed the rest of the army were
assembling.[1]

We now see this brilliant expedition in a very different plight.
On its arrival in Sicily time was lost through disagreements
between the generals. But finally Syracuse was almost invested
(its capture would have given the Athenians the island), when the

[1] VI. 30.   For the paean see p. 113 n.

Spartans threw a force under Gylippus into the city. Inspirited by this the Syracusans seized a position on some heights called Epipolae, which made the investment impossible. Athens now made a desperate effort and sent out large reinforcements which for a time turned the tables. But an Athenian night attack was disastrously defeated; and by the summer of 413 it became clear that they would not take Syracuse, and must retreat before it was too late. The chief Athenian generals were Nicias and Demosthenes; the latter a brave and efficient soldier, the former an honest and religious man, whose respectability had won the trust of Athens. But he was unequal to a great crisis, he had disliked the expedition from the first, and he was suffering from a mortal disease.

MEANWHILE the Athenian generals, troubled by their recent defeat and the utter discouragement which prevailed in the army, held a council of war. They saw that their attempts all failed, and that the soldiers were weary of remaining. For they were distressed by sickness, proceeding from two causes : the season of the year was that in which men are most liable to disease; and the place in which they were encamped was damp and unhealthy. And they felt that the situation was in every way hopeless. Demosthenes gave his voice against remaining; he said that the decisive attack upon Epipolae had failed, and, in accordance with his original intention, he should vote for immediate departure, while the voyage was possible and while, with the help of the ships which had recently joined them, they had the upper hand at any rate by sea.

Nicias in his own mind took the same gloomy view of their affairs; but he did not wish openly to confess their weakness, or by a public vote given in a numerous assembly to let their intention reach the enemy's ears, and so lose the advantage of departing secretly whenever they might choose to go. He had moreover still some reason to suppose that the Syracusans, of whose condition he was better informed than the other generals, were likely to be worse off than themselves if they would only persevere in the siege; they would be worn out by the exhaustion

of their resources ; and now the Athenians with their additional
ships had much greater command of the sea.—There was a party
in Syracuse itself which wanted to surrender the city to the
Athenians, and they kept sending messages to Nicias and advising
him not to depart. Having this information he was still wavering
and considering, and had not made up his mind. But in addressing the council he positively refused to withdraw the army ; he
knew, he said, that the Athenian people would not forgive their
departure if they left without an order from home. The men upon
whose votes their fate would depend [1] would not, like themselves,
have seen with their own eyes the state of affairs ; they would only
have heard the criticisms of others, and would be convinced by any
accusations which a clever speaker might bring forward. Indeed
many or most of the very soldiers who were now crying out that
their case was desperate would raise the opposite cry when they
reached home, and would say that the generals were traitors, and
had been bribed to depart ; and therefore he, knowing the
temper of the Athenians, would for his own part rather take his
chance and fall, if he must, alone by the hands of the enemy, than
die unjustly on a dishonourable charge at the hands of his
own people.[2]

Nicias carried the day ; departure was postponed, and more
reinforcements reached the Syracusans.

ON their arrival, the Syracusans immediately prepared to
renew their attack upon the Athenians, both by land and
sea. And the Athenian generals, seeing that their enemy had
been reinforced by a new army, and that their own affairs, instead
of improving, were daily growing worse in every respect, and being
especially troubled by the sickness of their troops, repented that
they had not gone before. Even Nicias now no longer objected,
but only made the condition that there should be no open voting.
So, maintaining such secrecy as they could, they gave orders for
the departure of the expedition ; the men were to prepare them-

[1] i.e. The Assembly in Athens.   [2] VII. 47 f.

selves against a given signal. The preparations were made and they were on the point of sailing, when the moon, being just then at the full, was eclipsed. The mass of the army was greatly moved and called upon the generals to remain. Nicias himself, who was too much under the influence of divination and such-like, refused even to discuss the question of their removal until they had remained thrice nine days, as the soothsayers prescribed. This was the reason why the departure of the Athenians was finally delayed.

This gave the Syracusans time to practise their fleet, and they began to close the Great Harbour with a barrier, thus preventing escape by sea. The Athenians were unrivalled sailors, but the morale of the men had suffered, their ships were foul, and they had already suffered a naval defeat. Yet they made a last attempt to regain command of the harbour, and Nicias addressed his men before they went on board. The account of the sea-fight is perhaps the most famous description in Thucydides.

NICIAS, overwhelmed by the situation, and seeing how great and how near the peril was (for the ships were on the very point of rowing out), feeling too, as men do on the eve of a great struggle,[1] that all which he had done was nothing, and that he had not said half enough, again addressed the captains, and calling each of them by his father's name, and his own name, and the name of his tribe, he entreated those who had made any reputation for themselves not to be false to it, and those whose ancestors were eminent not to tarnish their hereditary fame. He reminded them that they were the inhabitants of the freest country in the world, and how in Athens there was no interference with the daily life of any man. He spoke to them of their wives and children

[1] 'Thucydides is a gentleman whose truth I never appreciated so thoroughly before. He tells how the officers lectured and encouraged their men right up to the last moment, always remembering another word of counsel and wishing to say more, yet feeling all the time that however much they said it would still be inadequate. Just the same with us now. We've all lectured our platoons, but something still keeps turning up. . . . Well, we're parading in a minute.' Letter from the front, quoted in *The Times History of the War*, pt. 75.

and their fathers' Gods, as men will at such a time; for then
they do not care whether their commonplace phrases seem to be
out of date or not, but loudly reiterate the old appeals, believing
that they may be of some service at the awful moment. When
he thought that he had exhorted them, not enough, but as much
as the scanty time allowed, he retired, and led the land-forces to
the shore, extending the line as far as he could, so that they might
be of the greatest use in encouraging the combatants on board
ship. Demosthenes, Menander, and Euthydēmus, who had gone
on board the Athenian fleet to take the command, now quitted
their own station, and proceeded straight to the closed mouth of
the harbour, intending to force their way to the open sea where
a passage was still left.

The Syracusans and their allies had already put out with nearly
the same number of ships as before. A detachment of them
guarded the entrance of the harbour; the remainder were disposed all round it in such a manner that they might fall on the
Athenians from every side at once, and that their land-forces
might at the same time be able to co-operate wherever the ships
retreated to the shore. Sicānus and Agatharchus commanded
the Syracusan fleet, each of them a wing; Pythen and the Corinthians occupied the centre. When the Athenians approached the
closed mouth of the harbour the violence of their onset overpowered the ships which were stationed there; they then
attempted to loosen the fastenings. Whereupon from all sides the
Syracusans and their allies came bearing down upon them, and
the conflict was no longer confined to the entrance, but extended
throughout the harbour. No previous engagement had been so
fierce and obstinate. Great was the eagerness with which the
rowers on both sides rushed upon their enemies whenever the
word of command was given; and keen was the contest between
the pilots as they manœuvred one against another. The marines
too were full of anxiety that, when ship struck ship, the service on
deck should not fall short of the rest; every one in the place
assigned to him was eager to be foremost among his fellows.

Many vessels meeting—and never did so many fight in so small a space, for the two fleets together amounted to nearly two hundred—they were seldom able to strike in the regular manner, because they had no opportunity of first retiring or breaking the line ; they generally fouled one another as ship dashed against ship in the hurry of flight or pursuit. All the time that another vessel was bearing down, the men on deck poured showers of javelins and arrows and stones upon the enemy ; and when the two closed, the marines fought hand to hand, and endeavoured to board. In many places, owing to the want of room, they who had struck another found that they were struck themselves ; often two or even more vessels were unavoidably entangled about one, and the pilots had to make plans of attack and defence, not against one adversary only, but against several coming from different sides. The crash of so many ships dashing against one another took away the wits of the crews, and made it impossible to hear the boatswains, whose voices in both fleets rose high, as they gave directions to the rowers, or cheered them on in the excitement of the struggle. On the Athenian side they were shouting to their men that they must force a passage and seize the opportunity now or never of returning in safety to their native land. To the Syracusans and their allies was represented the glory of preventing the escape of their enemies, and of a victory by which every man would exalt the honour of his own city. The commanders too, when they saw any ship backing without necessity, would call the captain by his name, and ask, of the Athenians, whether they were retreating because they expected to be more at home upon the land of their bitterest foes than upon that sea which had been their own so long ; on the Syracusan side, whether, when they knew perfectly well that the Athenians were only eager to find some means of flight, they would themselves fly from the fugitives.

While the naval engagement hung in the balance the two armies on shore had great trial and conflict of soul. The Sicilian soldier was animated by the hope of increasing the glory which he had already won, while the invader was tormented by the fear that his fortunes might sink lower still. The last chance of the Athenians lay in their ships, and their anxiety was dreadful. The fortune of the battle varied ; and it was not possible that the spectators on the shore should all receive the same impression of it. Being quite close and having different points of view, they would some of them see their own ships victorious ; their courage would then revive, and they would earnestly call upon the Gods not to take from them their hope of deliverance. But others, who saw their ships worsted, cried and shrieked aloud, and were by the sight alone more utterly unnerved than the defeated combatants themselves. Others again, who had fixed their gaze on some part of the struggle which was undecided, were in a state of excitement still more terrible ; they kept swaying their bodies to and fro in an agony of hope and fear as the stubborn conflict went on and on ; for at every instant they were all but saved or all but lost. And while the strife hung in the balance you might hear in the Athenian army at once lamentation, shouting, cries of victory or defeat, and all the various sounds which are wrung from a great host in extremity of danger. Not less agonizing were the feelings of those on board. At length the Syracusans and their allies, after a protracted struggle, put the Athenians to flight, and triumphantly bearing down upon them, and encouraging one another with loud cries and exhortations, drove them to land. Then that part of the navy which had not been taken in the deep water fell back in confusion to the shore, and the crews rushed out of the ships into the camp. And the land-forces, no longer now divided in feeling, but uttering one universal groan of intolerable anguish, ran, some of them to save the ships, others to defend what remained of the wall ; but the greater number began to look to themselves and to their own safety. Never had there been a greater panic in an Athenian army than at that moment. After the rout of their fleet, they knew that they had no hope of saving themselves by land unless events took some extraordinary turn.

Thus, after a fierce battle and a great destruction of ships and men on both sides, the Syracusans and their allies gained the victory. They gathered up the wrecks and bodies of the dead, and sailing back to the city, erected a trophy. The Athenians, overwhelmed by their misery, never so much as thought of recovering their wrecks or of asking leave to collect their dead. Their intention was to retreat that very night. Demosthenes came to Nicias and proposed that they should once more man their remaining vessels and endeavour to force the passage at daybreak, saying that they had more ships fit for service than the enemy. For the Athenian fleet still numbered sixty, but the enemy had less than fifty. Nicias approved of his proposal, and they would have manned the ships, but the sailors refused to embark ; for they were paralysed by their defeat, and had no longer any hope of succeeding. So the Athenians all made up their minds to escape by land.

Hermocrates the Syracusan suspected their intention, and dreading what might happen if their vast army, retreating by land and settling somewhere in Sicily, should choose to renew the war, he went to the authorities, and represented to them that they ought not to allow the Athenians to withdraw by night (mentioning his own suspicion of their intentions), but that all the Syracusans and their allies should go out in advance, wall up the roads, and occupy the passes with a guard. They thought very much as he did, and wanted to carry out his plan, but doubted whether their men, who were too glad to repose after a great battle, and in time of festival—for there happened on that very day to be a sacrifice to Heracles—could be induced to obey. Most of them, in the exultation of victory, were drinking and keeping holiday, and at such a time how could they ever be expected to take up arms and go forth at the order of the generals ? On these grounds the authorities decided that the thing was impossible. Whereupon Hermocrates himself, fearing lest the Athenians should gain a start and quietly pass the most difficult places in the night, contrived the following plan : when it was growing dark he sent certain of his own acquaintance, accompanied by a few horsemen, to the Athenian camp. They rode up within earshot, and pretending to be friends (there were known to be men in the city who gave information to Nicias of what went on), called to some of the soldiers, and bade them tell him not to withdraw his army during the night, for the Syracusans were guarding the roads ; he should make preparation at leisure and retire by day. Having delivered their message they departed, and those who had heard them informed the Athenian generals.

On receiving this message, which they supposed to be genuine, they remained during the night. And having once given up the intention of starting immediately, they decided to remain during the next day, that the soldiers might, as well as they could, put together their baggage in the most excellent form, and depart, taking with them the bare necessaries of life, but nothing else.

Meanwhile the Syracusans and Gylippus, going forth before them with their land-forces, blocked the roads in the country by which the Athenians were likely to pass, guarded the fords of the rivers and streams, and posted themselves at the best points for receiving and stopping them. Their sailors rowed up to the beach and dragged away the Athenian ships. The Athenians themselves had burnt a few of them, as they had intended, but the rest the Syracusans towed away, unmolested and at their leisure, from the places where they had severally run aground, and conveyed them to the city.

On the third day after the sea-fight, when Nicias and Demosthenes thought that their preparations were complete, the army began to move. They were in a dreadful condition ; not only was there the great fact that they had lost their whole fleet, and instead of their expected triumph had brought the utmost peril upon Athens as well as upon themselves, but also the sights which presented themselves as they quitted the camp were painful to every eye and mind. The dead were unburied, and when any one saw the body of a friend lying on the ground he was smitten with sorrow and dread, while the sick or wounded who still survived but had to be left were even a greater trial to the living, and more to be pitied than those who were gone. Their prayers and lamentations drove their companions to distraction ; they would beg that they might be taken with them, and call by name any friend or relation whom they saw passing ; they would hang upon their departing comrades and follow as far as they could, and, when their limbs and their strength failed them, and they dropped behind, many were the imprecations and cries which they uttered. So that the whole army was in tears, and such was their despair that they could hardly make up their minds to stir, although they were leaving an enemy's country, having suffered calamities too great for tears already, and dreading miseries yet greater in the unknown future. There was also a general feeling of shame and self-reproach—indeed they seemed, not like an army, but like the fugitive population of a city captured after a siege ; and of a great city too. For the whole multitude who were marching together numbered not less than forty thousand. Each of them took with him anything he could carry which was likely to be of use. Even the heavy-armed and cavalry, contrary to their practice when under arms, conveyed about their persons their own food, some because they had no attendants, others because they could not trust them ; for they had long been deserting, and most of them had gone off all at once. Nor was the food which they carried sufficient ; for the supplies of the camp had failed. Their disgrace and the universality of the misery, although there might be some consolation in the very community of suffering, were nevertheless at that moment hard to bear, especially when they remembered from what pride and splendour they had fallen into their present low estate. Never had an Hellenic army experienced such a reverse. They had come intending to enslave others, and they were going away in fear that they would be themselves enslaved. Instead of the prayers and hymns with which they had put to sea, they were now departing amid appeals to heaven of another sort. They were no longer sailors, but lands-men, depending, not upon their fleet, but upon their infantry. Yet in face of the great danger which still threatened them all these things appeared endurable.

Nicias, seeing the army disheartened at their terrible fall, went along the ranks and encouraged and consoled them as well as he could. In his fervour he raised his voice as he passed from one to another and spoke louder and louder, desiring that the benefit of his words might reach as far as possible.

' Even now, Athenians and allies, we must hope : men have been delivered out of worse straits than these, and I would not have you judge yourselves too severely on account either of the reverses which you have sustained or of your present undeserved miseries. I too am as weak as any of you ; for I am quite prostrated by my disease, as you see. And although there was a time when I might have been thought equal to the best of you in the happiness of my private and public life, I am now in as great danger, and as much at the mercy of fortune, as the meanest. Yet my days have been passed in the performance of many a religious duty, and of many a just and blameless action. Therefore my hope of the future is still courageous, and our calamities do not appal me as they might. Who knows that they may not be lightened ? For our enemies have had their full share of success, and if we were under the jealousy of any God when our fleet started, by this time we have been punished enough. Others ere now have attacked their neighbours ; they have done as men will do, and suffered what men can bear. We may therefore begin to hope that the Gods will be more merciful to us ; for we now invite their pity rather than their jealousy. And look at your own well-armed ranks ; see how many brave soldiers you are, marching in solid array, and do not be dismayed ; bear in mind that wherever you plant yourselves you are a city already, and that no city in Sicily will find it easy to resist your attack, or can dislodge you if you choose to settle. Provide for the safety and good order of your own march, and remember every one of you, that on whatever spot a man is compelled to fight, there if he conquer he may find a native land and a fortress. We must press forward day and night, for our supplies are but scanty. The Sicels through fear of the Syracusans still adhere to us, and if we can only reach any part of their territory we shall be among friends, and you may consider yourselves secure. We have sent to them, and they have been told to meet us and bring food. In a word, soldiers, let me tell you that you must be brave ; there is no place near to which a coward can fly. And if you now escape your enemies, those of you who are not Athenians will see once more the home for which they long, while you Athenians will again rear aloft the fallen greatness of Athens. For men, and not walls or ships in which are no men, constitute a state.'

Thus exhorting his troops Nicias passed through the army, and wherever he saw gaps in the ranks or the men dropping out of line, he brought them back to their proper place. Demosthenes did the same for the troops under his command, and gave them similar exhortations. The army marched disposed in a hollow oblong : the division of Nicias leading, and that of Demosthenes following ; the hoplites [1] enclosed within their ranks the baggage-bearers and the rest of the host. When they arrived at the ford of the river Anápus they found a force of the Syracusans and of their allies drawn up to meet them ; these they put to flight, and getting command of the ford, proceeded on their march. The Syracusans continually harassed them, the cavalry riding alongside, and the light-armed troops hurling darts at them. On this day the Athenians proceeded about four and a half miles and encamped at a hill. On the next day they started early, and, having advanced more than two miles, descended into a level plain, and encamped. The country was inhabited, and they were desirous of obtaining food from the houses, and also water which they might carry with them, as there was little to be had for many miles in the country which lay before them. Meanwhile the Syracusans had gone forward, and at a point where the road ascends a steep hill called the Acraean height, and there is a precipitous ravine on either side, were blocking up the pass by a wall.

---

[1] Heavy-armed infantry.

On the next day the Athenians advanced, although again impeded by the numbers of the enemy's cavalry who rode alongside, and of their javelin-men who threw darts at them. For a long time the Athenians maintained the struggle, but at last retired to their own encampment. Their supplies were now cut off, because the horsemen circumscribed their movements.[1]

During an attempt to escape by night the forces of Nicias and Demosthenes were separated. The next day the latter was captured. The following was the fate of Nicias.

ON the following day he was overtaken by the Syracusans, who told him that Demosthenes had surrendered, and bade him do the same. He, not believing them, procured a truce while he sent a horseman to go and see. Upon the return of the horseman bringing assurance of the fact, he sent a herald to Gylippus and the Syracusans, saying that he would agree, on behalf of the Athenian state, to pay the expenses which the Syracusans had incurred in the war, on condition that they should let his army go ; until the money was paid he would give Athenian citizens as hostages, a man for a talent. Gylippus and the Syracusans would not accept these proposals, but attacked and surrounded this division of the army as they had the other, and hurled missiles at them from every side until the evening. They too were grievously in want of food and necessaries. Nevertheless they meant to wait for the dead of the night and then to proceed. They were just resuming their arms, when the Syracusans discovered them and raised the Paean. The Athenians, perceiving that they were detected, laid down their arms again, with the exception of about three hundred men who broke through the enemy's guard, and made their escape in the darkness as best they could.

When the day dawned Nicias led forward his army, and the Syracusans and the allies again assailed them on every side, hurling javelins and other missiles at them. The Athenians hurried on to the river Assinarus. They hoped to gain a little

[1] VII. 69 f.

relief if they forded the river, for the mass of horsemen and other troops overwhelmed and crushed them ; and they were worn out by fatigue and thirst. But no sooner did they reach the water then they lost all order and rushed in ; every man was trying to cross first, and the enemy pressing upon them at the same time, the passage of the river became hopeless. Being compelled to keep close together they fell one upon another, and trampled each other under foot : some at once perished, pierced by their own spears ; others got entangled in the baggage and were carried down the stream. The Syracusans stood upon the further bank of the river, which was steep, and hurled missiles from above on the Athenians, who were huddled together in the deep bed of the stream and for the most part were drinking greedily. The Peloponnesians came down the bank and slaughtered them, falling chiefly upon those who were in the river. Whereupon the water at once became foul, but was drunk all the same, although muddy and dyed with blood, and the crowd fought for it.

At last, when the dead bodies were lying in heaps upon one another in the water and the army was utterly undone, some perishing in the river, and any one who escaped being cut off by the cavalry, Nicias surrendered to Gylippus, in whom he had more confidence than in the Syracusans. He entreated him and the Lacedaemonians to do what they pleased with himself, but not to go on killing the men.[1]

Nicias and Demosthenes were put to death. Of the former Thucydides writes : ' No one of the Hellenes of my time was less deserving of so miserable an end : for he lived in the practice of every virtue.' The other prisoners were placed in the great Syracusan quarries.

THOSE who were imprisoned in the quarries were at the beginning of their captivity harshly treated by the Syracusans. There were great numbers of them, and they were crowded in a deep and narrow place. At first the sun by day was still scorching

[1] VII. 83 f.

and suffocating, for they had no roof over their heads, while the autumn nights were cold, and the extremes of temperature engendered violent disorders. Being cramped for room they had to do everything on the same spot. The corpses of those who died from their wounds, exposure to heat and cold, and the like, lay heaped one upon another. The smells were intolerable ; and they were at the same time afflicted by hunger and thirst. During eight months they were allowed only about half a pint of water and a pint of food a day. Every kind of misery which could befall man in such a place befell them. This was the condition of all the captives for about ten weeks. At length the Syracusans sold them, with the exception of the Athenians and of any Sicilian or Italian Greeks who had sided with them in the war. The whole number of the public prisoners is not accurately known, but they were not less than seven thousand.

Of all the Hellenic actions which took place in this war, or indeed, as I think, of all Hellenic actions which are on record, this was the greatest—the most glorious to the victors, the most ruinous to the vanquished ; for they were utterly and at all points defeated, and their sufferings were prodigious. Fleet and army perished from the face of the earth ; nothing was saved, and of the many who went forth few returned home.

Thus ended the Sicilian expedition.[1]

So closes the 7th book of Thucydides. The 8th book begins by telling how the news was brought to Athens.

The Athenians could not believe that the armament had been so completely annihilated, although they had the positive assurances of the very soldiers who had escaped from the scene of action. At last they knew the truth ; and then they were furious with the orators who had joined in promoting the expedition—as if they had not voted it themselves—and with the soothsayers, and prophets, and all who by the influence of religion had at the time inspired them with the belief that

[1] VII. 87.

they would conquer Sicily. Whichever way they looked there was trouble ; they were overwhelmed by their calamity, and were in fear and consternation unutterable. The citizens and the city were alike distressed ; they had lost a host of cavalry and hoplites and the flower of their youth, and there were none to replace them. And when they saw an insufficient number of ships in their docks, and no crews to man them, nor money in the treasury, they despaired of deliverance. They had no doubt that their enemies in Sicily, after the great victory which they had already gained, would at once sail against the Piraeus. Their enemies in Hellas, whose resources were now doubled, would likewise set upon them with all their might both by sea and land, and would be assisted by their own revolted allies. Still they determined, so far as their situation allowed, not to give way. They would procure timber and money by whatever means they might, and build a navy. They would make sure of their allies, and above all of Euboea.[1] Expenses in the city were to be economized, and they were to choose a council of the elder men, who should advise together, and lay before the people the measures which from time to time might be required. After the manner of a democracy, they were very amenable to discipline while their fright lasted.[2]

With splendid courage the Athenians prolonged the war for nine years, but they were doomed. Their subjects deserted them now that they could do so without fear, as was natural in an empire governed on Cleon's principles, and the Athenian Empire as a political force came to an end. That is the end of the *Real-Politik* of Cleon and his democracy, a lesson written for the world.

[1] A glance at the map will show why.   [2] VIII. 1.

VIII

HISTORY : XENOPHON

> The Anabasis . . . exemplifies the discipline, the endurance, the power
> of self-action and adaptation, the susceptibility of influence from speech
> and discussion, the combination of the reflecting obedience of citizens
> with the mechanical regularity of soldiers, which confer such immortal
> distinction on the Hellenic character.—G. GROTE.

In the late summer of 401 B.C. a Greek army of 10,000 men
found itself in the plains of Mesopotamia near Babylon. They were
mercenaries, whom Cyrus, the younger brother of the Persian
king, had engaged to assist him in an attempt to seize the throne.
A battle took place ; the Greeks were victorious, but Cyrus was
killed, their generals were entrapped and murdered by the
Persians, and there was nothing left but somehow to make their
way back to Greece. They had lost their leaders : to the west
there was desert, and on the north unknown mountains,
inhabited by wild and hostile tribes ; they had no guides or maps,
no knowledge of the country or of its language, no food or proper
commissariat arrangements, and winter was coming on. Close
by was a huge Persian army, estimated at 400,000 men. They
decided to follow the Tigris and try to reach the Black Sea.

Among them was a young Athenian called Xenophon, about
twenty-five years of age, who was chosen one of the new generals.
In later life he wrote the history of the Ten Thousand, calling
it the *Anabasis*—' The March Up Country '. We have several
other works from his hand, among which are a continuation of
Thucydides (the *Hellenica*), Memoirs of Socrates, the *Education of
Cyrus* (*Cyropaedia*), a kind of historical novel with Cyrus the
Great for hero, works on taxation, on hunting, on cavalry training,
and on household management (*Oeconomicus*) : the last named
gives a vivid picture of a Greek household and its mistress.
It was also ' the foundation on which Ruskin built all his studies
in Political Economy '.[1] He had it translated for his *Bibliotheca
Pastorum*, and says that ' it contains, first, a faultless definition
of wealth and explanation of its dependence for efficiency on

[1] Collected Works, XXXI, p. xv

the merits and faculties of its possessor ;—definition which cannot be bettered ; and which must be the foundation of all true Political Economy.[1] . . . Secondly, the most perfect ideal of kingly character and kingly government given in literature known to me. . . . Lastly and chiefly, this book contains the ideal of domestic life.'[2]

Yet Xenophon was a man of action rather than of letters. After his adventures with the Ten Thousand, he joined the Spartan forces who were fighting the Persians ; and on his banishment from Athens settled on a country estate in the Peloponnese, lived the life of a country squire, and spent his time in hunting and writing. In his history and in his writings about Socrates he challenges comparison with Thucydides and Plato, and at once reveals his inferiority to them in imagination and in intellectual power. Yet as a writer he is a master in his own particular way, and remained a model of that natural, unaffected style, so common and characteristic in Greek literature, which has no brilliance to dazzle the reader but which charms him by its perfect lucidity and grace. ' He has shown that the gravest and most important subjects can be treated by an educated man without any need to raise the voice.' As a man, he is a specimen of an ordinary Greek gentleman with literary interests, and the type, with its union of the active and the intellectual life, has an interest and value for all time. Though in no sense a great historian, in the *Hellenica* he is a valuable source for the history of his period, in the *Anabasis* he has left us a picture of a heroic action, and of a band of Greek soldiers of fortune and their leaders.

The following passage from the *Anabasis* gives scenes from a march in winter through the Armenian mountains. The Greeks had escaped from Mesopotamia. They now force a mountain pass and cross the Murad-su or eastern branch of the Euphrates ; what follows describes their adventures in the march to the hills above Trebizond by a route which we cannot now identify.

---

[1] The definition to which Ruskin refers is :
' The very same things are property to a man who knows how to use them, and not property to one who does not. . . . Suppose a man were to use his money to buy something which caused his body to be worse, his soul worse, his household worse, could we say that his money was any benefit to him ? . . . We may then exclude money from being counted as property, if it is in the hands of one who does not know how to use it.' Oec. i. § 10 f.
[2] ib., p. 27 f. The whole passage should be read.

THE next day they resolved to march without delay before the enemy could rally their forces, and seize the pass. So they packed their baggage, and set forward through deep snow with many guides ; that same day they passed the heights where Teribazus[1] designed to attack them, and encamped. Thence they made three marches through a desert, and came to the Euphrates, which they passed, the water coming up to the waist. It was said that the sources of the river were not far off. From here they made forty-five miles in three days, over a plain covered with deep snow. The last day's march was very hard, for the north wind, blowing full in their faces, wore the men out and benumbed them. One of their priests advised them to sacrifice to the wind ; this was done, and its violence visibly lessened. The snow was six feet deep, so that many of the slaves and baggage horses died, and about thirty soldiers. They made fires all night, for they found plenty of wood in the place where they encamped ; and those who came late having no wood, the others who had arrived earlier, and had made fires, would not allow them to warm themselves till they had given them a share of the wheat, or of the other provisions they had brought with them. By this exchange they relieved one another's wants. In the places where the fires were made, the snow melted, and large pits were formed which reached down to the earth ; this afforded an opportunity of measuring the depth of the snow.

They marched all the next day through the snow, and many of them began to suffer from ravenous hunger. Xenophon, who commanded the rear, saw men on the ground, but did not know what was wrong with them. Those who knew about the disease told him that it was clearly bulimy,[2] and that, if they ate anything, they would recover ; so he went to the baggage, and distributed all the food he found there, giving it to those who could walk, and telling them to divide among the sick. As soon as they had eaten something, they got up and continued their

[1] The Persian governor of Western Armenia.
[2] Lit. Ox-hunger.

march. So proceeding, Cheirisophus [1] came to a village just as it
was dark, and at a fountain outside the walls he found some
women and girls of the place carrying water. These inquired
who they were. The interpreter answered in Persian, that they
were going to the satrap from the King. [2] The women replied that
he was not there, but at a place about three miles away. As it
was late, they entered the walls, together with the women, and
went to the mayor of the town. Here Cheirisophus encamped
with all the able-bodied men. The rest, who were unable to
continue their march, passed the night without victuals or fire,
and some of them died. A party of the enemy following our
march, took some of the baggage-horses that could not keep pace
with the rest, and fought with one another about them. Some
of the men who had lost their sight by the snow, or whose toes
were frostbitten through the intenseness of the cold, were left
behind. The men protected their eyes against the snow by
wearing black bandages ; they protected their feet against the
cold by incessant motion, and by pulling off their shoes in the
night. If a man slept with his shoes on, the laces lacerated his
feet, and the shoes stuck to them, for when their old shoes were
worn out, the men wore brogues made of raw hides. These
accidents compelled us to leave some of our men behind ; and
they, seeing a piece of ground that appeared black, because there
was no snow upon it, concluded it was melted ; and melted it
was by steam that rose from a fountain in a valley near the place.
Thither they betook themselves, and sitting down, refused to
march any farther. Xenophon, who had charge of the rear, as
soon as he was informed of this, did his very best to persuade
them not to stay behind, telling them that the enemy had collected in great force, and were close behind. At last he grew
angry. But they told him to kill them, if he wished, for they
were not able to go on. Upon this, he thought the best thing
he could do was, if possible, to create a panic among the enemy

---

[1] A colleague of Xenophon.
[2] The King of Persia. The satrap is the Persian governor.

who were pursuing, to prevent them attacking these worn-out
stragglers. It was now dark, and the enemy came on, making
a great noise and quarrelling with one another about their booty.
Upon this, such of the rear-guard as were well rose and fell upon
them ; while those who were ill shouted out as loud as they
could, and struck their shields with their pikes. The enemy,
alarmed at this, threw themselves into the valley through the
snow, and were no more heard of.

Xenophon and his troops then resumed their march, assuring
the sick men, that the next day some people should be sent to
them ; but before they had gone half a mile, they found others
resting in the snow, and covered with it, and no watch kept.
Xenophon forced these to rise, and was told by them that the
men in front would not move forward. Xenophon, hearing this,
went on, and sending the fittest of the light-armed troops in
advance, ordered them to see what had caused the halt. They
reported that the whole army was resting. So Xenophon and
his men, after setting such a watch as they could, passed the
night there without either fire or food. When it was near day,
Xenophon sent the youngest of his men to oblige the sick to get
up and resume their march.

They managed to reach some villages, where they encamped.

HERE, Polycrates of Athens, one of the captains, asked
leave of absence, and taking with him some active men,
advanced at the double to the village allotted to Xenophon, where he surprised all the inhabitants, together with their
mayor, in their houses. He found here seventeen colts, that were
bred as a tribute for the King ; and also the mayor's daughter,
who had not been married above nine days : her husband, however, having gone to hunt hares, was not captured. The houses
were under ground ; the mouth resembling that of a well,
and widening out below ; there was an entrance dug for the cattle,
but the inhabitants descended by ladders. In these houses were
goats, sheep, cows, and fowls, with their young. All the cattle

were maintained with fodder within doors. There was also wheat,
barley and vegetables, and beer in jars ; the malt was level with
the brims of the vessels, and in it were straws, some large and
others small, without joints. When any one was thirsty, he took
one of these and sucked. The beer was very strong when un-
mixed with water, and very delicious to those who were used
to it.

The army stayed in these quarters for a week ; then resumed
its march and forced a mountain pass.

NEXT they came to the country of the Taochians,[1] making
in five marches ninety miles, and here their provisions
began to fail ; for the Taochians lived in fastnesses, into
which they had removed all their provisions. At last the army
arrived at a strong place, where there were neither houses nor
city, but where great numbers of men and women with their
cattle had collected. This place Cheirisophus ordered to be
attacked the moment he arrived : when the first line failed,
a second went up, and then another ; for the place was surrounded
with precipices and they could not attack it on all sides at once.
When Xenophon came up with the rear-guard, both light and
heavy-armed men, Cheirisophus said to him : ' You have come
in the nick of time ; for this place must be taken, otherwise the
army will be starved.'

A council of war was then summoned, and Xenophon asked
what was the difficulty in taking the place. Cheirisophus
answered : ' The only access is the one you see, and when any
of our men attempt to gain it, the enemy roll down stones from
the overhanging cliff, and you see what happens to those who are
hit ' ; and he pointed to some of the men whose legs and ribs
were broken. ' But,' says Xenophon, ' when they have used up
all the stones they have, what can hinder us then from going up ?
for I can see nothing to oppose us but a few men, and of these not
above two or three are armed. The space, as you see, which we

[1] The name seems to have survived in the modern Tao.

must cross under fire, is about one hundred and fifty feet, and of this one hundred feet is covered with large pines, growing in groups, behind which our men can shelter, and be out of the reach of the stones that are thrown or rolled down by the enemy. There remain not more than fifty feet, across which we must run as soon as the stones stop.' ' But,' said Cheirisophus, ' the moment we begin to approach the place covered with trees, they will shower down stones upon us.' ' That,' replied Xenophon, ' is the very thing we want, for their supply will come to an end all the sooner. However,' he continued, ' let us, if we can, advance to a place from which we shall have but a little way to run, and from which we can also, if desirable, easily retreat.'

Upon this, Cheirisophus and Xenophon advanced, with Callimachus of Parrhasia, who was the chief officer of the rear-guard for the day, all the rest of the officers standing out of danger. About seventy of the men advanced under the trees, not in a body, but one by one, each sheltering himself as well as he could. Then Callimachus made use of the following stratagem. He advanced two or three paces from the tree under which he stood, but as soon as the stones began to fly, he quickly retired ; each time that he advanced, more than ten cart-loads of stones were used up. When Agasius saw what Callimachus was doing, and that the eyes of the whole army were upon him, fearing that he would be the first man to enter the place, he advanced alone, intending to anticipate him. When Callimachus saw him passing by, he grasped the rim of his shield. In the meantime, Aristonymus, and after him Eurylochus, ran by them both ; for all these were ambitious of distinction, and constantly competing with one another. And so in competition, they took the place ; for the moment one of them had gained the ascent, there were no more stones thrown from above.

A dreadful sight followed ; the women first threw their children down the precipice, and then themselves. The men did the same. And here Aenēas the Stymphālian, a captain, seeing one of the natives, who was richly dressed, running to throw himself down, caught hold of him, and the other pulling him along, they both fell down the precipice together, and were dashed to pieces. We made very few prisoners, though we took a considerable quantity of oxen, asses, and sheep.

From here the Greeks advanced through the country of the Chalybes, and in seven marches made 150 miles. The Chalybes, who were the bravest tribe they met in all their march, attacked them. They had linen corslets, and instead of tassels[1] thick cords twisted. They had also greaves and helmets, and at their girdle a short sword like the Spartan dagger, with which they cut the throats of their defeated enemies, and afterwards cutting off their heads marched along with them. It was their way to sing and dance whenever they thought the enemy saw them. They had pikes 22 feet long, pointed at one end only. They stayed in their forts till the Greeks had marched past them, and then followed, harassing them perpetually. After that, they retired to their strongholds, into which they had conveyed their provisions : so that the Greeks could get no provisions in their country, and lived upon the cattle they had taken from the Taochians.

The Greeks then reached a district whose governor sent them a guide to conduct them through the territories of his enemies. He promised to take them in five days to a place from which they could see the sea. If not, he said that they might put him to death. When he had conducted them into the territories of his enemies, he asked them to lay waste the country with fire and sword; which showed that he came with this in view, and not from any goodwill he bore to the Greeks. The fifth day they arrived at a mountain called Thēches. As soon as the vanguard reached its top and saw the sea, they gave a great shout ; Xenophon and those in the rear heard it, and concluded that some other enemies were attacking them in front, for men from the country which they had just ravaged were hanging on their rear, and some had been killed by the rear-guard and others

[1] The Greek corslet ended in a fringe of leather.

captured in an ambush. Twenty wicker shields covered with raw ox-hides, with the hair on, had also been taken.

The noise still increased as they came nearer, and the men, as fast as they came up, joined those who still continued shouting ; the more the numbers grew, the louder was the shouting, so that Xenophon, thinking something extraordinary had happened, mounted on horseback, and taking with him the cavalry, rode up to their assistance. Suddenly they heard the soldiers calling out, ' SEA ! SEA ! '[1] and passing the news along. At this they all started running, the rear-guard as well as the rest, and the baggage animals and horses were driven forward. When they were all come up to the top of the mountain, they embraced one another, and also their generals and captains, with tears in their eyes ; and suddenly, by whose order it is not known, they collected a great many stones, and made a large cairn, upon which they placed a great quantity of shields made of raw ox-hides, staves, and shields taken from the enemy. The guide himself cut the bucklers in pieces, and urged the rest to do the same.[2] After this, the Greeks sent back their guide, giving him presents out of the public stock : these were a horse, a silver cup, a Persian dress, and eight pounds. He particularly asked the soldiers to give him some of their rings, and this many of them did.[3]

[1] Not only did the sight mean that they had escaped from the unknown mountains to waters lined with Greek settlements, but it was particularly welcome to men who at home were never far from the sea.

[2] To make them useless.

[3] Anabasis, iv. 5 f. I have adapted Spelman's translation.

IX

PHILOSOPHY: THE SOPHISTS AND SOCRATES

Socrates . . . a man unique in history, of a kind at all times needed, and seldom needed more than now.—JOHN STUART MILL.

WE have seen the origins of the history, and of the epic, lyric, and dramatic poetry of Europe ; we now pass to something even greater—the origin of European science and philosophy. It is greater in this sense. Man naturally sings and tells stories, and other nations have composed epics and lyrics which owe nothing to Greece. But Greece is the only creator of that spirit of free inquiry and scientific thought which in religion, morals, politics, and natural science make the civilization of the West what it is. As philosophical writers the great Greek thinkers have three transcendant merits. Living in an age less complex than our own, they saw the central problems unencumbered by lesser issues. Then, while modern philosophy is a specialized science with a technical vocabulary, Plato and Aristotle approach the problems of thought and conduct as the ordinary man approaches them, and for the most part use everyday language. Yet they are not ordinary men, but thinkers of genius who laid the foundations of European thought, raised most of its problems, solved many of them, and have left an indelible mark on it.

Philosophy and science are sisters, the children of reason. Between them they attempt to give a rational account of the universe, of the material world, of man as an animal with a body, and as a human being with reason and a personality, and of the laws that should regulate his conduct as a private individual and as a member of the state. The first attempt in the West to give such an account was made in Ionia about the year 600 B.C. Then was laid the first stone of what has since risen into the vast mansions of modern thought. In Greece science and philosophy continually went hand in hand. We shall reserve the science for later treatment : and we may ignore the early speculations of

Greek philosophy, which are principally of historical interest. **It**
is in the fifth century that it first demands our attention.

Conceive England without universities, without secondary
education, without printed books, and you have a picture of
fifth-century Greece. It would have mattered less under an
autocracy or an aristocracy, but a democracy is lost in such
conditions. To meet the need rose a class of men, called in their
own day ' Sophists ' : the word means wise men, and has originally
no bad meaning. They offered their age what we call higher
education, and this education naturally took the form of instruction in the art of speaking, which was the most indispensable
accomplishment of a citizen in a state where every man took an
active part in politics, and where, if you went to law, you had
to plead your case in person. Nor need such instruction be
a mean education. Liberally and widely viewed, it raises not
only such questions as the art of arranging, composing, and
delivering a speech, memory training, the art of writing (at one
end of which is grammar, at the other the meaning and nature
of literary style), but also every kind of philosophical question.
When a man has learnt the method of speaking, he must study its
topics, and that will take him into moral and political philosophy,
and beyond these to those problems of theology and metaphysics
to which in the last resort all avenues of thought lead. It was
in this spirit that the Sophists taught the pupils who flocked to
them. Their writings as a whole are lost, but some of the
fragments will show the ground they covered, and the many
intellectual hares they started, some of which are running still.

Perhaps the shortest way to an idea of their personality and
work is to glance at Hippias—a characteristic Sophist but not
the greatest of them.

EVEN in his old age Hippias had so powerful a memory,
that after hearing fifty names once he repeated them in
the order in which he heard them. He introduced into
his discourses such subjects as geometry, astronomy, music and
rhythm. He lectured too on painting and sculpture. At Sparta
he spoke about the genealogy of heroes, about colonizing and
about heroic deeds ; for the Spartans, with their political ambitions, enjoyed such subjects. He went on more missions than
any other Greek, representing his country, Elis, and in his speeches

and lectures never belied his reputation. Indeed he made large sums of money and received the citizenship of many states great and small.[1]

Plato, who treats Sparta and Hippias' adventures there in a lighter vein, bears witness to his range of subjects.

Socrates. What was it, Hippias, that won you the praise and delighted attention of the Spartans ? No doubt your astronomy, and the changes of the heavenly bodies, on which you are so expert ?

Hippias. Not at all. They would not tolerate the subject.

S. Then it was geometry that they enjoyed hearing about ?

H. Oh, no : few have any knowledge of that branch of mathematics.

S. Then they were anything but anxious to hear your disquisitions on arithmetic ?

H. Indeed they were.

S. And it would be the same with those subjects on which you are the leading authority, the significance of letters, syllables, rhythms and harmonies ?

H. Letters and harmonies at Sparta !

S. Then what was it that they enjoyed and praised ? Tell me yourself, as I have failed to guess.

H. The subjects they enjoy are the genealogies of heroes and men, and stories of the founding of cities, in fact every kind of ancient legend, so that I had to learn these topics by heart.[2]

Nor were Hippias' accomplishments only intellectual.

S. I KNOW that in most arts you are the wisest of men, as I have heard you stating in the market-place at the tables of the bankers, when you were setting forth the great and enviable stores of your wisdom ; and you said that upon one occasion, when you went to the Olympic games, all that you had on your person was made by yourself. You began with your ring, which

[1] Philostratus, V. S. i. id.   [2] Hipp. Major, 285.

was of your own workmanship, and you said that you could
engrave rings ; and you had another seal which was also of your
own workmanship, and a rubber and an oil flask, which you had
made yourself ; you said also that you had made the shoes which
you had on your feet, and the cloak and the short tunic ; but
what appeared to us all most extraordinary and a proof of singular
art, was the girdle of your tunic, which, you said, was as fine as
the most costly Persian fabric, and of your own weaving ; moreover, you told us that you had brought with you poems,
epic, tragic, and lyric, as well as prose writings of the most
various kinds ; and you said that your skill was also pre-eminent
in the arts which I was just now mentioning, and in the true
principles of rhythm and harmony and of orthography ; and if
I remember rightly, there were a great many other accomplishments in which you excelled. I have forgotten to mention your
art of memory, which you regard as your special glory, and I dare
say that I have forgotten many other things.[1]

The following fragments, taken at random, throw further light
on the wide range of the Sophists' interests :
' Protagoras made the following division of genders—masculine,
feminine, things ' (Aristotle).
' About the gods, I cannot know that they exist or that they
do not exist, or what is their nature : for many things hinder
knowledge—the obscurity of the subject, and the shortness of
human life ' (Protagoras).
' A man in an athletic contest hit Epitīmus of Pharsalus with
a javelin and killed him. Pericles spent a whole day with Protagoras discussing what was responsible, in the most precise
sense, for the accident—the javelin, or the man who threw it, or
the authorities in charge of the contest ' (Plutarch). We should
think an English prime minister mad if he spent a day in such
a way. Yet Pericles is one of the statesmen who have left their
mark on the world.
' According to Gorgias we need for the battle of life two virtues,
courage and wisdom : courage to endure danger, wisdom to
overcome it. Reason, like the proclamation at the Olympic
games, calls him who is willing and crowns him who is able.' It is

[1] Hipp. Minor, 368.

not for its ideas that I have quoted this extract from Gorgias, but because it is an example of the balanced and antithetical sentence (the Greek words tally and contrast precisely), which is one of the chief ingredients of style. Gorgias discovered this device, and greatly overdid it ; this was natural with a great discovery. But there is no great writer of English prose, from Hooker to Stevenson, whose pages are not coloured by these ' figures ', which the Greek Sophist made a principle of style.[1]

The Sophists were of immense importance in their own age, and the after-world owes them the first study of the technique of writing and of public speaking. Plato disliked them as professionals, who took money from their pupils instead of pursuing knowledge gratis and for its own sake : and more justly he blamed them as superficial and preferring practical success and immediate effect to truth. He gave the word sophist a bad meaning which it has never lost, and which men like Protagoras and Gorgias did not deserve. But we must pass to a man who put truth before everything and who in the realm of thought has perhaps influenced the world more deeply than any one. The following passage introduces us to him, shows the Sophists as we might have seen them in the year 433, and illustrates the extraordinary intellectual keenness of the Athenian. The speakers are Socrates and a young Athenian anxious to become a pupil of the Sophist Protagoras.

L AST night, or rather very early this morning, Hippocrates gave a tremendous thump with his staff at my door ; some one opened to him, and he came rushing in and bawled out : Socrates, are you awake or asleep ?

---

[1] Thus the following passages owe almost everything to the Gorgian balance and antithesis. ' Of Law there can be no less acknowledged, than that her seat is the bosom of God, her voice the harmony of the world : all things in heaven and earth do her homage, the very least as feeling her care, and the greatest as not exempted from her power : both Angels and men and creatures of what condition soever, though each in different sort and manner, yet all with uniform consent, admiring her as the author of their peace and joy ' (Hooker).

' Of this quality the world is impatient ; it chafes against it, rails at it, insults it, hates it ; it ends by receiving its influence, and undergoing its law. This quality at last inexorably corrects the world's blunders and fixes the world's ideals. It procures that the popular poet shall not finally pass for a Pindar, nor the popular historian for a Tacitus, nor the popular preacher for a Bossuet ' (M. Arnold).

I knew his voice, and said : Hippocrates, is that you ? and do you bring any news ?

Good news, he said ; nothing but good.

Delightful, I said ; but what is the news ? and why have you come hither at this unearthly hour ?

He drew nearer to me and said : Protagoras is come.

Yes, I replied ; he came two days ago : have you only just heard of his arrival ?

Yes, by the gods, he said ; but not until yesterday evening.

At the same time he felt for the truckle-bed, and sat down at my feet, and then he said : Yesterday, when we had done supper and were about to retire to rest, my brother said to me : Protagoras is come. I was going to you at once, and then I thought that the night was far spent. But the moment sleep left me after my fatigue, I got up and came hither direct.

I, who knew the very courageous madness of the man, said : What is the matter ? Has Protagoras robbed you of anything ?

He replied, laughing : Yes, indeed he has, Socrates, of the wisdom which he keeps from me.

But, surely, I said, if you give him money, and make friends with him, he will make you as wise as he is himself.

Would to heaven, he replied, that this were the case ! He might take all that I have, and all that my friends have, if he pleased. But that is why I have come to you now, in order that you may speak to him on my behalf ; for I am young, and also I have never seen nor heard him (when he visited Athens before I was but a child) ; and all men praise him, Socrates ; he is reputed to be the most accomplished of speakers. There is no reason why we should not go to him at once, and then we shall find him at home. He lodges, as I hear, with Callias the son of Hipponicus : let us start.

I replied : Not yet, my good friend ; the hour is too early. But let us rise and take a turn in the court and wait about there until day-break ; when the day breaks, then we will go.

Later they go to the house where Protagoras is staying, and stop in the porch to finish a discussion.

I THINK that the door-keeper, who was a eunuch, and who was probably annoyed at the great inroad of the Sophists, must have heard us talking. At any rate, when we knocked at the door, and he opened and saw us, he grumbled : They are Sophists—he is not at home ; and instantly gave the door a hearty bang with both his hands. Again we knocked, and he answered without opening : Did you not hear me say that he is not at home, fellows ? But, my friend, I said, you need not be alarmed ; for we are not Sophists, and we are not come to see Callias, but we want to see Protagoras ; and I must request you to announce us. At last, after a good deal of difficulty, the man was persuaded to open the door.

When we entered, we found Protagoras taking a walk in the cloister ; and next to him, on one side, were walking Callias, the son of Hipponicus, and Paralus, the son of Pericles. On the other side of him were Xanthippus, the other son of Pericles, also Antimoerus of Mende, who of all the disciples of Protagoras is the most famous, and intends to make sophistry his profession. A train of listeners followed him ; the greater part of them appeared to be foreigners, whom Protagoras had brought with him out of the various cities visited by him in his journeys, he, like Orpheus, attracting them by his voice, and they following. I should mention also that there were some Athenians in the company. Nothing delighted me more than the precision of their movements : they never got into his way at all ; but when he and those who were with him turned back, then the band of listeners parted regularly on either side ; he was always in front, and they wheeled round and took their places behind him in perfect order.

After him, as Homer says, ' I lifted up my eyes and saw ' Hippias the Ēlean sitting in the opposite cloister on a chair of state, and around him were seated on benches strangers whom he had brought with him from his native city of Elis, and some others : they were putting to Hippias certain physical and astronomical questions, and he, *ex cathedra*, was determining their several questions to them, and discoursing of them.

Also, 'my eyes beheld Tantalus'[1]; for Prodicus the Cean was at Athens : he had been lodged in a room which, in the days of Hipponicus, was a storehouse; but, as the house was full, Callias had cleared this out and made the room into a guest-chamber. Now Prodicus was still in bed, wrapped up in sheepskins and bedclothes, of which there seemed to be a great heap. I was very anxious to hear what Prodicus was saying, for he seems to be an all-wise and inspired man ; but I was not able to get into the inner circle, and his fine deep voice made an echo in the room which rendered his words inaudible.[2]

In this scene we have met one of the most famous figures in the history of thought. Socrates (469–399) wrote nothing. We rely for our knowledge of him chiefly on two of his followers, Plato and Xenophon.[3] There are thirty-five dialogues attributed to Plato, not all genuine, in which Socrates is a speaker, and four books of Socratic Memoirs with some other treatises by Xenophon. The pictures given by these two authorities differ. Xenophon, for instance, represents Socrates as discussing all kinds of practical matters, from housekeeping to military tactics ; in Plato he is occupied rather with ethical, political, and philosophical problems. One of the unsolved literary problems of the world is what the historic Socrates taught, how far Plato and Xenophon attributed their own views to him, and what truth lies in their pictures. The problem, however, only affects his views ; about his character and personality there is no dispute. Here are four pictures of him. The first is in the camp of the Athenian army besieging the town of

---

[1] A quotation from Homer, which continues ' in terrible pain '. The allusion is to the physical condition of P. and perhaps to his love of money—Tantalus being a type of unsatisfied desires. Note the urbane sarcasm with which Plato, no lover of the Sophists, treats them.

[2] Protagoras, 310. This and nearly all the following passages from Plato are in Jowett's translation.

[3] The Clouds (p. 136 f.) deals with Socrates in early life, before he had deserted science for the study of man, and is a caricature.

Potidaea in northern Greece. Socrates, then about thirty-five, was serving in the army, of whose life we here get a glimpse.

ALL this happened before he and I went on the expedition to Potidaea ; there we messed together, and I had the opportunity of observing his extraordinary power of sustaining fatigue. His endurance was simply marvellous when, being cut off from our supplies, we were compelled to go without food—on such occasions, which often happen in time of war, he was superior not only to me but to everybody ; there was no one to be compared to him. Yet at a festival he was the only person who had any real powers of enjoyment ; though not willing to drink, he could if compelled beat us all at that— wonderful to relate ! no human being had ever seen Socrates drunk. His fortitude in enduring cold was also surprising. There was a severe frost, for the winter in that region is really tremendous, and everybody else either remained indoors, or if they went out had on an amazing quantity of clothes, and were well shod, and had their feet swathed in felt and fleeces : in the midst of this, Socrates with his bare feet on the ice and in his ordinary dress marched better than the other soldiers who had shoes, and they looked daggers at him because he seemed to despise them.

I have told you one tale, and now I must tell you another, which is worth hearing,

' Of the doings and sufferings of the enduring man '

while he was on the expedition. One morning he was thinking about something which he could not resolve ; he would not give it up, but continued thinking from early dawn until noon—there he stood fixed in thought ; and at noon attention was drawn to him, and the rumour ran through the wondering crowd that Socrates had been standing and thinking about something ever since the break of day. At last, in the evening after supper, some Ionians out of curiosity (I should explain that this was not in winter but in summer), brought out their mats and slept in the open air that they might watch him and see whether he would stand all night.   There he stood until the following morning and with the return of light he offered up a prayer to the sun, and went his way.[1]

The next picture is on the stricken battle-field of Dēlium, where the Athenian army was disastrously defeated in 424.

THERE was another occasion on which his behaviour was very remarkable—in the flight of the army after the battle of Delium, where he served among the heavy-armed—I had a better opportunity of seeing him than at Potidaea, for I was myself on horseback, and therefore comparatively out of danger.   He and Laches were retreating, for the troops were in flight, and I met them and told them not to be discouraged, and promised to remain with them ; and there you might see him, Aristophanes, as you describe, just as he is in the streets of Athens, ' stalking like a pelican, and rolling his eyes ', calmly contemplating enemies as well as friends, and making very intelligible to anybody, even from a distance, that whoever attacked him would be likely to meet with a stout resistance ; and in this way he and his companion escaped—for this is the sort of man who is never touched in war ; those only are pursued who are running away headlong.[2]

The third picture is at the end of a dinner-party in Athens.

AGATHON arose in order that he might take his place on the couch by Socrates, when suddenly a band of revellers entered, and spoiled the order of the banquet.   Some one who was going out having left the door open, they had found their way in, and made themselves at home ; great confusion ensued, and every one was compelled to drink large quantities of wine.   Aristodēmus said that Eryximachus, Phaedrus, and others went away—

[1] *Symposium*, 219 f.
[2] *Symposium*, 221 f.   The words in inverted commas are a quotation from *The Clouds*.

SOCRATES

he himself fell asleep, and as the nights were long took a good rest:
he was awakened towards daybreak by a crowing of cocks, and
when he awoke, the others were either asleep, or had gone away ;
there remained only Socrates, Aristophanes, and Agathon, who
were drinking out of a large goblet which they passed round,
and Socrates was discoursing to them. Aristodemus was only
half awake, and he did not hear the beginning of the discourse ;
the chief thing which he remembered was Socrates compelling
the other two to acknowledge that the genius of comedy was the
same with that of tragedy, and that the true artist in tragedy was
an artist in comedy also. To this they were constrained to assent,
being drowsy, and not quite following the argument. And first
of all Aristophanes dropped off, then, when the day was already
dawning, Agathon. Socrates, having laid them to sleep, rose to
depart ; Aristodemus, as his manner was, following him. At the
Lycēum he took a bath, and passed the day as usual. In the
evening he retired to rest at his own home.[1]

The fourth passage shows what Socrates looked like, and how
he affected men. To estimate this effect, remember that the
speaker was the cleverest, most fashionable, and most unscrupulous young man in Athens, Alcibiades.

AND now, my boys, I shall praise Socrates in a figure which
will appear to him to be a caricature, and yet I speak,
not to make fun of him, but only for the truth's sake. I
say, that he is exactly like the busts of Silēnus, which are set up
in the statuaries' shops, holding pipes and flutes in their mouths ;
and they are made to open in the middle, and have images of
gods inside them. I say also that he is like Marsyas the satyr.
You yourself will not deny, Socrates, that your face is like that of
a satyr. Aye, and there is a resemblance in other points too.
And are you not a flute-player ? That you are, and a performer
far more wonderful than Marsyas. He indeed with instruments
used to charm the souls of men by the power of his breath, and

---

[1] Ib. 223 f. For Aristophanes, see p. 129 f. ; Agathon was a tragic poet.
The Lyceum was a famous gymnasium and park in Athens.

the players of his music do so still. But you produce the same effect with your words only, and do not require the flute : that is the difference between you and him. When we hear any other speaker, even a very good one, he produces absolutely no effect upon us, or not much, whereas the mere fragments of you and your words, even at second-hand, and however imperfectly repeated, amaze and possess the souls of every man, woman, and child who comes within hearing of them. And if I were not afraid that you would think me hopelessly drunk, I would have sworn as well as spoken to the influence which they have always had and still have over me. For my heart leaps within me, and my eyes rain tears when I hear them. And I observe that many others are affected in the same manner. I have heard Pericles and other great orators, and I thought they spoke well, but I never had any similar feeling ; my soul was not stirred by them, nor was I angry at the thought of my own slavish state. But this Marsyas has often brought me to such a pass, that I have felt as if I could hardly endure the life which I am leading ; and I am conscious that if I did not shut my ears against him, and fly as from the voice of the siren, my fate would be like that of others— he would transfix me, and I should grow old sitting at his feet. For he makes me confess that I ought not to live as I do, neglecting the wants of my own soul, and busying myself with the concerns of the Athenians ; therefore I hold my ears and tear myself away from him. And he is the only person who ever made me ashamed, which you might think not to be in my nature, and there is no one else who does the same. For I know that I cannot answer him or say that I ought not to do as he bids, but when I leave his presence the love of popularity gets the better of me. And therefore I run away and fly from him, and when I see him I am ashamed of what I have confessed to him. Many a time have I wished that he were dead, and yet I know that I should be much more sorry than glad, if he were to die : so that I am at my wits' end.[1]

---

[1] Ib. 215 f. Silenus was the drunken attendant of Dionysus, familiar to us in Rubens' and Titian's paintings.

Ugliness, physical strength, great personal fascination, originality, are the obvious traits of the man portrayed in these passages. Add to these a passion for intellectual things, which he pursues, not like a modern philosopher, in the study, but in everyday life, and among his fellow men.

It is reasonable to preface an account of Socrates with personal descriptions of him, because (and this is rare with philosophers) his greatness lies as much in his character and personality as in his teaching. He is one of the great creative thinkers of the world, but he is also one of its prophets and martyrs, and he stands out among the few men who have united intellectual to moral genius. He was born about 469 B.C., and while taking such part in public affairs as fell to the lot of all Athenians, he devoted his life to intellectual interests, first occupying himself with scientific questions, but deserting them for the study of man. He was to be found in the market, the gymnasia, and all places of public resort, asking and answering questions, ready to discuss anything in heaven and earth. Accused in 399 of irreligion and of corrupting the young, he was condemned and put to death. His defence is given in the *Apology* (or ' Reply of Socrates ') by Plato ; Xenophon has written another and obviously inferior version. The sentence was a judicial crime, but intelligible. Athens was nerve-racked and suspicious after a disastrous war ; among the pupils of Socrates were Alcibiades and many of the young aristocrats who had conspired against her democracy ; and, as we shall see, his teaching had a dangerous side.

Socrates did not believe in studying philosophy through books in which a writer states his opinion without its being tested or discussed. He preferred the method of conversation, pressing on by question and answer to the truth, exposing fallacies, and open to exposure himself. That explains why Plato's works are ' dialogues ', and why on first acquaintance they seem to be deserts of logic-chopping with occasional oases of fine and impressive writing. It was the habit of Socrates, when a phrase like justice, or friendship, or religiousness was used, to turn on the speaker, and asking what he really meant by it to dissect his definition. The Athenians used terms as loosely as we do, and the result is that definition after definition is tried and found wanting, and the dialogue often leaves us among the wrecks of discarded theories, still ignorant of what we set out to find. The following is a characteristic example of his method. He is discussing with the Thessalian Meno whether virtue is knowledge ;

in other words, whether one can learn to be good in the sense in which one can learn to carpenter or to plough.

Soc. The next question is, whether virtue is knowledge or of another species ?

Men. Yes.

Soc. Do we not say that virtue is a good ?

Men. Certainly.

Soc. Now, if there be any sort of good which is distinct from knowledge, virtue may be that good ; but if knowledge embraces all good, then we shall be right in thinking that virtue is knowledge ?

Men. True.

Soc. And virtue makes us good ?

Men. Yes.

Soc. And if we are good, then we are profitable ; for all good things are profitable ?

Men. Yes.

Soc. Then virtue is profitable ?

Men. That is the only inference.

Soc. Then now let us see what are the things which severally profit us. Health and strength, and beauty and wealth—these, and the like of these, we call profitable ?

Men. True.

Soc. And yet these things may also sometimes do us harm : would you not think so ?

Men. Yes.

Soc. And what is the guiding principle which makes them profitable or the reverse ? Are they not profitable when they are rightly used, and hurtful when they are not rightly used ?

Men. Certainly.

Soc. Next, let us consider the goods of the soul : they are temperance, justice, courage, quickness of apprehension, memory, magnanimity, and the like ?

Men. Surely.

Soc. And such of these as are not knowledge, but of another sort, are sometimes profitable and sometimes hurtful ; as, for example, courage wanting prudence, which is only a sort of confidence ? When a man has no sense he is harmed by courage, but when he has sense he is profited ?

Men. True.

Soc. And the same may be said of temperance and quickness of apprehension ; whatever things are learned or done with sense are profitable, but when done without sense they are hurtful ?

Men. Very true.

Soc. And in general, all that the soul attempts or endures, when under the guidance of wisdom, ends in happiness ; but when she is under the guidance of folly, in the opposite ?

Men. That appears to be true.

Soc. If then virtue is a quality of the soul, and is admitted to be profitable, it must be wisdom or prudence, since none of the things of the soul are either profitable or hurtful in themselves, but they are all made profitable or hurtful by the addition of wisdom or of folly ; and therefore if virtue is profitable, virtue must be a sort of wisdom or prudence ?

Men. I quite agree.

Soc. And the other goods, such as wealth and the like, of which we were just now saying that they are sometimes good and sometimes evil, do not they also become profitable or hurtful, accordingly as the soul guides and uses them rightly or wrongly ; just as the things of the soul herself are benefited when under the guidance of wisdom and harmed by folly ?

Men. True.

Soc. And the wise soul guides them rightly, and the foolish soul wrongly ?

Men. Yes.

Soc. And is not this universally true of human nature ? All good things hang upon the soul, and the things of the soul herself hang upon wisdom, if they are to be good ; and so wisdom is inferred to be that which profits—and virtue, as we say, is profitable ?

Men. Certainly.

Soc. And thus we arrive at the conclusion that virtue is either wholly or partly wisdom ?

Men. I think that what you are saying, Socrates, is very true.

Soc. But if this is true, then the good are not by nature good ?

Men. I think not.

Soc. If they had been, there would assuredly have been discerners of characters among us who would have known our future great men ; and on their showing we should have adopted them, and when we had got them, we should have kept them in the citadel out of the way of harm, and stamped them even more than we stamp gold, in order that no one might tamper with them ; and when they grew up they would have been useful to the state ?

Men. Yes, Socrates, that would have been the right way.

Soc. But if the good are not by nature good, are they made good by instruction ?

Men. There appears to be no other alternative, Socrates. On the supposition that virtue is knowledge, there can be no doubt that virtue is taught.

Soc. Yes, indeed ; but what if the supposition is erroneous ?

Men. I certainly thought just now that we were right.

Soc. Yes, Meno ; but a principle which has any soundness should stand firm not only just now, but always.

Men. Well ; and why are you so slow of heart to believe that knowledge is virtue ?

Soc. I will try and tell you why, Meno. I do not retract the assertion that if virtue is knowledge it may be taught ; but I fear that I have some reason in doubting whether virtue is knowledge : for consider now and say whether virtue, and not only virtue but anything that is taught, must not have teachers and disciples ?

Men. Surely.

Soc. And conversely, may not the art of which neither

teachers nor disciples exist be assumed to be incapable of being taught ?

Men. True ; but do you think that there are no teachers of virtue ?

Soc. I have certainly often inquired whether there were any, and taken great pains to find them, and have never succeeded.[1]

This is an instance of the spirit in which Socrates pursued truth, never content unless his principles ' stood firm, not only at the minute but for ever '. (Note how he throws over the conclusion which he seems to have reached, and proceeds to re-test and re-argue it again.) It is also an instance of the famous ' dialectic ' or ' conversation-method ', which uses question and answer, and is a far more promising means of reaching truth than the making of speeches or the writing of books, for the argument can be tested step by step as it proceeds. The method is that of the ' tutorial hour ' in our older universities, and of the tutorial class discussions of the Workers' Educational Association, and is strongly opposed to the modern tendency to trust in text-books and lectures. Socrates never confused, as we often do, education with information, or supposed that it consists in pumping facts and ideas into a passive mind. In the following fable he points out the drawbacks of books—their injury to the memory, their tendency to fill the mind with uncriticized and half-assimilated knowledge. Any one who really understands the fable will have grasped the most important thing in education.

AT the Egyptian city of Naucratis, there was a famous old god, whose name was Theuth ; the bird which is called the Ibis is sacred to him, and he was the inventor of many arts, such as arithmetic and calculation and geometry and astronomy and draughts and dice, but his great discovery was the use of letters. Now in those days the god Thamus was the king of the whole country of Egypt. To him came Theuth and showed his inventions, desiring that the other Egyptians might be allowed to have the benefit of them ; he enumerated them, and Thamus inquired about their several uses, and praised some of them and censured others, as he approved or disapproved of them.

[1] Meno, 87 f.

It would take a long time to repeat all that Thamus said to Theuth in praise or blame of the various arts. But when they came to letters, This, said Theuth, will make the Egyptians wiser and give them better memories ; it is a specific both for the memory and for the wit. Thamus replied : Most ingenious Theuth, the parent or inventor of an art is not always the best judge of the utility or inutility of his own inventions to the users of them. And in this instance, you who are the father of letters, from a paternal love of your own children have been led to attribute to them a quality which they cannot have ; for this discovery of yours will create forgetfulness in the learners' souls, because they will not use their memories ; they will trust to the external written characters and not remember of themselves. The specific which you have discovered is an aid not to memory, but to reminiscence, and you give your disciples not truth, but only the semblance of truth ; they will be hearers of many things and will have learned nothing ; they will appear to be omniscient and will generally know nothing ; they will be tiresome company, having the show of wisdom without the reality.[1]

The dialectic method is tedious to any but born disputants. It annoyed respectable Athenians who did not like their inconsistencies exposed or their conventional views upset. Even those who enjoyed talking with Socrates were disconcerted. ' Even before I talked with you, Socrates,' said one of them, ' I was told that you did nothing but puzzle yourself and others. In fact you seem to me just like the flat torpedo-fish, for you really make me numb—in soul and speech alike—and I don't know what answer to give you.' We may well believe that these conversations, with their negative result, had a bad effect on some young men, destroying their conventional views of right and wrong and substituting nothing for them. What then did Socrates think that he was doing, and why have these conversations of his had so profound an effect on the world ?

He shall answer for himself. The following is his own half-whimsical description and justification of his procedure. A friend of his was told by the Delphic oracle that Socrates was the wisest of mankind. The following is the comment of Socrates.

[1] Phaedrus, 274 f.

WHEN I heard the answer, I said to myself, What can the god mean? and what is the interpretation of his riddle? for I know that I have no wisdom, small or great. What then can he mean when he says that I am the wisest of men? And yet he is a god, and cannot lie; that would be against his nature. After long consideration, I thought of a method of trying the question. I reflected that if I could only find a man wiser than myself, then I might go to the god with a refutation in my hand. I should say to him, ' Here is a man who is wiser than I am; but you said that I was the wisest.' Accordingly I went to one who had the reputation of wisdom, and observed him—his name I need not mention; he was a politician whom I selected for examination—and the result was as follows: When I began to talk with him, I could not help thinking that he was not really wise, although he was thought wise by many, and still wiser by himself; and thereupon I tried to explain to him that he thought himself wise, but was not really wise; and the consequence was that he hated me, and his enmity was shared by several who were present and heard me. So I left him, saying to myself, as I went away: Well, although I do not suppose that either of us knows anything really beautiful and good, I am better off than he is—for he knows nothing, and thinks that he knows; I neither know nor think that I know. In this latter particular, then, I seem to have slightly the advantage of him. Then I went to another who had still higher pretensions to wisdom, and my conclusion was exactly the same. Whereupon I made another enemy of him, and of many others besides him.

Then I went to one man after another, being not unconscious of the enmity which I provoked, and I lamented and feared this: but necessity was laid upon me—the word of God, I thought, ought to be considered first. And I said to myself, Go I must to all who appear to know, and find out the meaning of the oracle. And I swear to you, Athenians, by the dog I swear!—for I must tell you the truth—the result of my mission was just this: I found that the men most in repute were all but the most foolish;

and that others less esteemed were really wiser and better. I will tell you the tale of my wanderings and of the ' Herculean ' labours, as I may call them, which I endured only to find at last the oracle irrefutable. After the politicians, I went to the poets. And there, I said to myself, you will be instantly detected ; now you will find out that you are more ignorant than they are. Accordingly, I took them some of the most elaborate passages in their own writings, and asked what was the meaning of them—thinking that they would teach me something. Will you believe me ? I am almost ashamed to confess the truth, but I must say that there is hardly a person present who would not have talked better about their poetry than they did themselves. Then I knew that not by wisdom do poets write poetry, but by a sort of genius and inspiration. The poets appeared to me to be much in the same case ; and I further observed that upon the strength of their poetry they believed themselves to be the wisest of men in other things in which they were not wise. So I departed, conceiving myself to be superior to them for the same reason that I was superior to the politicians. . . . This inquisition has led to my having many enemies of the worst and most dangerous kind, and has given occasion also to many calumnies. And I am called wise, for my hearers always imagine that I myself possess the wisdom which I find wanting in others : but the truth is, men of Athens, that God only is wise ; and by his answer he intends to show that the wisdom of men is worth little or nothing ; he is not speaking of Socrates, he is only using my name by way of illustration, as if he said, He, O men, is the wisest, who, like Socrates, knows that his wisdom is in truth worth nothing. And so I go about the world, obedient to the god, and search and make inquiry into the wisdom of any one, whether citizen or stranger, who appears to be wise ; and if he is not wise, then in vindication of the oracle I show him that he is not wise ; and my occupation quite absorbs me, and I have no time to give either to any public matter of interest or to any concern of my own, but I am in utter poverty by reason of my devotion to the god.[1]

[1] Apology, 21 f.

So in a half-parable Socrates describes that complete open-mindedness, that conviction of fallibility and ignorance, which is the chief stimulus and the indispensable condition in all progress towards knowledge. It would be easy to apply to modern politicians, men of letters, &c., the tests which Socrates applied to his contemporaries ; and the results would be the same.

We think of missions as religious. Socrates had a mission no less than Isaiah or Wesley, but it was intellectual : he spent his life in convincing the Athenians, not of sin, but of ignorance. Of the motives and character of his amazing conversations we can form some idea from the following :

SOME one will say : And are you not ashamed, Socrates, of a course of life which is likely to bring you to an untimely end? To him I may fairly answer : There you are mistaken : a man who is good for anything ought not to calculate the chance of living or dying ; he ought only to consider whether in doing anything he is doing right or wrong—acting the part of a good man or of a bad. For wherever a man's place is, whether the place which he has chosen or that in which he has been placed by a commander, there he ought to remain in the hour of danger ; he should not think of death or of anything but of disgrace. And this, men of Athens, is true.

Strange, indeed, would be my conduct, O men of Athens, if I who, when I was ordered by the generals whom you chose to command me at Potidaea and Amphipolis and Delium, remained where they placed me, like any other man, facing death—if now, when, as I conceive and imagine, God orders me to fulfil the philosopher's mission of searching into myself and other men, I were to desert my post through fear of death, or any other fear ; that would indeed be strange, and I might justly be arraigned in court for denying the existence of the gods, if I disobeyed the oracle because I was afraid of death, fancying that I was wise when I was not wise. For the fear of death is indeed the pretence of wisdom, and not real wisdom, being a pretence of knowing the unknown ; and no one knows whether death, which men in their fear apprehend to be the greatest evil, may not be the greatest good. Is not this ignorance of a disgraceful sort, the ignorance which is the conceit that a man knows what he does not know ? And in this respect only I believe myself to differ from men in general, and may perhaps claim to be wiser than they are :—that whereas I know but little of the world below, I do not suppose that I know : but I do know that injustice and disobedience to a better, whether God or man, is evil and dishonourable, and I will never fear or avoid a possible good rather than a certain evil. And therefore if you let me go now, and are not convinced by Anytus, who said that since I had been prosecuted I must be put to death ; if you say to me, Socrates, this time we will not mind Anytus, and you shall be let off, but upon one condition, that you are not to inquire and speculate in this way any more, and that if you are caught doing so again you shall die ;—if this was the condition on which you let me go, I should reply : Men of Athens, I honour and love you ; but I shall obey God rather than you, and while I have life and strength I shall never cease from the practice and teaching of philosophy, exhorting any one whom I meet and saying to him after my manner : You, my friend—a citizen of the great and mighty and wise city of Athens—are you not ashamed of heaping up the greatest amount of money and honour and reputation, and caring so little about wisdom and truth and the greatest improvement of the soul, which you never regard or heed at all ? And if the person with whom I am arguing says : Yes, but I do care ; then I do not leave him or let him go at once ; but I proceed to interrogate and examine and cross-examine him, and if I think that he has no virtue in him, but only says that he has, I reproach him with undervaluing the greater, and over-valuing the less. And I shall repeat the same words to every one whom I meet, young and old, citizen and alien, but especially to the citizens, inasmuch as they are my brethren. For know that this is the command from God ; and I believe that no greater good has ever happened in the state than my service to the God. For I do nothing but go about persuading you all, old and young alike, not to take thought for your persons or your properties, but first and chiefly to care about the greatest improvement of the soul. I tell you that virtue is not given by money, but that from virtue comes money and every good of man, public as well as private. This is my teaching, and if this is the doctrine which corrupts the youth, I am a mischievous person.[1]

This is preaching not less ardent than that of a Hebrew prophet, though different in form and spirit ; but it is also one of the most momentous steps in the history of thought. ' Socrates', says Aristotle, ' taught men to define their general terms.' If he were alive to-day he would still be busy at the same task, forcing us to say what we mean, questioning journalists and politicians on their latest ' cry ', and dissipating the thick fog that hangs about ' self-determination ' or ' socialism ' or ' liberty ' or ' democracy ' or the latest catchword of the day. Till the distant hour when mankind come to say what they mean and mean what they say, their greatest intellectual need will be a Socrates.

This is not due to his doctrines. We do not believe the famous theory which guided his thought and inspired his mission, that all wrongdoing is the result of ignorance, and that if men know what is good they will do it ; though we may be reminded that most of the evil in the world is due to false opinions about what is right. Fools are responsible for at least as much evil as knaves ; and even knaves often ' know not what they do '. But his significance for us lies in the fact that he is the first and most perfect example of the spirit of science—if science is the pursuit of truth for its own sake. He has the ideal of science ; he used to say that there was only one good, knowledge, and only one evil, ignorance. He has its ardour, and at the age of seventy is still so keen in the pursuit of truth, that his last hours were given to it. He has its patience and caution : that is why his dialogues often end without a conclusion ; for he would rather admit ignorance than accept an untested or unsatisfactory answer. He has its self-control and self-suppression, and never loses his temper in a discussion, is never discourteous or unfair. He has its courage, and is never frightened or shocked or irritated by any view, but always ready dispassionately to examine it. He has its perfect disinterestedness, and is as ready to test his own opinions as well as those of others : for he remembered what disputants generally

---

[1] Apology, 28 f. The extract is from Socrates' defence when on trial. Anytus is one of his accusers.

forget, his own ignorance and fallibility. A passage in the *Phaedo* illustrates this, where, with but a few hours to live, he is discussing immortality. The argument seems to have shown that the soul is immortal, and at such a moment the mind might well have allowed itself to rest in pleasant or comforting thoughts. Socrates felt the temptation, but he checks himself.

AT this moment I am sensible that I have not the temper of a philosopher ; like the vulgar, I am only a partisan. Now the partisan, when he is engaged in a dispute, cares nothing about the rights of the question, but is anxious only to convince his hearers of his own assertions. And the difference between him and me at the present moment is merely this—that whereas he seeks to convince his hearers that what he says is true, I am rather seeking to convince myself ; to convince my hearers is a secondary matter with me. And do but see how much I gain by the argument. For if what I say is true, then I do well to be persuaded of the truth ; but if there be nothing after death, still, during the short time that remains, I shall not distress my friends with lamentations, and my ignorance will not last, but will die with me, and therefore no harm will be done. This is the state of mind, Simmias and Cebes, in which I approach the argument. And I would ask you to be thinking of the truth and not of Socrates : agree with me, if I seem to you to be speaking the truth ; or if not, withstand me might and main, that I may not deceive you as well as myself in my enthusiasm, and like the bee, leave my sting in you before I die.

And now let us proceed, he said.[1]

Passages like these remind us that character is not less necessary than intellect to great achievements in the world of thought. Their union in Socrates explains his power over his associates, and his influence in the world is due to the fact that he died as well as lived for truth, and is perhaps the first of her martyrs. When death overtook him, he faced it with perfect serenity and courage. This is the speech which Plato puts on his lips when the death sentence was passed :

[1] *Phaedo*, 91.

NOT much time will be gained, O Athenians, in return for the evil name which you will get from the detractors of the city, who will say that you killed Socrates, a wise man; for they will call me wise, even although I am not wise, when they want to reproach you. If you had waited a little while, your desire would have been fulfilled in the course of nature. For I am far advanced in years, as you may perceive, and not far from death. I am speaking now not to all of you, but only to those who have condemned me to death. And I have another thing to say to them: You think that I was convicted because I had no words of the sort which would have procured my acquittal—I mean, if I had thought fit to leave nothing undone or unsaid. Not so; the deficiency which led to my conviction was not of words—certainly not. But I had not the boldness or impudence or inclination to address you as you would have liked me to do, weeping and wailing and lamenting, and saying and doing many things which you have been accustomed to hear from others, and which, as I maintain, are unworthy of me. I thought at the time that I ought not to do anything common or mean when in danger: nor do I now repent of the style of my defence; I would rather die having spoken after my manner, than speak in your manner and live. For neither in war nor yet at law ought I or any man to use every way of escaping death. Often in battle there can be no doubt that if a man will throw away his arms, and fall on his knees before his pursuers, he may escape death; and in other dangers there are other ways of escaping death, if a man is willing to say and do anything. The difficulty, my friends, is not to avoid death, but to avoid unrighteousness; for that runs faster than death. I am old and move slowly, and the slower runner has overtaken me, and my accusers are keen and quick, and the faster runner, who is unrighteousness, has overtaken them. And now I depart hence condemned by you to suffer the penalty of death—they too go their ways condemned by the truth to suffer the penalty of villainy and wrong; and I must abide by my award—let them abide by theirs. I suppose that these things may be regarded as fated—and I think that they are well.[1]

After a few words to those who had condemned him, he addresses those who voted for his acquittal, closing his speech with some reflections on death.

LET us reflect and we shall see that there is great reason to hope that death is a good; for one of two things—either death is a state of nothingness and utter unconsciousness, or, as men say, there is a change and migration of the soul from this world to another. Now if you suppose that there is no consciousness, but a sleep like the sleep of him who is undisturbed even by dreams, death will be an unspeakable gain. For if a person were to select the night in which his sleep was undisturbed even by dreams, and were to compare with this the other days and nights of his life, and then were to tell us how many days and nights he had passed in the course of his life better and more pleasantly than this one, I think that any man, I will not say a private man, but even the great king will not find many such days and nights, when compared with the others. Now if death be of such a nature, I say that to die is gain; for eternity is then only a single night. But if death is the journey to another place, and there, as men say, all the dead abide, what good, my friends and judges, can be greater than this? If indeed when the pilgrim arrives in the world below, he is delivered from the professors of justice in this world, and finds the true judges who are said to give judgement there, Mīnos and Rhadamanthus and Aeacus and Triptolemus, and other sons of God who were righteous in their own life, that pilgrimage will be worth making. What would not a man give if he might converse with Orpheus and Musaeus and Hesiod and Homer? Nay, if this be true, let me die again and again. I my-self, too, shall have a wonderful interest in there meeting and conversing with Palamēdēs, and Ajax the son of Telamon, and any other ancient hero who has suffered death through an unjust

[1] Apology, 38 f.

judgement; and there will be no small pleasure, as I think, in comparing my own sufferings with theirs. Above all, I shall then be able to continue my search into true and false knowledge; as in this world, so also in the next; and I shall find out who is wise, and who pretends to be wise, and who is not. What would not a man give, my judges, to be able to examine the leader of the great Trojan expedition; or Odysseus or Sisyphus, or numberless others, men and women too! What infinite delight would there be in conversing with them and asking them questions! In another world they do not put a man to death for asking questions: assuredly not. For besides being happier than we are, they will be immortal, if what is said is true.

Wherefore, my judges, be of good cheer about death, and know of a certainty, that no evil can happen to a good man, either in life or after death. He and his are not neglected by the gods; nor has my own approaching end happened by mere chance. I am not angry with my condemners, or with my accusers; they have done me no harm, although they did not mean to do me any good; and for this I may gently blame them.

Still I have a favour to ask of them. When my sons are grown up, I would ask you, my friends, to punish them, and I would have you trouble them, as I have troubled you, if they seem to care about riches, or anything, more than about virtue; or if they pretend to be something when they are really nothing—then reprove them, as I have reproved you, for not caring about that for which they ought to care, and thinking that they are something when they are really nothing. And if you do this, both I and my sons will have received justice at your hands.

The hour of departure has arrived, and we go our ways—I to die, and you to live. Which is better God only knows.

The following is the account of his last hours, one of the great descriptive passages in literature, in its union of profound feeling with perfect simplicity and reticence. The story is told by one of Socrates' disciples, Phaedo, to another who had not been present at the end.

I WILL begin at the beginning, and endeavour to repeat the entire conversation. On the previous days we had been in the habit of assembling early in the morning at the court in which the trial took place and which is not far from the prison. There we used to wait talking with one another until the opening of the doors (for they were not opened very early) ; then we went in and generally passed the day with Socrates. On the last morning we assembled sooner than usual, having heard on the day before when we quitted the prison in the evening that the sacred ship had come from Dēlos ; and so we arranged to meet very early at the accustomed place. On our arrival the jailer who answered the door, instead of admitting us, came out and told us to stay until he called us. ' For the Eleven ', he said, ' are now with Socrates ; they are taking off his chains, and giving orders that he is to die to-day.' He soon returned and said that we might come in. On entering we found Socrates just released from chains, and Xanthippè sitting by him, and holding his child in her arms. When she saw us she uttered a cry and said, as women will : ' O Socrates, this is the last time that either you will converse with your friends, or they with you.' Socrates turned to Crito and said : ' Crito, let some one take her home.' Some of Crito's people accordingly led her away, crying out and beating herself.[1]

There follows the famous discussion on immortality, which is the subject of the dialogue. At its close his disciples ask for his last commands.

WHEN he had done speaking, Crito said : And have you any commands for us, Socrates—anything to say about your children, or any other matter in which we can serve you ?

Nothing particular, Crito, he replied : only, as I have always told you, take care of yourselves ; that is a service which you may be ever rendering to me and mine and to all of us, whether

---

[1] Phaedo, 59 f. The ' sacred ship ' went annually to Delos ; during its absence no executions could take place. ' The Eleven ' were the chief police officials. Xanthippe is Socrates' wife.

you promise to do so or not. But if you have no thought for yourselves, and care not to walk according to the rule which I have prescribed for you, not now for the first time, however much you may profess or promise at the moment, it will be of no avail.

We will do our best, said Crito : And in what way shall we bury you ?

In any way that you like ; but you must get hold of me, and take care that I do not run away from you. Then he turned to us and added with a smile :—I cannot make Crito believe that I am the same Socrates who have been talking and conducting the argument ; he fancies that I am the other Socrates whom he will soon see, a dead body—and he asks, How shall he bury me ? And though I have spoken many words in the endeavour to show that when I have drunk the poison I shall leave you and go to the joys of the blessed—these words of mine, with which I was comforting you and myself, have had, as I perceive, no effect upon Crito. And therefore I want you to be surety for me to him now, as at the trial he was surety to the judges for me : but let the promise be of another sort ; for he was surety for me to the judges that I should remain, but go away and depart ; and then he will suffer less at my death, and not be grieved when he sees my body being burned or buried. I would not have him sorrow at my hard lot, or say at the burial, Thus we lay out Socrates, or, Thus we follow him to the grave or bury him ; for false words are not only evil in themselves, but they infect the soul with evil. Be of good cheer then, my dear Crito, and say that you are burying my body only, and do with that whatever is usual, and what you think best.

When he had spoken these words, he arose and went into a chamber to bathe ; Crito followed him and told us to wait. So we remained behind, talking and thinking of the subject of our discourse, and also of the greatness of our sorrow ; he was like a father of whom we were being bereaved, and we were about to pass the rest of our lives as orphans. When he had taken his

bath his children were brought to him (he had two young sons
and an elder one) ; and the women of his family also came, and
he talked to them and gave them a few directions in the presence
of Crito ; then he dismissed them and returned to us.

Now the hour of sunset was near, for a good deal of time had
passed while he was within. When he came out, he sat down
with us again after his bath, but not much was said. Soon the
jailer, who was the servant of the Eleven, entered and stood by
him, saying : To you, Socrates, whom I know to be the noblest
and gentlest and best of all who ever came to this place, I will
not impute the angry feelings of other men, who rage and swear
at me, when, in obedience to the authorities, I bid them drink the
poison—indeed, I am sure that you will not be angry with me ;
for others, as you are aware, and not I, are to blame. And so
fare you well, and try to bear lightly what must needs be—you
know my errand. Then bursting into tears he turned away and
went out.

Socrates looked at him and said : I return your good wishes,
and will do as you bid. Then turning to us, he said, How charming
the man is : since I have been in prison he has always been coming
to see me, and at times he would talk to me, and was as good to
me as could be, and now see how generously he sorrows on my
account. We must do as he says, Crito ; and therefore let the cup
be brought, if the poison is prepared[1] : if not, let the attendant
prepare some.

Yet, said Crito, the sun is still upon the hill-tops, and I know
that many a one has taken the draught late, and after the
announcement has been made to him, he has eaten and drunk,
and enjoyed the society of his beloved ; do not hurry—there is
time enough.

Socrates said : Yes, Crito, and they of whom you speak are
right in so acting, for they think that they will be gainers by the
delay ; but I am right in not following their example, for I do not
think that I should gain anything by drinking the poison a little

---

[1] Hemlock poison was used in cases of capital punishment.

later ; I should only be ridiculous in my own eyes for sparing and saving a life which is already forfeit. Please then do as I say, and not to refuse me.

Crito made a sign to the servant, who was standing by ; and he went out, and having been absent for some time, returned with the jailer carrying the cup of poison. Socrates said : You, my good friend, who are experienced in these matters, shall give me directions how I am to proceed. The man answered : You have only to walk about until your legs are heavy, and then to lie down, and the poison will act. At the same time he handed the cup to Socrates, who in the easiest and gentlest manner, without the least fear or change of colour or feature, looking at the man with all his eyes, Echecrates, as his manner was, took the cup and said : What do you say about making a libation out of this cup to any god ? May I, or not ? The man answered : We only prepare, Socrates, just so much as we deem enough. I understand, he said : but I may and must ask the gods to prosper my journey from this to the other world—even so—and so be it according to my prayer. Then raising the cup to his lips, quite readily and cheerfully he drank off the poison. And hitherto most of us had been able to control our sorrow ; but now when we saw him drinking, and saw too that he had finished the draught, we could no longer forbear, and in spite of myself my own tears were flowing fast ; so that I covered my face and wept, not for him, but at the thought of my own calamity in having to part from such a friend. Nor was I the first ; for Crito, when he found himself unable to restrain his tears, had got up, and I followed ; and at that moment, Apollodōrus, who had been weeping all the time, broke out in a loud and passionate cry which made cowards of us all. Socrates alone retained his calmness : What is this strange outcry ? he said. I sent away the women mainly in order that they might not misbehave in this way, for I have been told that a man should die in peace. Be quiet then, and have patience. When we heard his words we were ashamed, and refrained our tears ; and he walked about until, as he said, his legs began to fail, and then he lay on his back, according to the directions, and the man who gave him the poison now and then looked at his feet and legs ; and after a while he pressed his foot hard, and asked him if he could feel ; and he said, No ; and then his leg, and so upward and upwards, and showed us that he was cold and stiff. And he felt them himself, and said : When the poison reaches the heart, that will be the end. He was beginning to grow cold about the groin, when he uncovered his face, for he had covered himself up, and said—they were his last words—he said : Crito, I owe a cock to Asclēpius ;[1] will you remember to pay the debt ? The debt shall be paid, said Crito ; is there anything else ? There was no answer to this question ; but in a minute or two a movement was heard, and the attendants uncovered him ; his eyes were set, and Crito closed his eyes and mouth.

Such was the end, Echecrates, of our friend ; concerning whom I may truly say, that of all the men of his time whom I have known, he was the wisest and justest and best.

[1] Cocks were sacrificed to Asclepius, in whose temples the sick slept for treatment. ' Socrates hopes to awake cured like these ' (Burnet).

PLATO

X

PHILOSOPHY: PLATO

Plato was essentially a poet—the truth and splendour of his imagery, and the melody of his language, are the most intense that it is possible to conceive.—SHELLEY.

Must do my Plato. I'm never well without that.—RUSKIN (1876).

AMONG the young aristocrats who associated with Socrates was one in birth, temperament, genius and life, very different from his master. Yet so deep was the impression made on Plato (427–347) by his teacher that Socrates is the hero of nearly all his dialogues : of himself we hear only incidentally. He was twenty-eight when Socrates was put to death. He went abroad, travelled for twelve years, returned to Athens, bought a house and garden in a public park called the Academy, and there for forty-one years, in the company of pupils and friends, studied and lectured in most branches of thought, but with a special bias towards mathematics and astronomy. Socrates had a mission to Athens, and talked in its public places to any one who would listen. Plato's school in the Academy is more like a private university for teaching and research : it lasted for nearly 800 years after his death. His teaching was interrupted by one experiment in practical politics. At the age of sixty he was asked to undertake the education of the young prince of Syracuse ; his attempt to train a model ruler failed, not entirely through Plato's fault. We have probably twenty-seven dialogues from his hand. Of these, the following are most suited to the general reader : the *Apology* (Socrates' defence at his trial), *Phaedo* (his death-bed discussion of immortality), *Symposium* and *Phaedrus* (dealing with beauty and love), *Gorgias* and *Protagoras* (two discussions turning on whether pleasure is the good), *Critias*, a picture of a prehistoric Golden Age, and the *Republic*.[1]

The greatness of Socrates lies largely in a unique force of personality and character, that of Plato in his thought and writings. With his great work in logic, metaphysics, and mathematics, we will not concern ourselves. Yet his philosophy starts

[1] In dealing with the philosophers, I have not attempted to give a complete sketch of their views, but have quoted characteristic passages from them.

in a logical problem ; how, in the changing, manifold world around us, are we to attain knowledge ? How do we know that these pieces of wood of different shapes, which we call tables, are tables ? In virtue of what do we call beautiful the countless different things to which we apply the word ? The reply is : we have this knowledge in virtue of a general ' idea ' of a table, and a general ' idea ' of beauty ; these ' ideas ' exist not on earth, or for our senses, but for our minds, and, to Plato's mind, have a higher reality than the fleeting objects of sense.

That is a standing problem of technical philosophy—the question what knowledge is. But in Plato it grows into something much wider. It raises the questions ; What is the Soul ? What should men pursue—money, power, the various material things which we live among, or something else ? Why do we take pleasure in beauty—a beautiful face, violets scattered along a hedge foot, the words of a great poet ? What value have these beautiful things ? These are real problems, and if the reader will first give his own answer to them, he will better appreciate Plato's. For Plato, Soul controls the world and is the supreme reality. It exists, entirely pure, as God ; but it is also present in all living things, more dominant in some than others, though in all mixed with and impeded by earthly elements. It lives not by food and drink or the material things which surround it, but by intercourse with unseen spiritual realities, wisdom, truth, beauty, and the other supreme ideas. Its problem in life is to keep these before its mind, escaping to them from the material world, which affords glimpses of them, and especially, through beautiful things, of beauty. Our soul before birth saw the unseen world of Eternal Being where reside God and the eternal ' ideas ' of beauty, truth, goodness, and all that exists on earth. To this world it must return by memory and the use of reason so far as, among the shadows of earth, it can.

Plato was the first to propound this view of the world, which has influenced poets and religious teachers more deeply perhaps than any philosophic theory. We hear its echoes alike in Words-worth and Shelley, and it has coloured many a passage of English poetry. S. Paul expresses essentially the same doctrine, when he talks of living in the Spirit and not in the Flesh, and says, ' We look not at the things which are seen but at the things which are not seen : for the things which are seen are temporal ; but the things which are not seen are eternal.' In the following passage Plato puts this doctrine in the form of a ' myth ' or fable, describing the human soul as a chariot, in which reason, the charioteer, drives two horses, one of animal desire, the other of the nobler, 'spirited' emotions. The myth describes our soul's adventures before birth, and how the soul comes to decline from its heavenly state to a lower life on earth. It explains the spiritual value of truth, wisdom, beauty, and why beauty moves us, recalling to the soul the heavenly world from which it came.

OF the nature of the soul, though her true form be ever a theme of large and more than mortal discourse, let me speak briefly, and in a figure. And let the figure be composite—a pair of winged horses and a charioteer. Now the winged horses and the charioteers of the gods are all of them noble and of noble descent, but those of other races are mixed ; the human charioteer drives his in a pair ; and one of them is noble and of noble breed, and the other is ignoble and of ignoble breed ; and the driving of them of necessity gives a great deal of trouble to him. I will endeavour to explain to you in what way the mortal differs from the immortal creature.

The inanimate world is in the charge of Soul, which pervades the whole heaven, in divers forms appearing ;—when perfect and fully winged she soars upward, and orders the whole world ; whereas the imperfect soul, losing her wings and drooping in her flight, at last settles on the solid ground—there, finding a home, she receives an earthly frame which appears to be self-moved, but is really moved by her power ; and this composition of soul and body is called a living and mortal creature. And now let us ask the reason why the soul loses her wings !

The wing is the corporeal element which is most akin to the divine, and which by nature tends to soar aloft and carry that which gravitates downwards, into the upper region, which is the habitation of the gods. The divine is beauty, wisdom, goodness, and the like ; and by these the wing of the soul is nourished, and grows apace ; but when fed upon evil and foulness and the opposite of good, wastes and falls away. Zeus, the mighty lord holding the reins of a winged chariot, leads the way in heaven, ordering all and taking care of all; and there follows him the array of gods and demi-gods, marshalled in eleven bands; Hestia [1] alone abides at home in the house of heaven; of the rest they who are reckoned among the princely twelve march in their appointed order. They see many blessed sights in the inner heaven, and there are many ways to and fro, along which the blessed gods are passing, every one doing his own work; he may follow who will and can, for jealousy has no place in the celestial choir. But when they go to banquet and festival, then they move up the steep to the top of the vault of heaven. The chariots of the gods in even poise, obeying the rein, glide rapidly; but the others labour, for the vicious steed goes heavily, weighing down the charioteer to the earth when his steed has not been thoroughly trained :—and this is the hour of agony and extremest conflict for the soul. For the immortals, when they are at the end of their course, go forth and stand upon the outside of heaven, and the revolution of the spheres carries them round, and they behold the things beyond. But of the heaven which is above the heavens, what earthly poet ever did or ever will sing worthily? It is such as I will describe; for I must dare to speak the truth, when truth is my theme. There abides the Very Being with which true knowledge is concerned; the colourless, formless, intangible essence, visible only to mind, the pilot of the soul. The divine intelligence, being nurtured upon mind and pure knowledge, and the intelligence of every soul which is capable of receiving the food proper to it, rejoices at beholding Reality, and once more gazing upon truth, is replenished and made glad, until the revolution of the worlds brings her round again to the same place. In the revolution she beholds Justice, and Temperance, and Knowledge Absolute; and beholding the other True Existences in like manner, and feasting upon them, she passes down into the interior of the heavens and returns home; and there the charioteer,

---

[1] The goddess of the hearth. 'The twelve' are the chief gods of the Greek pantheon.

putting up his horses at the stall, gives them ambrosia to eat and nectar to drink.

Such is the life of the gods ; but of other souls, that which follows God best and is likest to him lifts the head of the charioteer into the outer world, and is carried round in the revolution, troubled indeed by the steeds, and with difficulty beholding True Being ; while another only rises and falls, and sees, and again fails to see by reason of the unruliness of the steeds. The rest of the souls are also longing after the upper world and they all follow, but not being strong enough they are carried round below the surface, plunging, treading on one another, each striving to be first ; and there is confusion and perspiration and the extremity of effort ; and many of them are lamed or have their wings broken through the ill-driving of the charioteers ; and all of them after a fruitless toil, not having attained to the mysteries of True Being, go away, and feed upon Opinion.[1] The reason why the souls exhibit this exceeding eagerness to behold the plain of Truth is that pasturage is found there, which is suited to the highest part of the soul ; and the wing on which the soul soars is nourished with this. And there is a law of Destiny, that the soul which attains any vision of Truth in company with a god is preserved from harm until the next period, and if attaining always is always unharmed. But when she is unable to follow and fails to behold the Truth, and through some ill-hap sinks beneath the double load of forgetfulness and vice, and her wings fall from her and she drops to the ground, the law ordains that this soul shall at her first birth pass, not into any other animal, but only into man ; and the soul which has seen most of Truth shall come to the birth as a philosopher, or artist, or some musical and loving nature ; that which has seen Truth in the second degree shall be some righteous king or warrior chief ; the soul which is of the third class shall be a politician, or economist, or trader ; the fourth shall be a great athlete, or a physician ; the fifth shall lead the life of a prophet or hierophant ; to the sixth

[1] As opposed to Knowledge.

the character of a poet or some other imitative artist will be assigned ; to the seventh the life of an artisan or husbandman ; to the eighth that of a sophist or demagogue ; to the ninth that of a prince ;—all these are states of probation, in which he who does righteously improves, and he who does unrighteously, deteriorates his lot.[1]

Ten thousand years must elapse before the soul of each one can return to the place from whence she came, for she cannot grow her wings in less ; only the soul of a philosopher, guileless and true, or the soul of a lover, who is not devoid of philosophy, may acquire wings in the third of the recurring periods of a thousand years ; he is distinguished from the ordinary good man who gains wings in three thousand years :—and they who choose this life three times in succession have wings given them, and go away at the end of three thousand years. But the others receive judgement when they have completed their first life, and after the judgement they go, some of them to the houses of correction which are under the earth, and are punished ; others to some place in heaven whither they are lightly borne by justice, and there they live in a manner worthy of the life which they led here when in the form of men. And at the end of the first thousand years [2] the good souls and also the evil souls both come to draw lots and choose their second life, and they may take any which they please. The soul of a man may pass into the life of a beast, or from the beast return again into the man. But the soul which has never seen the truth will not pass into the human form. For a man must

[1] The position of the trader, doctor, and poet in this hierarchy of lives may surprise us. But Plato's conception of the true ' business man ' may be seen on p. 308. The doctor is placed low, because he deals with human nature in disease, not in health ; the poet, because Plato regarded the literary life as unreal, and its creations as mere shadows of the real world ; the prophet, because he and the ' hierophant ' (connected with religious initiations) were tainted with quackery. ' Economist ', i.e. manager of a household ; whose work in a slave-owning state may be heavy enough to be classed with that of a business man.

[2] Human life is taken as 100 years: we atone for our sins and are rewarded for our good deeds ten times over. This makes our life in the underworld 1,000 years, after which we are reborn. This cycle of 1,000 years must be repeated ten times, before we can return to the divine. See the myth on p. 312 f.

have intelligence of universals, and be able to proceed from the many particulars of sense to one conception of reason ; [1]—this is the recollection of those things which our soul once saw while following God—when she raised her head up towards the True Being. And therefore the mind of the philosopher alone has wings ; and this is just, for he is always, according to the measure of his abilities, clinging in recollection to those things in which God abides, and in beholding which He is what He is. And he who employs aright these memories is ever being initiated into perfect mysteries and alone becomes truly perfect. But, as he forgets earthly interests and is rapt in the divine, the vulgar deem him mad, and rebuke him ; they do not see that he is inspired.

Thus far I have been speaking of the kind of madness which is imputed to him who, when he sees the beauty of earth, is transported with the recollection of the true Beauty ; he would like to fly away, but he cannot ; he is like a bird fluttering and looking upward and careless of the world below ; and he is therefore thought to be mad. And I have shown this of all inspirations to be the noblest and highest and the offspring of the highest to him who has or shares in it, and that he who loves the beautiful is called a lover because he partakes of it. For, as has been already said, every soul of man has in the way of nature beheld True Being; this was the condition of her passing into the form of man. But all souls do not easily recall the things of the other world ; they may have seen them for a short time only, or they may have been unfortunate in their earthly lot, and, having had their hearts turned to unrighteousness through some corrupting influence, they may have lost the memory of the holy things which once they saw. Few only retain an adequate remembrance of them ; and they, when they behold here any image of that other world, are rapt in amazement ; but they are ignorant of what this rapture means, because they do not clearly perceive. For there

---

[1] Unlike an animal, which merely has a succession of particular sensations, man must be able to form general ideas.

is no light of Justice or Temperance or any of the higher Ideas, which are precious to souls, in the earthly copies of them : they are seen through a glass dimly ; and there are few who, going to the images, behold in them the realities,[1] and these only with difficulty. There was a time when with the rest of the happy band they saw Beauty shining in brightness—we philosophers following in the train of Zeus, others in company with other gods ; and then we beheld the beatific vision and were initiated into a mystery which may be truly called most blessed, celebrated by us in our state of innocence, before we had any experience of evils to come, when we were admitted to the sight of apparitions innocent and simple and calm and happy, which we beheld shining in pure light, pure ourselves and not yet enshrined in that living tomb which we carry about, now that we are imprisoned in the body, like an oyster in his shell. Let me linger over the memory of scenes which have passed away.

But of Beauty, I repeat again that we saw her there shining in company with the celestial Forms ; and coming to earth we find her here too, shining in clearness through the clearest aperture of sense. For sight is the most piercing of our bodily senses ; though not by that is Wisdom seen ; her loveliness would have been transporting if there had been a visible image of her, and the other Ideas, if they had visible counterparts, would be equally lovely. But this is the privilege of beauty, that being the loveliest she is also the most palpable to sight. Now he who is not newly initiated or who has become corrupted, does not easily rise out of this world to the sight of true beauty in the other ; he looks only at her earthly namesake, and, instead of being awed at the sight of her, he is given over to pleasure. But he whose initiation is recent, and who has been the spectator of many glories in the other world, is amazed when he sees any one having a godlike face or form, which is the expression of divine beauty ; and at first a shudder runs through him, and again the old awe steals

[1] The ' images ' are beautiful, &c., things on earth, which remind us of the ' realities ', i.e. the ideal Beauty, &c., in heaven.

over him ; then looking upon the face of his beloved as of a god he reverences him, and if he were not afraid of being thought a downright madman, he would sacrifice to his beloved as to the image of a god ; then while he gazes on him there is a sort of reaction, and the shudder passes into an unusual heat and perspiration ; for, as he receives the effluence of beauty through the eyes, the wing moistens and he warms. And as he warms, the parts out of which the wing grew, and which had been hitherto closed and rigid, and had prevented the wing from shooting forth, are melted, and as nourishment streams upon him, the lower end of the wing begins to swell and grow from the root upwards ; and the growth extends under the whole soul—for once the whole was winged.

After describing how love makes the wing of the soul to grow, Plato proceeds :

AS I said at the beginning of this tale, I divided each soul into three—two horses and a charioteer ; and one of the horses was good and the other bad : the division may remain, but I have not yet explained in what the goodness or badness of either consists, and to that I will now proceed. The right-hand horse is upright and cleanly made ; he has a lofty neck and an aquiline nose ; his colour is white, and his eyes dark ; he is a lover of honour and modesty and temperance, and the follower of true glory ; he needs no touch of the whip, but is guided by word and admonition only. The other is a crooked lumbering animal, put together anyhow ; he has a short thick neck ; he is flat-faced and of a dark colour, with grey eyes and blood-red complexion ; the mate of insolence and pride, shag-eared and deaf, hardly yielding to whip and spur. Now when the charioteer beholds the vision of love, and has his whole soul warmed through sense, and is full of the prickings and ticklings of desire, the obedient steed, then as always under the government of shame, refrains ; but the other, heedless of the pricks and of the blows of the whip, plunges and runs away, giving all manner of trouble to his companion and the charioteer. They at first indignantly oppose him and will not be urged on to do terrible and unlawful deeds ; but at last, when he persists in plaguing them, they yield and agree to do as he bids them. And now they are on the spot and behold the flashing beauty of the beloved ; which when the charioteer sees, the memory is carried to the true beauty, whom he beholds in company with Modesty like an image placed upon a holy pedestal. He sees her, but he is afraid and falls backward in adoration, and by his fall is compelled to pull back the reins with such violence as to bring both the steeds on their haunches, the one willing and unresisting, the unruly one very unwilling. And when this has happened several times and the villain has ceased from his wanton way, he is tamed and humbled, and follows the will of the charioteer, and when he sees the beautiful one he is ready to die of fear. And from that time forward the soul of the lover follows the beloved in modesty and holy fear.

After this their happiness depends upon their self-control ; if the better elements of the mind which lead to order and philo-sophy prevail, then they pass their life here in happiness and harmony—masters of themselves and orderly—enslaving the vicious and emancipating the virtuous elements of the soul ; and when the end comes, they are light and winged for flight, having conquered in one of the three heavenly or truly Olympian victories ; nor can human discipline or divine inspiration confer any greater blessing on man than this.[1]

These extracts give us a glimpse of Plato's philosophic and religious ideas. It would be difficult to find anywhere a loftier conception of God and of human life than the following passage conveys.

Theod. If you could only persuade everybody, Socrates, as you do me, of the truth of your words, there would be more peace and fewer evils among men.

Soc. Evils, Theodorus, can never pass away ; for there must

[1] Phaedrus, 246 f. The wrestling match at the Olympic games had three rounds.

always remain something which is antagonistic to good. Having no place among the gods in heaven, of necessity they hover around the mortal nature and this earthly sphere. Wherefore we ought to fly away from earth to heaven as quickly as we can ; and to fly away is to become like God, as far as this is possible ; and to become like him is to become holy, just, and wise. But, my friend, you cannot easily convince mankind that they should pursue virtue or avoid vice for other reasons than a good reputation, which is the reason given by the world. Whereas, the truth is that God is never in any way unrighteous—he is perfect righteousness ; and he of us who is the most righteous is most like him. Herein we see whether a man is really clever or whether he is worthless and no true man. For to know this is true wisdom and virtue, and ignorance of this is manifest folly and vice. All other kinds of wisdom or cleverness, which seem only, such as the wisdom of politicians, or the wisdom of the arts, are coarse and vulgar. The unrighteous man, or the sayer and doer of unholy things, had far better not be encouraged in the illusion that his roguery is clever ; for men glory in their shame— they fancy that they hear others saying of them, ' These are not mere good-for-nothing persons, mere burdens of the earth, but such as men should be who mean to dwell safely in a state.' Let us tell them that they are all the more truly what they do not think they are because they do not know it ; for they do not know the penalty of injustice, which above all things they ought to know—not stripes and death, as they suppose, which evil-doers often escape, but a penalty which cannot be escaped.

Theod. What is that ?

Soc. There are two patterns eternally set before them ; the one blessed and divine, the other godless and wretched : but they do not see them, or perceive that in their utter folly and infatuation they are growing like the one and unlike the other, by reason of their evil deeds ; and the penalty is, that they lead a life answering to the pattern which they are growing like.[1]

[1] Theaet. 176.

The philosophy of Plato, with its ascetic tinge, turning from the visible to the invisible, from earth to heaven, is one of the permanent modes of the human mind, one of the ways in which some spirits of every thinking generation interpret the world. It is the same with his political writings. Here too we find an attitude to the state, a view of life, which continually recurs in history, warmly championed by some thinkers, bitterly contested by others. Perhaps no writer contains so many seminal thoughts ; thoughts often hidden in paradoxes, but never losing their fertility and continually germinating afresh in the minds where the seed falls.

For Plato's political views the reader should study the *Republic*, his greatest work, which raises question after question of moral and metaphysical philosophy, but at the bottom is a discussion of the ideal ordering of human life in the state. Plato's youth had seen the fall of the Athenian Empire, and we, who in recent years have been within sight of a general downfall of European civilization, can read with sympathy this attempt to devise an ideal and stable community. It was suggested by a practical need, but the proposals in the *Republic* are not practical. This must always be remembered. Some writers, like Aristotle, Adam Smith, Mill (to mention no moderns), can be treated as practical guides in politics. Others, like the Hebrew prophets, Plato, Ruskin, live less in the world of actual institutions than among the ideal principles, which are never fully realized, but in the light of which human practice is continually being tested and revised. In a later work, the *Laws*, Plato sketched a constitution that he believed practical. In the *Republic*, with a characteristic Greek freedom of thought, ignoring prejudice and existing custom, he pictures the state which, in a better world, mankind might enjoy ; and just because he has not to consider the compromises and reticences necessary in practical politics, he can raise and face the fundamental problems of politics that beset and puzzle every age. The chief of these problems he conceives to be the unwisdom that hinders men from seeing the right, the selfishness that makes them prefer their private interests to it, the position of women, the uses of education, the disunion caused by the divergent interests of different classes, the influence of literature and art on the citizen. Now, as then, these, if we leave foreign relations aside, are the root problems of politics. The lines along which Plato wishes to solve them are as follows.

The nation must be ruled by the best and most intelligent people in it, or, in his words, by ' philosopher-kings '. ' Until philosophers are kings, or the kings and rulers of this world have the spirit of philosophy, until political power and wisdom are united, until those commoner natures, who pursue either to the exclusion of the other, stand aside, states will never have rest from their evils—no, nor, I believe, will the human race ; then only will this state of ours have a possibility of life and behold the light of day.' [1]

This idea surprises us, for whom a philosopher is a man writing on difficult subjects in obscure language. But to Plato he was a lover of wisdom, who had the desire to know truth and the will to live by it. Here are two pictures of the philosopher, the first a whimsical portrait of his position in an uncongenial community. He is shown (by contrast with the narrow, practical ' man of the world') lost in a society where money, power, and high birth are worshipped, yet a worthier citizen of the universe than the worldling.

AND thus, my friend, on every occasion, private as well as public, as I said at first, when he appears in a law court, or in any place in which he has to speak of things which are at his feet and before his eyes, he is the jest of the general herd, tumbling into every sort of disaster through his inexperience. His awkwardness is fearful, and gives the impression of imbecility. When he is abused, he has nothing personal to say in answer to the civilities of his adversaries, for he knows no scandals of any one and they do not interest him ; and therefore he is laughed at for his sheepishness ; and when others are being praised and glorified, in the simplicity of his heart he cannot help going into fits of laughter, so that he seems to be a downright idiot. When he hears a prince or king eulogized, he fancies that he is listening to the praises of some keeper of cattle—a swineherd, or shepherd, or perhaps a cowherd, who is congratulated on the quantity of milk which he squeezes from them ; and he remarks that the

---

[1] Plato is undemocratic in so far as he has a poor opinion of the brains and character of most of mankind, democratic in so far as he believes in a career open to talent, and draws his rulers from every class.

creature whom they tend, and out of whom they squeeze the
wealth, is of a less tractable and more insidious nature. Then,
again, he observes that the great man is of necessity as ill-
mannered and uneducated as any shepherd—for he has no
leisure, and he is surrounded by a wall, which is his mountain-pen.
Hearing of enormous landed proprietors of ten thousand acres
and more, our philosopher deems this to be a trifle, because he has
been accustomed to think of the whole earth ; and when they
sing the praises of aristocracy, and say that some one is a gentleman because he can show seven generations of wealthy ancestors,
he thinks that their sentiments only betray a dull and narrow
vision in those who utter them, and who are not educated enough
to look at the whole, nor to consider that every man has had
thousands and ten thousands of progenitors, and among them
have been rich and poor, kings and slaves, Hellenes and barbarians,
innumerable.   And when people pride themselves on having
a pedigree of twenty-five ancestors, which goes back to Heracles,
the son of Amphitryon, he cannot understand their poverty of
ideas.   Why are they unable to calculate that Amphitryon had
a twenty-fifth ancestor, who might have been anybody, and was
such as fortune made him, and that he had a fiftieth, and so on ?
He amuses himself with the notion that they cannot count, and
thinks that a little arithmetic would have got rid of their senseless
vanity.[1]

This picture is deliberately overdrawn. The following passage
shows in sober statement what Plato thought the real philosopher
to be like, and why he believed him the right ruler for the state.
Incidentally, it is an admirable statement of the moral value
of a liberal education. Plato points out that the philosopher,
by his profession, has a clearer vision of principle than the
ordinary man, who lives from hand to mouth and deals with
each case as the moment suggests ; he will therefore be more set
on ordering the world in accordance with principle, and in
particular with the principles among which his mind lives—
beauty, truth, justice, &c. He continues :

[1] Theaet. 174.

IS there not another quality which philosophers should possess ?

What quality ?

Truthfulness : they will never intentionally receive into their mind falsehood, which is their detestation, and they will love the truth.

Yes, that may be safely affirmed of them.

' May be ', my friend, I replied, is not the word ; say rather, ' must be affirmed ' : for a lover cannot help loving all that belongs or is akin to the object of his affections.

Right, he said.

And is there anything more akin to wisdom than truth ?

How can there be ?

Can the same nature be a lover of wisdom and a lover of falsehood ?

Never.

The true lover of learning then must from his earliest youth, as far as in him lies, desire all truth ?

Assuredly.

But then again, as we know by experience, he whose desires are strong in one direction will have them weaker in others ; they will be like a stream which has been drawn off into another channel.

True.

He whose desires are drawn towards knowledge in every form will be absorbed in the pleasures of the soul, and will hardly feel bodily pleasure—I mean, if he be a true philosopher and not a sham one.

That is most certain.

Such an one is sure to be temperate and the reverse of covetous ; for the motives which make another man desirous of having and spending have no place in his character.

Very true.

Another criterion of the philosophical nature has also to be considered.

What is that ?

There should be no secret corner of illiberality ; nothing can be more antagonistic than meanness to a soul which is ever longing after the whole of things both divine and human.

Most true, he replied.

Then how can he who has magnificence of mind and is the spectator of all time and all existence, think much of human life ?

He cannot.

Or can such an one account death fearful ?

No indeed.

Then the cowardly and mean nature has no part in true philosophy ?

Certainly not.

Or again : can he who is harmoniously constituted, who is not covetous or mean, or a boaster, or a coward—can he, I say, ever be unjust or hard in his dealings ?

Impossible.[1]

The permanent truth in these ideas is that a man who has 'meditated much upon God, the human mind and the *Summum Bonum*' is likely to be better, not intellectually only but morally, than one who has not : nobler interests leave less room for the petty and base. And such characters the state needs. Plato knew, as Burke knew, that ' a great empire and little minds go ill together', and that no one without imagination and idealism could be a true statesman. But, as the *Theaetetus* passage shows, he divined the truth that there are communities in which the ideally best rulers are disastrous practical failures, that the wise and good will not succeed if they have to govern a too uncongenial society, where they may seem as absurd and out of place as a sober man in a company of drunkards.

Plato's first problem is to find his rulers. Here he relies on eugenics (he is the first eugenist) to give him a stock of first-class ability. Then, as the ablest men are liable to be corrupted, Plato calls to his aid education and devises a training to develop and strengthen alike the body and the mind. Finally, because he sees that private interests and ambitions may still warp his rulers' characters, he enjoins on his governing classes community of possessions and of wives and children. He is here more far-

[1] Republic, 485.

sighted and logical than our communists, who forget that the ultimate root of individualism lies as much in the private family as in private property. *Un père de famille est capable de tout.*[1] So Plato believes himself to have secured the ideal statesman, naturally able, highly trained, with no interests to consider except those of his fellow men, with no temptation to exploit the community.

Plato's communism seems to most of us impracticable and repellent, and he himself admitted that it could not be realized. Its interest is that it points to the disease that saps the strength of all nations, that selfishness for which it is a desperate remedy. And here too, as in his view of the universe, he represents a permanent mood of the human mind, which reappears in age after age. His vision of a state, free from the temptations and weaknesses of private property, ruled by an *élite* in the interests of mankind, continually haunts the dreams of men, and has been incorporated in experiments more or less noble, which reveal its practical difficulties. Plato is the spiritual ancestor equally of the Mediaeval Church and of the idealists among the Bolsheviks.

Plato saw that education is the foundation of political and social progress. His system rests on it, and he is the first great educational thinker of the world. Much that is interesting and suggestive in his system must here be passed over : his insistence on a ' liberal ' education, the important part assigned to mathematics and science, the even balance kept (as we have not always kept it) between the extremes of those who condemn and those who exaggerate athletics. I will here only call attention to two principles, emphasized by him, to which our eyes are but now opening—if indeed they are open at all—the importance of continuing education in later life, and the significance of sub-conscious influences. The following passage shows that Plato divined the importance of the sub-conscious element in education. In theory we accept, in practice we ignore, the view he urges ; but our education can never be satisfactory till we have grappled with the problem.

BUT shall our superintendence go no further, and are the poets only to be required by us to express the image of the good in their works, on pain, if they do anything else, of expulsion from our state ? Or is the same control to be

[1] Quoted by A. E. Taylor, *Plato*, to whom I owe one or two other points.

extended to other artists, and are they also to be prohibited from exhibiting the opposite forms of vice and intemperance and meanness and indecency in sculpture and building and the other creative arts ; and is he who cannot conform to this rule of ours to be prevented from practising his art in our state, lest the taste of our citizens be corrupted by him ? We would not have our rulers grow up amid images of moral deformity, as in some noxious pasture, and there browse and feed upon many a baneful herb and flower day by day, little by little, until they silently gather a festering mass of corruption in their own soul. Let our artists rather be those who are gifted to discern the true nature of the beautiful and graceful ; then will our youth dwell in a land of health, amid fair sights and sounds, and receive the good in everything ; and beauty, the effluence of fair works, shall flow into the eye and ear, like a health-giving breeze from a purer region, and insensibly draw the soul from earliest years into likeness and sympathy with the beauty of reason.[1]

If Plato's requirements are met in the beautiful surroundings of schools like Winchester, Eton, and others, they are totally ignored in Bethnal Green or Poplar, where, in the name of liberty, and in the interests of trade, the state allows the children of the poor to be infected from childhood with the moral and artistic ugliness of cinema and advertisement.

But, however well brought up, men are liable to be corrupted by the world. In the following passage Plato shows how men come to lose the ideals with which they go into life. ' The public ', he says, ' complains that individual teachers, like Socrates (we can substitute modern parallels at will), corrupt the young men : the real corrupter is the public itself.' Plato is speaking primarily of politics, but his words apply equally to all occupations and all ages. Then, as now, men were bullied or seduced into dropping their principles, and ' giving the public what it wants '. What Plato here describes happens every day in every land.

DO not great crimes and the spirit of pure evil spring out of a fullness of nature ruined by education rather than from any inferiority, whereas weak natures are scarcely capable of any very great good or very great evil ?

[1] Republic, 401.

There I think that you are right.

And our philosopher follows the same analogy—he is like a plant which, having proper nurture, must necessarily grow and mature into all virtue, but, if sown and planted in an alien soil, becomes the most noxious of all weeds, unless he be preserved by some divine power. Do you really think, as people so often say, that our youth are corrupted by Sophists? Are not the public who say these things the greatest of all Sophists? And do they not educate to perfection young and old, men and women alike, and fashion them after their own hearts?

When is this accomplished? he said.

When they meet together, and the world sits down at an assembly, or in a court of law, or a theatre, or a camp, or in any other popular resort, and there is a great uproar, and they praise some things which are being said or done, and blame other things, equally exaggerating both, shouting and clapping their hands, and the echo of the rocks and the place in which they are assembled redoubles the sound of the praise or blame—at such a time will not a young man's heart, as they say, leap within him? Will any private training enable him to stand firm against the overwhelming flood of popular opinion? or will he be carried away by the stream? Will he not have the notions of good and evil which the public in general have—he will do as they do, and as they are, such will he be?

Yes, Socrates; necessity will compel him.[1]

Once corrupted, he will find many people to show him how the public can be flattered. Plato compares these politicians to

A MAN who should study the tempers and desires of a mighty strong beast who is fed by him—he would learn how to approach and handle him, also at what times and from what causes he is dangerous or the reverse, and what is the meaning of his several cries, and by what sounds, when another utters them, he is soothed or infuriated;

[1] Ib. 491 fin.

and you may suppose further, that when, by continually attending upon him, he has become perfect in all this, he calls his knowledge wisdom, and makes of it a system or art, which he proceeds to teach, although he has no real notion of what he means by the principles or passions of which he is speaking, but calls this honourable and that dishonourable, or good or evil, or just or unjust, all in accordance with the tastes and tempers of the great brute. Good he pronounces to be that in which the beast delights and evil to be that which he dislikes.

Plato's remedy is striking, and it is one of the points in which he is in advance of us. He prescribes yet more education, and an education that continues through life. He saw the absurdity of systems like our own in which education ceases at twenty-three or earlier, and in which after that age, as if there were nothing else to be learnt, hardly any one does any systematic thinking or study. Therefore his ruler class, after finishing what we should call their university course, are to embark on a special course of study (largely mathematical and scientific) till the age of thirty-five, when they are to enter politics for fifteen years, then to be released to study, then return to politics, and so on. The modern movement for Adult Education is a return to Plato.

The ideal community is an ' aristocracy ' : government by the best, that is, by the wise. But Plato describes other types of state. He has Greek conditions in his mind, and he describes each type in its extreme form, but much that he says applies to our own times. Second in merit comes ' timocracy ', where ' honour ' is the guiding principle. Plato is thinking of Sparta, but his picture recalls pre-war Prussia, and, at points, the rule of the landed-gentlemen class in England : indeed it is very much what we should call aristocracy. ' Timocracy ' is followed by ' oligarchy ', which corresponds to unrestricted capitalism. Plato puts his finger on the political weakness of such a state—the sharp division between rich and poor and the growth of a class made desperate by poverty. He begins by showing how his ' timocratic ' class becomes infected by capitalism—a similar change in nineteenth-century England is a favourite theme of modern novelists.

OUGHT I not to begin by describing how the change from timocracy to oligarchy arises ?

Yes.

Well, I said, no eyes are required in order to see how the one passes into the other.

How ?

The accumulation of gold in the treasury of private individuals is the ruin of timocracy. One, seeing another grow rich, seeks to rival him, and thus the great mass of the citizens become lovers of money.

Likely enough.

And so they grow richer and richer, and the more they think of making a fortune the less they think of virtue ; for when riches and virtue are placed together in the scales of the balance, the one always rises as the other falls.

True.

And in proportion as riches and rich men are honoured in the state, virtue and virtuous are dishonoured.

Clearly.

And so at last, instead of loving contention and glory, men become lovers of trade and money ; they honour and look up to the rich man, and make a ruler of him. And this, speaking generally, is the way in which oligarchy is established.

Yes, he said ; but what are the characteristics of this form of government, and what are the defects of which we were speaking ?

First of all, I said, consider the nature of the qualification. Just think of what would happen if pilots were to be chosen according to their property, and a poor man were refused permission to steer, even though he were a better pilot ?

You mean that they would shipwreck ?

Yes ; and is not this true of the government of anything ?

I should imagine so.

Except a state ?—or would you include a state ?

Nay, he said, the case of a state is the strongest of all, inasmuch as its rule is the greatest and most difficult of all.

This, then, will be the first great defect of oligarchy ?
Clearly.
And here is another defect which is quite as bad.
What defect ?
The inevitable division : such a state is not one, but two states, the one of poor, the other of rich men ; and they are living on the same spot and always conspiring against one another.
That, surely, is at least as bad.
Another discreditable feature is, that, for a like reason, they are incapable of carrying on any war. Either they arm the multitude, and then they are more afraid of them than of the enemy ; or, if they do not call them out in the hour of battle, they are oligarchs indeed, few to fight as they are few to rule. And at the same time their fondness for money makes them unwilling to pay taxes.[1]

There follows the growth of an unemployed pauper class. These Plato compares to walking drones in a hive.

OF these walking drones God has made some without stings, but others have dreadful stings ; of the stingless class are those who in their old age end as paupers ; of the stingers come all the criminal class, as they are termed.
Most true, he said.
Clearly then, whenever you see paupers in a state, somewhere in that neighbourhood there are hidden away thieves and cut-purses and robbers of temples, and all sorts of malefactors.
Clearly.
Well, I said, and in oligarchical states do you not find paupers ?
Yes, he said ; nearly everybody is a pauper who is not a ruler.
And may we be so bold as to affirm that there are also many criminals to be found in them, rogues who have stings, and whom the authorities are careful to restrain by force ?
Certainly, we may be so bold.

Ib. 550.

The existence of such persons is to be attributed to want of education, ill-training, and an evil constitution of the state?

True.

Such, then, is the form and such are the evils of oligarchy; and there may be many other evils.

Plato then sketches the capitalist at his very worst. 'The " oligarchical man " is the man who makes it his highest good to command the things which money can buy, and the money which can buy them. His maxim is to make a profit out of everything, and to work hard, and deny himself the full indulgence of his appetites, in order to be sure of getting his profit. Education he naturally despises, honesty he values in general as the " best policy ", but his real opinion of it is betrayed when he gets the chance to make a dishonest profit with impunity.' [1]

HE takes [Plato says] to money-making and by mean and miserly savings and hard work gets a fortune together. Is not such an one likely to seat the concupiscent and covetous element on the vacant throne and to suffer it to play the great king within him, girt with tiara and chain and scimitar?

Most true, he replied.

And when he has made reason and spirit sit down on the ground obediently on either side of their sovereign, and taught them to know their place, he compels the one to think only of how lesser sums may be turned into larger ones, and will not allow the other to worship and admire anything but riches and rich men, or to be ambitious of anything so much as the acquisition of wealth and the means of acquiring it.[2]

Plato then draws a parallel between the capitalist and the capitalist state.

FIRST then, they resemble one another in the value which they set upon wealth?

Certainly.

Also in their penurious, laborious character; the individual

[1] Taylor, *o. c.*   [2] Republic, 553.

only satisfies his necessary appetites, and confines his expenditure to them ; his other desires he subdues, under the idea that they are unprofitable.

True.

He is a shabby fellow, who saves something out of everything and makes a purse for himself ; and this is the sort of man whom the vulgar applaud. You see that he is not a man of cultivation, I said.

I imagine not, he said ; had he been educated he would never have made a blind god[1] his master, or given him chief honour.

Excellent ! I said. Yet consider : Must we not further admit that owing to this want of cultivation there will be found in him dronelike desires as of pauper and rogue, which are forcibly kept down by his general habit of life ?

True.

Do you know where you will have to look if you want to discover his rogueries ?

Where must I look ?

You should see him where he has some great opportunity of acting dishonestly.

Aye.

It will be clear enough then that in his ordinary dealings which give him a reputation for honesty he coerces his bad passions by an enforced virtue ; not making them see that they are wrong, or taming them by reason, but by necessity and fear constraining them, and because he trembles for his possessions.

To be sure.

For these reasons such an one will be more respectable than most people ; yet the true virtue of a unanimous and harmonious soul will flee far away and never come near him.

No man could say that this is a picture of the average capitalist : but it is a type to be found in all industrial communities.

It is to the passion for money that Plato ascribes the degeneracy

---

[1] i.e. money.

of states. In his unfinished *Critias* he drew a picture of the ideal community of Atlantis and of its corruption.

SUCH was the vast power which the god settled in the lost island of Atlantis. For many generations, as long as the divine nature lasted in them, they were obedient to the laws, and well-affectioned toward the god, whose seed they were ; for they possessed true and in every way great spirits, uniting gentleness with wisdom in the various chances of life, and in their intercourse with one another. They despised everything but virtue, caring little for their present state of life, and thinking lightly of the possession of gold and other property, which seemed only a burden to them ; neither were they intoxicated by luxury ; nor did wealth deprive them of their self-control ; but they were sober, and saw clearly that all these goods are increased by virtue and friendship with one another, whereas by too great regard and respect for them they are lost and friendship with them. By such reflections and by the continuance in them of a divine nature, the qualities which we have described grew and increased among them ; but when the divine portion began to fade away, and became diluted too often and too much with the mortal admixture, and the human nature got the upper hand, they then, being unable to bear their fortune, behaved unseemly, and to him who had an eye to see, grew visibly debased, for they were losing the fairest of their precious gifts ; but to those who had no eye to see the true happiness, they appeared glorious and blessed at the very time when they were full of avarice and unrighteous power.[1]

We may here add a passage which shows Plato's gift of diagnosing the diseases of human society. Why, he asks, are commerce and industry so unsatisfactory ? His reply is that those employed in them regard the occupation as a means of making money, not of benefiting the community. Instead of remembering that his function in life is to house and entertain men, the hotel-keeper only thinks of making money out of them. And so

[1] *Critias,* 542.

in all trades. For this the remedy is to get the best men (and women) into trade, and to change its ideal. The cause and cure of industrial disease have never been more simply stated.

FEW, dear Cleinias, are the men—they need rare natural gifts and the best of education—who can show moderation when assailed by wants and desires ; few, who are sober when they have a chance of making large sums of money, and who are content with moderate profits. The mass of mankind are the exact opposite ; their desires are unbounded, their appetite for gain unlimited. This explains the attacks on such occupations as retail business, commerce, and hotel-keeping, and the disrepute under which they lie. I am going to make a ridiculous suggestion ; it will never be acted on and I hope it will not. But suppose that we were to compel the best men everywhere to become retailers or to manage hotels or to carry on some similar business : or, if fate and necessity compelled the best women to follow similar callings, then we should realize how agreeable and attractive these occupations were, and if they were managed on uncorrupt principles, they would be honoured as we honour a mother and a nurse. As it is, men go to lonely spots and build houses of entertainment, and receive necessitous guests in welcome rest-houses, and give them peace and calm when storm-tost, and cool shade in hot weather : and then, instead of treating them as friends, and doing the duties of hospitality, they treat them like enemies or captives at their mercy, and do not release them till they have paid unjust, abominable, extortionate ransoms. It is these bad practices which have discredited an occupation that in fact is the relief of human necessity.[1]

The *Republic* is a great work because of the vision with which Plato divines fundamental problems, and of the boldness and frankness with which he treats them. Always he shows that detachment which enabled the Greeks to originate philosophy and science, the power to ignore the prejudices and customs of his own day, to consider each question *de novo*, and (as he would

[1] Laws, 918. See Ruskin, *Unto This Last*, c. 1, for the same doctrine.

have phrased it) to follow the argument where it led instead of compelling it to follow him. Thus, though slavery was as completely a part of Athenian civilization as machinery is of our own, Plato conceives a state in which slavery disappears. Thus, though Athenian women were peculiarly backward and repressed, he treats the problem of women with a frankness and openness which probably no writer before the nineteenth century has equalled, arguing that though men may be on the whole the abler sex, nothing in feminine nature unfits women for political life, and concluding that it should be open to them as fully as to men. To-day this is accepted : but only rare insight and courage could have led a thinker to enounce it more than two thousand years ago.

Of one element of greatness in the *Republic,* an English translation gives little idea. It is a literary masterpiece. It is characteristic of Plato that he inspired two schools of philosophy which have nothing in common, the Sceptics and the Mystics of antiquity. Plato combined, as no other philosopher has done, different and apparently inconsistent powers, uniting the greatest literary and artistic gifts to the close-reasoning power of the dialectician. At one time he spins fine-drawn, abstract arguments, at another he writes pure poetry. The concluding extracts illustrate his humour, imagination, and power of writing. We have already witnessed the setting of one Socratic dialogue (p. 255 f.) ; the following passage gives the scene of another. It takes place in the country outside Athens and shows how mistaken is the belief that the Greeks did not care for nature ; though Socrates, like Dr. Johnson, preferred the human interest of the town. Notice the Greek fairy story about the cicada.

Soc. Let us turn aside and go by the Ilissus ; we will sit down at some quiet spot.

Phaedr. I am fortunate in not having my sandals, and as you never have any, I think that we may go along the brook and cool our feet in the water ; this will be the easiest way, and at midday and in the summer is pleasant.

Soc. Lead on, and look out for a place in which we can sit down.

Phaedr. Do you see that tallest plane-tree in the distance ?

Soc. Yes.

Phaedr. There are shade and gentle breezes, and grass on which we may either sit or lie down. I should like to know, Socrates, whether the place is not somewhere here at which Boreas is said to have carried off Orithyia from the banks of the Ilissus ?

Soc. Such is the tradition.

Phaedr. And is this the exact spot ? The little stream is delightfully clear and bright ; I can fancy that there might be maidens playing near.[1]

After some conversation they reach the plane-tree.

Soc. By Herè, a fair resting-place, full of summer sounds and scents. Here is this lofty and spreading plane-tree, and the agnus castus high and clustering, in the fullest blossom and the greatest fragrance ; and the stream which flows beneath the plane-tree is deliciously cold to the feet. Judging from the ornaments and images, this must be a spot sacred to Achelous[2] and the Nymphs. How delightful is the breeze : so very sweet ; and there is a sound in the air shrill and summerlike which makes answer to the chorus of the cicadae. But the greatest charm of all is the grass, like a pillow gently sloping to the head. My dear Phaedrus, you have been an admirable guide.

Phaedr. What an incomprehensible being you are, Socrates : when you are in the country, as you say, you really are like some stranger who is led about by a guide. Do you ever cross the border ? I rather think that you never venture even outside the gates.

Soc. Very true, my good friend ; and I hope that you will excuse me when you hear the reason, which is, that I am a lover of knowledge, and the men who dwell in the city are my teachers, and not the trees or the country. Though I do indeed believe that you have found a spell with which to draw me out of the city into the country, like a hungry cow before whom a bough or a bunch of fruit is waved. For only hold up before me in like manner a book, and you may lead me all round Attica, and over

[1] Phaedrus, 229.
[2] The greatest of Greek rivers, used by them to personify water.

the wide world. And now having arrived, I intend to lie down, and do you choose any posture in which you can read best. Begin. There is time enough. And I believe that the grasshoppers chirruping after their manner in the heat of the sun over our heads are talking to one another and looking down at us. What would they say if they saw that we, like the many, are not conversing, but slumbering at midday, lulled by their voices, too indolent to think ? Would they not have a right to laugh at us ? They might imagine that we were slaves, who, coming to rest at a place of resort of theirs, like sheep lie asleep at noon around the well. But if they see us discoursing, and like Odysseus sailing past them, deaf to their siren voices, they may perhaps, out of respect, give us of the gifts which they receive from the gods that they may impart them to men.

Phaedr. What gifts do you mean ? I never heard of any.

Soc. A lover of music like yourself ought surely to have heard the story of the grasshoppers, who are said to have been human beings in an age before the Muses. And when the Muses came and song appeared they were ravished with delight ; and singing always, never thought of eating and drinking, until at last in their forgetfulness they died. And now they live again in the grass-hoppers ; and this is the return which the Muses make to them—they neither hunger, nor thirst, but from the hour of their birth they are always singing, and never eating or drinking ; and when they die they go and inform the Muses in heaven who honours them on earth.[1]

Plato's poetic genius is shown in the ' myths ' or fables, which he uses in many of his dialogues to convey by allegory truths that human reason can only imperfectly express. The following example is from the *Republic*. It is a vision of what happened to our souls before birth and of what will happen to them after death. Note Plato's belief in eternal punishment, his doctrine of free will, and his insistence that right conduct must be based on definite principles : if it merely proceeds from habit and the absence of temptation, it seems to him built on sand. The

[1] Ib. 259.

symbolism of the myth is derived from contemporary Orphic doctrines which taught rebirth ; these Orphic theories on a future life have deeply coloured Christian eschatology. The close of the myth illustrates how near lie the borders of poetry and prose.

WELL, I will tell you a tale ; a tale of a hero, Er the son of Armenius, a Pamphylian by birth. He was slain in battle, and ten days afterwards, when the bodies of the dead were taken up already in a state of corruption, his body was found unaffected by decay, and carried away home to be buried. And on the twelfth day, as he was lying on the funeral pile, he returned to life and told them what he had seen in the other world. He said that when his soul left the body he went on a journey with a great company, and that they came to a mysterious place at which there were two openings in the earth ; they were near together, and over against them were two other openings in the heaven above. In the intermediate space there were judges seated, who commanded the just, after they had given judgement on them and had bound their sentences in front of them, to ascend by the heavenly way on the right hand ; and in like manner the unjust were bidden by them to descend by the lower way on the left hand ; these also bore the symbols of their deeds, but fastened on their backs. He drew near, and they told him that he was to be the messenger who would carry the report of the other world to men, and they bade him hear and see all that was to be heard and seen in that place. Then he beheld and saw on one side the souls departing at either opening of heaven and earth when sentence had been given on them ; and at the two other openings other souls, some ascending out of the earth dusty and worn with travel, some descending out of heaven clean and bright. And arriving ever and anon they seemed to have come from a long journey, and they went forth with gladness into the meadow, where they encamped as at a festival ; and those who knew one another embraced and conversed, the souls which came from earth curiously inquiring about the things above, and the souls which came from heaven about the things

beneath. And they told one another of what had happened by
the way, those from below weeping and sorrowing at the remembrance of the things which they had endured and seen in their
journey beneath the earth (now the journey lasted a thousand
years), while those from above were describing heavenly delights
and visions of inconceivable beauty. The story, Glaucon, would
take too long to tell; but the sum was this: He said that for
every wrong which they had done to any one they suffered ten-
fold; or once in a hundred years—such being reckoned to be the
length of man's life, and the penalty being thus paid ten times
in a thousand years. If, for example, there were any who had
been the cause of many deaths, or had betrayed or enslaved states
or armies, or been guilty of any other evil behaviour, for each
and all their offences they received punishment ten times over,
and the rewards of beneficence and justice and holiness were in
the same proportion. He mentioned that he was present when one
of the spirits asked another, ' Where is Ardiaeus the Great ? '
(Now this Ardiaeus lived a thousand years before the time of Er:
he had been the tyrant of some city of Pamphylia, and had
murdered his aged father and his elder brother, and was said to
have committed many other abominable crimes.) The answer
of the other spirit was: ' He comes not hither and will never
come.' ' And this ', said he, ' was one of the dreadful sights which
we ourselves witnessed. We were at the mouth of the cavern, and,
having completed all our experiences, were about to reascend,
when of a sudden Ardiaeus appeared and several others, most of
whom were tyrants; and there were also besides the tyrants
private individuals who had been great criminals: they were
just, as they fancied, about to return to the upper world, but the
mouth, instead of admitting them, gave a roar, whenever any of
these incurable sinners or some one who had not been sufficiently
punished tried to ascend; and then wild men of fiery aspect, who
were standing by and heard the sound, seized and carried them
off; and Ardiaeus and others they bound head and foot and hand,
and threw them down and flayed them with scourges, and

dragged them along the road at the side, carding them on thorns like wool, and declaring to the passers-by what were their crimes, and that they were being taken away to be cast into hell.' And of all the many terrors which they had endured, he said that there was none like the terror which each of them felt at that moment, lest they should hear the voice ; and when there was silence, one by one they ascended with exceeding joy. These, said Er, were the penalties and retributions, and there were blessings as great.[1]

After seven days the spirits are taken to the place where they draw lots for their future existence.

WHEN Er and the spirits arrived, their duty was to go at once to Lachesis ;[2] but first of all there came a prophet who arranged them in order ; then he took from the knees of Lachesis lots and samples of lives, and having mounted a high pulpit, spoke as follows : ' Hear the word of Lachesis, the daughter of Necessity. Mortal souls, behold a new cycle of life and mortality. Your genius[3] will not be allotted to you, but you will choose your genius ; and let him who draws the first lot have the first choice, and the life which he chooses shall be his destiny. Virtue is free, and as a man honours or dishonours her he will have more or less of her ; the responsibility is with the chooser—God is justified.' When the Interpreter had thus spoken he scattered lots indifferently among them all, and each of them took up the lot which fell near him, all but Er himself (he was not allowed), and each as he took his lot perceived the number which he had obtained. Then the Interpreter placed on the ground before them the samples of lives ; and there were many more lives than the souls present, and they were of all sorts. There were lives of every animal and of man in every condition. And there were

---

[1] Republic, 614.
[2] The three Fates were Lachesis (the Allotter), Clotho (the Spinner), Atropos (the Unturning One). The first allotted, the second spun, the third made irrevocable, the thread of life.
[3] The spirit, the personification of his destiny, that attends each man through life.

despotisms among them, some lasting out the despot's life, others which broke off in the middle and came to an end in poverty and exile and beggary ; and there were lives of famous men, some who were famous for their form and beauty as well as for their strength and success in games, or, again, for their birth and the qualities of their ancestors ; and some who were the reverse of famous for the opposite qualities. And of women likewise. There was not, however, any definite character in them, because the soul, when choosing a new life, must of necessity become different. But there was every other quality, and they all mingled with one another, and also with elements of wealth and poverty, and disease and health ; and there were mean states also. And here, my dear Glaucon, is the supreme peril of our human state ; and therefore the utmost care should be taken. Let each one of us leave every other kind of knowledge and seek and follow one thing only, if peradventure he may be able to learn and may find some one who will make him able to learn and discern between good and evil, and so to choose always and everywhere the better life as he has opportunity. He should consider the bearing of all these things which have been mentioned severally and collectively upon virtue ; he should know what the effect of beauty is when combined with poverty or wealth in a particular soul, and what are the good and evil consequences of noble and humble birth, of private and public station, of strength and weakness, of cleverness and dullness, and of all the natural and acquired gifts of the soul, and the operation of them when conjoined ; he will then look at the nature of the soul, and from the consideration of all these qualities he will be able to determine which is the better and which is the worse ; and so he will choose, giving the name of evil to the life which will make his soul more unjust, and good to the life which will make his soul more just ; all else he will disregard. For we have seen and know that this is the best choice both in life and after death. A man must take with him into the world below an adamantine faith in truth and right, that there too he may be undazzled by the desire of wealth or the other allurements of evil, lest, coming upon despotisms and similar fortunes, he do irremediable wrongs to others and suffer yet worse himself ; but let him know how to choose the mean and avoid the extremes on either side, as far as possible, not only in this life but in all that which is to come. For this is the way of happiness.

And according to the report of the messenger from the other world this was what the prophet said at the time : ' Even for the last comer, if he chooses wisely and will live diligently, there is appointed a happy and not undesirable existence. Let not him who chooses first be careless, and let not the last despair.' And when he had spoken, he who had the first choice came forward and in a moment chose the greatest despotism ; his mind having been darkened by folly and sensuality, he had not thought out the whole matter before he chose, and did not at first sight perceive that he was fated, among other evils, to devour his own children. But when he had time to reflect, and saw what was in the lot, he began to beat his breast and lament over his choice, forgetting the proclamation of the prophet ; for, instead of throwing the blame of his misfortune on himself, he accused chance and the gods, and everything rather than himself. Now he was one of those who came from heaven, and in a former life had dwelt in a well-ordered state, but his virtue was a matter of habit only, and he had no philosophy. And it was true of others who were similarly overtaken, that the greater number of them came from heaven and therefore they had never been schooled by trial, whereas the pilgrims who came from earth having themselves suffered and seen others suffer were not in a hurry to choose. And owing to this inexperience of theirs, and also because the lot was a chance, many of the souls exchanged a good destiny for an evil or an evil for a good. For if a man had always on his arrival in this world dedicated himself from the first to sound philosophy, and had been moderately fortunate in the number of the lot, he might, as the messenger reported, be happy here, and also his journey to another life and return to this, instead of being rough and underground, would be smooth and heavenly. Most curious, he said, was the spectacle—sad and laughable and strange; for the choice of souls was in most cases based on their experiences of a previous life. There he saw the soul which had once been Orpheus choosing the life of a swan out of enmity to the race of women, hating to be born of a woman because they had been his murderers; he beheld also the soul of Thamyras[1] choosing the life of a nightingale; birds, on the other hand, like the swan and other musicians, wanting to be men. The soul which obtained the twentieth lot chose the life of a lion, and this was the soul of Ajax the son of Telamon, who would not be a man, remembering the injustice which was done him in the judgement about the arms. The next was Agamemnon, who took the life of an eagle, because, like Ajax, he hated human nature by reason of his sufferings. About the middle came the lot of Atalanta; she, seeing the great fame of an athlete, was unable to resist the temptation: and after her there followed the soul of Epēus the son of Panopēus passing into the nature of a woman cunning in the arts; and far away among the last who chose, the soul of the jester Thersītēs was putting on the form of a monkey. There came also the soul of Odysseus having yet to make a choice, and his lot happened to be the last of them all. Now the recollection of former toils had disenchanted him of ambition, and he went about for a considerable time in search of the life of a private man who had no cares; he had some difficulty in finding this, which was lying about and had been neglected by everybody else; and when he saw it, he said that he would have done the same had his lot been first instead of last, and that he was delighted to have it. And not only did men pass into animals, but I must also mention that there were animals tame and wild who changed into one another and into corresponding human natures—the good into the gentle and the evil into the savage, in all sorts of combinations.

---

[1] Orpheus, refusing after his wife's death to marry again, was killed by the Thracian women (see *Lycidas*). Thamyras, a legendary poet. Ajax, the Homeric hero, failed to obtain the arms of Achilles, which after Achilles' death were to be given to the bravest of the Greeks. Epeus made the wooden horse by which the Greeks took Troy. Thersites: see *Troilus and Cressida*.

All the souls had now chosen their lives, and they went in the order of their choice to Lachesis, who sent with them the genius whom they had severally chosen, to be the guardian of their lives and the fulfiller of the choice : this genius led the souls first to Clōtho, and drew them within the revolution of the spindle impelled by her hand, thus ratifying the destiny of each ; and then, when they were fastened to this, carried them to Atropos, who spun the threads and made them irreversible, whence without turning round they passed beneath the throne of Necessity ; and when they had all passed, they marched on in a scorching heat to the plain of Forgetfulness, which was a barren waste destitute of trees and verdure ; and then towards evening they encamped by the river of Unmindfulness, whose water no vessel can hold ; of this they were all obliged to drink a certain quantity, and those who were not saved by wisdom drank more than was necessary ; and each one as he drank forgot all things. Now after they had gone to rest, about the middle of the night there was a thunderstorm and earthquake, and then in an instant they were driven upwards in all manner of ways to their birth, like stars shooting. He himself was hindered from drinking the water. But in what manner or by what means he returned to the body he could not say ; only, in the morning, awaking suddenly, he found himself lying on the pyre.

And thus, Glaucon, the tale has been saved and has not perished, and will save us if we are obedient to the word spoken ; and we shall pass safely over the river of Forgetfulness and our soul will not be defiled. Wherefore my counsel is, that we hold fast ever to the heavenly way and follow after justice and virtue always, considering that the soul is immortal and able to endure every sort of good and every sort of evil. Thus shall we live dear to one another and to the gods, both while remaining here and when we receive our reward. And it shall be well with us both in this life and in the pilgrimage of a thousand years which we have been describing.

ARISTOTLE

XI

PHILOSOPHY : ARISTOTLE

Aristotle penetrated into the whole universe of things and subjected its scattered wealth to intelligence : to him the greater number of the philosophical sciences owe their origin and differentiation.—HEGEL.

ARISTOTLE was born about 385 of a medical family in the small town of Stagīra in Macedonia, on the fringe of Greek civilization. From his eighteenth to his thirty-eighth year he was a student in Plato's school at Athens. On Plato's death he joined a fellow student, who from a slave had become banker, and from banker prince of Assos in Northern Asia Minor, where he maintained Macedonian interests against the Persian king till he met a violent end. On his death Aristotle fled, and in 343 became tutor of the Macedonian prince, who was to conquer Persia and carry Hellenism to the East. These were his two contacts with practical life and the outside world. In 335 he retired to Athens, to found his famous school or university at the Lyceum, and spend his last years in teaching and research. He died in 322. His will, like Shakespeare's, shows a nature practical, considerate, affectionate.

Aristotle is a different type from his two great predecessors, and had neither the personality of the one nor the vision and imagination of the other. His achievement is indicated by the fact that no modern book on him treats satisfactorily alike his scientific and his philosophical and political works. Aristotle covers a field wider than the modern writer can command. He belongs to that finest and rarest type of human intellect in which the great humanist and the great man of science meet. On logic, moral philosophy, politics, metaphysics, psychology, physics, zoology (including embryology), poetry, the technique of speaking and writing, he wrote epoch-making works, which governed thought for more than a thousand years, and some of which serve as text-books to the present day. Neither before or since has any human being covered so many fields of knowledge. Nor was his study superficial. We know, for instance, some of his studies preparatory to his writing his work on politics ; they include a collection of 158 constitutions, works *On Government by Princes, On the Laws of Non-Greek States, On the Territorial Claims of States, On Monarchy, On Colonies, On the Statesman, On Justice, On Economics.*

It is a feature of Greek Literature that its writers are often complementary to each other, one exhibiting the features that another lacks. This is so with Thucydides and Herodotus, as with Aeschylus, Sophocles, and Euripides ; and it is so with Plato and Aristotle. They have points of resemblance. Both founded schools for teaching and research ; both were scientific by temperament, though Plato inclined to mathematics and the more abstract subjects, Aristotle to the natural sciences. The first difference which strikes the reader is between the easy and brilliant style of Plato and the dry, abrupt, ill-arranged sentences of Aristotle ; this unlikeness is due to the accident that, though both published works written in attractive style for the public, and both lectured privately to their pupils, it is the lecture notes of Aristotle and the published works of Plato which have survived. Yet the differences between the two men are fundamental. Plato stood to Aristotle somewhat as Ruskin stood to J. S. Mill. Plato has a poet's impetuous and soaring temperament which, impatient of anything less than the ideal, breaks through the fetters of fact and re-shapes the world to the lines of his vision. Aristotle in the temper of natural science starts in politics or morals, as in biology, from the world of observed phenomena, collects, classifies, and analyses facts, never losing sight of earth. Thus he commences in his *Ethics* and *Politics* with the views generally held in his day, in his *Poetics* with the drama of the fifth and fourth centuries, building up his theories from these. He accepts things as he finds them, sometimes too contentedly, for he defends slavery, conceives no other state than the Greek ' city', and has no eyes for the new world, which, even as he wrote, Alexander was bringing to birth. A comparison of the *Republic* with the *Politics* illustrates the difference between the two men. Aristotle has the defects and the merits of the practical man and the scientific observer ; his vision is precise and accurate, but it has a narrower range than Plato's. The politician will go to Plato for inspiration, to Aristotle for practical advice.

Of Aristotle's science we shall see something later (p. 424). His writings on Physics, deep as is the mark which they have set on thought, have cramped as much as forwarded it, and are probably his least successful work. His metaphysical and psychological writings are technical and unsuited to quotation. His most living writings are his *Ethics* (edited by his son Nicomachus), *Politics*, *Poetics*, and *Rhetoric*. Of these the *Ethics* is an admirable introduction to moral philosophy, for it is a textbook by a man of genius, and its errors are known ; the *Politics* is full of insight, though Aristotle wrote for the Greek city-state, and never conceived the new problems of the great communities of to-day. The *Rhetoric* is less famous, and deals with less momentous issues, but is a model of philosophic treatment of a practical subject. A study of the art of persuading an audience, it ranges from the laws of style to the study of character, from the principles of proof to the art of delivery, treating its subject with an admirable mixture of breadth and precision, and with a scientific realism which often seems cynical. These works are not easy reading ; they have the defects of lecture-notes and are dry, ill-arranged, and not free from contradictions ; but the gold they contain is worth the pains of extraction.

My first extracts come from his *Ethics*.

In the following passage Aristotle defines the object of human life, or what he calls the Good for man. He does not find it, where others have found it, in pleasure, fame, power, or moral excellence.

IN every pursuit and art the Chief Good is that for the sake of which all that we do is done ; this in medicine is health, in war victory, in house-building the house. In every action, in every moral choice, this is the End,[1] all and everything else is directed and subordinated to achieving it. So if in all action there is an End proposed, this End will be the practical Good ; or if there are several Ends, it will be these. . . . Now since there are clearly many Ends, and of these we choose some (e. g. wealth) with a view to others, it will be clear that all are not Final Ends ; but the Chief Good is plainly something final. . . . Now we call absolutely final that which is always chosen for its own sake, and

[1] A fundamental idea in Aristotle's thought is that all things, men and states included, have each their own ' end ', a final aim or conclusion to which they tend and which is the goal or fulfilment of their being. Coleridge's phrase illustrates and plays on this meaning of the word : ' when every man is his own end, all things will come to a bad end.' When used in this technical sense, ' end ' is here printed with a capital.

not for the sake of something else. And that is just what Happiness pre-eminently seems to be. For we always choose it for its own sake and not for any other purpose : we choose pleasure and honour and intellect and all other Goods partly for their own sake (we should choose them, even if nothing further came of them), but partly for the sake of Happiness, to which we suppose them to lead ; whereas no one chooses Happiness with a view to these subordinate Goods, or with a view to any other thing at all, except itself.[1]

If Happiness is the object of life, what is Happiness ? Aristotle's discussion of this shows that by the word so translated (*Eudaimonia*), he does not mean happiness in a vulgar sense.

THE best way of defining Happiness is by ascertaining what is the function of man. With a musician, a sculptor and every artist, and in general with all persons who have a function and a work, their Good and Excellence seems to reside in their function : it would seem to be the same with man, if he has a function. But while a carpenter and a cobbler has a work and function, has man none ? . . . What can it be ? Not mere life, because clearly he shares this with plants, and we are looking for something peculiar to him. We must therefore dismiss the life of mere nourishment and growth. There follows the faculty of sensation. But this again man clearly shares with horses, oxen, and all animals. There remains the activity of the Rational Faculty. . . .

The function then of man is an activity[2] of the soul in accordance with the Reason, or at any rate not independently of it. . . . And the Good for man is an activity of the soul in accordance with goodness[3] (and if there are various types of goodness, in

---

[1] Ethics, i. 7. 1097 a (extracts).

[2] Aristotle wishes to emphasize that Happiness is not a mere passive state, but an activity.

[3] An instance of the difficulty of translating Greek. *Aretē*, the word here translated ' goodness ', does not necessarily mean moral goodness. Everything has an *aretē*, defined by Aristotle as ' what makes a thing be in a sound condition and do its work well. Thus the " goodness " of the eye makes the eye good and makes it see well : the " goodness " of a horse

accordance with the best and most perfect type). And we must add, in a complete life; for as one swallow or one fine day does not make spring, so one day or a short time of happiness does not make a man happy.[1]

Aristotle then deals with the problem whether 'happiness' is independent of circumstances. Later the Stoics were to take the view that 'good consists in the virtues, wisdom, righteousness, courage, temperance, &c., and evil in their opposites, unwisdom, unrighteousness, &c., while life, health, pleasure, beauty, strength, wealth, fame, good birth, and their opposites death, illness, labour, ugliness, weakness, poverty, disrepute, and low birth are neutral and indifferent'.[2] But far as he was from materialism, the ordinary Greek kept his feet firmly on the earth, and Aristotle holds that

HAPPINESS requires the addition of external goods: without material aids it is difficult, if not impossible, to do noble actions. For there are many things which we effect by means of friends, wealth, or political power, which serve us as tools. Further, Happiness is marred by the want of certain things, such as good birth, good looks, happiness in one's children. A man who is completely ugly or low-born or solitary or childless cannot be entirely happy: this is still more so if his friends or children are wicked, or if he has had good ones and lost them by death.[3]

Happiness then is the activity of the highest part of our nature. This Aristotle regards as our reason; but his conception of reason is wide, and the 'contemplation' of which he speaks covers the life of the theologian, philosopher, scientist, and artist, as far as these are not mere technical experts, but are occupied with the essential reality of things. The intellectual life seems to him to be Happiness, because it has the following characteristics: it is

makes the horse good, and good at carrying its rider; the " goodness " of man makes man good and able to perform his proper function in life well. Again, the " goodness " of the moral faculty is what we should call virtue, the " goodness " of the intellect is its perfect vigour. . . .' In the above passage Aristotle means that happiness is an activity of the soul, connected with its highest ' goodness '. [1] Ib. i. 7. 1097 b.
[2] Diog. Laert. vii. 112. [3] Ethics, i. 8. 1099 a.

pleasant ; it is desired for itself and not for anything beyond itself ; we can enjoy it more continuously than any other ; it is the most independent and needs fewest adjuncts ; it is the highest faculty in us.

Plato and Aristotle are agreed in putting the life of thought above any other. They regard the practical life as concerned with transitory things, and therefore inferior, while philosophy and science contemplate eternal realities.

One weakness of this view is obvious. Unlike Christianity, it excludes from ' Happiness ' the mass of humanity. Yet we must admit that the Moral Ideal, which finds the good in practical life, ' leads on to the thought of an Ideal beyond and above it which alone gives it meaning, but which seems to escape definite conception by man '. It is this further Ideal which Aristotle is attempting to define. The reasons he gives for his view are easier to reject than to refute.

I F Happiness is an activity in accordance with goodness,[1] that goodness must be the highest ; that is, it must be the goodness of the best part of us. Whether this is Reason, or some other principle in us, that naturally rules and directs, and conceives of divine and noble things, whether divine itself or the most divine thing in us, its activity in accordance with its own proper goodness would be perfect Happiness. That it is Contemplative has already been stated. This activity is the highest : for the Reason is the highest thing in us, and the world with which Reason deals is the highest thing we know. Further, it is the most continuous : for we are more able to contemplate, than to act, continuously. Again, it is considered that there should be an element of pleasure in Happiness : and the activity of wisdom is admittedly the most pleasant of all good activities. The purity and the security of philosophy [2] seem to make it wonderfully pleasant. Further of all Goods Contemplation is the most independent : for wise men, like just men and like everybody else, require the necessities of life : but among those who are sufficiently provided with these, the just man and the temperate and the brave and the other virtuous types need objects and company for the exercise

---

[1] See p. 322, note 1.　　　　[2] In which Aristotle includes Science.

of their virtues, while the wise can contemplate even in solitude, and can do so the more, the wiser they are. Perhaps it is better to have fellow workers : still, in fact, the wise man is the most independent. Besides Contemplation would seem to be the only thing desired for itself. It has no result except itself, while from all moral activities we expect to get something, more or less, besides the mere doing of them.

Now if political and military activities are the greatest and noblest of moral activities, but if they are not chosen for their own sakes but aim at some End beyond themselves, whereas the Contemplative Activity of the Reason seems to be the most serious of activities, and to aim at no end beyond itself, and to carry with it its own pleasure, and if such independence and leisure and absence of weariness as man is capable of are attendant on this activity, then the Activity of the Reason will be the final Happiness for man, assuming that it is accompanied by a sufficient length of life, for in Happiness there is no incompleteness.

And such a life is higher than human. For a man will live it in virtue of something divine in him and not of his humanity. If Reason compared with our human nature is divine, then the life of Reason is divine in comparison with human life. We should not listen to those who tell us that human beings should think like men, and mortals think like mortals, but we should achieve such immortality as we may, and strain every nerve to live by the highest things in us. They may be small in substance, but in price and power they are far beyond all else. And if this life has a higher reality and excellence, it would seem to be our nature. Now it would be strange if men chose something other than their natural life. Here comes in what we have already said. Everything finds best and most agreeable that which is proper to its nature : so man finds the life of Reason best, since in it he finds his true nature. Therefore the life of Reason must be the happiest.[1]

---

[1] Ib. x. 7. 1177 a.

The following passage is a good example of Aristotle's dry light, and matter-of-fact arguing, which is as salutary as it is often annoying. It is pleasanter and easier to lose oneself with Sir Thomas Browne in an *O altitudo* ! But it does not make for clear thinking, as does this sober logic.

THERE is a further proof that Happiness is a Contemplative Activity. We regard the gods as especially happy and blessed. Now what kind of actions are we to attribute to them ? Are we to suppose them as occupied in being just ? Is it not ridiculous to conceive of them as forming contracts, restoring deposits, and so on ? Or are we to picture them as brave, facing dangers and supporting terrors, because it is noble to do so ? Or as liberal ? But to whom will they make presents ? It is absurd to fancy them as having money or anything of the kind. And how could they be temperate ? Would it not be a poor honour to praise them for having no bad desires ? And every kind of moral action we can enumerate will be found trifling and unworthy of the gods. Yet it is universally admitted that the gods live and are active. Now if you take away Action and, still more, Creation, from a living being, what is left except Contemplation. So the supremely blessed activity of God must be Contemplation. And of human activities the one most closely related to this will be the happiest.

A further proof is, that all other animals than man are completely deprived of this activity, and do not enjoy Happiness. The whole life of the gods is happy : and that of man is happy, so far as he possesses something like this activity. But no other animal is happy, because they have no share in Contemplation. . . .

It is the activity of Reason and the disposition and devotion to this that is best and dearest to God. If the gods have any care for human things, as it appears they do, it is reasonable to suppose that they take pleasure in what is best and most akin to themselves (and this must be the Reason), and that they requite those who love and honour it most, because such men care for what the gods love and because their life is right and noble.[1]

[1] Ib. x. 8. 1179 a, f.

How does a man learn to be good? Socrates would have answered, 'By knowing what goodness is': and that is a plausible idea. But Aristotle's answer is the true one, and explains the importance which he attaches to education. He saw the all-importance of habit in making character for good or ill.

THERE are two kinds of goodness, moral and intellectual. The latter in the main originates in and is developed by instruction; but the former is the creation of habit. We acquire moral goodness neither by nature nor in spite of nature. Nature gives us the capacity for it, and our capacity is perfected by habit. We acquire moral goodness by first performing moral actions; the various arts are similarly acquired. By doing we learn what the learning fits us to do. Men become builders by building, harpists by playing the harp. Similarly we become just by doing just acts, temperate by acting temperately, brave by behaving bravely.

What happens in states is an evidence of this. Legislators make their citizens good by habituation. That is the intention of every legislator; those who carry it out badly fail; and here lies the difference between good and bad systems of government.[1]

So with moral goodness, it is by our behaviour in our relations with our fellow men that we become just or the reverse; and it is by our behaviour in danger and by the acquisition of habits of courage or cowardice that we become brave or cowardly. It is the same with desire and passion. Some men become temperate and gentle, others immoral and passionate; the former by one kind of behaviour, the latter by another. In short our dispositions resemble our acts, and are produced by them. And so we must give a certain character to our acts, for our habits depend directly on them. To acquire such or such habits from our childhood is not of small, but of very great consequence; indeed it is everything.[2]

Can we find any common characteristic in the different virtues?

[1] This paragraph contains a whole philosophy of statecraft.
[2] Ib. ii. 1. 1103 a.

Is there any element common e. g. to courage, justice, generosity, by reason of which we call them virtues ? Aristotle's theory, that all virtues are Means or ' middles ' lying between two Extremes, is typical of the Greek instinct for moderation, and is too famous not to be quoted. He has been arguing that in the various arts success consists in doing neither too much nor too little but just the right amount. (This is true equally of building, music, boot-making, &c.)

SIMILARLY with moral virtue, the field of which is feeling and action. Here, too, there is excess and defect, and a mean. With fear, confidence, anger, pity, pleasure, and pain generally, one can feel too much and too little, and both too much and too little are wrong. To feel them at the right time, in the right circumstances, to the right people, for the right reasons, and in the right way, is the Mean and the best and the mark of goodness. So, too, with actions, there is excess and defect and a Mean.[1]

Most virtues can be described as Means : but the doctrine does not really explain the nature of virtue, and it breaks down when applied to justice and truthfulness. Aristotle is more helpful when he discusses the different virtues. His clear-headedness and good sense can be seen in the following discussion of Courage.

COURAGE has to do with fear and confidence and is a Mean. Men may have too little fear or too much confidence : [2] there is no word to describe the former of these, but an excess of confidence is called rashness. An excess of fear or deficiency of confidence is called cowardice.[3]

Aristotle then points out that we ought to fear some things, such as disgrace, and that the supreme test of courage is facing death, ' for it is an end, and the dead are not affected either by evil or by good.' He then draws some curious distinctions, which reflect the Greek mind, and which he tries to justify.

[1] Ib. ii. 5. 1106 b.
[2] This seems an odd distinction. But there is a difference, as will be seen on p. 329, par. 2.
[3] ii 6. 1107 a.

YET courage is not shown in facing every kind of death, for instance, death at sea or by disease. In what circumstances then is it shown ? Surely in the noblest, like those of war, where the danger is the greatest and the most honourable. Still the courageous man is fearless also in disease and on the sea, though not with the fearlessness of the seaman. The seaman is confident because of his experience, but the landsman despairs of safety and dislikes the idea of such a death as drowning. Courage comes into play, where a brave resistance can be made or where death is honourable ; but there is no question of honour or resistance in death by drowning or disease. Of some terrors we say that they are beyond human endurance. These excite fear in any rational being. But the brave man is as unterrified as a man may be. He will be afraid of such things, but, as he ought and as reason bids, he will face them for the sake of honour, which is the End of courage. So I call brave the man who endures and fears and is bold with respect to the right objects, for the right cause, in the right manner, and at the right time. His actions and feelings follow reason and right.[1]

Having shown the sense in which courage is a mean, Aristotle deals with the excesses which lie on either side of it.

EXCESSIVE want of fear has no name. But a man who was not afraid of anything, even of waves and earthquakes (as they say the Celts [2] are not), would be mad or insensible. Excessive confidence in the face of terrors is called rashness. The rash seem to be impostors who profess bravery. They wish to seem to be what the brave man is, and therefore they copy him where they can. For this reason they are generally braggarts. They are precipitate and anxious for danger before it comes, but they collapse in its presence, while the brave are keen in the hour of action but quiet before it. The man who shows an excess

---

[1] iii. 6. 1115 a (shortened).
[2] Shakespeare has preserved the legend about the Celts attacking the waves in his metaphor of ' taking arms against a sea of troubles '.

of fear is a coward. He fears the wrong things in the wrong way. He is deficient in confidence, but he is more often detected by his excessive distress. He is despondent, for he is afraid of everything.[1]

Aristotle then points out that there are spurious kinds of courage. This is the best part of his discussion.

THERE are five other types of courage, so called. First is civic courage, the closest to the real kind. To the citizen legal penalties, disgrace, and honours are motives for facing danger. That is why the bravest nations are those where the brave are honoured and the cowards disgraced. This type of courage closely resembles true courage, because its motive is virtue ; for it springs from a sense of shame and a desire to win honour (which is noble), and to avoid disgrace (which is ignoble). In the same class we should place those who act under compulsion from their leaders ; but their courage is of a lower type, for their motive is not shame but fear, and it is not dishonour that they shrink from, but pain. For their masters apply compulsion, like Hector, who said

But if I find a man fleeing and cowering afar from the battle,
Let him not think to escape the dogs.[2]

So with commanders who flog their troops if they retreat, or station them with trenches and other obstacles in their rear. All apply compulsion. But honour, not compulsion, should be the motive for courage.

Another so-called type of courage is special experience. This is the origin of Socrates' idea that courage was knowledge. There are various instances of this kind of courage : in military matters it is shown by the professional soldier.[3] There are many empty terrors in war, which in general the professional appreciates ; this makes him appear brave in comparison with the amateur

[1] iii. 7. 1115 b.
[2] Homer, Il. ii. 391. A misquotation. Agamemnon is the speaker.
[3] Mercenaries were common in Aristotle's time.

who does not understand their nature. Besides experience enables professional soldiers to hurt the enemy without being themselves hurt, for they understand the use of arms and have resources at their command which enable them to do this. So they are like armed men matched with the unarmed, or athletes contending with amateurs. But professionals become cowardly when the danger is excessive and they are inferior in equipment and numbers. Then, while the citizen armies die at their post, feeling flight to be dishonourable and death preferable to safety at such a price, the professional soldiers are the first to fly. They face the danger at first, believing themselves the stronger side; but when they discover the truth, they run away, being more afraid of death than of dishonour. That is not courage.

Again, mere animal spirit is sometimes included in courage, and because the brave are spirited, the word brave is applied to those who are actuated merely by animal spirit, like wild beasts who charge the man who wounds them. Now the brave man's motive is honour, and animal spirit co-operates here. But beasts are actuated by pain, because they are wounded or frightened; if they are left at peace in their own haunts they do not attack men. We cannot call creatures brave that are goaded by pain or by animal spirit to rush into danger, without an idea of what it is: otherwise hungry donkeys must be brave, for blows will not drive them from their food. Similarly adulterers are induced by their desires to do many bold actions. This animal type of courage is the most natural kind, and, if purpose and motive are added to it, it becomes true courage.

There is pain in anger and pleasure in revenge. Those who fight from these motives may be pugnacious but are not courageous. Their motive is not honour nor their guide reason; they are inspired by passion. There is, however, some resemblance between them and the brave.

Nor, again, are the sanguine brave. They have won many victories over numerous foes, and that gives them confidence in danger. Like the brave, they are confident ; but the brave are confident for the reasons I have given, while the sanguine are confident from supposing themselves the stronger and unlikely to suffer a reverse. (It is much the same with drunkards, who become sanguine.) When their expectations are not realized, they run away ; while the brave face what is and seems terrible, because it is honourable to do so and dishonourable not to do so. So it is a greater proof of courage to be fearless and unmoved in sudden alarms than in those which are expected. Courage is then the outcome of character, there being less question of preparation. When danger is foreseen a man might take his line from calculation and reasoning ; where it is sudden, he acts according to his character.

Finally the ignorant appear to be brave. They resemble the sanguine, but are inferior, as they have no opinion of themselves. The sanguine have such an opinion, and that is why they make a stand : whereas the ignorant run away the moment they know or suspect matters to be otherwise than they had thought ; like the Argives, who attacked the Spartans under the impression that they were men of Sicyon. This concludes my account of real courage and of its spurious forms.[1]

We now pass to Aristotle's political writings. In reading these, four things particularly should be remembered.

(1) The Greek state was a small city. It was not therefore troubled by many of the problems that beset the huge modern communities.

(2) Though in practice the individual at Athens was at least as well off as with us, in theory he counted for far less. Such a phrase as ' the rights of the individual ' is unknown to Aristotle ; nor would he have understood thinkers, who place the individual's duty to God and to his conscience above his duty to the state.[2] He does not face the possibility of a conflict between these duties. Here, owing chiefly to the influence of Christianity, we have advanced beyond him. But the result has been that the significance of the state is sometimes minimized, and though war

---

[1] iii. 8. 1116 a.   [2] Here Plato is nearer our modern views.

brings out the instinctive loyalty of the citizen, he is apt at other times to forget the state except when he has occasion to grumble at it. Yet the life of the community will be healthier, and political problems easier of solution, if the citizen considers himself as a member of a society existing to realize high ideals. Aristotle viewed him thus, and here supplies a corrective to some modern tendencies.

(3) As the individual counted for less with Aristotle, so the state counted for more. It occupied the position which in theory God occupies with us, and was the highest object of the citizen's allegiance.

(4) This was largely due to the character of Greek religion. With us religion is a powerful influence, separable from the state. It can, or could, be trusted to watch and train men's morals, while the state deals with other sides of their life. In Greece religion had little to do with morals, and occupied a very different position. Hence far more was thrown on the state. With the decline in the power of the Churches, the modern state is obliged to think more of its members' morals, and is coming nearer to the Greek position. Unless the Churches recover their power, it will be obliged to become something like what Aristotle thought it should be.

In the following passage Aristotle answers the questions, Why the state comes into being? What is its aim? Is it natural? His answer contains an implicit reply to the Anarchist, who considers the state an evil, and to the thinker who believes (as modern German philosophers have believed) that it has nothing to do with morality. His words are simple, but they are profound.

WHEN several villages are united in a single complete community, large enough to be nearly or quite self-sufficing, the state comes into existence, originating in the bare needs of life, and continuing in existence for the sake of a good life. And therefore, if the earlier forms of society are natural, so is the state, for it is the End of them, and the nature of a thing is its End.[1] For what each thing is when fully developed, we call its nature, whether we are speaking of a man, a horse, or a family.

Hence it is evident that the state is a creation of nature, and

[1] Used here and below in the technical sense (p. 321).

that man is by nature a political animal. And he who by nature and not by mere accident is without a state, is either a bad man or above humanity ; he is like the

         ' Tribeless, lawless, hearthless one,'

whom Homer denounces—the natural outcast is forthwith a lover of war ; he may be compared to an isolated piece at draughts.

Now, that man is more of a political animal than bees or any other gregarious animals is evident. Nature, as we often say, makes nothing in vain, and man is the only animal whom she has endowed with the gift of speech. And whereas mere voice is but an indication of pleasure or pain, and is therefore found in other animals (for their nature attains to the perception of pleasure and pain and the intimation of them to one another, and no further), the power of speech is intended to set forth the expedient and inexpedient, and therefore likewise the just and the unjust. And it is a characteristic of man that he alone has any sense of good and evil, of just and unjust, and the like, and the association of living beings who have this sense makes a family and a state.

The proof that the state is a creation of nature is that the individual, when isolated, is not self-sufficing ; and therefore he is like a part in relation to the whole. But he who is unable to live in society, or who has no need because he is sufficient for himself, must be either a beast or a god : he is no part of a state. A social instinct is implanted in all men by nature, and yet he who first founded the state was the greatest of benefactors. For man, when perfected, is the best of animals, but, when separated from law and justice, he is the worst of all ; since armed injustice is the more dangerous, and he is equipped at birth with arms, meant to be used by intelligence and virtue, which he may use for the worst ends. And so, if he have not virtue, he is the most unholy and the most savage of animals, and the most full of lust and gluttony. But justice is the bond of men in states, for the administration of justice, which is the determination of what is just, is the principle of order in political society.[1]

A state exists for the sake of a good life, and not for the sake of life only. Hence it may be further inferred that virtue must be the care of a state which is truly so called, and not merely enjoys the name : for without this End the community becomes a mere alliance which differs only in place from alliances of which the members live apart ; and law is only a convention, ' a surety to one another of justice,' and has no real power to make the citizens good and just.[2]

The object of the state then is neither conquest nor trade nor empire nor anything but ' the good life '. And by this Aristotle means, not conduct in the narrow sense, but the ideal life for man. The state exists to give its citizens leisure to lead this.

THE whole of life is divided into two parts, business and leisure, war and peace, and of actions some aim at what is necessary and useful, and some at what is honourable. And the preference given to one or the other class of actions must necessarily be like the preference given to one or other part of the soul and its actions over the other ; there must be war for the sake of peace, business for the sake of leisure, things useful and necessary for the sake of things honourable. All these points the statesman should keep in view when he frames his laws ; he should consider the parts of the soul and their functions, and above all the better and the End ; he should also remember the diversities of human lives and actions. For men must be able to engage in business and go to war, but leisure and peace are better ; they must do what is necessary and indeed what is useful, but what is honourable is better.[3]

These ends Aristotle thinks most likely to be secured under an aristocracy ; by which he means the rule, not of the rich or the well-born, but of the best men in the state. He sees, however,

---

[1] Politics, i. 2, § 8 f. This and the following quotations are in Jowett's version. [2] iii. 9, § 6 f. vii. 14, § 12 f.

the justification as well as the dangers of democracy, which gives power to all citizens alike, without asking whether they are good and wise.

THERE is also a doubt as to what is to be the supreme power in the state :—Is it the multitude ? Or the wealthy ? Or the good ? Or the one best man ? Or a prince ? Any of these alternatives seems to involve disagreeable consequences. If the poor, for example, because they are more in number, divide among themselves the property of the rich—is not this unjust ? No (will be the reply), for the supreme authority justly willed it. But if this is not injustice, pray what is ? Again, when in the first division all has been taken, and the majority divide anew the property of the minority, is it not evident, if this goes on, that they will ruin the state ? Yet surely, virtue is not the ruin of those who possess her, nor is justice destructive of a state ; and therefore this law of confiscation clearly cannot be just. If it were, all the acts of a tyrant must of necessity be just ; for he only coerces other men by superior power, just as the multitude coerce the rich. But is it just then that the few and the wealthy should be the rulers ? And what if they, in like manner, rob and plunder the people—is this just ? If so, the other case will likewise be just. But there can be no doubt that all these things are wrong and unjust.

Then ought the good to rule and have supreme power ? But in that case everybody else, being excluded from power, will be dishonoured. For the offices of a state are posts of honour ; and if one set of men always hold them, the rest must be deprived of them. Then will it be well that the one best man should rule ? Nay, that is still more oligarchical, for the number of those who are dishonoured is thereby increased. Some one may say that it is bad in any case for a man, subject as he is to all the accidents of human passion, to have the supreme power, rather than the law. But what if the law itself be democratical or oligarchical, how will that help us out of our difficulties ? Not at all ; the same consequences will follow.

Most of these questions may be reserved for another occasion. The principle that the multitude ought to be supreme rather than the few best is one that is maintained, and, though not free from difficulty, yet seems to contain an element of truth. For the many, of whom each individual is but an ordinary person, when they meet together may very likely be better than the few good, if regarded not individually but collectively, just as a feast to which many contribute is better than a dinner provided out of a single purse. For each individual among the many has a share of virtue and prudence, and when they meet together they become in a manner one man, who has many feet, and hands, and senses.[1]

There is a danger in allowing them to share the great offices of state, for their folly will lead them into error, and their dishonesty into crime. But there is a danger also in not letting them share, for a state in which many poor men are excluded from office will necessarily be full of enemies.[2]

In practice Aristotle thinks that a government by what we should call the middle and professional classes is best. It is an interesting fact that, though Greece was the mother of democracy, the three great Greek political thinkers, Thucydides (the author of the finest description of the democratic ideal), Plato, and Aristotle, all came to disbelieve in it as a form of government. That is no argument against democracy[3]; but it is a salutary warning to those who fancy that by uttering the word democracy we establish heaven on earth.

NOW in all states there are three elements : one class is very rich, another very poor, and a third in a mean.[4] It is admitted that moderation and the mean are best, and therefore it will clearly be best to possess the gifts of fortune in moderation ; for in that condition of life men are most ready

---

[1] iii. 10 f.   [2] iii, § 7 f.

[3] The weakness of the executive and the absence of any representative system were peculiar defects of Athenian democracy. The assembly—or parliament—of Athens consisted of the entire people, not of representatives of it.   [4] In the technical sense (p. 328).

to follow rational principle. But he who greatly excels in beauty, strength, birth, or wealth, or on the other hand who is very poor, or very weak, or very much disgraced, finds it difficult to follow rational principle. Of these two the one sort grow into violent and great criminals, the others into rogues and petty rascals. Again, the middle class is least likely to shrink from rule, or to be over-ambitious for it ; both of which are injuries to the state. Again, those who have too much of the goods of fortune, strength, wealth, friends, and the like, are neither willing nor able to submit to authority. The evil begins at home ; for when they are boys, by reason of the luxury in which they are brought up, they never learn, even at school, the habit of obedience. On the other hand, the very poor, who are in the opposite extreme, are too degraded. So that the one class cannot obey, and can only rule despotically ; the other knows not how to command and must be ruled like slaves. Thus arises a city, not of freemen, but of masters and slaves, the one despising, the other envying ; and nothing can be more fatal to friendship and good fellowship in states than this : for good fellowship springs from friendship ; when men are at enmity with one another, they would rather not even share the same path. But a city ought to be composed, as far as possible, of equals and similars ; and these are generally the middle classes. Therefore the city which is composed of middle-class citizens is necessarily best constituted in respect of the elements of which we say the fabric of the state naturally consists. And this is the class of citizens which is most secure in a state, for they do not, like the poor, covet their neighbours' goods ; nor do others covet theirs, as the poor covet the goods of the rich ; and as they neither plot against others, nor are themselves plotted against, they pass through life safely.

Thus it is manifest that the best political community is formed by citizens of the middle class, and that those states are likely to be well administered, in which the middle class is large, and stronger if possible than both the other classes, or at any rate than either singly ; for the addition of the middle class turns the scale, and prevents either of the extremes from being dominant. Great then is the good fortune of a state in which the citizens have a moderate and sufficient property ; for where some possess much, and the others nothing, there may arise an extreme democracy, or a pure oligarchy ; or a tyranny may grow out of either extreme ; but it is not so likely to arise out of the middle constitutions and those akin to them.[1]

Aristotle's criticism of Plato's communism (p. 298) is based on its unsuitability to human nature, and applies equally to communism in our own day. The following passage is characteristic of Aristotle's common sense, knowledge of human nature, and dispassionate and evenly-balanced mind.

NEXT let us consider what should be our arrangements about property : should the citizens of the perfect state have their possessions in common or not ? Three cases are possible : (1) the soil may be appropriated, but the produce may be thrown for consumption into the common stock; and this is the practice of some nations. Or (2), the soil may be common, and may be cultivated in common, but the produce divided among individuals for their private use ; this is a form of common property which is said to exist among certain foreign peoples. Or (3), the soil and the produce may be alike common.

When the agriculturists are not the owners, the case will be different and easier to deal with ; but when they till the ground for themselves the question of ownership will give a world of trouble. If they do not share equally in enjoyments and toils, those who labour much and get little will necessarily complain of those who labour little and receive or consume much. There is always a difficulty in men living together and having all human relations in common, but especially in their having common property. The partnerships of fellow travellers are an example to the point ; for they generally fall out over everyday matters

[1] iv. ii, § 4 f.

and quarrel about any trifle which turns up. So with servants : we are most liable to take offence at those with whom we most frequently come into contact in daily life.

These are only some of the disadvantages which attend the community of property ; the present arrangement, if improved as it might be by good customs and laws, would be far better, and would have the advantages of both systems. Property should be in a certain sense common, but, as a general rule, private ; for, when every one has a distinct interest, men will not complain of one another, and they will make more progress, because every one will be attending to his own business. And yet among the good, and in respect of use, ' Friends ', as the proverb says, ' will have all things common.' Even now there are traces of such a principle, showing that it is not impracticable, but, in well-ordered states, exists already to a certain extent and may be carried further. For, although every man has his own property, some things he will place at the disposal of his friends, while of others he shares the use with them. The Lacedaemonians, for example, use one another's slaves, and horses, and dogs, as if they were their own ; and when they lack provisions on a journey, they appropriate what they find in the fields throughout the country. It is clearly better that property should be private, but the use of it common ; and the special business of the legislator is to create in men this benevolent disposition. Again, how immeasurably greater is the pleasure when a man feels a thing to be his own ; for surely the love of self is a feeling implanted by nature and not given in vain, although selfishness is rightly censured ; this, however, is not the mere love of self, but the love of self in excess, like the miser's love of money ; for all, or almost all, men love money and other such objects in a measure. And further, there is the greatest pleasure in doing a kindness or service to friends or guests or companions, which can only be rendered when a man has private property. These advantages are lost by excessive unification of the state. No one, when men have all things in common, will any longer set an example of liberality or do any liberal action ; for liberality consists in the use which is made of property.

Communistic legislation may have a specious appearance of benevolence; men readily listen to it, and are easily induced to believe that in some wonderful manner everybody will become everybody's friend, especially when some one is heard denouncing the evils now existing in states, suits about contracts, convictions for perjury, flatteries of rich men and the like, which are said to arise out of the possession of private property. These evils, however, are due to a very different cause—the wickedness of human nature. Indeed, we see that there is much more quarrelling among those who have all things in common, though there are not many of them when compared with the vast numbers who have private property.

Again, we ought to reckon, not only the evils from which the citizens will be saved, but also the advantages which they will lose. The life which they are to lead appears to be quite impracticable. The error of Socrates must be attributed to the false notion of unity from which he starts. Unity there should be, both of the family and of the state, but in some respects only. For there is a point at which a state may attain such a degree of unity as to be no longer a state, or at which, without actually ceasing to exist, it will become an inferior state, like harmony passing into unison, or rhythm which has been reduced to a single foot. The state, as I was saying, is a plurality, which should be united and made into a community by education ; and it is strange that the author of a system of education which he thinks will make the state virtuous, should expect to improve his citizens by regulations of this sort, and not by philosophy or by customs and laws. Let us remember that we should not disregard the experience of ages ; in the multitude of years these things, if they were good, would certainly not have been unknown.[1]

To Aristotle, as to Plato, education is of supreme importance.

[1] ii. 5 f.

In the following passage he gives an interesting argument for
keeping it in the hands of the state, though elsewhere he admits
certain advantages in private education. He then raises the
question whether it should aim at the training of character or at
higher knowledge, or at merely utilitarian ends. His conclusion
is that it must be not ' vocational ' but ' liberal ' (the phrase
originates with Aristotle).   It may be noticed how he decides
these questions by reference to ultimate general principles :
the right education is that which will produce the Good for
man. It must be remembered (1) that general Greek education
was not carried much beyond the elementary stage : those who
wished for higher education got it for themselves, and Aristotle
does not deal with their problems : (2) that music was much
more important in Greek education than in our own.

N O one will doubt that the legislator should direct his
attention above all to the education of youth ; for the
neglect of education does harm to the constitution. The
citizen should be moulded to suit the form of government under
which he lives. For each government has a peculiar character
which originally formed and which continues to preserve it. The
democratic character creates democracy, and the oligarchic
character creates oligarchy ; and always the better the character,
the better the government.

Again, for the exercise of any faculty or art a previous training
and habituation are required ; clearly therefore they are required
for the practice of virtue. And since the whole city has one End,
it is clear that education should be one and the same for all, and
that it should be public and not private—not as at present, when
every one looks after his own children separately, and gives them
separate instruction of the sort which he thinks best ; the training
in things which are of common interest should be the same for all.
Neither must we suppose that any one of the citizens belongs to
himself, for they all belong to the state, and are each of them
a part of the state, and the care of each part is inseparable from
the care of the whole. In this particular as in some others the
Lacedaemonians are to be praised, for they take the greatest

pains about their children, and make education the business of the state.

That education should be regulated by law and should be an affair of state is not to be denied, but what should be the character of this public education, and how young persons should be educated, are questions which remain to be considered. As things are, there is disagreement about the subjects. For there is no general agreement about the things to be taught. Neither is it clear whether education is more concerned with intellectual or with moral virtue. The existing practice is perplexing ; no one knows on what principle we should proceed—should the useful in life, or should virtue, or should the higher knowledge, be the aim of our training ; all three opinions have been entertained. There can be no doubt that children should be taught those useful things which are really necessary, but not all useful things ; for occupations are divided into liberal and illiberal ; and to young children should be imparted only such kinds of knowledge as will be useful to them without vulgarizing [1] them. And any occupation, art, or science, which makes the body or soul or mind of the freeman less fit for the practice or exercise of virtue, is vulgar.

The customary branches of education are in number four ; they are—(1) reading and writing, (2) gymnastic exercises, (3) music, to which is sometimes added (4) drawing. Of these, reading and writing and drawing are regarded as useful for the purposes of life in a variety of ways, and gymnastic exercises are thought to infuse courage. Concerning music a doubt may be raised—in our own day most men cultivate it for the sake of pleasure, but originally it was included in education, because nature herself, as has been often said, requires that we should be able, not only to work well, but to use leisure well ; for, as I must repeat once again, the first principle of all action is leisure. Both are required, but leisure is better than occupation and is its End ;

---

[1] The Greek word is *banausos*, and was originally used of mechanical occupations, which were thought degrading to a free man.

and therefore the question must be asked, what ought we to do when at leisure ? Clearly we ought not to be amusing ourselves, for then amusement would be the end of life.[1]

After remarking that amusement, though not the object of leisure, is necessary for hard-worked persons as a relaxation, Aristotle continues.

IT is clear then that there are branches of learning and education which we must study merely with a view to leisure spent in intellectual activity, and these are to be valued for their own sake ; whereas those kinds of knowledge which are useful in business are to be deemed necessary, and exist for the sake of other things. And therefore our fathers admitted music into education, not on the ground either of its necessity or utility, for it is not necessary, nor indeed useful in the same manner as reading and writing, which are useful in money-making, in the management of a household or estate, in the acquisition of knowledge and in political life, nor like drawing, useful for a more correct judgement of the works of artists, nor again like gymnastic, which gives health and strength ; for neither of these is to be gained from music. There remains, then, the use of music for intellectual enjoyment in leisure ; which is in fact evidently the reason of its introduction, this being one of the ways in which it is thought that a freeman should pass his leisure.[2]

Aristotle then sums up.

IT is evident, then, that there is a sort of education in which parents should train their sons, not as being useful or necessary, but because it is liberal or noble. Whether this is of one kind only, or of more than one, and if so, what they are, and how they are to be imparted, must hereafter be determined. Thus much we are now in a position to say, that the ancients witness to us : for their opinion may be gathered from the fact that music is one of the received and traditional branches of education.

[1] viii. 1.   [2] viii. 3, § 6.

Further, it is clear that children should be instructed in some useful things—for example, in reading and writing—not only for their usefulness, but also because many other sorts of knowledge are acquired through them. With a like view they may be taught drawing, not to prevent their making mistakes in their own purchases, or in order that they may not be imposed upon in the buying or selling of articles, but perhaps rather because it makes them judges of the beauty of the human form. To be always seeking after the useful does not become free and exalted souls.

The following passage is from the *Rhetoric*. Its subject may seem an odd topic for a treatise on the art of speaking. But the Greeks studied the subject far more methodically than the moderns, and analysis of human character seemed to them an essential part of the orator's equipment. If Aristotle here seems exaggerated and cynical, it must be remembered that he is describing a type, not an individual, and viewing it from the angle of the professional lawyer or politician.

THE young are in character prone to desire and ready to carry any desire they may have formed into action. They are changeful too and fickle in their desires, which are as transitory as they are vehement ; for their wishes are keen without being permanent, like a sick man's fits of hunger and thirst. They are passionate, irascible, and apt to be carried away by their impulses. They are the slaves too of their passion, as their ambition prevents their ever brooking a slight and renders them indignant at the mere idea of enduring an injury. And while they are fond of honour, they are fonder still of victory ; for superiority is the object of youthful desire, and victory is a species of superiority. Again, they are fonder both of honour and of victory than of money, the reason why they care so little for money being that they have never yet had experience of want. They are charitable rather than the reverse, as they have never yet been witnesses of many villainies ; and they are trustful, as they have not yet been often deceived. They are sanguine too ;

for the young are heated by Nature as drunken men by wine ;
besides they have not yet experienced frequent failures.   Their
lives are lived principally in hope, as hope is of the future and
memory of the past, and while the future of youth is long, its
past is short ; for on the first day of life the field of memory is
empty, the field of hope infinite.   For the same reason they are
easily deceived, as being quick to hope.   They are inclined to be
courageous ; for they are full of passion, which excludes fear,
and of hope, which inspires confidence, as anger is incompatible
with fear, and the hope of something good is itself a source of
confidence.   They are bashful too, having as yet no independent
standard of honour and having lived entirely in the school of
convention.   They have high aspirations ; for they have never
yet been humiliated by the experience of life, but are unacquainted
with the limiting force of circumstances ; and a great idea of
one's own deserts, such as is characteristic of a sanguine disposition, is itself a form of high aspiration.   Again, in their actions
they prefer honour to expediency, as it is habit rather than
calculation which controls their lives, and, while calculation
pays regard to expediency, virtue pays regard exclusively to
honour.   Youth is the age when people are most devoted to their
friends or relations or companions, as they are then extremely
fond of social intercourse and have not yet learnt to judge their
friends or indeed anything else by the rule of expediency.   If the
young commit a fault, it is always on the side of excess ; for they
carry everything too far, whether it be their love or hatred or
anything else.   They regard themselves as omniscient and are
positive in their assertions ; this is in fact the reason of their
carrying everything too far.   Also their offences take the line
of insolence and not of meanness.   They are compassionate from
supposing all people to be virtuous or at least better than they
really are ; for as they estimate their neighbours by their own
innocence, they regard the evils which befall them as undeserved.
Finally, they are fond of laughter and consequently facetious,
facetiousness being disciplined insolence.

Such being the character of the young, it may be said generally that elder men who have passed their prime have characters mostly composed of the qualities opposite to these. For as they have lived many years and have been often the victims of deception and error, and as vice is the rule rather than the exception in human affairs, they are never positive about anything and always err on the side of too little excess. They ' suppose ', they never ' know ' anything ; and in discussion they always add ' perhaps ' or ' possibly ', expressing themselves invariably in this guarded manner, but never positively. They are uncharitable too, i. e. they are ready to put the worst construction upon everything. Again, they are suspicious of evil from not trusting anybody, and they do not trust anybody from having had experience of human wickedness. Hence too they have no strong loves or hatreds ; but their love is such as may some day be converted into hatred and their hatred such as may some day be converted into love. Their temper of mind is neither grand nor generous ; not the former, for they have been so much humiliated by the experience of life as to have no desire of any great or striking object or of anything but the mere appliances of life ; nor the latter, for property is a necessity of life, and they have learnt by experience the difficulty of acquiring it and the facility with which it may be lost. They are cowards and perpetual alarmists, their disposition being exactly contrary to that of the young ; for as they are not fervent like the young, but have cooled down, their old age has in consequence paved the way for cowardice, fear itself being a sort of cooling process. They are fond of life, and never so fond of it as on their last day ; for it is the absent which is the object of all desire, and that which we most lack we are most desirous to possess. They are selfish to a fault, selfishness again being a species of mean-mindedness. And from their selfishness it follows that their standard of life is too apt to be expediency rather than honour ; for expediency is what is good to the individual, and honour what is good in an absolute sense. They are apt to be shameless rather than the contrary ; for as they pay less regard to honour than to expediency, they are able to disregard appearances. They are despondent too partly from their experience of life—for the generality of things which occur in the world are bad or at least do not turn out so well as they might—and partly from their cowardly disposition. Again, they live by memory rather than by hope ; for while the remainder of their life is necessarily short, its past is long, and the future is the sphere of hope, the past the sphere of memory. This too is the explanation of their garrulity ; they are perpetually talking over what has happened in the past because of the pleasure they feel in recollection. It is calculation rather than character which regulates their lives ; for the end of calculation is expediency, but the end of character is virtue. The offences which they commit take the line of petty meanness rather than of insolence. The old are compassionate as well as the young, not however for the same reason ; for in the one case the reason is humanity, and in the other infirmity, as the old suppose all manner of suffering to be at their door, and this is a state of mind which, as we have said, excites compassion. Hence they are querulous, not facetious nor fond of laughter.

As to persons who are in the prime of life, it is evident that in character they will occupy a position intermediate between the young and the old. They will be exempt from the excess of either ; they will be neither excessively confident, as excess of confidence is foolhardiness, nor excessively fearful, but will preserve a proper balance of confidence and fear ; they will be neither universally trustful nor universally distrustful, but will rather form their judgement in accordance with the facts ; their rule of life will be neither honour only nor expediency only but both, and neither parsimony nor extravagance but a proper Mean. The same will be true in regard to passion and desire. They will combine temperance with valour and valour with temperance, these being qualities which are distributed separately among the young and the old ; for the young are brave and licentious and the old are temperate and cowardly. It may indeed be said generally that, wherever there are advantages distributed between youth and age, persons in the prime of life enjoy both, and that, wherever there are excesses or defects inherent in youth and age, they observe moderation in respect to them. The body, I may say, is at its prime from 30 to 35, and the soul about 49.[1]

The treatise known as the *Art of Poetry* or the *Poetics* is all that remains of a larger work : it deals chiefly with tragedy, and should be read in connexion with Greek Drama.

The first impression of this book is unpleasing. Aristotle is totally unlike the great English critics, such as Coleridge, Shelley, or Matthew Arnold. (Contrast, for instance, Shelley's *Defence of Poetry* with the passage on the origin of literature quoted below.) Aristotle lays poetry on the operating table and dissects it. The artist's and the anatomist's view of the same subject are very different, and the latter's is the less attractive. Yet it is not the less interesting and instructive. Aristotle tried to form an idea of the essence of tragedy and the rules that should be observed in writing it. These he deduced from Greek Drama, with its limitations and peculiarities. It is hardly credible that, with no other guide, any critic could produce a book of permanent value. Yet if the reader takes Aristotle and applies his doctrines to Shakespeare or to later drama, he will be surprised to find how little of the treatise is out of date, how living are its conceptions, how few of them a modern playwright can afford to disregard. ' The book is of permanent value as . . . an original or first-hand statement of what we may call the classical view of artistic criticism. It does not regard poetry as a matter of unanalysed inspiration ; it makes no concession to personal whims or fashion or ennui. It tries by rational methods to find out what is good in art and what makes it good, accepting the belief that there is just as truly a good way and many bad ways in poetry as in morals or in playing billiards.' [2] A reader will be better able to judge of the merits of the *Poetics*, if he answers for himself the questions implied in the headings below, and then reads Aristotle's answers.

[1] ii. 12 f. (tr. Welldon).
[2] G. Murray, Preface to Aristotle on the Art of Poetry.

The origin of literature

Poiëtikë, the Greek word translated in the following passage by 'poetry', means 'making' or, as we might say, 'creation'. Aristotle does not use the word in our narrow sense, but includes in 'poetry' all creative literature, considering the real distinction to be between such literature, whether in prose or poetry, and the mere statement of facts, like a science text-book or the *Annual Register*. Those who try to find any fundamental distinction between, say, Ruskin's description of the Campagna and a descriptive passage of Wordsworth or Tennyson, will discover the justification for such a view. The truth of Aristotle's general theory may be seen in the earliest works of art.

IT is clear that the general origin of poetry was due to two causes, each of them part of human nature. Imitation is natural to man from childhood, one of his advantages over the lower animals being this, that he is the most imitative creature in the world, and learns at first by imitation. And it is also natural for all to delight in works of imitation. The truth of this second point is shown by experience : though the objects themselves may be painful to see, we delight to view the most realistic representations of them in art, the forms for example of the lowest animals and of dead bodies. The explanation is to be found in a further fact : to be learning something is the greatest of pleasures not only to the philosopher but also to the rest of mankind, however small their capacity for it ; the reason of the delight in seeing the picture is that one is at the same time learning—gathering the meaning of things, e. g. that the man there is so-and-so ; for if one has not seen the thing before, one's pleasure will not be in the picture as an imitation of it, but will be due to the execution or colouring or some similar cause. Imitation, then, being natural to us—as also the sense of harmony and rhythm, metres being obviously species of rhythms—it was through their original aptitude, and by a series of improvements for the most part gradual on their first efforts, that men created poetry out of their improvisations.[1]

[1] Poetics, c. 4.

A definition of tragedy

RESERVING Epic and Comedy for consideration hereafter, let us proceed now to the discussion of Tragedy ; before doing so, however, we must gather up the definition resulting from what has been said. A tragedy, then, is the imitation of an action that is serious[1] and also complete in itself ; in language with pleasurable accessories, each kind brought in separately in the parts of the work ; in a dramatic, not in a narrative form ; with incidents arousing pity and fear, wherewith to accomplish its purgation[2] of such emotions. Here by ' language with pleasurable accessories ' I mean that with rhythm and harmony or song superadded ; and by ' the kinds separately ' I mean that some portions are worked out with verse only, and others in turn with song.[3]

The most important element of Drama

Aristotle then points out six ingredients of drama, Spectacle (i.e. scenery, the actors' dress, &c.), Character, Plot or Story, Diction, Song and Music, Thought. He lays the chief stress on the third of these, condemning plays which are mere studies of character—a common type on the modern stage. Observe the admirable criticism of dramas which rely on staging for their effect.

THE most important of the six is the combination of the incidents of the story. Tragedy is essentially an imitation not of persons but of action and life, of happiness and misery. All human happiness or misery takes the form of action ; the end for which we live is a certain kind of activity, not a quality. Character gives us qualities, but it is in our actions—what we do—that we are happy or the reverse. In a play accordingly they do not act in order to portray the Characters ; they include the Characters for the sake of the action. So that

[1] As opposed to Comedy.
[2] Bywater quotes fifty-eight interpretations of these words. Tragedy arouses emotions of pity and fear, but these do not injure us, for at the same time, like a drug, it carries them off. See Milton's preface to *Samson Agonistes*.
[3] i.e. dialogue and chorus respectively.

it is the action in it, i.e. its Fable or Plot, that is the end and purpose of the tragedy ; and the end is everywhere the chief thing. Besides this, a tragedy is impossible without action, but there may be one without Character. And again : one may string together a series of characteristic speeches of the utmost finish as regards Diction and Thought, and yet fail to produce the true tragic effect ; but one will have much better success with a tragedy which, however inferior in these respects, has a Plot, a combination of incidents, in it. A further proof is in the fact that beginners succeed earlier with the Diction and Characters than with the construction of a story ; and the same may be said of nearly all the early dramatists. We maintain, therefore, that the first essential, the life and soul, so to speak, of Tragedy is the Plot ; and that the Characters come second—compare the parallel in painting, where the most beautiful colours laid on without order will not give one the same pleasure as a simple black-and-white sketch of a portrait. We maintain that Tragedy is primarily an imitation of action, and that it is mainly for the sake of the action that it imitates the personal agents. Third comes the element of Thought, i.e. the power of saying whatever can be said, or what is appropriate to the occasion.[1] One must not confuse it with Character. Character in a play is that which reveals the moral purpose of the agents, i.e. the sort of thing they seek or avoid. Fourth among the literary elements is the Diction of the personages, i.e. as before explained, the expression of their thoughts in words, which is practically the same thing with verse as with prose. As for the two remaining parts, the musical element is the greatest of the pleasurable accessories of Tragedy. The Spectacle, though an attraction, is the least artistic of all the parts, and has least to do with the art of poetry. The tragic effect is quite possible without a public performance and actors ; and besides, the getting-up

[1] The argumentative speeches, so common in Euripides, in which speakers justify their position, come under this head, as would the law-court speeches of Portia and Hermione.

of the Spectacle is more a matter for the costumier than the poet.[1]

The right length for a play

BEAUTY is a matter of size and order, and therefore impossible either (1) in a very minute picture, since our perception becomes indistinct as it approaches instantaneity; or (2) in a picture of vast size—one, say, 1,000 miles long—as in that case, instead of the object being seen all at once, the unity and wholeness of it is lost to the beholder. Just in the same way, then, as a beautiful whole made up of parts, or a beautiful living creature, must be of some size, a size to be taken in by the eye, so a story or Plot must be of some length, but of a length to be taken in by the memory. As for the limit of its length, so far as that is relative to public performances and spectators, it does not fall within the theory of poetry. The limit, however, set by the actual nature of the thing is this : the longer the story, consistently with its being comprehensible as a whole, the finer it is by reason of its magnitude. As a rough general formula, ' a length which allows of the hero passing by a series of probable or necessary stages from misfortune to happiness, or from happiness to misfortune ', may suffice as a limit for the magnitude of the story.[2]

A definition of Unity of Plot

In the following passage, with equal subtlety and sense, Aristotle defines for all time a principle that underlies the making of dramas or epics.

THE Unity of a Plot does not consist, as some suppose, in its having one man as its subject. An infinity of things befall that one man, some of which it is impossible to reduce to unity ; and in like manner there are many actions of one man which cannot be made to form one action. One sees, therefore, the mistake of all the poets who have written a *Heracleid*, a *Theseid*, or similar poems; they suppose that, because Heracles was

[1] c. 6.   [2] c. 7.

one man, the story also of Heracles must be one story. Homer, however, evidently understood this point quite well, whether by art or instinct, just in the same way as he excels the rest in every other respect. In writing an *Odyssey*, he did not make the poem cover all that ever befell his hero—instead of doing that, he took an action with a Unity of the kind we are describing as the subject of the *Odyssey*, as also of the *Iliad*. The truth is that, just as in the other imitative arts one imitation is always of one thing, so in poetry the story, as an imitation of action, must represent one action, a complete whole, with its several incidents so closely connected that the transposal or withdrawal of any one of them will disjoin and dislocate the whole. For that which makes no perceptible difference by its presence or absence is no real part of the whole.[1]

How far History is suitable as a subject for Drama

It is obvious that Shakespeare, dramatizing the story of Henry V, leaves out much which a historian would record. Aristotle here states the principle on which a dramatist makes his selection. A historian may give us isolated facts; but the events in a drama must lead one to another, like links in a chain. A historian may tell us ' what is true only of some particular person at a particular time' : in the characters of drama we feel, behind the individual, a certain type of character. That is what Aristotle means by calling poetry more philosophic and universal than history.

FROM what we have said it will be seen that the poet's function is to describe, not the thing that has happened, but a kind of thing that might happen, i. e. what is possible as being probable or necessary. The distinction between historian and poet is not in the one writing prose and the other verse —you might put the work of Herodotus into verse, and it would still be a species of history; it consists really in this, that the one

---

[1] c. 8. Aristotle did not, as is often supposed, lay down the famous doctrines of the unity of Time and Place, which for so long fettered drama. These were the work of his successors : Aristotle is careful, in discussing the problem, to leave the dramatist free.

describes the thing that has been, and the other a kind of thing that might be. Hence poetry is something more philosophic and of graver import than history, since its statements are of the nature rather of universals, whereas those of history are singulars. By a universal statement I mean one as to what such or such a kind of man will probably or necessarily say or do—which is the aim of poetry, though it affixes proper names to the characters ; by a singular statement, one as to what, say, Alcibiades did or had done to him.[1]

Aristotle then remarks that Greek tragedy avoids plays with imaginary characters, and draws its plots from legend. What follows shows his open-mindedness. Though the Drama he knew avoided plays on historical or imaginary subjects, he admits that there is no objection to them.

NEVERTHELESS even in Tragedy there are some plays with but one or two known names in them, the rest being inventions ; and there are some without a single known name, e. g. Agathon's *Antheus*, in which both incidents and names are of the poet's invention ; and it is no less delightful on that account. So that one must not aim at a rigid adherence to the traditional stories on which tragedies are based. And if a poet should come to take a subject from actual history, he is none the less a poet for that ; since some historic occurrences may very well be in the probable and possible order of things ; and it is in that aspect of them that he is their poet.

Of simple Plots and actions the episodic are the worst. I call a Plot episodic when there is neither probability nor necessity in the sequence of its episodes.

What should be the character of the ideal Tragic Hero ? Should Tragedies [2] have an unhappy ending ?

To see how far they are true, test Aristotle's views on the first point by the heroes of Shakespeare's tragedies.

[1] c. 9.
[2] The Greek word does not imply, as with us, an unhappy ending.

WE assume that, for the finest form of Tragedy, the Plot must imitate actions arousing pity and fear, since that is the distinctive function of Tragedy. It follows, therefore, that there are three forms of Plot to be avoided. (1) A good man must not be seen passing from happiness to misery, or (2) a bad man from misery to happiness. The first situation is not fear-inspiring or piteous, but simply odious to us. The second is the most untragic that can be ; it has no one of the requisites of Tragedy ; it does not appeal either to the human feeling in us, or to our pity, or to our fears. Nor, on the other hand, should (3) an extremely bad man be seen falling from happiness into misery. Such a story may arouse the human feeling in us, but it will not move us to either pity or fear ; pity is occasioned by undeserved misfortune, and fear by that of one like ourselves ; so that there will be nothing either piteous or fear-inspiring in the situation. There remains, then, the intermediate kind of personage, a man not pre-eminently virtuous and just, whose misfortune, however, is brought upon him not by vice and depravity but by some error, of the number of those in the enjoyment of great reputation and prosperity, e. g. Oedipus, Thyestes, and the men of note of similar families. The perfect Plot, accordingly, must have a single, and not (as some tell us) a double issue ; the change in the hero's fortunes must be not from misery to happiness, but on the contrary from happiness to misery ; and the cause of it must lie not in any depravity, but in some great error on his part ; the man himself being either such as we have described, or better, not worse, than that. The theoretically best tragedy, then, has a Plot of this description. The critics, therefore, are wrong who blame Euripides for taking this line in his tragedies, and giving many of them an unhappy ending. It is, as we have said, the right line to take. The best proof is this : on the stage, and in the public performances, such plays, properly worked out, are seen to be the most truly tragic ; and Euripides, even if his execution be faulty in every other point, is seen to be nevertheless the most tragic certainly of the dramatists. After this comes the construction of Plot which some rank first, one with a happy end for the good characters, and an unhappy end for the bad. It is ranked as first only through the weakness of the audiences ; the poets merely follow their public, writing as its wishes dictate. But the pleasure here is not that of Tragedy. It belongs rather to Comedy, where the bitterest enemies in the piece walk off good friends at the end, with no slaying of any one by any one.[1]

We have concentrated on the three greatest stars in the firmament of Greek philosophy and may ignore its countless lesser lights, who for the most part are mere names to us, though famous and powerful in their generation. Three great philosophic movements we can only mention. The first two of these are sharply contrasted. Epicurus (341–270 B.C.), scientist and materialist, taught that the object of life is pleasure, though ' we cannot live with pleasure unless our life is honourable, just, and wise '. The Stoics, starting with Zeno (336–264), taught the idealists of later Greece and of Rome to follow virtue and sustain the evils of life without flinching, till the New Platonists brought the consolations of mysticism to the death-bed of the Graeco-Roman world. Though they survive only in fragments, there were more Stoics and Epicureans than there ever were Platonists and Aristotelians. For four hundred years they divided the thinking world between them, and for those who reject Christianity still provide perhaps the best alternative reasoned philosophy of life.

[1] c. 13. Students of the *Poetics* are recommended to read Butcher, *Aristotle's Theory of Poetry and the Fine Arts* (Macmillan).

XII

ORATORY: DEMOSTHENES

The greatest oration of the greatest of orators.—LORD BROUGHAM on Demosthenes' ' Speech on the Crown '.

THE oratory of a past generation is the least interesting part of its literature. The occasions which called it forth belong to a long-dead day ; it is inextricably intertwined with transitory interests and sordid passions ; nor can we hear it delivered, as it was meant to be, by the living voice of its creators. Its interest is historical, for the scholar ; or technical, as an example of the art of pleading a case ; or philosophical, as with Burke, because it contains profound political thought ; or literary, from the brilliance of its purple patches.

Speakers and eloquence have existed ever since men formed themselves into societies, but here, as in so many things, the Greeks laid the foundation of a scientific treatment of the subject, and were the creators of the art of oratory. We have speeches by eleven orators, all belonging to the fourth century, when the art reached its perfection and Athens was still free. Some of these were delivered in the Assembly, but most in the law courts. An Athenian who went to law was obliged to plead in person, but he had his speech written by an expert, and these ' private' speeches which survive are from the hands of famous orators, though they were actually delivered by ordinary citizens. They have great technical interest for a barrister who wishes to see how an ancient pleader put his case, otherwise they are apt to disappoint us. There are few purple passages, for these speakers were more concerned to win their case than to make a literary display ; there is little political thought in them, for they were addressed not to posterity, but to a jury met to decide a particular issue.

Three out of the eleven speakers have a special interest for the general reader. There is Lysias (about 458–380), who, if ease, wit, refinement, lucidity, naturalness were the aim of a writer, would be perhaps the greatest stylist among them. Addison, with his eloquence, clearness, and charm, would have been an English

DEMOSTHENES

Lysias, had there been professional speechwriters in England and had he taken to the art. There is Isocrates (436–338), not only one of the most far-seeing politicians and influential educators of Greece, but the originator of three great forces in modern Europe. He was too nervous to speak in public, and published his views on politics and education in the form of speeches. Thus he is the father of political journalism. He is also the author of that theory of education which rejects the Platonic ideal of precise and scientific knowledge, and aims at a general, widely-based culture, that makes the student's mind supple and well-informed and puts into his hands a skeleton key, fitting no lock precisely, but capable of turning them all. Thirdly, he is the great-grandfather of Johnsonese, and perfected a style that, adopted and popularized by Cicero, with its rolling periods and its balanced sentences, was to be the basis for all ages of stately prose ; we hear its echoes in Milton and Jeremy Taylor, in Landor and Ruskin. Finally, there is Demosthenes.

With Lysias and Isocrates we shall not deal. The qualities of Lysias are lost in translation. Much of Isocrates belongs merely to his own age, the rest has been absorbed into the general current of world culture. But we must glance at Demosthenes (384–322), to whom a great English orator gave the title at the head of this chapter. A delicate boy, shy and inclined to stammer, he became in his manhood the leader of the war-party in Athens. He detected the designs of Philip, and set himself to persuade the peaceful, good-natured democracy of Athens to spend on war money which they preferred to use for social needs at home, and to sacrifice their own lives on the field of battle instead of paying mercenaries to take their place. He did persuade the people ; but it awoke too late from dreams of peace, and found that policies cannot be improvised at a moment's notice and that tardy self-defence was useless against an enemy who knew exactly what he wanted to do and had made every preparation to do it. We, who a few years ago were at war with an adventurer nation, can read Demosthenes with understanding as he denounces the designs of an adventurer king ; and as he warns the Athenians of their unpreparedness and implores them to awake to the situation, can recognize that his words might have been applied to other democracies beside that of Athens.

Demosthenes is not, like Burke, a storehouse of political wisdom. The Englishman soared above the immediate battle, the Greek lived too much in its dust and heat to take distant or philosophic

views.   He has the defects as well as the merits of a practical
statesman (which Burke was not), and his speeches are too
apposite to the occasions of their delivery, too full of the politics
of the day to make easy reading two thousand years after they
were spoken.   Yet there is a universal element in them which
appeals to every age.   They are the very breath of patriotism,
if patriotism is the passionate devotion to the greatness and
traditions of a country, the recognition of an unlimited duty of
maintaining its fame by energy, courage, and self-sacrifice.

The following passage, which we might have heard delivered
in the Assembly in the spring of 341 B.C., is an example of the
spirit and method of Demosthenes.   He has just illustrated the
danger of Athens from the fate of three Greek towns, Olynthus,
Eretria, and Ōreus, which had listened to advocates of peace, had
declined to make war against Philip, and had been destroyed by
him.   He urges Athens to remember their ruin, and act before
it is too late.   Omit the local illustrations, and almost every word
might have been used by a speaker in the English House of
Commons in the days before the war.

PERHAPS you are surprised that the Olynthians favoured
the champions of Philip's interest rather than their own.
Why was it ?   What happens here, happened there.
Sometimes the advocates of the wise policy are unpopular, however much they regret it, for they have to consider what is best
for their country :   while their opponents serve the interests of
Philip by measures that please the people.   The patriots demanded
increased taxation, Philip's friends said it was needless.   The
one said ' Fight and mistrust ', the other said ' Keep the peace '—
till Olynthus was in the toils.   It was the same in everything ;—
I will not tell the story in detail.   One party said what would
gratify their audience, the other said what would save it.   And
in the end the people submitted to much, not with their eyes
shut, not to please themselves, but merely lying down under
it because they thought their cause lost.   I am afraid that
this will be your fate, when you come to review your situation,
and see that there is nothing left for you to do.   May it never
come to that, my countrymen.   It is better to die ten thousand

deaths than to adopt a policy to humour Philip, and to sacrifice speakers who are maintaining your interests.

It is foolish and wicked to indulge such hopes, blundering in your policy, doing nothing that you should, listening to the pro-Philip party and fancying that Athens is too big to sustain any disaster—come what may. It is shameful to say afterwards: ' Who would have thought it ? yes, we ought to have done this, and not done that.' The Olynthians could mention many points where foreknowledge would have saved them from ruin—so could the people of Oreus, so could the Phōcians, so could each of the states that Philip has overthrown. How does that help them ? While the ship is safe, be it small or great, sailor and pilot and all aboard should be active to watch that no one intentionally or unintentionally capsizes her. Once the sea is over her decks, their efforts are vain. So, Athenians, while we are safe, with our great city, our abundant resources, our glorious name, what are we to do ? Perhaps there are some sitting in the audience who have long been wishing to put that question to me. I will tell you, and I will propose a motion, so that you can vote it if you wish. Defend yourselves in person, make your preparations—with ships, with money, with men, I mean. Even if the rest of the world submits to be slaves, you must fight for freedom. . . . (Here follow practical proposals.) Those are the measures for a city with your reputation. You are wrong, if you think that Chalcis or Megara will save Greece, while you run away from your responsibilities. We may be thankful if they save themselves. In this it is you who must act. That is the privilege which your ancestors faced many great dangers to win, and which they have bequeathed to you. But if every one sits down, trying to please himself, and thinking how he personally may evade acting, in the first place you will never find any one to act, and in the second, I am afraid that all at once we shall be driven to the very action which we are anxious to avoid. That is my speech, my proposal. If you accept it, I believe that even now we can be saved. If any one has something better to suggest, let him give his advice. And may whatever decision you take, be for your good. So grant it, all ye gods in heaven ! [1]

' Is this supreme oratory ? ' the reader may ask. ' It is vigorous stuff, but hardly what we expected and there is not even a peroration.' Certainly it is not like the finest English eloquence with its richness of phrase and stately movement. It is the oratory, not of the North, but of the South, and it has the rarest of qualities, intense passion, behind it. The speaker makes no epigrams and indulges in no flowers of speech. He is too much in earnest. His mind sees the sword hanging over Athens ready to fall, and he cares for nothing but to rouse her from sleep before it is too late. His emotion is betrayed in the abrupt, rasping phrases, the emphasis, the sudden transitions from argument to apostrophe, from question to exclamation, here a prayer, here a plain statement, here an imaginary interruption—and this is not a particularly vehement piece. If you wish to judge of its effect, imagine it delivered by Demosthenes, and try to deliver it yourself. He himself said that delivery was the first, second, and third point in successful oratory, and used to speak with a vehemence such as we never hear in England. A Greek critic tells us that he behaved as if he were possessed ; his rival Aeschines talks of him weeping, screaming, and rushing about the platform, and compares him to a wild beast. Yet he is anything but a ranter or rhetorician. Vehement as his speeches are, they are full of argument. Many orators have been able to move the passions, many have been close and cogent reasoners. Demosthenes united both these powers, as perhaps no speaker has ever done, and it is the secret of his greatness. He attacked the walls of the intellect and the emotions at the same moment, and, so assaulted, the fortress almost inevitably falls.

A reader who wishes to study Demosthenes should commence either with one of the *Philippics*, or with the speech *On the Chersonēse*, or with his masterpiece, the speech *On the Crown*, delivered when his policy had failed, and triumphantly vindicating it against his critics. But, as I have said, he must expect to find, not a string of purple patches, but hard argument on the question before the house. Here I shall only quote the most famous passage in Demosthenes. He is replying to an impeachment by his enemy Aeschines, and has the extremely difficult task of defending

---

[1] Philippic, iii. 63 f.

a policy that has ended in disaster. His opponents said, in effect: 'You spent our treasure and sacrificed our young men—for nothing. Athens did what you wished, she was beaten, and Philip's heel is upon her. Are you a statesman worthy of the confidence of your country ? ' This is the answer of Demosthenes. Note the vehemence and variety of the manner to which attention has been already called.

A S Aeschines lays such stress on the consequences of my policy, I wish to make a statement that may startle you. And in God's name I beg you not to be surprised at my paradox, but to give it your favourable consideration. If the secrets of the future were revealed to us, if every one had foreseen them, and if you, Aeschines, had prophesied them, and shouted and screamed your protestations—and you never opened your lips—not even then ought Athens to have turned aside from her path, if she had any regard for her fame or her past or for the ages to come. At present our policy seems a failure ; all men may fail if it is God's will ; but if Athens had surrendered her post to Philip in the hour when she claimed to be the champion of Greece, she would have been shamed as a traitor to all. Gentlemen, suppose Athens had abandoned without an effort a cause for which your fathers faced every danger that man can face, who would not have pointed the finger of scorn at you—at you, Aeschines—not at Athens, Heaven forbid, nor at me. How, in God's name, could we have looked in the face strangers who came to our city, if this present revolution in Greece had taken place, and Philip had become the master and leading power in the Greek world, and others—without us—had carried on the struggle against such a consummation ; and that, though Athens in days past had never preferred peace without honour to the dangerous battle for the right. Is there a Greek, is there any one outside Greece, who does not know that Thebes, and before Thebes, Sparta, and earlier still the king of Persia, would have been willing and thankful to give Athens what she wished, and leave her in possession of what she had, if she would do what they asked, and leave another nation to lead Greece ? But such an idea was intolerable ; it was not in our nature ; it was not in our traditions. No one from the beginning of time has ever persuaded us to throw in our lot with might that was not right, to accept the security of slaves, or to shirk at any moment of our history the risks of the battle for pre-eminence, for honour, and for renown. So august, so consonant with your character do you think such principles that the Athenians of the past whom you chiefly praise are those that have observed them. You are right. Could any one fail to admire the courage of the men who would not take orders from a foreigner, but rather endured to embark and leave their country and city, choosing as their general, Themistocles, who had proposed this policy, and stoning Cyrsilus who urged them to comply with the Persians' demands.[1] They stoned him, and their wives stoned his wife. The Athenians of the age of Marathon did not look for statesmen and generals who would make them prosperous slaves : they would not live, if they could not live in freedom. Each of them considered himself born for his country as well as for his father and mother. Where is the difference ? Why, a man who looks on himself as born for his parents waits for the day of doom and the coming of death ; the other will go to meet death to keep his country free, and is less afraid of it than of the insults and dishonour that a defeated people must endure.

If I presumed to say that it was I who inspired you with a spirit worthy of your past, there is not a man present who might not properly rebuke me. But my point is that these principles of conduct were your own, that this spirit existed in the city before me, but that in its particular application I had merely my share as your servant. Aeschines, however, denounces our policy as a whole, invokes your resentment against me as responsible for the city's terrors and risks, and in his anxiety to wrest from me the distinction of an hour, robs you of glories which will endure for ever. If you decide that my policy was wrong, you will make

---

[1] He alludes to the Persian invasion of 480, when for strategic reasons the Athenians evacuated their town and allowed the enemy to occupy it.

it seem that your misfortunes are due, not to the unkindness of fortune, but to a mistake of your own. But it is not true, gentlemen, it is not true that you were mistaken when you took upon you that peril for the freedom and safety of Greece. No, by our fathers, who were first to face the danger at Marathon ; by those who stood in the ranks at Plataea ; by the fleets of Salamis and Artemisium ; by all those many others who lie in the sepulchres of the Nation, brave men whom Athens honoured and buried, all alike, Aeschines, not the successful only, nor only the victorious. She did well. They have all done what brave men may ; their fate is that which God assigned.[1]

The following extract from the treatise ' On the Sublime ' (first or second century A.D.), which goes under the name of Longinus, contains a subtle analysis of the above passage and is a good example of later Greek literary criticism.

DEMOSTHENES is producing an argument in favour of his policy. What was the natural way to treat it ? Something like this : ' You were not wrong when you took upon you that peril for the freedom of Greece. Your history proves it ; for the fighters of Marathon, Salamis, and Plataea were not wrong.' Instead, as by a sudden divine inspiration, he utters the oath by the heroes of Greece ; ' You were not wrong, no, by those who were first to face the danger at Marathon.' He seems by this apostrophe to deify the ancestors of his audience ; he suggests by his phrase that we ought to swear by men who died thus, as we swear by gods. He infuses into the minds of his judges the spirit of these fighters, and transforms a logical argument into transcendent and sublime emotion and into the conviction which so novel and extraordinary an oath extorts. At the same time he insinuates the healing and antiseptic thought, that they should be as proud of their struggle with Philip as of the victories of Marathon and Salamis. . . . He has framed his oath for men who were beaten, so that Chaeronea might cease to

[1] On the Crown, 199 f.

seem a disaster. . . . He was open to the retort : 'You are speaking of a defeat that occurred in your administration, and yet you
invoke the memory of a victory.' So he adjusts his language to
avoid this objection, teaching that even in our inspiration we
should keep a steady head. 'By those', he says, 'who were the
first to face the danger at Marathon ; by the fleets of Salamis
and Artemisium ; by those who stood in the ranks at Plataea.'
He never uses the word 'conquered', but suppresses any phrase
indicating the result, since the Persian Wars were a triumph,
and Chaeronea the opposite. Then, before his hearers can reflect,
he carries them off their feet with the words 'whom Athens
honoured and buried ; all alike, Aeschines, not the successful
only '.[1]

[1] c. 16.

XIII

THEOCRITUS AND THE EPIGRAMMATISTS

' I should be content to die, if I had written anything equal to this.'
    TENNYSON, after reading the 13th Idyll of Theocritus.[1]

*Two years after his great victory at Chaeronea Philip dies, and
is succeeded by his son, the nineteen-year-old Alexander. Greece
sees her chance, revolts, and is at once struck down. A year later
Alexander, aged twenty-one, is chosen commander-in-chief of the
Greek forces, for a campaign against Persia. The Macedonian
conquest has proved a blessing in disguise. At last Greece is united :
her arms, so long used against herself, are turned against a foreign
enemy : she goes out to achieve the spiritual and intellectual conquest
of the world, and to carry to others the culture hitherto almost confined
to her own land. It is the birth of Hellenism—a development comparable to the change of Christianity from a Jewish sect to a world
mission, and hardly less momentous.*

*In the next ten years we see Alexander as conqueror of Persia,
Syria, Palestine, Egypt : he crosses the Indus and reaches the
Beas ; then returns to die in Babylon, after a drinking bout,
in 323, at the age of thirty-two. He leaves behind him cities such
as Alexandria, centres of Greek culture in Eastern lands, and
a great empire that falls asunder into kingdoms, ruled by Hellenized
monarchs, the descendants of his generals. The most important of
these kingdoms, Macedonia (with Greece), Syria, and Egypt, bear
rule with varying fortunes till, one by one, they are eaten up by
Rome, Macedonia in 146, Syria in 64, Egypt in 30 B.C.*

*By its prestige Athens remains the mother city of Hellenism :
but other centres, especially Alexandria, become not less important.
The chief poets, the great scientists of the period live in Sicily,*

---

[1] The lines specially referred to are those describing Heracles calling to
the boy Hylas, who had been carried off by the water nymphs.

> τρὶς μὲν Ὕλαν ἄυσεν . . .
> τρὶς δ᾽ ἄρ᾽ ὁ παῖς ὑπάκουσεν, ἀραιὰ δ᾽ ἵκετο φωνὰ
> ἐξ ὕδατος· παρεὼν δὲ μάλα σχεδὸν εἴδετο πόρρω.

' Thrice he called Hylas . . . and thrice the boy heard him, and thin his
voice came from the water, and though very near he seemed far away.'

Alexandria, and elsewhere. As a political force Greece is null, as a world influence she is supreme. Greek culture, like a flood, saturates everything in its reach. Rome takes from Greece her philosophy and science, her models and chief inspiration in every branch of literature, her doctors and artists and professors. A Roman poet wrote, ' Conquered Greece took her conqueror captive ', and paradoxical Germans have held (quite falsely) that the chief value of Roman literature is as the vehicle of Greek ideas to the after-world. Her gifts are welcomed, except in one place. The struggles of the Maccabees, the second-century patriots of Judaea, are against the Hellenism which their Syrian masters wish to impose ; yet S. Paul and the evangelists write in Greek, and not only is the doctrine of the first chapter of S. John cast in Greek philosophical terms, but Christian thought from the first is moulded by Greek ideas and developed by Greek thinkers.

At last the splendid flame of Hellenism is buried under the ruins of the Roman Empire, or survives pallid and flickering in the Greek Empire of Constantinople, till, rediscovered by the West, it lights the fires of the Renaissance.

Greek literature did not end with Greek independence ; it became cosmopolitan and continued to flower in widely diffused centres of Hellenism. Menander, the chief master of comedy, was an Athenian, but, to take five famous later names, the poet Theocritus came from Sicily, the philosophers Epictetus and Dio Chrysostom from towns in Asia Minor, the satirist Lucian from Samosata in Syria, the epigrammatist Meleager from Gadara in Palestine. Jews like Philo, Josephus, S. Paul, Romans like M. Aurelius and Aelian, write in Greek. The most important centre of Greek culture in the third century B. C. was Alexandria, where literature and science flourished under the Ptolemies.

It would require pages to enumerate the different varieties of this literature, which ranges from philosophy to novels, from epics to guide-books, from science to sermons. Its quality is not contemptible. Much of it indeed is *belles-lettres* rather than literature, the work of scholars and men of letters, who understood the art of writing and lived in an educated and cultured society ; some of it is disfigured by the affectations of the *littérateur* or the pedantry of the scholar. Yet the vast majority of Greek epigrams were written after 300 B. C. And as the after-world has produced no epic to rival Homer, so it has produced no body of epigrams comparable to these. The *Bucolics* of

Theocritus again are perfect in their kind, and many English readers, if asked their preference in Greek poetry, would probably choose them after Homer. Yet neither Menander nor Theocritus nor the epigrams can be ranked with the great writers of the earlier age. In literary art they are at least equal. But whereas in tragedy and epic we see human nature at the fullest tension of its energies, the highest reach of its power, buffeted by all the storms of life, the later writers sail their small boats on the easy waters of a landlocked bay. One cannot put their works by the side of Aeschylus or Euripides any more than one can put the *Double Dealer* or *Oenone* or the *Scholar Gipsy* by the side of *King Lear*. Their interests are narrower, their outlook less heroic. Liberty is lost and they have none of the activities of a free political life. They are touched by the withering effect of cosmopolitanism. Unlike the great Athenians, who were soldiers and politicians as well as writers, they are nearly all ' literary men ', viewing the world from study windows. But that is the one reason why we can understand them, and in their kind they are perfect. I propose here only to give specimens of the epigrammatists and of three eminent writers.

The most delightful and the greatest of the Alexandrian poets is Theocritus. Born probably in Sicily (about 305 B.C.), he enjoyed the patronage both of the Syracusan and Egyptian courts. Under the title of Idylls (the closest translation is *genre*) twenty-nine poems attributed to him have survived, mainly in hexameters and in Doric dialect. Most of them are Bucolics or Pastorals. Theocritus is the father of the pastoral in literature and far superior to his numerous but unattractive offspring: and he has set many echoes ringing in later literature, from Virgil's *Eclogues* to Milton's *Lycidas*, from *Adonais* to *Thyrsis* and the *Scholar Gipsy*. There are also occasional poems and some pieces called Mimes by the Greeks. The latter are short and semi-dramatic: Anstey's *Voces Populi* and the *Dolly Dialogues* would be classed as mimes. No Greek poetry is more modern than Theocritus; none needs less adjustment of our minds for its appreciation. His merits explain themselves. He is perhaps chiefly enjoyed because of his feeling for Nature. There is indeed plenty of this elsewhere in Greek; but in Theocritus it is predominant. He does not, it is true, like Wordsworth, give Nature a soul and find in her an interpretation of life: the Greek mind is too direct and concrete for that. But we meet in his poems, idealized yet never wholly conventional, the Sicilian shepherds of his time, and walk with him the Greek country-side.

In the following pastoral a shepherd and a goatherd meet : the former sings of Daphnis, who died for love. The interest of the poem is twofold : the figures on the cup are admirably described ; and the song shows what Milton's *Lycidas* owes to Theocritus, and also how a great poet borrows. Milton has used the Greek for the framework of his poem (as Virgil and as Shelley in *Adonais* used it), but his poetry is his own.

THYRSIS.

SWEET are the whispers of yon pine that makes
Low music o'er the spring, and, Goatherd, sweet
Thy piping ; second thou to Pan alone.

GOATHERD.

Shepherd, thy lay is as the noise of streams
Falling and falling ay from yon tall crag.

THYRSIS.

Pray, by the Nymphs, pray, Goatherd, seat thee here
Against this hill-slope in the tamarisk shade,
And pipe me somewhat, while I guard thy goats.

GOATHERD.

I durst not, Shepherd, O I durst not pipe
At noontide ; fearing Pan, who at that hour
Rests from the toil of hunting. Harsh is he ;
Wrath at his nostrils ay sits sentinel.
But, Thyrsis, thou canst sing of Daphnis' woes ;
High is thy name for woodland minstrelsy :
Then rest we in the shadow of the elm
Fronting Priāpus and the Fountain-nymphs.
There, where the oaks are and the Shepherd's seat,
Sing as thou sang'st erewhile, when matched with him
Of Libya, Chrŏmis ; and I'll give thee, first,
To milk, aye thrice, a goat—she suckles twins,
Yet ne'ertheless can fill two milkpails full :—

Next, a deep drinking-cup, with sweet wax scoured,
Two-handled, newly-carven, smacking yet
O' the chisel. Ivy reaches up and climbs
About its lip, gilt here and there with sprays
Of woodbine, that enwreathed about it flaunts
Her saffron fruitage. Framed therein appears
A damsel ('tis a miracle of art)
In robe and snood : and suitors at her side
With locks fair-flowing, on her right and left,
Battle with words, that fail to reach her heart.
She, laughing, glances now on this, flings now
Her chance regards on that : they, all for love
Wearied and eye-swoln, find their labour lost.
Carven elsewhere an ancient fisher stands
On the rough rocks : thereto the old man with pains
Drags his great casting-net, as one that toils
Full stoutly : every fibre of his frame
Seems fishing ; so about the grey-beard's neck
(In might a youngster yet) the sinews swell.
Hard by that wave-beat sire a vineyard bends
Beneath its graceful load of burnished grapes ;
A boy sits on the rude fence watching them.
Near him two foxes : down the rows of grapes
One ranging steals the ripest ; one assails
With wiles the poor lad's scrip, to leave him soon
Stranded and supperless. He plaits meanwhile
With ears of corn a right fine cricket-trap,
And fits it on a rush : for vines, for scrip,
Little he cares, enamoured of his toy.
I jest not : up, lad, sing : no songs thou'lt own
In the dim land where all things are forgot.

THYRSIS [*sings*].
Begin, sweet Maids, begin the woodland song.
The voice of Thyrsis. Aetna's Thyrsis I.

Where were ye, Nymphs, oh where, while Daphnis pined ?
In fair Penēus' or in Pindus' glens ?[1]
For great Anāpus' stream was not your haunt,
Nor Aetna's cliff, nor Ācis' sacred rill.
　　　Begin, sweet Maids, begin the woodland song.
O'er him the wolves, the jackals howled o'er him ;
The lion in the oak-copse mourned his death.
　　　Begin, sweet Maids, begin the woodland song.
The kine and oxen stood around his feet,
The heifers and the calves wailed all for him.
　　　Begin, sweet Maids, begin the woodland song.
First from the mountain Hermes came, and said,
' Daphnis, who frets thee ? Lad, whom lov'st thou so ? '
　　　Begin, sweet Maids, begin the woodland song.
Came herdsmen, shepherds came, and goatherds came ;
All asked what ailed the lad. Priapus came
And said, ' Why pine, poor Daphnis ? while the maid
Foots it round every pool and every grove,
O lack-love and perverse, in quest of thee.'
　　　Begin, sweet Maids, begin the woodland song.[2]

The song continues in the same strain and ends with the death
of Daphnis.

A scene at midday during harvest in the island of Cos.

　　　　　. . . . . . there we lay
Half-buried in a couch of fragrant reed
And fresh-cut vine-leaves, who so glad as we ?
A wealth of elm and poplar shook o'erhead :
Hard by a sacred spring flowed gurgling on
From the Nymphs' grot, and in the sombre boughs
The sweet cicada chirped laboriously.

---

[1] Pindus is a mountain, Peneus a river, in Thessaly. The places following are in Sicily.
[2] Idyll i. 1–81 (extracts). The translations are by Calverley. That
of Idyll xv is from Matthew Arnold, Pagan and Mediaeval Religious
Sentiment (in *Essays in Criticism*, 1st series).

Hid in the thick thorn-bushes far away
The treefrog's note was heard ; the crested lark
Sang with the goldfinch ; turtles made their moan,
And o'er the fountain hung the gilded bee.
All of rich summer smacked, of autumn all :
Pears at our feet, and apples at our side
Rolled in luxuriance ; branches on the ground
Sprawled, overweighed with damsons ; while we brushed
From the cask's head the crust of four long years.
Say, ye who dwell upon Parnassian peaks,
Nymphs of Castalia, did old Chīron e'er
Set before Heracles a cup so brave
In Pholus' cavern—did as nectarous draughts
Cause that Anāpian shepherd, in whose hand
Rocks were as pebbles, Polyphēme the strong,[1]
Featly to foot it o'er the cottage lawns :—
As, ladies, ye bid flow that day for us
All by Dēmēter's shrine at harvest-home ?
Beside whose cornstacks may I oft again
Plant my broad fan : while she stands by and smiles,
Poppies and cornsheaves on each laden arm.[2]

A scene on the sea-shore in Sicily, before dawn.

WANT quickens wit : Want's pupils needs must work,
O Diophantus : for the child of toil
Is grudged his very sleep by carking cares :
Or, if he taste the blessedness of night,
Thought for the morrow soon warns slumber off.
  Two ancient fishers once lay side by side
On piled-up sea-wrack in their wattled hut,
Its leafy wall their curtain. Near them lay
The weapons of their trade, basket and rod,
Hooks, weed-encumbered nets, and cords and oars,
And, propped on rollers, an infirm old boat.

[1] See p. 52.   The Centaur Chiron brought up Hercules and other heroes.
Demeter, goddess of the earth and its crops.   [2] Id. vii.

Their pillow was a scanty mat, eked out
With caps and garments : such the ways and means,
Such the whole treasury of the fishermen.
They knew no luxuries : owned nor door nor dog ;
Their craft their all, their mistress Poverty :
Their only neighbour Ocean, who for ay
Round their lorn hut came floating lazily.
   Ere the moon's chariot was in mid-career,
The fishers girt them for their customed toil,
And banished slumber from unwilling eyes.

Asphalion, one of the old men, tells the other of a dream he
has just had.

ASPHALION.

' LAST evening, as I plied my watery trade,
   (Not on an o'erfull stomach—we had made
Betimes a meagre meal, as you can vouch,)
I fell asleep ; and lo ! I seemed to crouch
Among the boulders, and for fish to wait,
Still dangling, rod in hand, my vagrant bait.
A fat fellow caught it : (e'en in sleep I'm bound
To dream of fishing, as of crusts the hound :)
Fast clung he to the hooks ; his blood outwelled :
Bent with his struggling was the rod I held :
I tugged and tugged : my efforts made me ache :
" How, with a line thus slight, this monster take ? "
Then gently, just to warn him he was caught,
I twitched him once ; then slacked and then made taut
My line, for now he offered not to run ;
A glance soon showed me all my task was done.
'Twas a gold fish, pure metal every inch
That I had captured. I began to flinch :
" What if this beauty be the sea-king's joy,
Or azure Amphitrīte's treasured toy ! "
With care I disengaged him—not to rip

With hasty hook the gilding from his lip :
And with a tow-line landed him, and swore
Never to set my foot on ocean more,
But with my gold live royally ashore.
So I awoke : and, comrade, lend me now
Thy wits, for I am troubled for my vow.'

COMRADE.

' Ne'er quake : you're pledged to nothing, for no prize
You gained or gazed on. Dreams are naught but lies.
Yet may this dream bear fruit ; if, wide-awake
And not in dreams, you'll fish the neighbouring lake.
Fish that are meat you'll there mayhap behold,
Not die of famine, amid dreams of gold.'[1]

The realistic gifts of Theocritus can be judged from the two
following poems, both mimes. The power of the first is obvious :
it lies in the romantic setting and in the painting of the bitterest
of human emotions ; and fully to appreciate it, a reader must see
the one and feel the other. It is a moonlit, windless night. Two
girls, Sīmaetha and her servant Thestylis, are standing by a fire,
on which from time to time they throw corn and herbs, meanwhile spinning a wheel. They have a wax doll in the shape
of a man. Simaetha has been deserted by her lover, Delphis,
and is using ' sympathetic ' magic to recover his love.

WHERE are the bay-leaves, Thestylis, and the charms ?
    Fetch all ; with fiery wool the caldron crown ;
Let glamour win me back my false lord's heart !
Twelve days the wretch hath not come nigh to me,
Nor made inquiry if I die or live,
Nor clamoured (oh unkindness !) at my door.
Sure his swift fancy wanders otherwhere,
The slave of Aphrodīte and of Love.
I'll off to Tīmagētus' wrestling-school

[1] Id. xxi. The poem is almost certainly not by Theocritus. Amphitrite
is a sea-goddess.

At dawn, that I may see him and denounce
His doings; but I'll charm him now with charms.
So shine out fair, O moon! To thee I sing
My soft low song: to thee and Hecate [1]
The dweller in the shades, at whose approach
E'en the dogs quake, as on she moves through blood
And darkness and the barrows of the slain.
All hail, dread Hecate: companion me
Unto the end, and work me witcheries
Potent as Circe or Mēdēa wrought,
Or Perimēde of the golden hair!
 Turn, magic wheel, draw homeward him I love.
First we ignite the grain. Nay, pile it on!
Where are thy wits flown, timorous Thestylis?
Shall I be flouted, I, by such as thou?
Pile, and still say, ' This pile is of his bones.'
 Turn, magic wheel, draw homeward him I love.
Delphis racks me: I burn him in these bays.
As, flame-enkindled, they lift up their voice,
Blaze once, and not a trace is left behind:
So waste his flesh to powder in yon fire!
 Turn, magic wheel, draw homeward him I love.
E'en as I melt, not uninspired, the wax,
May Mindian Delphis melt this hour with love:
And, swiftly as this brazen wheel whirls round,
May Aphrodite whirl him to my door.
 Turn, magic wheel, draw homeward him I love.
Next burn the husks. Hell's adamantine floor
And aught that else stands firm can Artemis move.
Thestylis, the hounds bay up and down the town:
The goddess stands i' the cross-roads: sound the gongs.
 Turn, magic wheel, draw homeward him I love.
Hushed are the voices of the winds and seas;
But O not hushed the voice of my despair.

---

[1] Goddess of the underworld: also identified with Artemis.

He burns my being up, who left me here
No wife, no maiden, in my misery.

    Turn, magic wheel, draw homeward him I love.

Thrice I pour out ; speak thrice, sweet mistress, thus :
' What face soe'er hangs o'er him be forgot
Clean as, in Dīa,[1] Thēseus (legends say)
Forgat his Ariadne's locks of love.'

    Turn, magic wheel, draw homeward him I love.

The coltsfoot grows in Arcady, the weed
That drives the mountain-colts and swift mares wild.
Like them may Delphis rave : so, maniac-wise,
Race from his burnished brethren home to me.

    Turn, magic wheel, draw homeward him I love.

He lost this tassel from his robe ; which I
Shred thus, and cast it on the raging flames.
Ah baleful Love ! why, like the marsh-born leech,
Cling to my flesh, and drain my dark veins dry ?

    Turn, magic wheel, draw homeward him I love.

From a crushed eft to-morrow he shall drink
Death ! But now, Thestylis, take these herbs and smear
That threshold o'er, whereto at heart I cling
Still, still—albeit he thinks scorn of me—
And spit, and say, ' 'Tis Delphis' bones I smear.'

    Turn, magic wheel, draw homeward him I love.

                               [Exit Thestylis.

Now, all alone, I'll weep a love whence sprung
When born ? Who wrought my sorrow ? Anaxo came,
Her basket in her hand, to Artemis' grove.
Bound for the festival, troops of forest beasts
Stood round, and in the midst a lioness.[2]

    Bethink thee, mistress Moon, whence came my love.

Theucharidas' slave, my Thracian nurse now dead
Then my near neighbour, prayed me and implored

[1] The island of Naxos where Theseus deserted Ariadne who had saved
him from the Minotaur.
[2] A religious procession, of which wild beasts were a feature.

To see the pageant : I, the poor doomed thing,
Went with her, trailing a fine silken train,
And gathering round me Clearista's robe.

    Bethink thee, mistress Moon, whence came my love.

Now, the mid-highway reached by Lycon's farm,
Delphis and Eudāmippus passed me by.
With beards as lustrous as the woodbine's gold
And breasts more sheeny than thyself, O Moon,
Fresh from the wrestler's glorious toil they came.

    Bethink thee, mistress Moon, whence came my love.

I saw, I raved, smit (weakling) to my heart.
My beauty withered, and I cared no more
For all that pomp ; and how I gained my home
I know not : some strange fever wasted me.
Ten nights and days I lay upon my bed.

    Bethink thee, mistress Moon, whence came my love.

And wan became my flesh, as 't had been dyed,
And all my hair streamed off, and there was left
But bones and skin. Whose threshold crossed I not,
Or missed what grandam's hut who dealt in charms ?
For no light thing was this, and time sped on.

    Bethink thee, mistress Moon, whence came my love.

At last I spake the truth to that my maid :
' Seek, an thou canst, some cure for my sore pain.
Alas, I am all the Mindian's ! But begone,
And watch by Timagetus' wrestling-school :
There doth he haunt, there smoothly takes his rest.

    Bethink thee, mistress Moon, whence came my love.

Find him alone : nod softly : say, " she waits " ;
And bring him.' So I spake : she went her way,
And brought the lustrous-limbed one to my roof.
And I, the instant I beheld him step
Lightfooted o'er the threshold of my door,

    (*Bethink thee, mistress Moon, whence came my love,*)

Became all cold like snow, and from my brow

Brake the damp dewdrops : utterance I had none,
Not e'en such utterance as a babe may make
That babbles to its mother in its dreams ;
But all my fair frame stiffened into wax.

    Bethink thee, mistress Moon, whence came my love.
He bent his pitiless eyes on me ; looked down,
And sate him on my couch, and sitting, said :
'Thou hast gained on me, Simaetha, (e'en as I
Gained once on young Philīnus in the race,)
Bidding me hither ere I came unasked.

    Bethink thee, mistress Moon, whence came my love.
For I had come, by Eros I had come,
This night, with comrades twain or maybe more,
The fruitage of the Wine-god in my robe,
And, wound about my brow with ribbons red,
The silver leaves so dear to Heracles.[1]

    Bethink thee, mistress Moon, whence came my love.
Had ye said " Enter ", well : for, 'mid my peers
High is my name for goodliness and speed :
I had kissed that sweet mouth once and gone my way.
But had the door been barred, and I thrust out,
With brand and axe would we have stormed ye then.

    Bethink thee, mistress Moon, whence came my love.
Now be my thanks recorded, first to Love,
Next to thee, maiden, who didst pluck me out,
A half-burned helpless creature, from the flames,
And badst me hither. It is Love that lights
A fire more fierce than his of Lipara,[2]

    (*Bethink thee, mistress Moon, whence came my love.*)
Scares, mischief-mad, the maiden from her bower,
The bride from her warm couch.' He spake : and I,
A willing listener, sat, my hand in his.
Till yesterday he found no fault with me,

[1] i.e. a wreath of poplar.
[2] The volcanic Liparaean islands, north of Sicily.

Nor I with him. But lo, to-day there came
Philista's mother—hers who flutes to me—
With her Melampo's ; just when up the sky
Gallop the mares that chariot rose-limbed Dawn :
And divers tales she brought me, with the rest
How Delphis loved, she knew not rightly whom :
But this she knew ; that of the rich wine ay
He poured ' to Love ' ; and at the last had fled,
To line, she deemed, the fair one's halls with flowers.
Such was my visitor's tale, and it was true :
For thrice, nay four times, daily he would stroll
Hither, leave here full oft his Dorian flask :
Now—'tis a fortnight since I saw his face.
Doth he then treasure something sweet elsewhere ?
Am I forgot ? I'll charm him now with charms.
But let him try me more, and by the Fates
He'll soon be knocking at the gates of hell.
Spells of such power are in this chest of mine,
Learned, lady, from mine host in Palestine.

    Lady, farewell : turn ocean-ward thy steeds :
As I have purposed, so shall I fulfil.
Farewell, thou bright-faced Moon ! Ye stars, farewell,
That wait upon the car of noiseless Night.[1]

The following poem takes us, first into a house, and then into
the streets in third-century Alexandria.

A couple of Syracusan women, staying at Alexandria, agreed
on the occasion of a great religious solemnity—the feast of
Adōnis—to go together to the palace of King Ptolemy Phila-
delphus, to see the image of Adonis, which the queen Arsinoe,
Ptolemy's wife, had decorated with peculiar magnificence. A
hymn, by a celebrated performer, was to be recited over the
image. The names of the two women are Gorgo and Praxinoe ;
their maids, who are mentioned in the poem, are called Eunoe and
Eutychis. Zōpyrio is Praxinoe's child. Gorgo comes by
appointment to Praxinoe's house to fetch her, and there the
dialogue begins :

[1] Id. ii.

Gorgo. Is Praxinoe at home ?

Praxinoe. My dear Gorgo, at last ! Yes, here I am. Eunoe, find a chair—get a cushion for it.

G. It will do beautifully as it is.

Pr. Do sit down.

G. Oh, this gad-about spirit ! I could hardly get to you, Praxinoe, through all the crowd and all the carriages. Nothing but heavy boots, nothing but men in uniform. And what a journey it is ! My dear child, you really live *too* far off.

Pr. It is all that insane husband of mine. He has chosen to come out here to the end of the world, and take a hole of a place—for a house it is not—on purpose that you and I might not be neighbours. He is always just the same—anything to quarrel with one ! anything for spite !

G. My dear, don't talk so of your husband before the little fellow. Just see how astonished he looks at you. Never mind, Zopyrio, my pet, she is not talking about papa.

Pr. Good heavens ! the child does really understand.

G. Pretty papa !

Pr. That pretty papa of his the other day (though I told him beforehand to mind what he was about), when I sent him to a shop to buy soap and rouge, brought me home salt instead—stupid, great, big, interminable animal !

G. Mine is just the fellow to him. . . . But never mind now, get on your things and let us be off to the palace to see the Adonis. I hear the Queen's decorations are something splendid.

Pr. In grand people's houses everything is grand. What things you have seen in Alexandria ! What a deal you will have to tell to anybody who has never been here !

G. Come, we ought to be going.

Pr. Every day is holiday to people who have nothing to do. Eunoe, pick up your work ; and take care, lazy girl, how you leave it lying about again ; the cats find it just the bed they like. Come, stir yourself, fetch me some water, quick ! I wanted the water first, and the girl brings me the soap. Never mind ; give it me. Not all that, extravagant! Now pour out the water—stupid! why don't you take care of my dress? That will do. I have got my hands washed as it pleased God. Where is the key of the large wardrobe? Bring it here—quick!

G. Praxinoe, you can't think how well that dress, made full, as you have got it, suits you. Tell me, how much did it cost—the dress by itself, I mean.

Pr. Don't talk of it, Gorgo : more than eight guineas of good hard money. And about the work on it I have almost worn my life out.

G. Well, you couldn't have done better.

Pr. Thank you. Bring me my shawl, and put my hat properly on my head—properly. No, child (*to her little boy*), I am not going to take you ; there 's a bogy on horseback, who bites. Cry as much as you like ; I'm not going to have you lamed for life. Now we'll start. Nurse, take the little one and amuse him ; call the dog in, and shut the street-door. (*They go out.*) Good heavens! what a crowd of people! How on earth are we ever to get through all this? They are like ants : you can't count them. My dearest Gorgo, what will become of us ? here are the royal Horse Guards. My good man, don't ride over me ! Look at that bay horse rearing bolt upright ; what a vicious one ! Eunoe, you mad girl, do take care !—that horse will certainly be the death of the man on his back. How glad I am now, that I left the child safe at home !

G. All right, Praxinoe, we are safe behind them ; and they have gone on to where they are stationed.

Pr. Well, yes, I begin to revive again. From the time I was a little girl I have had more horror of horses and snakes than of anything in the world. Let us get on ; here 's a great crowd coming this way upon us.

G. (*to an old woman*). Mother, are you from the palace ?

Old Woman. Yes, my dears.

G. Has one a tolerable chance of getting there ?

Old Woman. My pretty young lady, the Greeks got to

Troy by dint of trying hard ; trying will do anything in this world.

G. The old creature has delivered herself of an oracle and departed.

Pr. Women can tell you everything about everything, Jupiter's marriage with Juno not excepted.

G. Look, Praxinoe, what a squeeze at the palace gates !

Pr. Tremendous ! Take hold of me, Gorgo ; and you, Eunoe, take hold of Eutychis !—tight hold, or you'll be lost. Here we go in all together. Hold tight to us, Eunoe ! Oh, dear ! oh, dear ! Gorgo, there 's my scarf torn right in two. For heaven's sake, my good man, as you hope to be saved, take care of my dress !

Stranger. I'll do what I can, but it doesn't depend upon me.

Pr. What heaps of people ! They push like a drove of pigs.

Stranger. Don't be frightened, ma'am, we are all right.

Pr. May you be all right, my dear sir, to the last day you live, for the care you have taken of us ! What a kind, considerate man ! There is Eunoe jammed in a squeeze. Push, you goose, push ! Capital ! We are all of us the right side of the door, as the bridegroom said when he had locked himself in with the bride.

G. Praxinoe, come this way. Do but look at that work, how delicate it is !—how exquisite ! Why, they might wear it in heaven.

Pr. Heavenly patroness of needlewomen, what hands were hired to do that work ? Who designed those beautiful patterns ? They seem to stand up and move about, as if they were real— as if they were living things, and not needlework. Well, man is a wonderful creature ! And look, look, how charming he lies there on his silver couch, with just a soft down on his cheeks, that beloved Adonis—Adonis, whom one loves even though he is dead !

Another Stranger. You wretched women, do stop your incessant chatter ! Like turtles, you go on for ever. They are enough to kill one with their broad lingo—nothing but *a, a, a.*

G. Lord, where does the man come from ? What is it to you if we *are* chatterboxes ? Order about your own servants ! Do you give orders to Syracusan women ? If you want to know, we came originally from Corinth, as Bellerophon did ; we speak Peloponnesian. I suppose Dorian women may be allowed to have a Dorian accent.

Pr. Oh, honey-sweet Proserpine, let us have no more masters than the one we've got ! We don't the least care for *you* ; pray don't trouble yourself for nothing.

G. Be quiet, Praxinoe ! That first-rate singer, the Argive woman's daughter, is going to sing the *Adonis* hymn. She is the same who was chosen to sing the dirge last year. We are sure to have something first-rate from *her*. She is going through her airs and graces ready to begin.

Then follows the religious hymn : and then a speech of the incorrigible Gorgo concludes the poem.

' Praxinoe, certainly women are wonderful things. That lucky woman to know all that ! and luckier still to have such a splendid voice ! And now we must see about getting home. My husband has not had his dinner. That man is all vinegar, and nothing else ; and if you keep him waiting for his dinner, he 's dangerous to go near. Adieu, precious Adonis, and may you find us all well when you come next year ! '[1]

Epigram means inscription, and the derivation betrays the epigram's origin and use. Relatives wished to preserve the memory of their dead ; donors that of gifts to temples or cities. So a literary form arose which in time was applied to other uses. The earliest surviving Greek epigrams date from the seventh century B. C. ; in the Alexandrian age, when poets understood the technique of writing but had not the power of invention and imagination necessary for an epic or a tragedy, they welcomed a form which gave scope for the one and did not require the other. It was the age of scholars, and the epigram is the literary form most adapted to a scholar's gifts.[2] Consequently most though perhaps not the greatest Greek epigrams were written

---

[1] Id. xv. The Greek is in hexameter verse.
[2] As Mr. A. E. Housman's poems show. Though not technically epigrams, they are essentially epigrammatic.

after 300 B. C.; they continued to be written until late in the Christian era, and they are the most uniformly successful branch of the literature of the period. They were collected at various times into anthologies, of which the last was made at Constantinople by a fourteenth-century monk.

Two characteristics of the Greek epigram will strike any reader. First, it is not what we call epigrammatic. There is no straining after effect, no obvious attempt to make points. It is perfectly natural, not rhetorical. Least of all is there any of the falsity that marks, for instance, the conclusion of Ben Jonson's epigram on Salathiel Pavy (p. 5). Second, it is essentially *economical* in the sense in which I have before used that word. Observe for instance how differently Pope and Simonides approach the same task. Both are writing an epitaph on a woman; and if the length of an inscription should be adjusted to the distinction of its subject, the epigram of Simonides should have been the longer of the two: for Archedike was a great lady in her day. Pope expands himself in a rather miscellaneous way over the virtues of Mrs. Corbet, ending with an effective line.

On Mrs. Corbet, who died of a Cancer

Here rests a Woman, good without pretence,
Blest with plain Reason and with sober Sense:
No Conquests she, but o'er herself, desired,
No Arts essayed, but not to be admired.
Passion and Pride were to her soul unknown,
Convinced that Virtue only is our own.
So unaffected, so composed a mind;
So firm, yet soft; so strong, yet so refined;
Heaven, as its purest gold, by Tortures tried;
The Saint sustained it, but the Woman died.[1]

Simonides, who might have found even more to say about the wife of the prince of Athens, omits all but two points, her great position in the world, and one trait in her character, closely related to her position.

First in his day of Greeks was Hippias,
Whose wife, Archedikē, this dust doth hide;

---

[1] In St. Margaret's, Westminster. Johnson thought it Pope's 'most valuable' epitaph. English can of course show many epitaphs and epigrams as 'economical' as the Greek.

Children she bore who sat on princely thrones,
To princes she was daughter, sister, bride ;
Yet was her heart not lifted up to pride.[1]

Tastes will no doubt differ about the respective merits of these epitaphs, and some may think Simonides colourless. Yet they may find that, with long acquaintance, Simonides rises in the scale while Pope falls ; and the best test of great literature is, if it improves with re-reading. In any case Simonides illustrates the method of the Greek epigram—omission and concentration. Ascetics in nothing else, the Greeks were ascetics in literature ; here they practised a rigid self-denial. The tradition perpetuated itself, and the economy and naturalness which mark the epigrams of the seventh century B.C., mark those which Greeks were writing 1,200 years later. The following selections will give an idea of the variety of subject and tone in these epigrams.

LOVE POEMS

MY star, you watch the stars. Were I yon skies,
To see you with a thousand starry eyes ![2]

* * *

O LOVE that flew so lightly to my heart,
Why are thy wings so feeble to depart ?[3]

* * *

LIKE the calm sea beguiling with those blue eyes of hers
Asclepias tempteth all men to be love's mariners.[4]

* * *

SAY Heliodore and Heliodore, and still say Heliodore,
And let the music of her name mix with the wine you pour.
And wreathe me with the wreath she wore, that holds the scent
    of myrrh,
For all that it be yesterday's, in memory of her.
The rose that loveth lovers, the rose lets fall a tear
Because my arms are empty, because she is not here.[5]

* * *

---

[1] Simonides, fr. 111. Cp. the epitaph on the Countess of Pembroke, beginning ' Underneath this sable hearse '.
[2] Plato. [3] Meleager (first century B.C.), tr. R. Garnett.
[4] Meleager, tr. Sir Rennell Rodd. [5] Id.

TEARS for thee, Heliodore, and bitter tears to shed,
If all that love has left to give can reach thee with the dead ;
Here at thy grave I offer, that tear-drenched grave of thine,
Libation of my longing before affection's shrine.
Forlorn I mourn thee, dearest, in the land where shadows dwell,
Forlorn, and grudge the tribute death could have spared so well.
Where is the flower I cherished ?   Plucked by the god of doom ;
Plucked, and his dust has tarnished the scarce unbudded bloom.
I may but pray thee, mother earth, who givest all thy best,
Clasp her I mourn for ever close to thy gentle breast.[1]

EPITAPHS

On the Spartans who fell at Plataea in 479 B.C.

INTO the dark death-cloud they passed, to set
    Fame on their own dear land for fadeless wreath,
And dying died not. Valour lifts them yet
    Into the splendour from the night beneath.[2]

On the Athenians who fell in the same battle

IF the best merit be to lose life well,
    To us beyond all else that fortune came :
In war, to give Greece liberty, we fell,
    Heirs of all time's imperishable fame.[3]

On a Boy

THESE mounded stones the boy Cleoetes hide ;
Pity him, who was beautiful and died.[4]

On a Girl

FOR Crēthis' store of tales and pleasant chat
Oft sigh the Samian maidens, missing that
Which cheered their tasks ; but she, beyond their call,
Sleeps here the sleep that must be slept by all.[5]

---

[1] Id.   [2] Simonides (b. 556 B.C.), tr. H. Macnaghten.
[3] Simonides, tr. W. Headlam.   [4] Anon.
[5] Callimachus (third century B.C.), tr. R. Garnett

Three Epitaphs on Children

FULL oft of old the islands changed their name,
And took new titles from some heir of fame;
Then dread not ye the wrath of gods above,
But change your own and be the ' isles of Love '.
For Love's own name and shape the infant bore,
Whom late we buried on your sandy shore.
Break softly there, thou never-weary wave,
And earth, lie lightly on his little grave.[1]

———

DEAD ! my firstborn ? no ! to a better country departed,
Living in happy islands that know no maid so lighthearted.
There thou goest rejoicing along the Elysian pasture—
Soft the flowers around thee—away from every disaster.
Winter nor chills thee, nor summer burns, nor sickness makes
    sorry ;
Thou nor hungerest more, nor thirstest, and robbed of its glory
Seems to thee now this life of ours, for thou dwellest securely—
Innocent, there where the rays of Olympus enhallow thee
    purely ![2]

———

I HAD but sipped the cup of life, a little child, when Death,
For good or ill, I know not which, deprived me of breath.
Oh greedy Death ! why so unkind ? Why bear a child away ?
Why make me pay so soon the debt which all alike must pay ?[3]

Two Epitaphs on Friends

THEY told me, Heraclitus, they told me you were dead ;
They brought me bitter news to hear and bitter tears to shed.
I wept as I remembered how often you and I
Had tired the sun with talking and sent him down the sky.

———

[1] Crinagoras (first century B.C.), tr. J. W. Burgon.
[2] Anon., tr. W. M. Hardinge.
[3] Anon., tr. G. B. Grundy.

And now that thou art lying, my dear old Carian guest,
A handful of grey ashes, long, long ago at rest,
Still are thy pleasant voices, thy nightingales awake,
For Death, he taketh all away, but them he cannot take.[1]

THIS stone, beloved Sabinus, on thy grave
  Memorial small of our great love shall be.
I still shall seek thee lost ; from Lēthe's wave
  Oh ! drink not thou forgetfulness of me.[2]

Two Epitaphs on Enemies

LIGHT lie the earth, Nearchus, on thy clay,
That so the dogs may easier find their prey.[3]

AFTER much eating, drinking, lying, slandering,
Timocreon of Rhodes rests here from wandering.[4]

On the philosopher Epictētus

SLAVE, poor as Īrus, halting as I trod,
I, Epictetus, was the friend of God.[5]

On a Slave Girl

O ZŌSIMA, your soul was ever free
And now your body too hath liberty.[6]

On a Fowler

WITH reeds and bird-lime from the desert air
Eumēlus gathered free, though scanty, fare.
No lordly patron's hand he deigned to kiss ;
Nor luxury knew, save liberty, or bliss.
Thrice thirty years he lived, and to his heirs
His reeds bequeathed, his bird-lime, and his snares.[7]

[1] Callimachus, tr. W. Cory. [2] Anon., tr. Goldwin Smith.
[3] Ammianus (second century A. D.), tr. J. H. Merivale.
[4] Simonides, tr. J. H. Merivale. [5] Anon., tr. H. Macnaghten.
[6] Damascius (sixth century A. D.), tr. J. A. Pott.
[7] Isidorus (first century A. D.), tr. W. Cooper.

On a Fisherman

THIS oar and net, and fisher's wicker snare,
   Themiscus placed above his buried son ;
Memorials of the lot in life he bare,
   The hard and needy life of Pelagon.[1]

Miscellaneous Epitaphs

THOU wert the morning-star among the living,
   Ere thy fair light had fled ;
Now having died thou art as Hesperus, giving
   New splendour to the dead.[2]

———

A STRANGER ! Who ? A shipwrecked corpse unknown
Leontichas entombed beneath this stone ;
Mourning his own sad life, that finds no rest,
Like seabirds wandering still on ocean's breast.[3]

———

HERE lies a sailor, there a peasant swain !
Alike to thee, O Death, the land and main.[4]

———

FOR sixty years I bore an evil lot :
No child I had—and would my sire had not.[5]

———

MY name and country were . . . no matter what !
Noble my race . . . who cares though it were not ?
The fame I won in life . . . is all forgot !
Now here I lie and no one cares a jot.[6]

———

MINE haven 's found ; Fortune and Hope adieu ;
Mock others now, for I have done with you.[7]

[1] Sappho, tr. C. Elton.   [2] Plato, tr. Shelley.
[3] Callimachus, tr. H. Milman.   [4] Id.   [5] Anon., tr. J. A. Pott.
[6] Paulus Silentiarius (sixth century A. D.), tr. J. A. Pott.
[7] Anon., tr. R. Burton.

DEDICATIONS

By a Soldier

THE crooked bow and arrow-spending case
  Promachus hangs up in this holy place,
Phoebus, to thee. The shafts remain apart,
For each is buried in a foeman's heart.[1]

By an Old Beauty

LAIS, now old, that erst all-tempting lass,
To goddess Venus consecrates her glass ;
For she herself hath now no use of one,
No dimpled cheek hath she to gaze upon :
She cannot see her springtide damask grace,
Nor dare she look upon her winter face.[2]

By a Shipwrecked Man

POSEIDON, and all Ocean-deities,
Lucilius, 'scaped from shipwreck on the seas,
Doth dedicate to ye who bade him live
His hair, for nothing else is left to give.[3]

The four following poems, of which three are dedications,
illustrate the Greek feeling for Nature.

On a Shrine of the Nymphs

NYMPHS of the fount, who in this cool retreat
Walk the clear waters with your rosy feet,
Hail, and preserve Cleonymus, your shrines
Who placed beneath the tall and whispering pines.[4]

The God of the Cross Roads

I, HERMES, by the grey sea-shore
  Set where the three roads meet,
Outside the wind-swept garden,
  Give rest to weary feet ;
The waters of my fountain
  Are clear and cool and sweet.[5]

[1] Mnasalcas (third century B. C.), tr. R. Garnett.   [3] Plato.
[2] Lucian (second century A. D.), tr. R. Garnett.
[4] Moero (a Byzantine poetess), tr. H. Milman.
[5] Anyte (a fourth ? century B. C. poetess), tr. Sir Rennell Rodd.

The Well Head

PAUSE not here to drink thy fill
Where the sheep have stirred the rill,
And the pool lies warm and still—
Cross yon ridge a little way,
Where the grazing heifers stray,
And the stone-pine branches sway
O'er a creviced rock below ;
Thence the bubbling waters flow
Cooler than the northern snow.[1]

A Starry Night

I, RAPT in scrutiny as Night unbars
The thick and mazy glories of the stars,
Though earth on Earth, no more am linked to her,
But sit in Jove's own hall, a banqueter.[2]

On a Yacht

THEY say that I am small and frail,
    And cannot live in stormy seas ;
It may be so ; yet every sail
    Makes shipwreck in the swelling breeze.
Not strength nor size can then hold fast ;
    But Fortune's favour, Heaven's decree :
Let others trust in oar and mast ;
    But may the gods take care of me.[3]

[1] Leonidas of Tarentum, tr. Sir R. Rodd.

[2] Ptolemy—the famous mathematician, astronomer, and geographer (second century A. D.), tr. R. Garnett.

[3] Leonidas of Tarentum (third century B.C.), tr. Goldwin Smith.

HUMOROUS EPIGRAMS

An Unfounded Scandal

SOME say, Nicylla, that you dye your hair:
Those jet-black locks you purchased at the fair![1]

On a Singer

THE screech-owl sings; death follows at her cries:
Demophilus strikes up; the screech-owl dies.[2]

The Viper and the Cappadocian

A VIPER stung a Cappadocian's hide,
And poisoned by his blood that instant died.[3]

The three following epigrams are on doctors.

THE physician who killed me,
Neither bled, purged or pilled me,
Nor counted my pulse; but it comes to the same,
In the height of my fever I thought of his name.[2]

Scientific Surgery

THE patient surely had been lame for life,
So Scalpel, pitying, killed him with his knife.[4]

The Doctor and the Statue

YESTERDAY the Zeus of stone from the doctor had a call:
Though he 's Zeus and though he 's stone, yet to-day 's his
    funeral.[5]

[1] Lucilius (first century A. D.), tr. G. B. Grundy.
[2] Nicarchus (first century A. D.), tr. H. Wellesley.
[3] Demodocus (fifth century A. D. ?), tr. J. H. Merivale.
[4] Nicarchus, tr. Earl of Cromer.   [5] Nicarchus, tr. G. B. Grundy.

After these uncomplimentary epigrams I must add one by an unknown writer.

On a great Doctor

HERE lies great Oreibasius, now dead,
Who many a victory over death hath won.
Fate feared him so, she often left the thread
  Of life half-spun.[1]

On a Lecturer

SEVEN pupils he hath who list to his lore,
For the benches are three and the walls are four.[2]

A Nursery Rhyme

HUMPY tortoise, what do you here ?
I'm weaving the wool and the thread, my dear.
What of your grandson, and how died he ?
White horses have carried him out to sea.[3]

[1] Anon., tr. G. B. Grundy. [2] Anon., tr. J. A. Pott. [3] Id.

XIV

PLUTARCH

Ce même notre Plutarque, si parfait et excellent juge des actions humaines.—MONTAIGNE.

THE epigram has brought us into Roman, and then into Byzantine, times ; we must return to the first century A.D. Hellenism in this period is even more cosmopolitan than before. Its task was to give a culture to the Roman Empire. It inspired Roman poets, orators, and men of letters ; it supplied the philosophies by which the educated Roman regulated his life ; education, science, and medicine were largely in the hands of Greeks. But Greece received, as well as gave : she was a part of the Roman Empire, and that empire and the qualities which built it up attracted the attention and won the admiration of her writers. This is eminently true of Plutarch.

Plutarch (A.D. 46–120) was born in Boeotia, and spent most of his life there, but visited Egypt and Italy. To-day he would have been a professor, probably of philosophy, for no other subject could cover his various interests. As it was, he was a man of letters, and spent his time in reading, writing, and discussing with his many friends religion, philosophy, politics, history, archaeology, and literature, with the wide range of a man of liberal education. He has left a great body of writings, which fall under two heads. There are the works, collected under the misleading title of *Moral Writings*, which include essays on subjects as different as Advice on Marriage, How to read Poetry to the Young, Superstition, the Delays of God's Vengeance, the Use of Enemies, the Face in the Moon, Conversations at Dinner, with many more.[1] Interesting as many of these are, Plutarch's fame rests not on them but on his *Parallel Lives*, biographies of famous Greeks and Romans. Fifty of these have survived, mostly in couples, a Greek and a Roman, with a brief comparison at the end. To read these

---

[1] Selected essays from these are published in translation by the Oxford University Press.

is not merely to peruse a number of isolated biographies, but to walk through a picture-gallery of the ancient world, and to form an idea of what the Greek and the Roman character have meant in history.

Plutarch is not a great historian. He has not the intellectual power or the scientific spirit of Thucydides ; he does not view his subject as a whole or divine the forces that underlie and explain the course of history. But he shows us what the Athenian did not trouble to show—the faces, lives, and characters of the actors. He is essentially a biographer, with an eye for picturesque detail, a memory for stories and a gift of telling them, a dramatic sense and a knowledge of character. His interest was double— intellectual and moral : he enjoyed re-creating famous figures and scenes, and this makes him delightful to read. Shakespeare's Roman plays are a testimony to this side of Plutarch—his richness in dramatic scenes and heroic figures : and Shakespeare left unused far more subjects than he took. But Plutarch also studied history for what it could teach of the art of living. Few men have known better what candour, simplicity, large-mindedness, courage, self-sacrifice, and patriotism are : few have loved them more. These are the qualities in men that attracted Plutarch ; and this temper, pervading the *Lives* though never obtrusive or self-conscious, makes them a better lesson in conduct than the most moral of his moral essays.

The following passage describes a scene from the death-bed of the great aristocrat who led and did much to make the Athenian democracy.

ABOUT that time Pericles was attacked by the plague. . . . When he was near his end, the most distinguished men in Athens and his surviving friends were sitting by him, talking of his great qualities and his power, and recalling his achievements and the number of his victories. They were conversing together, thinking that he had lost consciousness and could not understand. But it happened that he had listened to it all, and breaking into their conversation he expressed his surprise, that they mentioned with praise acts in which fortune had had a share and which many other generals had rivalled, but said nothing of his noblest and greatest achievement.

for these qualities had made them quite great enough. He used to say that he would rather lose the reward for his good actions than escape punishment for his bad ones : and that he could pardon all offenders except himself. He said that he regretted three things in his life : that he had ever trusted a woman with a secret, that he had ever gone by sea when he could go on foot, and that he had remained a whole day intestate. Speaking to a vicious old man he said : ' Age has many deformities : do not add to it those of vice.'

After recounting Cato's military achievements, Plutarch continues :

Ten years after his consulship he stood for the office of censor.[1] The aristocracy opposed his election, and put forward seven candidates, who courted the electors by fair promises, as though they wanted an indulgent and easy government. Cato on the other hand was the opposite of mild. He openly threatened evil-doers from the hustings, exclaiming that the city needed a thorough purge, and asking the masses, if they were wise, to choose not the pleasantest doctor, but the most rigorous. And so truly great and worthy of its great men was Rome, that it did not fear the grimness and severity of Cato but rejected the flatterers who showed themselves ready to do everything to please it.

Plutarch then mentions some cases where Cato showed severity, and continues.

He caused most annoyance by retrenching people's luxury. To destroy it outright was impossible, so widespread and fatal was the disease : but he took it in flank, causing all dress, carriages, women's ornaments, and household furniture, which cost more than £60, to be rated at ten times their value, with the idea of raising heavier taxation on the increased assessment. He also imposed a capital tax so as to discourage those on

[1] The chief financial official at Rome, with wide powers over the status of citizens.

whom the burden fell and who saw the modest and frugal liver paying less. Cato paid no attention to complaints, and became still more rigid.

He was a good father, a good husband, and a good man of business. He married his wife for her birth, not for money : his view was that the rich and the aristocratic were equally haughty and proud, but that the latter had a stronger sense of honour. He said that a man who struck wife or child was laying hands on the most sacred of things. He thought it more creditable to be a good husband than a great politician, and what he most admired in Socrates was his gentleness and considerateness to his shrewish wife and stupid children. When his child was born, nothing except business of state was so urgent as to keep him from being at home when his wife bathed and dressed it. When the boy was of an age, Cato took him and taught him to read and write, though he had a good slave tutor who taught many boys. But, as he says, he did not want his son to be indebted for such important instruction to a slave. He says that he wrote stories in big characters and with his own hand, that the boy could learn and profit at home by the deeds of the Romans of old : and he was as careful to avoid a coarse word in his son's presence, as in that of the Vestal Virgins.

He never paid more than £60 for a slave : for he never bought handsome and luxurious ones but only sturdy hard workers. When they grew old, he thought it well to sell them and not to feed useless heads. He considered that nothing superfluous was cheap : even if it cost a farthing, it was dear. Slaves in his house had either to be doing some work or else sleeping. When he grew richer and gave dinners to his friends and colleagues in office, as soon as the meal was over he used to flog with a leather strap those who had waited or served carelessly. He also managed that there should be some quarrels among his slaves, looking with suspicion and fear on agreement between them.

He was an old man when there came to Rome an embassy from Athens, of which Carneades the Platonist was a member. The most studious young Romans at once visited these Greeks, and attended their lectures with enthusiasm. Cato was disgusted to see this passion for study making its way into Rome and, afraid that the younger generation would transfer their ambitions to it and forsake the glory of war and active life for that of speaking, he resolved to have the philosophers all sent away on some good pretext. He rose in the senate and blamed the magistrates for allowing an embassy of men who could easily persuade any one of anything they wished, to stay so long without settling their business. He urged the senate to come to an immediate decision on the subject of the embassy, so that they could return to their schools and talk to Greek children, and leave young Romans to listen to the laws and the magistrates as they used to do. Cato did this because he had fallen foul of philosophy and out of pride scoffed at all Greek culture and literature. He declared that Socrates was a garrulous and seditious man, who tried to seize power in his country by the means at his disposal, undermining old customs and drawing the Athenians to views contrary to the laws. To prejudice his son against Hellenism he used a phrase on which a man of his age should not have ventured, uttering an oracular warning that Rome would lose her power when she became infected with Greek literature. Time has shown the vanity of his condemnation, for Rome has at one and the same time risen to the height of her power and grown familiar with all Greek literature and thought.

He composed various books and histories. One of these is on farming, in which he deals with making cakes and preserving fruit : for he had an ambition to be original and expert in everything. In the country his table was rather more lavish than elsewhere. He regularly invited his acquaintances among his neighbours and passed the time in gaiety with them. He was agreeable and a favourite not only with his contemporaries but with the young, for he knew much of many things and had heard and seen much that was memorable. The praise of good and honourable citizens was a frequent topic at his board, while the useless and vicious were ignored. For Cato would not allow a word to be spoken of them either in praise or blame.

Of the numerous striking death scenes in Plutarch, taken from a century when so many came to violent ends, I select the murder of Caesar, partly that the reader may compare Shakespeare with the Greek to whom he went for his facts. In one point Plutarch is the more impressive of the two. The series of omens, warnings, and accidents, that all but frustrated the plot, have in Plutarch's cumulative rehearsal an extraordinarily dramatic effect.

The passage is preceded by a description of the discontent excited by Caesar's supposed desire to restore the monarchy.

THIS turned the thoughts of men to Marcus Brutus, who was supposed to be descended from the tyrannicide Brutus. But the honours and favours which he had received from Caesar blunted any personal instincts to overthrow the monarchy. Not only had he been himself pardoned after Pompey's defeat at Pharsalia, and by his intercessions saved the lives of many of his friends, but he was greatly trusted by Caesar. When the conspiracy was in being and some declared that Brutus was involved, Caesar refused to listen, and touching his body said to the accusers, 'Brutus is waiting for my skin,' implying that the qualities of Brutus fitted him for Caesar's position, but that he would not show himself base and ungrateful to win it. Those who desired a change and regarded Brutus as the only or the best man to effect it, did not dare to suggest it to him personally, but filled his chair of office with letters, mostly to such purport as 'You are sleeping, Brutus' and 'You are not Brutus'. Noticing that these produced some stirrings of ambition, Cassius pressed and urged him more than before. He had private reasons for hating Caesar. But Caesar suspected him and used to say to his friends: 'What do you think of Cassius's intentions ? I don't like him, he is so pale.' Again, when Dolabella and Antony were accused to him of plotting, he said: ' I am not afraid of these fat, long-haired fellows, but of those pale, thin men,' referring to Cassius and Brutus.

It seems that we may foreknow destiny, though we cannot escape it, for they say that strange sights and signs were seen. In so momentous a tragedy it is not perhaps worth mentioning lights in the sky, wandering noises at night, and solitary birds settling in the Forum. The philosopher Strabo relates that men on fire were seen in the streets ; that a great flame proceeded from the hand of a soldier's servant, and that the man seemed to the bystanders to be in a blaze, without being any the worse when it was extinguished ; that when Caesar was sacrificing, the victim's heart could not be found—an ominous portent, for no animal could exist without a heart. One finds in many authorities, that a seer warned him to beware of a great danger on the 15th of March, called by the Romans the Ides ; when the day came Caesar greeted the seer on his way to the senate and said mockingly : ' The Ides of March are come.' ' Yes,' replied the prophet quietly, ' they are come, but they are not past.' The day before, he was dining with Marcus Lepidus, and, as was his habit, was signing some letters at table ; the conversation turned on the question, which was the best kind of death, when Caesar, before any one could speak, exclaimed, ' An unexpected one.'

Afterwards when he was in bed, as usual, with his wife Calpurnia, all the doors and windows of the house flew open at once. The noise disturbed him, and by the light of the moon he saw his wife in a deep sleep and heard her mutter indistinct words and inarticulate groans. She fancied she was holding his murdered body in her arms and weeping over him. When it was day, she implored Caesar, if possible, not to go out but to adjourn the meeting of the senate : or, if he disregarded her dreams, to inquire about the future by sacrifices and other means. Even Caesar had some apprehensions and fears, for he had never previously known Calpurnia a victim to feminine superstitions, and he now saw her greatly agitated : so that when the priests had repeatedly sacrificed and reported the omens as unfavourable, he decided to send Antony to dismiss the senate.

On this Decimus Brutus, surnamed Albinus, in whom Caesar had such confidence as to have made him his second heir, but who was in the conspiracy with the other Brutus and Cassius, afraid that a day's delay might result in the truth becoming known, laughed at the seers and warned Caesar that he was exposing himself to criticism and to a charge of treating the senate in cavalier fashion. They had met by his instructions and were ready to vote unanimously that he should be declared king of all the provinces outside Italy and be allowed to wear a crown anywhere but in Italy. If he told them to adjourn their sitting for the present and meet again when Calpurnia had better dreams, what would his detractors say, and who would listen to his friends, when they argued that his behaviour was not arbitrary and tyrannical ? If he was determined to declare it a non-dies, it would be better for him to appear in person and to adjourn the senate after addressing it. With these words Brutus took Caesar's arm and led him out. He had only gone a short way from his house when a strange slave tried to get word with him. Prevented by the thronging crowd round Caesar, he forced his way into the house and put himself in Calpurnia's hands, begging her to keep him till Caesar returned, for he had an important message to him.

Artemidōrus of Cnīdus, a Greek professor, whose occupation had made him intimate with some of Brutus's circle, so that he knew most of what was going on, came with the information he intended to give in writing. He saw that Caesar took any petitions and handed them to his attendants, so coming very near, he said : ' Read this, Caesar, alone and at once, for it deals with a matter of serious importance to you.' Caesar took the paper and tried several times to read it, but was prevented by the crowds that pressed to speak to him. He kept it in his hand and it was the only paper he had when he entered the senate.

All these things might happen accidentally. But we see the guiding and ordaining finger of God in the place in which the senate met that day and in which the struggle and the murder took place. It was one of the buildings which Pompey had raised and dedicated along with his theatre, and a statue of Pompey stood there. They say that Cassius before the act turned his eyes to this statue and silently invoked it ; he was inclined to the doctrines of Epicurus,[1] but the hour and the imminence of danger inspired him with emotions that made him forget his theories. Antony who was a powerful man and loyal to Caesar was kept out of the way by Brutus Albinus, who purposely arranged a long interview with him. When Caesar entered, the senate rose out of respect for him. Some of Brutus's confederates took up their position behind his chair ; others went towards him as though to support Tillius Cimber's petition on behalf of his exiled brother, and followed Tillius to Caesar's seat. Caesar sat down and waved their petitions away. They became more vehement in their requests and he showed annoyance, till Tillius seized his robe with both hands and began to pull it off his neck. This was the signal for the attack.

Casca gave him the first blow, striking him in the neck. He was naturally nervous at the opening of their great venture, and the wound was a slight one and not mortal. Caesar turned, and seizing the dagger held it, at the same time crying out in Latin, ' Miserable Casca, what are you doing ? ' while his murderer shouted in Greek, ' Brother, help.' So the murder began. Those who were not in the conspiracy were too horrified and panic-stricken at what they saw either to run away or to help, and did not even venture to cry out. The conspirators

---

[1] An anti-theological materialism.

all drew their naked daggers and Caesar found himself surrounded. Wherever he turned, he met blows, saw steel levelled
at his face and eyes, and found himself driven like a wild beast
and penned in by all their hands. It had been agreed that each
of them should draw blood and flesh their swords, and that
is why Brutus dealt him a single blow, striking him in the
groin. Some say that he fought the others, twisting this way
and that and shouting, but that when he saw the sword of
Brutus drawn, he pulled his robe over his face and threw himself down by the base of Pompey's statue—either by accident
or because his murderers pushed him there. It was drenched
with his blood, and men thought that Pompey presided in
vengeance over the death of his enemy, who lay at his feet
and gasped his life out from a multitude of wounds. He is
said to have received twenty-three : and many of his murderers
wounded each other as they rained their blows on his body.

XV

SCIENCE: HIPPOCRATES, ARISTOTLE, THEOPHRASTUS

Most people, when they think of the Greek genius, naturally call to mind its masterpieces in literature and art. . . . But the Greek, with his insatiable desire to know the true meaning of everything in the universe and to be able to give a rational explanation of it, was just as irresistibly driven to natural science, mathematics, and logic.—SIR T. L. HEATH.

GREEK scientific works are on different footing from Greek literature and philosophy. The latter are living and instructive to-day : time has antiquated the former, as it antiquates the science of every age, and we should only read them for their historical interest, or because, however wrong in detail, they are in some sort preserved from corruption by the still indwelling genius that created them. For this reason the following chapter treats a great topic very briefly. I have kept it to the end, so that the subject could be seen as a whole. But what is isolated in this chapter was not isolated in life. Science rose in the seventh century B.C. and thenceforward ran an unbroken course, continually influencing Greek thought. Unlike our own science, it went in the company of philosophy, and flowed from the same source.

I have called Greece the sole creator of that spirit of free inquiry and scientific thought which in religion, morals, politics, and physical science makes the civilization of the West what it is. That seems a big claim. It does not of course mean that the achievements of modern science were anticipated by the Greeks; obviously such an idea is absurd. But achievements in science and philosophy are made possible mainly by a certain attitude to life, a certain way of looking at the world. This way is first found in Greece. There is no trace of it elsewhere in Europe, and if the Greeks had never existed, there is no sign that the West would have evolved either philosophy or science. So much would be universally admitted. Obviously there is nothing in our intellectual life (I am not speaking of religion) which does not ultimately spring from seeds sown in Greece. Our Anglo-Saxon ancestors contribute nothing, and Rome learnt her philosophy as she learnt her poetry, from Greek models.

And not Europe only, but the whole world, is passing under the dominion of the Greek spirit. The nineteenth century began the transformation, still incomplete, of India, Japan, China, Egypt, Turkey, by European influences, as two centuries before the civilization of America had been transformed. Those countries have learnt or are learning from us a particular way of looking at life and the world. That way is Greek. Important as are the philosophies of India and China, they are imaginative rather than scientific in spirit, the independent scientific achievement of those countries is small, and it is not Eastern thought that is mastering the West but Western thought that is mastering the East. The germ of that thought was sown in Mitylēne about 600 B.C.; it seeded itself in all departments of life and covered the Greek and Roman world. It fell with the fall of the Roman Empire, into whose framework it had grown, and civilization for a thousand years fell back from the heights which it had attained. It was not till Greek literature had been re-discovered that the Renaissance came and the modern world began. At that time the kingdoms of the East were more advanced and more powerful than those of the West. But from that day the West slowly began to overtake them, and to-day the East turns to Europe, and imports not merely European manufactures but European thought. At the origin of this thought we will now look. It begins in science and mathematics, and this chapter, which covers some eight centuries, is confined to their origin and development.

To appreciate what the Greeks did, imagine yourself in the atmosphere in which a Greek boy grew up in the seventh century B.C., that is, without any of the scientific knowledge which we automatically acquire, because those about us possess it. What would you suppose to be the shape and size of the earth? How would you map it? What would you think of the lights that burn, far out of reach, by day or by night, in the sky above, and how would you explain their motions, disappearances or eclipses? Of what are they and the earth composed? How would you class the millions of living things that inhabit the earth? If you or your neighbours were ill, how would you treat them? Some of these questions would never suggest themselves, and it would be a colossal task to answer any of them; the more difficult because we should not start with an open mind. Tradition would tell how Chaos was the first of things : how her children, Darkness and Night, gave birth to Aether and Day : how the world was a flat plate surrounded by the river of Ocean, and roofed by a solid bowl which rested on pillars, and in which the heavenly bodies were set. How would we emancipate ourselves from these beliefs, and what would we substitute for them ? The man who took the first step was Thāles of Milētus (b. 625 B.C.). He predicted an eclipse, foresaw a good olive harvest, and made a corner in oil-presses, diverted a river for King Croesus, and tried to unite the Ionian towns against the foreigner ; but his life is a landmark in the history of thought because he declared that all things were made out of water. It is a less foolish idea than at first sight appears. ' Water ', he had noticed, ' is everywhere, and enters into everything. It lapped, a blue liquid, on the shores of his home ; it fell, a white solid, in hail and snow on the hills ; it blew across them, a transitory vapour, in wreaths of mist. It was in the sky over his head, and on rainy days fell and gave fertility to the soil of his fields. It appeared suddenly on the ground as dew, it welled up in springs, it ascended on sunny days in great shafts to the sky. It ran as blood through his own veins, and as sap through the trunks of his olives ; he could squeeze it out of their berries, and as oil it fed the flame of his lamps. Surely this omnipresent thing was the element from which everything was made. Even legend sanctioned the belief, for were not Tēthys and Oceanus called the parents of all things, and did not the gods swear by the waters of the Styx ? ' [1] But it is the question and not the answer that we should admire. The momentous fact is that it has occurred to some one to look behind the infinite variety of nature for some single principle to which all can be reduced. The originality of such an idea cannot be appreciated too highly. It opened the way to those who, by different theories more or less plausible, led up to the answer of Leucippus (fl. 435 B.C.), that the world is made of atoms combined in an infinite void, a conception which is the parent of modern physics. This example of Hellenic scientific thought is characteristic. It shows the Greeks' acute and quick intelligence, their power of breaking off from all prepossessions, of trying to see things as they are, and above all their instinct for rational explanations. If we under-estimate this achievement, it is because we have not imagination enough to go back to pre-scientific times and to

[1] *The Greek Genius*, p. 204.

realize how difficult it is for men living in a world of superstitious and traditional beliefs to rise above them.

This is not the place for an account of Greek science and mathematics. But we can glance at their achievements and give some specimens. The history of Greek science falls into four periods. It begins in the rich commercial cities of Ionia, and is carried thence across the sea to the Greek settlements in Sicily and Southern Italy. Here we meet Pythagoras (fl. 530), ' one of the most original figures in Greece and indeed in human history ',[1] a great traveller, the founder of a mysterious political brother-hood, a teacher of the transmigration of souls, the first man to maintain the spherical shape of the earth and the heavenly bodies, the first to give a scientific explanation of the different pitch of musical notes, the founder of scientific mathematics, and of scientific medicine. To him or to his school we owe the abstract conceptions underlying mathematics—point, line, magnitude, surface, body—the foundation of plane geometry, and the first theory of proportion. His idea that the universe in the last resort consists of numbers was partly mystical ; but there is method in the madness of this audacious conception. Our science conceives the world in terms of formulae, and the electrons to which it has reduced the universe are mathematical abstrac-tions, whose existence and properties are inferences from mathe-matical reasoning. For modern science as for Pythagoras, matter is number, and much as he would have to learn and modify, he would understand a conception which he was the first dimly to form.[2]

With the fall of Ionia, and the rise of Athens, the centre of learning shifts to Greece, and the second period of Greek science begins. Here the greatest names are Democritus, Plato (to whose school mathematics owes an immense debt), and Aristotle, unique for his mastery of almost every field of learning from politics to mechanics, from poetry to physics ; in science his great achieve-ments were the foundation of comparative anatomy and zoology ; with him we should mention his pupil Theophrastus, the father of botany. Before Aristotle, the makers of Greek science show amazing acuteness, audacity, independence of mind, and a natural gift for abstract thought, but they often remind us of born shots

[1] Gomperz.
[2] Pythagoras also founded a famous medical school. Other schools were at Cnidus and Cos in Ionia : in the latter island lived Hippocrates, the greatest of Greek doctors.

shooting in the dark. As the light grows, their bullets increasingly find the mark, but it is not till Aristotle that we find ourselves in an atmosphere like that of modern science. He is the father of organized and methodical research, elaborately collecting material and laying massive foundations for the palace of knowledge. This tendency developed when Greece sank into political un-importance, and learning followed the shift of material power to the capitals of the successors of Alexander the Great.

Chief among these was Alexandria, which for two hundred years remained the intellectual centre of the world. This is the third period of Greek science. Time, place, and man were favourable to science. The conquests of Alexander had opened up a new world ; East and West met in the streets of a city which was the door to both ; creative litera-ture declined with the loss of liberty, and human energy turned to the acquisition of knowledge. To crown this, a line of cultivated monarchs liberally endowed learning. Ptolemy founded, under the name of the 'Museum', or Temple of the Muses, the first public library and university of the world, the home of poets, astronomers, mathematicians, literary critics, and researchers in nearly every branch of knowledge. To this age belong Herophilus, the first investigator of the nervous system and the founder of human anatomy, Erasistratus, who recognized the connexion of human intelligence with the convolutions of the brain, Euclid, whose work on geometry remained a text-book in English schools till a few years ago, Apollōnius of Perga who wrote the first great work on conic sections, Eratosthenes, the founder of geography, the originator of parallels of longitude and latitude, the first to adapt a map to the spherical shape of the earth, Aristarchus of Samos, who anticipated Copernicus in perceiving that the sun was the centre of our system, Hipparchus the Bithynian, the greatest astronomer of antiquity, who, more than any one, reminds us in his methods of a modern man of science. It is not merely that he ' fixed the chief data of astronomy —the lengths of the tropical and sidereal year, of the various months, and of the synodic periods of the five planets ; de-termined the obliquity of the ecliptic and the moon's path, the place of the sun's apogee, the eccentricity of his orbit, and the moon's horizontal parallax—all with approximate accuracy' ; [1] that he invented trigonometry and applied it to astronomy; that he catalogued some 900 fixed stars. But he had an attitude

[1] Article on Astronomy in *Encycl. Britannica.*

worth more than his discoveries, the patient waiting on truth which is the heart of science. He mistrusted theories and pursued facts ; he criticized Eratosthenes for writing on geometry before he had the complete material for scientific certainty ; and he compiled his catalogue of stars that observers in the future might be able to check any variations in them.

But the greatest of Greek mathematicians is Archimēdes (287–212), whose work is thus summarized by Sir Thomas Heath in his *History of Greek Mathematics*.

' In geometry Archimedes' work consists in the main of original investigations into the quadrature of curvilinear plane figures and the quadrature and cubature of curved surfaces. These . . . gave birth to the calculus of the infinite, conceived and brought to perfection by Kepler and others. He performed in fact what is equivalent to *integration* in finding the area of a parabolic segment and of a spiral, the surface and volume of a sphere and the segment of a sphere, and the volumes of any segments of the solids of revolution of the second degree. In arithmetic he calculated approximations to the value of π, in the course of which calculation he shows that he could approximate to the value of square roots of large or small non-square numbers ; he further invented a system of arithmetical terminology by which he could express in language any number up to that which we should now write down with 1 followed by 80,000 million million ciphers. In mechanics he not only worked out the principles of the subject but advanced so far as to find the centre of gravity of a segment of a parabola, a semi-circle, a cone, a hemisphere, a segment of a sphere, a right segment of a paraboloid and a spheroid of revolution. Lastly, he invented the whole science of hydrostatics, which again he carried so far as to give a most complete investigation of the positions of rest and stability of a right segment of a paraboloid of revolution floating in a fluid with its base either upwards or downwards, but so that the base is either wholly above or wholly below the surface of the fluid. This represents a sum of mathematical achievement unsurpassed by any one man in the world's history.' [1]

---

[1] ii. 19 f. The surviving works of A. are too technical for quotation here. A translation of them may be found in Sir T. L. Heath, *The Works of Archimedes*. The ordinary reader is likely to be most interested by the Arēnārius or Sand-reckoner, in which A. shows that a mass of sand equal to the magnitude of the earth would contain fewer grains than the number which his system of notation, mentioned above, could express.

In the second century B. C. the brilliance begins to fade. Research continues : additions are made to knowledge ; and there are great men even in the Roman epoch ; like Galen, who concentrated the medical knowledge of the past, and was the channel of its preservation in the Middle Ages, or Ptolemy, who summarized the astronomical and geographical learning of the ancient world, providing in the former a plausible, if erroneous, theory of the movements of the heavenly bodies that dominated the world till the coming of Copernicus. Later still, Diophantus laid the foundations of algebra. And the flame continues alight, if faint, throughout Byzantine times till the fall of Constantinople (A. D. 1453). But the creative originality of the earlier period is gone. There is no ground for attributing this decay to the practical and materialistic temper of the Romans ; for, though no Roman reaches even the second rank in science, there is no evidence that its pursuit was discouraged among the Greeks. It is more likely that vast accumulations of knowledge and theory are unfavourable to originality ; the mind is too busy assimilating what others have left it, to see the world freshly for itself. But the cause of this, as of many other phenomena of the mysterious spirit of man, remains obscure. No less mysterious is the reason why the Greeks, having achieved so much, did not achieve a little more and anticipate the work of modern science. Partly it is that they were handicapped by the want of the microscope and of the elaborate instruments of modern research ; that in medicine, Greek and Roman public opinion was hostile to dissection of the human body—only in Alexandria was it permitted—and that the Greeks, with a passion for disinterested knowledge, thought it vulgar to employ science for practical or commercial purposes. Greek science was never brought into connexion with industry or commerce, and it is noteworthy that the Greeks achieved nothing in chemistry, the science most closely allied with industry. It thus missed what has been in the modern world a great indirect stimulus to the advance of knowledge.

To sum up the value and significance of Greek science and mathematics—we have some brilliant anticipations of modern discoveries—the starting of nearly every branch of science, and a considerable achievement. On Greek knowledge or so much of it as survived, the world subsisted, till the Renaissance set the human mind free once more, and, still under Greek inspiration, it entered the path that led to modern science. There are many errors ; some are inconceivably gross in men who knew so much, if we did not remember that they were starting from zero or near it. The greatest and most permanent advance was made in mathematics, and this is natural. Greek science did not possess our accumulated masses of knowledge and its instruments for experiment were rudimentary—the Greeks had not even proper chronometers. These weaknesses were far less felt in mathematics, which is an *a priori* science, and requires abstract reasoning rather than experiment or collection of facts. How much the Greeks could achieve where they were unhampered we can see from the fact that ' no advance was made on Euclid till modern times, and no change, even in form, was attempted till quite recently '.[1]

But the real achievement of the Greeks was not in what they discovered, but in the fact that they wanted to discover, and that by some instinct they knew the way to set about it. There they differ from the Egyptians and Babylonians who had observed the stars and learnt the elements of surveying for practical purposes, but who show no sign of interest in the theory of either. The Greeks, on the other hand, were far more interested in the theory than in the practice, in knowing than in doing. So they started science on the right lines and in the right spirit ; and science once so started, the hardest part of the work was done.

When I speak of ' right lines ', I am thinking especially of four qualities. The first is the desire to know. The second is the determination to find a rational explanation for phenomena. The third is open-mindedness and candour. The fourth is industry and observation. If these qualities are present, the coming of science is assured. Their presence in the Greeks may be judged from what follows. I give, first some quotations to illustrate the spirit in which they worked, then some specimens of their work.

' ANAXAGORAS said that thought [2] and the freedom which it gives are the end of life.'

' Thought is the most excellent of things ; and wisdom consists in telling the truth and acting as Nature bids, listening to her ' [3] (Heraclītus).

[1] Article on Science in *Encycl. Britannica*.
[2] The Greek word means contemplation and includes the scientific and philosophic life.
[3] An anticipation of Bacon's maxim that we conquer Nature by obeying her.

' It is not by the body or by wealth that man is made happy, but by rightness and completeness of understanding ' (Democritus).

' Culture is an ornament to the fortunate, a refuge for the unhappy ' (id.).

' Three things come from wisdom, right reasoning, right speaking, and right conduct (id.).

' Know thyself ' (inscribed on the temple at Delphi).

' All men have the power of knowing themselves and becoming wise ' (Heraclitus).

' We must honour truth before friendship ' (Aristotle).

' I am one of those who are very willing to be refuted, if I say what is untrue, and quite as ready to be refuted as to refute. For I hold it the greater gain of the two—just as the gain is greater of being cured of some great evil than of curing some one else ' (Socrates).

' I pray heaven that, so far as they are right, my words may endure : if unintentionally I have said anything wrong, I pray that God will impose on me the punishment which those who are wrong deserve : and this is that they should be set right ' (Socrates).

' A life that is not questioned is not worth living ' (Socrates).

' It is better to detect our own errors than those of our neighbours ' (Democritus).

' The real philosopher is marked by the feeling of wonder, which is the only source of philosophy ' (Plato).

' In reality we know nothing ; truth lies in the depths ' (Xenophanes).

' If you do not expect the unexpected, you will not find truth : she is hard to discern and reach ' (Heraclitus).

' Much knowledge does not teach understanding ' (id.).

' Aim at much thought rather than at much knowledge ' (Democritus).

' Nothing happens without a cause but everything for a reason and by necessity ' (Leucippus).

There follow some specimens of early Greek science, which illustrate its audacity, its freedom, its insight, its errors. In reading them it must be remembered that these thinkers started at scratch. The following are the dates of the thinkers quoted : Anaximander (b. 610), Anaximenes (fl. 550), Xenophanes (fl. 540), Heraclītus (fl. 500), Anaxagoras (500–428), Empedocles (fl. 445), Dēmocritus (fl. 420).

THE earth is an independent body in the air, keeping its position by its equidistance from all other bodies. It is round and cylindrical in shape, like a stone pillar. One of its surfaces is the earth on which we tread, the other is antipodal to it. The heavenly bodies are a fiery ring, surrounded by mist : there are tubular apertures in this mist, through which we see them. When these apertures are blocked, eclipses occur (Anaximander).

> What mankind call Iris,[1] this too is only a mist,
> Purple and red and green to the eye (Xenophanes).

Anaxagoras declared that mind and matter were the beginning of everything, mind as creative, matter as coming into being. Everything was together, and then mind came and ordered them. . . . He said that the rise of the Nile proceeded from the snow melting in the extreme south and coming down as water in the summer : and that the sun, moon, and stars were red-hot stones carried round in the revolution of the heavens. The moon was lower than the sun and nearer to us. The sun was bigger than the Peloponnese ; the moon had no light of its own but derived it from the sun. The eclipses of the moon are due to the sun's light being cut off by the earth or, sometimes, by the bodies below the moon.

Democritus said that there is an unlimited number of universes, differing in size. Some have no sun or moon, some have them greater than ours, some have several suns and moons. The distances between the universes are unequal : here there are more, there fewer ; some are in growth, others at their acme, others in decline ; here they are coming into existence, there

---

[1] In Greek mythology the rainbow is the goddess Iris.

they are perishing. They are destroyed by collision with each other. Some universes are destitute of animals, plants, and all moisture.

In the two following passages we have an anticipation of a theory of evolution.

ANAXIMANDER says that man originated from animals of a different species : for all other animals are quickly able to feed themselves, but man needs a long period of nursing. Therefore he would not have originally survived (if he had been what he is now).

Hair and foliage and the thick plumage of birds are one in nature (Empedocles).

The following is interesting as the first instance of an argument from geology.

Xenophanes thinks that sea and earth were once in one, and that in time the earth was separated from the water. The proofs he gives are the discovery of shells on the mainland and on mountains, and he says that the outline of a fish and of seals [1] have been found in the quarries of Syracuse, and the outline of a sardine in Paros deep in the rock, and in Malta flat figures of every kind of sea creature.

The writers hitherto quoted survive only in fragments : Hippocrates (b. 460) can be judged from extant works. He belonged to the famous medical school in the Ionian island of Cos. Writings of many men gather round his name (perhaps a quarter of the 53 treatises attributed to him are genuine), and down to the Middle Ages the great representatives of medical science wrote commentaries on his works. That he achieved much can be judged from such comments as those of Dr. Francis Adams, writing in 1849 on the treatise *On Articulations* : ' Several sections of the work are perfect masterpieces, as the parts which relate to dislocations at the shoulder and hip-joint, and more especially the latter, in which, as it appears to me, he has given a fuller history of everything relating to the subject.

[1] Some read ' sea-weeds '.

than is to be found in any single work, even at the present day.' [1] But he is called the Father of Medicine not for his discoveries, but because he laid down the principles on which that art is founded. To appreciate what he did, glance before proceeding at Babylonian and Egyptian medicine, or at a mediaeval book of prescriptions. In returning to Hippocrates the reader emerges from an air thick with magic and superstition, into the rational atmosphere, free from prejudice or prepossession, which is the heritage of modern science. The following extract illustrates his attitude.

Primitive peoples are irresistibly tempted to consider disease as a supernatural infliction. Insanity or epidemics seem direct visitations of heaven. The Jews of Christ's era regarded epileptics as ' possessed with a devil ', and the fifth-century Greek called their mysterious complaint ' the sacred illness '. The following passage from Hippocrates' treatise on epilepsy shows how firmly he rejected such ideas, and laid down the momentous principle that all disease is natural in origin and to be cured, not by magic or incantation, but by natural means. He is attacking the view that epilepsy is sent by God.

I DO not consider that the body of man is polluted by God, the most perishable by the most holy of things ; for even if it were defiled, or in any way affected by something else, it would be likely to be purified and sanctified rather than polluted by God. . . . This disease seems to me to be no more divine than the rest ; but it is as natural as all other diseases, and has a cause for all its symptoms ; . . . it has the same origin as all other diseases, and is curable just as they are, except where from length of time it is confirmed, and has become too strong for the remedies administered. In origin it is hereditary like all other diseases. For if a phlegmatic person be born of a phlegmatic, and a bilious of a bilious, and a phthisical of a phthisical, and a hypochondriac of a hypochondriac, what is to hinder it from happening that where the father and mother were subject to this disease, certain of their offspring should be subject also ? Another great proof that it is in no way more divine than any other disease is, that it occurs in those who are of a phlegmatic constitution, but does not

[1] Sydenham Society—Translation of Hippocrates, ii. 557. In the translations below I have occasionally used this.

attack the bilious. Yet, if it were more divine than the others, this disease ought to attack all alike, and make no distinction between the bilious and the phlegmatic. The brain is the cause of this complaint, as it is of all the other chief diseases, and in what manner I will now plainly declare. . . . And again : This so-called Sacred Disease arises from the same cause as the others, namely, those things which enter and quit the body, such as cold, the sun and the winds, which are ever changing and never at rest. And these things are divine, so that there is no necessity for making a distinction, and holding this disease to be more divine than others, but all are divine, and all human ; each has its own peculiar nature and power, and none is beyond our control or skill.[1]

In treating disease Hippocrates has two main principles. It is not enough to be a clever empiric, treating symptoms and having practical remedies. The doctor must go beyond these to the cause of illness, and be a master of theory as well as of practice.

IN my opinion every doctor must have a knowledge of nature, and, if he is to do his duty, make every effort to learn the relation of the human organism to articles of food and drink, and to every kind of habit, and the effects produced on each individual by each. It is not enough simply to think that cheese is a bad article of diet, because it disagrees with those who eat heavily of it : we must know how it disagrees and why and with what element in the human body. For there are many other kinds of food and drink which are naturally deleterious, and they affect people differently. . . . Cheese, to return to the example I have taken, does not hurt all persons alike : some eat freely of it without suffering at all, and it is extremely sustaining to the persons with whom it agrees. Others do not bear it well. The two classes are differently constituted, and the difference is as follows. Some who have a physical element incompatible with cheese, find this element set in active commotion by it. Those

---

[1] On the Sacred Disease.

in whose bodies this humour is abundant and prevalent naturally suffer most. If it had been harmful to the human constitution in general, it would have hurt everybody. Any one who knows this can avoid suffering from it.

During convalescence, and during long illnesses, many disorders occur, some spontaneously, others from the treatment that happens to be applied. If the patient happens to have done something novel that day, bathing or walking or eating something unusual, even though it was really the right thing to do, I know that, nevertheless, most doctors, like the amateur, ascribe the fault to one or other of the new things he has done. They do not know the real cause, and possibly they deprive the patient of something which was highly advantageous to him. That is wrong. Instead one must know the effects of a bath improperly administered and the effects of fatigue. Like everything else, like a full meal, like particular foods, they produce different effects. Whoever does not know the particular relation of each thing to the human constitution will never know their effects nor their use.[1]

But in spite of his insistence on theory, Hippocrates knew that medical knowledge rested on observation : and his greatness resides in his combination of broad principle with minute attention to symptoms. Of the following passage which gives his principles, Dr. Adams says, ' What an admirable and comprehensive enumeration of all the circumstances upon which prognosis and diagnosis of diseases are to be founded ! Here we find nothing either wanting or redundant.'

WE form our opinion with regard to illnesses on our knowledge of the general character of all, and the particular character of each, on our knowledge of the complaint, the patient, the treatment applied, and the person applying it— for these have a favourable or unfavourable effect. We take into account climate in general, and the particular season and locality ; the patient's habits, way of life, occupation, and age ; his words,

[1] On Ancient Medicine, 20 f.

ways, silence, thoughts, sleep or its absence, dreams (their character and occasion), picking, scratching, tears, paroxysms, discharges, sneezing, sickness. We note the number and character of the successive changes and developments of the illness towards a crisis or a fatal termination ; we observe perspiration, coldness, rigor, cough, sneezing, hiccup, breathing, haemorrhage. These and their results are what we must bear in view.[1]

Hippocrates' powers of observation may be illustrated by a page from his case-book. These accounts of cases are among his most interesting writings. Observe that he gives his patient's address.

ERASINUS, who lived near the Torrent of Boötes, was seized with fever after supper ; passed a disturbed night. During the first day quiet, but in suffering at night. On the second, symptoms all exacerbated ; at night delirious. On the third day suffering ; very delirious. On the fourth very uncomfortable ; had no sound sleep at night ; dreams and talking ; then worse symptoms, aggravated and dangerous, terror, discomfort. Early on the fifth day became composed : took everything in : but a little before midday went out of his mind and could not restrain himself : extremities cold and discoloured. Died about sunset. (There follow medical details about the symptoms.) [2]

The following passages show Hippocrates' wide interests and philosophic power. In these discussions of the effects of climate on character we have the first instance in European literature of the application of science to political thought. After discussing the differences in appearance between Europeans and Asiatics and the causes of these, Hippocrates proceeds.

THE Asiatic is fainthearted and unmanly, less warlike than the European and gentler.[3] The chief cause of this is the seasonal climate ; there are no great changes either to cold or to heat ; the seasons are alike. There is neither mental excitement nor any violent physical change, which might produce

---

[1] Epidemics, i. 23. I have omitted some medical details.
[2] Epidemics, i, Case 8.   [3] H. has the Persians chiefly in mind.

a passionate temper and induce a hardy and spirited disposition. For it is by changes that the human mind is excited and prevented from stagnating. This seems to me the cause of the feebleness of Asiatics, and their government is a further reason. The greater part of Asia is a monarchy. Now where men are not free or their own masters, but are under an autocrat, they do not trouble about military exercises ; their aim is to appear unwarlike. For they and their rulers are not on a level. The subject is compelled in the interests of the ruler to campaign and suffer hardships and death, far from his children and wife and friends. All his gallant and good actions tend to the advancement and aggrandisement of his masters, while his own reward is danger and death. So by avoiding anything warlike they inevitably grow soft, and even those who are naturally brave and courageous have their character changed by their institutions. The following is a strong proof of this. Those Greeks and native peoples in Asia, who are not under an autocracy, but who are independent and reap the fruits of the hardships they undergo, are the most warlike : for the dangers they incur are incurred in their own interests, and they are personally rewarded for their courage as they are punished for their cowardice.[1]

In Europe too there are peoples differing from each other in size, figure, and courage. Those who inhabit a mountainous, rugged, high, and well-watered region, where the differences between the seasons are marked, are likely to be tall and naturally hardy and courageous : they are apt to have a considerable element of wildness and ferocity in their nature. The inhabitants of low-lying country, hot plains, where the winds and the waters are generally warm, will not be tall nor of normal proportions, but broad in build, fleshy, and black-haired. They are inclined to have a dark complexion and to be phlegmatic rather than choleric : their dispositions will not be naturally so hardy and courageous, though these qualities may be created by their institutions. If there are rivers in the country which remove the

[1] About Airs, Waters, and Places, 16.

rainfall and stagnant waters, they will be healthy and fair, but if there are no rivers and if they drink standing water from pools and marshes, they will have over-developed stomachs and enlarged spleens. The inhabitants of high, level, windy, and well-watered countries will be tall and uniform, but rather gentle and effeminate in disposition. Where the country is bare, waterless, rugged, parched by the sun in summer and by the cold in winter, the inhabitants will be hard, wiry, well-built, sinewy, hairy, quick, active, and restless in disposition ; self-willed and opiniative in temper and habit ; more inclined to be fierce than mild ; quicker and more intelligent in the arts and better at war.[1]

In treating disease Hippocrates used drugs and violent remedies as little as possible, leaving the curative powers of nature to assert themselves. Those interested in his methods should read his *Aphorisms*, but as they are chiefly of medical interest I do not quote from them. The physician's oath, attributed to him, shows his ideals for his profession.

I SWEAR by Apollo the physician, and by Asclepius, and Health, and All-Heal, and I call all gods and goddesses to witness that, according to my ability and judgement, I will keep this Oath and this Bond—to reckon him who taught me this Art equally dear to me as my parents, to share my substance with him, and in the hour of his need impart what he requires, to look upon his offspring in the same footing as my own brothers, and to teach them this art if they wish to learn it, without fee or stipulation. . . . I will follow the system of regimen which, according to my ability and judgement, I consider for the benefit of my patients, and abstain from whatever is deleterious and mischievous. I will give no deadly medicine if asked, nor suggest any such plan ; so too, I will not produce abortion. With purity and with holiness I will pass my life and practise my Art. . . Into whatever houses I enter I will go into them for the benefit

---

[1] Ib. 24. Here he thinks successively of Sparta, the marshy Boeotian country, and Attica ; he describes the Athenian character as it was before the days of Pericles.

of the sick, and will abstain from every voluntary act of mischief and corruption. . . . Whatever in my professional practice or outside it in the life of the world I see or hear, which ought not to be spoken of abroad, I will not divulge, considering that such things should be kept secret. While I continue to keep this Oath unviolated, may I be allowed to enjoy life and the practice of the art, respected by all men, in all times. But should I trespass and violate this Oath, may the reverse be my lot.[1]

With Aristotle we come still closer to the modern world. His interests are universal. He wrote on physics, meteorology, astronomy, mechanics, mathematics, optics, anatomy, physiology, psychology, biology, botany, agriculture, anthropology. In physics he stepped back rather than forward. His great scientific work was in biology. ' Wherever the line between the visible and the invisible is crossed, Aristotle's powers are paralysed.' Where he could use his eyes, his genius for observation had full scope. His minuteness, his amazing knowledge, and, in spite of many errors, his general accuracy make him one of the greatest biologists. Nor did he only collect information. He was the first to make a satisfactory classification of the animal world, and his system held the field till the work of Cuvier. If any one wishes to judge the greatness of this achievement, let him set about the work, starting where Aristotle did. Of his biological writings [2] we possess treatises on embryology, the locomotion of animals, the organs of animals, as well as the long *Historia Animalium.* My quotations, which are from the biological works, may illustrate Aristotle's method, but give no more idea of his work than a few stones would give of a great building.

The Study of Biology

DOUBTLESS the contemplation of the heavenly bodies fills us with more delight than we get from the contemplation of lowly things ; for the sun and stars are born not, neither do they decay, but are eternal and divine. But the heavens are high and afar off, and of celestial things the know-

---

[1] The Oath.
[2] De Generatione Animalium (considered by some judges his greatest scientific work), De Motu Anim., De Incessu Anim., De Partibus Anim.

ledge that our senses give us is scanty and dim. On the other hand, the living creatures are nigh at hand, and of each and all of them we may gain ample and certain knowledge if we so desire. If a statue please us, shall not the living fill us with delight ; all the more if in the spirit of philosophy we search for causes and recognize the evidences of design. Then will Nature's purpose and her deep-seated laws be everywhere revealed, all tending in her multitudinous work to one form or another of the Beautiful.[1]

A discussion of the senses of taste, hearing, and smell in fish

THERE is no doubt but that fishes have the sense of taste, for a great number of them delight in special flavours ; and fishes freely take the hook if it be baited with a piece of flesh from a tunny or from any fat fish, obviously enjoying the taste and the eating of food of this kind. Fishes have no visible organs for hearing or for smell ; for what might appear to indicate an organ for smell in the region of the nostril has no communication with the brain. These indications, in fact, in some cases lead nowhere, like blind alleys, and in other cases lead only to the gills ; but for all this fishes undoubtedly hear and smell. For they are observed to run away from any loud noise, such as would be made by the rowing of a galley, so as to become easy of capture in their holes ; for, by the way, though a sound be very slight in the open air, it has a loud and alarming resonance to creatures that hear under water. And this is shown in the capture of the dolphin ; for when the hunters have enclosed a shoal of these fishes with a ring of their canoes, they set up from inside the canoes a loud splashing in the water, and by so doing induce the creatures to run in a shoal high and dry up on the beach, and so capture them while stupefied with the noise. And yet, for all this, the dolphin has no organ of hearing discernible. Furthermore, when engaged in their craft, fishermen are particularly careful to make no noise with oar or net ; and after they have spied a shoal, they let down their nets at a spot so far off that they count upon no noise being likely to reach the shoal,

[1] De Part. An. i. 5, tr. D'Arcy Thompson.

occasioned either by oar or by the surging of their boats through the water ; and the crews are strictly enjoined to preserve silence until the shoal has been surrounded. And, at times, when they want the fish to crowd together, they adopt the stratagem of the dolphin-hunter ; in other words they clatter stones together, that the fish may, in their fright, gather close into one spot, and so they envelop them within their nets. Further, when fishermen see a shoal of fish feeding at a distance, disporting themselves in calm bright weather on the surface of the water, if they are anxious to descry the size of the fish and to learn what kind of a fish it is, they may succeed in coming upon the shoal whilst yet basking at the surface if they sail up without the slightest noise, but if any man make a noise previously, the shoal will be seen to scurry away in alarm. Again, there is a small river-fish called the *cottus* or bull-head ; this creature burrows under a rock, and fishers catch it by clattering stones against the rock, and the fish, bewildered at the noise, darts out of its hiding-place. From these facts it is quite obvious that fishes can hear ; and indeed some people, from living near the sea and frequently witnessing such phenomena, affirm that of all living creatures the fish is the quickest of hearing.

The case is similar in regard to the sense of smell. Thus, as a rule, fishes will not touch a bait that is not fresh, neither are they all caught by one and the same bait, but they are severally caught by baits suited to their several likings, and these baits they distinguish by their sense of smell ; and, by the way, some fishes are attracted by malodorous baits, as the saupe, for instance, is attracted by excrement. Again, a number of fishes live in caves ; and accordingly fishermen, when they want to entice them out, smear the mouth of a cave with strong-smelling pickles, and the fish are soon attracted to the smell. And the eel is caught in a similar way ; for the fisherman lays down an earthen pot that has held pickles, after inserting a ' weel ' in the neck thereof. As a general rule, fishes are especially attracted by savoury smells. For this reason, fishermen roast the fleshy parts of the cuttle-fish and use it as bait on account of its smell, for fish are peculiarly attracted by it ; they also bake the octopus and bait their fish-baskets or weels with it, entirely, as they say, on account of its smell. Furthermore, gregarious fishes, if fish-washings or bilge-water be thrown overboard, are observed to scud off to a distance, from apparent dislike of the smell. And it is asserted that they can at once detect by smell the presence of their own blood ; and this faculty is manifested by their hurrying off to a great distance whenever fish-blood is spilt in the sea. And, as a general rule, if you bait your weel with a stinking bait, the fish refuse to enter the weel or even to draw near ; but if you bait the weel with a fresh and savoury bait, they come at once from long distances and swim into it. It is manifest, then, that the animals above mentioned are in possession of all the five senses.[1]

The habits of the sheat-fish and of the sepia

OF river-fish, the male of the sheat-fish is remarkably attentive to the young. The female after parturition goes away ; the male stays and keeps on guard where the spawn is most abundant, contenting himself with keeping off all other little fishes that might steal the spawn or fry, and this he does for forty or fifty days, until the young are sufficiently grown to make away from the other fishes for themselves. The fishermen can tell where he is on guard : for, in warding off the little fishes, he makes a rush in the water and gives utterance to a kind of muttering noise. He is so earnest in the performance of his parental duties that the fishermen at times, if the eggs be attached to the roots of water-plants deep in the water, drag them into as shallow a place as possible ; the male fish will still keep by the young, and, if it so happen, will be caught by the hook when snapping at the little fish that come by ; if, however, he be sensible by experience of the danger of the hook, he will still keep by his charge, and with his extremely strong teeth will bite the hook in pieces.[2]

[1] H. A. 533 a, f, tr. and notes by D'Arcy Thompson.
[2] Ib. 621 a.

Of molluscs the sepia is the most cunning, and is the only species that employs its dark liquid for the sake of concealment as well as from fear: the octopus and calamary make the discharge solely from fear. These creatures never discharge the pigment in its entirety; and after a discharge the pigment accumulates again. The sepia, as has been said, often uses its colouring pigment for concealment; it shows itself in front of the pigment and then retreats back into it; it also hunts with its long tentacles not only little fishes, but oftentimes even mullets. The octopus is a stupid creature, for it will approach a man's hand if it be lowered in the water; but it is neat and thrifty in its habits: that is, it lays up stores in its nest, and, after eating up all that is eatable, it ejects the shells and sheaths of crabs and shell-fish, and the skeletons of little fishes. It seeks its prey by so changing its colour as to render it like the colour of the stones adjacent to it; it does so also when alarmed. By some the sepia is said to perform the same trick; that is, they say it can change its colour so as to make it resemble the colour of its habitat. The only fish that can do this is the angel-fish, that is, it can change its colour like the octopus. The octopus as a rule does not live the year out. It has a natural tendency to run off into liquid; for, if beaten and squeezed, it keeps losing substance and at last disappears. The female after parturition is peculiarly subject to this colliquefaction; it becomes stupid; if tossed about by waves, it submits impassively; a man, if he dived, could catch it with the hand; it gets covered over with slime, and makes no effort to catch its wonted prey. The male becomes leathery and clammy. As a proof that they do not live into a second year there is the fact that, after the birth of the little octopuses in the late summer or beginning of autumn, it is seldom that a large-sized octopus is visible, whereas a little before this time of year the creature is at its largest. After the eggs are laid, they say that both the male and the female grow so old and feeble that they are preyed upon by little fish, and with ease dragged from their holes; and that this could not have been done previously; they say also that this is not the case with the small and young octopus, but that the young creature is much stronger than the grown-up one. Neither does the sepia live into a second year. The octopus is the only mollusc that ventures on to dry land ; it walks by preference on rough ground ; it is firm all over when you squeeze it, excepting in the neck.[1]

The following passage on hair in animals shows that Aristotle is not a mere observer. He lays down the principle of compensation in nature. Note the teleological interpretation of nature, of which he is the father. Here, and elsewhere, it leads him to false explanations.

ALL animals that have hairs on the body have lashes on the eyelids ; but birds and animals with scale-like plates, being hairless, have none.[2] The Libyan ostrich, indeed, forms an exception ; for, though a bird, it is furnished with eyelashes. This exception, however, will be explained hereafter. Of hairy animals, man alone has lashes on both lids. For in quadrupeds there is a greater abundance of hair on the back than on the under side of the body ; whereas in man the contrary is the case, and the hair is more abundant on the front surface than on the back. The reason for this is that hair is intended to serve as a protection to its possessor. Now, in quadrupeds, owing to their inclined attitude, the under or anterior surface does not require so much protection as the back, and is therefore left comparatively bald, in spite of its being the nobler of the two sides. But in man, owing to his upright attitude, the anterior and posterior surfaces of the body are on an equality as regards need of protection. Nature therefore has assigned the protective covering to the nobler of the two surfaces ; for invariably she brings about the best arrangement of such as are possible. This then is the reason that there is no lower eyelash in any quadruped ; though in some a few scattered hairs sprout out under the lower lid.[3] This

[1] H. A. 621 b.
[2] Birds, as a rule, have no eyelashes. There are, however, a few exceptions, and of these the ostrich is one.
[3] So far as I can ascertain it is true that man is the only mammal with a distinct marginal lower eyelash, with the exception of some monkeys,

also is the reason that they never have hair in the axillae, as man has. Their hair, then, instead of being collected in these parts, is either thickly set over the whole dorsal surface, as is the case for instance in dogs, or, sometimes, forms a mane, as in horses and the like, or as in the male lion, where the mane is still more flowing and ample. So, again, whenever there is a tail of any length, nature decks it with hair, with long hair if the stem of the tail be short, as in horses, with short hair if the stem be long, regard also being had to the condition of the rest of the body. For nature invariably gives to one part what she subtracts from another. Thus when she has covered the general surface of an animal's body with an excess of hair, she leaves a deficiency in the region of the tail. This, for instance, is the case with bears.[1]

The first European works on botany which we possess come from Theophrastus of Lesbos (372–287), a pupil of Aristotle. He wrote on almost as many subjects as his master, and two of his scientific works, *Inquiries about Plants* and *The Causes of Plants*, have survived. The former, in nine books, is the more valuable. The Lyceum (p. 319) contained a botanical garden, where methodical observations could be made, and Alexander's expedition to the East led to increased knowledge of Oriental plants —as the last of the following extracts shows.

THE beech presents no differences, there being but one kind. It is a straight-growing, smooth, and unbranched tree, and in thickness and height is about equal to the silver-fir, which it also resembles in other respects ; the wood is of a fair colour, strong, and of good grain, the bark smooth and thick, the leaf undivided, longer than a pear-leaf, spinous at the tip, the roots neither numerous nor running deep ; the fruit is smooth like an acorn, enclosed in a shell, which is, however, without prickles and smooth, not spinous, like the chestnut, though in

an exception elsewhere (H. A. ii. 8. 502^b 31) recognized by A., and some few antelopes. In very many mammals, especially the smaller kinds, there are no eyelashes at all. In the larger kinds, as a rule, the upper lash is well developed and marginal, while the lower lash is represented, as A. rightly says, by some long straggling hairs set below the lid, not on its margin.

[1] De Part. Anim. 658 a, tr. W. Ogle.

sweetness and flavour it resembles it. In mountain country it also grows white and has timber which is useful for many purposes, for making carts, beds, chairs and tables, and for shipbuilding ; while the tree of the plains is black and useless for these purposes ; but the fruit is much the same in both.

The yew has also but one kind, is straight-growing, grows readily, and is like the silver-fir, except that it is not so tall and is more branched. Its leaf is also like that of the silver-fir, but glossier and less stiff. As to the wood, in the Arcadian yew it is black or red, in that of Ida bright yellow and like prickly cedar ; so they say that dealers practise deceit, selling it for that wood : for that it is all heart, when the bark is stripped off ; its bark also resembles that of prickly cedar in roughness and colour, its roots are few, slender, and shallow. The tree is rare about Ida, but common in Macedonia and Arcadia ; it bears a round fruit a little larger than a bean, which is red in colour and soft ; and they say that if beasts of burden eat of the leaves they die, while ruminants take no hurt. Even men sometimes eat the fruit, which is sweet and harmless.[1]

The ivy has many forms ; one kind grows on the ground, another grows tall, and of the tall-growing ivies there are several kinds. However the three most important seem to be the white, the black, and the *helix*. And of each of these there are several forms. Of the ' white ', one is white only in its fruit, another in its leaves also. Again to take only white-fruited sorts, one of these has its fruit well formed, close and compact like a ball. Another kind is smaller and loose in growth like the black ivy.

The *helix* presents the greatest differences ; the principal difference is in the leaves, which are small, angular, and of more graceful proportions, while those of the ivy proper are rounder and simple ; there is also difference in the length of the twigs, and further in the fact that this tree is barren. For, as to the view that the *helix* by natural development turns into the ivy, some insist that this is not so, the only true ivy according to

---

[1] Hist. Plant. iii. 10. The translations from Theophrastus are by Sir A. Hort (Loeb Library).

these being that which was ivy from the first (whereas if, as some say, the *helix* invariably turns into ivy, the difference would be merely one of age and condition, and not of kind, like the difference between the cultivated and the wild pear). However the leaf even of the full-grown *helix* is very different from that of the ivy, and it happens but rarely and in a few specimens that in this plant a change in the leaf occurs as it grows older, as it does in the abele and the castor-oil plant. There are several forms of the *helix*, of which the three most conspicuous and important are the green ' herbaceous ' kind (which is the commonest), the white, and the variegated, which some call the ' Thracian ' *helix*. Each of these appears to present variations ; of the green, one form is slenderer and has more regular and also closer leaves, the other has all these characteristics in a less degree. Of the variegated kind again one sort has a larger, one a smaller leaf, and the variegation is variable. Similarly the various forms of the white *helix* differ in size and colour. The ' herbaceous ' kind is the most vigorous and covers most space. They say that the form which is supposed to turn into ivy is clearly marked not only by its leaves, because they are larger and broader, but also by its shoots ; for these are straight from the first, and this form does not bend over like the other ; also because the shoots are slenderer and larger, while those of the ivy-like form are shorter and stouter. The ivy too, when it begins to seed, has its shoots upward-growing and erect.

All ivies have numerous close roots, which are tangled together, woody and stout, and do not run very deep ; but this is specially true of the black kind and of the roughest and wildest forms of the white. So it is mischievous to plant this against any tree ; for it destroys and starves any tree by withdrawing the moisture. This form also more than the others grows stout and becomes tree-like, and in fact becomes itself an independent ivy tree, though in general it likes to be against another tree, and is, as it were, parasitic.

From the first it has also this natural characteristic, that it regularly puts forth roots from the shoots between the leaves, by means of which it gets a hold of trees and walls, as if these roots were made by nature on purpose. And so by withdrawing and drinking up the moisture it starves its host, while, if it is cut off below, it is able to survive and live. There are also other not inconsiderable differences in the fruit ; both in the white and in the black kind, it is in some cases rather sweet, in others extremely bitter ; in proof of this, birds eat one but not the other. Such are the facts about ivy.[1]

India has its so-called 'fig-tree' (banyan), which drops its roots from its branches every year ; and it drops them, not from the new branches, but from those of last year or even from older ones ; these take hold of the earth and make a kind of fence about the tree, so that it becomes like a tent, in which men sometimes even live. The roots as they grow are easily distinguished from the branches, being whiter, hairy, crooked, and leafless. The foliage above is also abundant, and the whole tree is round and very large. They say that it extends its shade for as much as 400 yards : and the thickness of the stem is in some instances more than sixty paces, while many specimens are as much as forty paces through. The leaf is quite as large as a shield, but the fruit is very small, only as large as a chick-pea, and it resembles a fig. And this is why the Greeks named this tree a 'fig-tree'. The fruit is curiously scanty, not only relatively to the size of the tree but absolutely. The tree also grows near the river Akesines.[2]

Passionately devoted to knowledge for its own sake, the Greek inclined to despise applied science. The following somewhat trivial instances of it are from the *Pneumatics* of the Alexandrian mathematician Heron (1st cent. A. D. ?). The book is chiefly composed of descriptions of some eighty mechanical devices, including an automatic machine for coins, a hydraulic organ, a self-trimming lamp, an odometer, mechanical birds that sing, a trumpet sounded by hydraulic means, &c. The following is interesting as an anticipation of the principle of the steam-engine.

[1] Hist. Plant. iii. 18. 6. Note his knowledge of the ivy's aerial roots.
[2] Hist. Plant. iv. 4. 4.

To move a ball by steam.

A FIRE is lighted under a cauldron, A B, containing water, and covered at the mouth by the lid C D: with this the bent tube E F G communicates, the extremity of the tube being fitted into a hollow ball, H K. Opposite

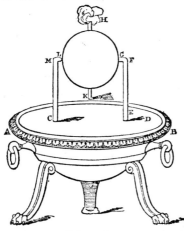

to the extremity G place a pivot, L M, resting on the lid C D; and let the ball contain two bent pipes, communicating with it at the opposite extremities of a diameter, and bent in opposite directions, the bends being at right angles and across the lines F G, L M. As the cauldron gets hot it will be found that the steam, entering the ball through E F G, passes out through the bent tubes towards the lid, and causes the ball to revolve.[1]

A Fire-Engine.

TAKE two vessels of bronze, A B C D, E F G H, having the inner surface bored in a lathe to fit a piston (like the barrels of water-organs), K L, M N being the pistons fitted to the boxes. Let the cylinders communicate with each other by means of the tube X O D F, and be provided with valves, P, R, such as have been explained above, within the tube X O D F and opening outwards from the cylinders. In the bases of the cylinders pierce circular apertures, S, T, covered with polished hemispherical cups, V Q, W Y, through which insert spindles soldered to, or in some way connected with, the bases of the cylinders, and provided with

[1] ii. 11, tr. Woodcroft (*The Pneumatics of Hero of Alexandria*, 1851).

shoulders at the extremities that the cups may not be forced off the spindles. To the centre of the pistons fasten the vertical rods S E, S E, and attach to these the beam A′ A′, working, at its centre, about the stationary pin D, and about the pins B, C, at the rods S E, S E. Let the vertical tube S′ E′ communicate with the tube X O D F, branching into two arms at S′, and provided with small pipes through which to force up water, such as were explained above in the description of the machine for producing a water-jet by means of the compressed air. Now, if the cylinders, provided with these additions, be plunged into a vessel containing water, I J U Z, and the beam A′ A′ be made to work at its extremities A′ A′, which move alter-nately about the pin D, the pistons, as they descend, will drive out the

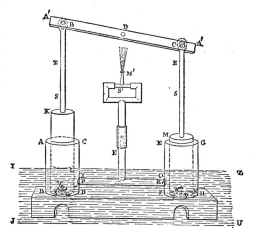

water through the tube E′ S′ and the revolving mouth M′. For when the piston M N ascends it opens the aperture T, as the cup W Y rises, and shuts the valve R; but when it descends it shuts T and opens R, through which the water is driven and forced upwards. The action of the other piston, K L, is the same. Now the small pipe M′, which waves backward and forward, ejects the water to the required height but not in the required direc-tion, unless the whole machine be turned round; which on urgent occasions is a tedious and difficult process. In order, therefore, that the water may be ejected to the spot required, let the tube E′ S′ consist of two tubes, fitting closely together lengthwise, of which one must be attached to the tube x o d f, and the other to the part from which the arms branch off at s'; and thus, if the upper tube be turned round, by the inclination of the mouthpiece m' the stream of water can be forced to any spot we please. The upper joint of the double tube must be secured to the lower, to prevent its being forced from the machine by the violence of the water. This may be effected by holdfasts in the shape of the letter L, soldered to the upper tube, and sliding on a ring which encircles the lower.[1]

[1] Ib. i. 28. Among the extant works of Heron are the Dioptra on land-surveying, the Belopoiica on engines of war, and the Automatopoietica, a description of an automatic theatre, said to have suggested the machinery of the famous Strasbourg clock.

PRINTED IN GREAT BRITAIN AT THE UNIVERSITY PRESS, OXFORD
BY CHARLES BATEY, PRINTER TO THE UNIVERSITY